The Universe in the Image
of *Imago Dei*

The Universe in the Image of *Imago Dei*

The Dialogue between Theology and Science as a Hermeneutics of the Human Condition

ALEXEI V. NESTERUK

◆PICKWICK *Publications* • Eugene, Oregon

THE UNIVERSE IN THE IMAGE OF *IMAGO DEI*
The Dialogue between Theology and Science as a Hermeneutics of the Human Condition

Copyright © 2022 Alexei V. Nesteruk. All rights reserved. Except for brief quotations in critical publications or reviews, no part of this book may be reproduced in any manner without prior written permission from the publisher. Write: Permissions, Wipf and Stock Publishers, 199 W. 8th Ave., Suite 3, Eugene, OR 97401.

Pickwick Publications
An Imprint of Wipf and Stock Publishers
199 W. 8th Ave., Suite 3
Eugene, OR 97401

www.wipfandstock.com

PAPERBACK ISBN: 978-1-6667-1123-3
HARDCOVER ISBN: 978-1-6667-1124-0
EBOOK ISBN: 978-1-6667-1125-7

Cataloguing-in-Publication data:

Names: Nesteruk, Alexei V., 1957– [author].

Title: The universe in the image of image Dei : the dialogue between theology and science as a hermeneutics of the human condition / Alexei V. Nesteruk.

Description: Eugene, OR: Pickwick Publications, 2022 | Includes bibliographical references and index.

Identifiers: ISBN 978-1-6667-1123-3 (paperback) | ISBN 978-1-6667-1124-0 (hardcover) | ISBN 978-1-6667-1125-7 (ebook)

Subjects: LCSH: Religion and science | Image of God—History of doctrines | Image of God—Biblical teaching | Theological anthropology—Christianity | Christology | Theology | Cosmology

Classification: BX320.3 N47 2022 (paperback) | BX320.3 (ebook)

VERSION NUMBER 030722

Scripture quotations marked (KJV) are from The Authorized (King James) Version. Rights in the Authorized Version in the United Kingdom are vested in the Crown. Reproduced by permission of the Crown's patentee, Cambridge University Press.

Scripture quotations marked (ESV) are from The ESV® Bible (The Holy Bible, English Standard Version®), copyright © 2001 by Crossway, a publishing ministry of Good News Publishers. Used by permission. All rights reserved.

In memoriam of George Horton

CONTENTS

Illustrations | x
Preface | xi
Acknowledgments | xv
Abbreviations | xvi

INTRODUCTION: THE INTERPLAY BETWEEN ANTHROPOLOGY AND COSMOLOGY IN THE DIALOGUE BETWEEN THEOLOGY AND SCIENCE | 1

PART 1: HUMANITY AS A CENTRAL THEME OF THE DIALOGUE BETWEEN THEOLOGY AND SCIENCE | 27

1 THE DIALOGUE BETWEEN THEOLOGY AND SCIENCE: ITS SENSE AND PHILOSOPHICAL FOUNDATIONS | 29

Why the relation between the terms in the dialogue of theology with science cannot be symmetric? | 30

Theology needs science—science needs theology | 38

How to make philosophically the distinction in the modes of the given in the natural sciences and theology? | 42

How to make a theological distinction in the modes of the given in the natural sciences and theology? | 50

2 THE UNKNOWABILITY OF HUMANITY AND THE PARADOX OF SUBJECTIVITY AT THE INCEPTION OF THE DIALOGUE BETWEEN THEOLOGY AND SCIENCE | 64

From the unknowability of humanity to the paradox of subjectivity | 65

The unknowability of humanity as oblivion of origins | 80

The unknowability as the primary forgetting | 93

The primacy of life and a pneumatological dimension of the dialogue between theology and science | 101

3   THE DIALOGUE BETWEEN THEOLOGY AND SCIENCE AS AN OPEN-ENDED HERMENEUTIC OF THE HUMAN CONDITION | 114

    The incarnational logic of the human condition | 115

    The dialogue between theology and science as an open-ended hermeneutics of the human condition | 132

    The human phenomenon and the dialogue between theology and science as an expression of life's self-affectivity | 138

    Human life's self-affectivity as a geocentric corporeity and hypostatic omnipresence | 144

    The dialogue between theology and science as a self-affective life's response to the saturated phenomenon of the universe | 153

PART 2: THE UNIVERSE IN THE IMAGE OF *IMAGO DEI* OR HUMANITY AS HYPOSTASIS OF THE UNIVERSE | 159

    Introduction | 160

    Theological thinking of the universe and the mystery of the human existence | 163

    Cosmology as explication of the human | 170

    The human condition and Christian faith in creation: a philosophical explication | 180

    Creation in Greek philosophy and Patristic theology | 184

    Creation as origination of the universe in modern cosmology | 189

    Creation in the natural attitude or how not to speak about creation: A patristic insight in the issue of "Why not sooner of creation?" | 199

    Creation in the natural attitude or how not to speak about creation: Kant's insight in the issue of "Why not sooner of creation?" | 208

    A possible theologico-scientific synthesis in responding to the issue of "Why not sooner of creation?" | 216

    The universe as the "place" of self-affective life or the universe as a saturated phenomenon | 223

    From creation of the world to creation of humanity: the narrative of the Incarnation | 231

    Humanity as hypostasis of the universe: praise as exploration | 243

CONCLUSION: THE TRANSFIGURATION OF THE UNIVERSE THROUGH THE DEIFIED KNOWLEDGE OR THE UNIVERSE IN THE IMAGE OF *IMAGO DEI* | 258

Appendix 1: Glossary of philosophical terms | 271

Appendix 2: Glossary of basic terms and ideas from physical cosmology (in the order of logical necessity) | 284

Bibliography | 293

Index | 303

ILLUSTRATIONS

Figure 1: The unity of the universe as generated from the Big Bang | 254

Figure 2: From a theogenic uniformity of the universe to its cosmographic uniformity | 257

PREFACE

THE TITLE OF THIS book contains three basic components of any Christian theological and philosophical discourse, namely God, the created world (the universe), and humanity, thus reflecting a known truth that cosmology, anthropology and Christology operate together. This implies that one cannot talk about the structure of the world without human presence in it, as well as it is impossible to produce any reasonable understanding of humanity without positioning it in the created universe. In the same fashion, in order to comprehend where the human capacity of predicating the whole universe comes from, one needs to appeal to humanity's Divine Image (*Imago Dei*), that is, to its archetype in the incarnate Christ (who is present in the universe and at the same time, by creating and sustaining it, "contains" the universe hypostatically). Because of being in the *Imago Dei* all human beings are theologians to a certain extent, so that all cosmological and anthropological propositions intrinsically contain the traces of the human created condition in communion with God. At the same time the very possibility of being theologians in the conditions of the world has cosmological foundations to the same extent as the Incarnation of Christ is possible only in the very special physical and biological conditions. The link between cosmology and anthropology becomes seen as the impossibility of studying the order of the cosmos without taking into account the conditions of the Incarnation of Christ as the inaugural event in the order of the human history.

To say that the universe is given in the image of humanity (that is, in the image of *Imago Dei*) is equivalent to saying that the image of humanity itself can only be seen through the prism of its existence in that universe which can accommodate the incarnate Christ. Humanity (as *Imago Dei*) turns out to be in the epistemologically central position because it is humanity that is gifted with the capacity to initiate all enquiries in the sense of itself as well as in the sense of the universe. This epistemological centrality of humanity in the universe is accentuated through those aspects of its cognitive behavior that include its symbolic, mythological and rational dimensions. The issue of this centrality as the question of origin of these patterns of behavior would be difficult to address without appealing to religious experience as a particular historical form of such a behavior. In this sense the dialogue between theology and science represents an enquiry into the interplay of different cognitive patterns of behavior exercised by humanity since its dawn. Said philosophically, the dialogue attempts to formalise the relationship between two types of phenomenality with which the human subject deals: that one related to experience of sheer existence (the phenomenality of life as exceeding a capacity of its discursive apprehension), and another one in which humanity's existence is presented as a constituent part of the physical universe (organic life in the phenomenality of objects).

Since humanity forms the centre of disclosure and manifestation of the universe its epistemological centrality is interpreted theologically through a relationship between humanity and God—creator and termed as *communion with God, participation in God,* or *life of (Divine) Life* conferring to humanity the dignity of *Imago Dei*. Christians believe that there is something unique in the human phenomenon since the first among humans was created in the Divine Image (Gen 1:26–28). However, at present such scientific disciplines as evolutionary biology, palaeoanthropology, archaeology, medical biology, the sciences of the artificial intelligence, epistemology, psychology and others, directly and radically challenge the literal and sometimes abstract vision of humanity as a unique formation in the world, thus challenging in turn the traditional doctrine of *Imago Dei*. All these disciplines place humans in a mediocre position in the world accompanied by the feeling of anxiety, insecurity, and non-attunement to the universe. Theology needs to respond to these challenges by incorporating into its scope the data from the sciences in order to neutralise these anxieties by arguing that the true and ultimate home of humanity is not this evolutionary universe with its decay into nothingness, but the promised Kingdom of God where love for life and existence will be unconditional. It is from within such a perspective that the sense of all cosmological theories can be instituted in the perspective of humanity's infinite tasks related to the history of salvation.

The inseparability of anthropology, cosmology, and Christology is approached in the book in the context of the dialogue between theology and science. Since Orthodox Christianity treats theology as a reflection upon experience of communion with God while being in the physical universe, so that life as such is treated as communion, all human activities (including a scientific one) originate in this communion. Science means not only a way of human thinking, but expresses the dynamism of the human existence as related to communion. In this case the symmetry between theology and science assumed in many versions of the dialogue is not sustainable because life, understood as communion and the condition of disclosure and manifestation of the universe, phenomenologically precedes its own explication through the sciences. This asymmetry between life and science forms the dialogue's *existential commitment*. Being a commitment, it entails a method of explication of the coherence between human rationality and the rationality of the cosmos that are both assumed in the foundation of the sciences. The essential feature of this method is to elucidate the intuition that since both, science and theology, originate in life of one and the same human person, no existential separation and contradiction between them is possible. It is in this sense that the Eastern Orthodox Christian approach to the dialogue between theology and science (compared with the Western Christianity's versions of this dialogue) tends not only to elucidate the distinctive characteristics but also to step over the boundary between them. The existential commitment reveals the underlying origin of the dialogue in the ambiguous position of humanity in the world (being an object in the world and subject for the world) leading to the split between a scientific perception of existence and its immediate givenness through communion. Since no metaphysical reconciliation between two opposites in such a dualistic hermeneutics of the subject is possible, the issue of the facticity of the human subjectivity, as the sense-bestowing centre of being, acquires theological dimensions. First of all this is expressed in the human inability to know itself, the inability which, theologically, follows from the unknowability of God in whose image humanity is made. It is this unknowability of humanity by itself that stops any attempts of reconciling science and theology. The "dialogue" between them rather demonstrates the working of *formal* purposefulness in such a "reconciliation" as an intrinsic characteristic of the human condition in the Divine Image. This means that the dialogue between science and theology can be considered as a *teleological activity without an ontologically achievable purpose* thus representing *de facto* an open-ended hermeneutics of the human condition.

Since a scientific counterpart of the dialogue is dealing with the natural world as it is articulated by humanity, the knowledge of the universe cannot be complete to the same extent as the knowledge of humanity by itself. Thus cosmology, through the dialogue with theology, contributes to an open-ended hermeneutics of the human condition by being a *teleological activity of studying the universe without an ontologically achievable purpose.* Yet, since the disclosure and manifestation of the universe is initiated from within the human phenomenon, there is an existential asymmetry between theology (interpreting the human phenomenon as life from the Divine Life) and science (that constitutes the image of the universe formed through the given cognitive faculties). In spite of the fact that the human existence is articulated theologically as a special creation characterized by those hypostatic features which cannot be deduced from the worldly causality and are usually associated with Christ's archetype, cosmology is implicitly present in this articulation not only as a medium of embodiment, but because of the ultimate perennial correlation between the question of origin of the universe and that of the fleshly humanity. Cosmological accounts of creation form the description of the *necessary* conditions of the human existence while the theological accounts of humanity's creation and its salvific history form the hermeneutics of the *sufficient* conditions of existence of human beings and their articulate image of the universe. Theology elucidates the radical difference between humanity and the rest of creation by referring humanity to its archetype in the incarnate Christ. The Incarnation, being a motive of creation, thus falls under a rubric of the inaugural event endowing humanity with that *Imago Dei* which lies in the foundation and possibility of any further articulations of the universe. By being granted the hypostatic properties humanity produces the image of the universe by bringing the latter to self-articulation manifesting trough humanity the self-affectivity of the Divine Life itself. Being life from Life, humanity endows the universe with existence in the phenomenality of life, thus being hypostasis of the universe. It is because of this that to the same extent as any theological proposition implicitly contains the cosmological conditions of its very possibility, any cosmological formula and any assertion of the universe imply the presence of humanity, that is, of life from the Divine Life. Thus that which is called the *dialogue* between science and theology is *de facto* the dialogue between two phenomenological structures in one and the same human subject: on the one hand seeing its own life as conditioned by the physical universe and, on the other hand, sensing this life as having its transcendent origin in the Divine Life. The sense of this dialogue is to provide a hermeneutics of the human condition understanding in advance that its mystery will always remain humanity's infinite task.

ACKNOWLEDGMENTS

I WOULD LIKE TO express my feeling of gratitude for an academic support while this book has been written to Adrian Lemeni, Vasillios Makrides, Christopher Knight, Kirill Kopeikin, Tatiana Litvin, Konstantin and Sophia Litvinenko, Ruslan Loshakov, Efthymios Nicolaides, Sr. Tereza Obolevitch, Andrei Pavlenko, Ted Peters, Kostas Tampakis, Elizabeth Theokritoff, Olga Sekiro, Alexander Shevchenko, Alexander Soldatov, Alexander Spaskov, Stoyan Tanev, Roman Turovsky, Gayle Woloschak. I am grateful to the University of Portsmouth for all routine support required to prepare this book, as well as to Russian Christian Academy of Humanities in St. Petersburg, and St. Petersburg State Marine Technical University for the opportunity to approve some of the book's ideas through teaching courses. Special thanks to my wife Zhanna Sizova sharing all theoretical and practical aspects of my life when this book was coming into existence. Some parts of the book have been made possible through participation in the project "Science and Orthodoxy around the World" run by the National Hellenic Research Foundation in Greece and sponsored by the World Charity Templeton Foundation in 2016–19, as well as through the grant "PH Philosophy In Neopatristics: New Figures and New Interpretations" from The National Science Centre, Poland (DEC–2018/31/B/HS1/01861).

ABBREVIATIONS

NPNF: *The Nicene and Post-Nicene Fathers of the Christian Church.* Edited by Philip Schaff and Henry Wace. Edinburgh: T. & T. Clark, 1989–94.

Philokalia: *The Philokalia: The Complete Text.* Translated and edited by G. E. H. Palmer et al. Vol. 2. London: Faber & Faber, 1990.

INTRODUCTION

The Interplay between Anthropology and Cosmology in the Dialogue between Theology and Science

THE TOPIC OF THIS book is related to the dialogue between theology and science that became a matter of intensive scholarly discussions during the last forty to fifty years. Then one wonders whether this dialogue in the form it has been carried out, succeeded so far, that is, achieved some results which have had impact on both science and theology? The author believes that the negative answer to this question is provided by the unceasing scientific and technological advance that continues with no recourse to the dialogue between theology and science whatsoever. All discussions on whether science and theology are in conflict, or in "peaceful coexistence" do not have existential implications: the problem of finding a "common" ground for science and theology remains and its ongoing presence points to something basic and unavoidable in the human condition. Such a state of affairs indicates that the method of conducting this dialogue at present is unsatisfactory because it does not address the major question as to what is the foundation of the *distinction, difference, and division* between science and religion as those modes of activity and knowledge which originate in one and the same human subject. This leads to the question of facticity of that consciousness which lies in the foundation of theology and science, that is, the facticity[1] of the human existence and life in general. Theology itself can respond to this question from within the explicitly belief-based ground, namely faith in that knowledge of the world represents a natural revelation accessible to humanity because of the God-given faculties. Knowledge is

---

1. In philosophy, the term *facticity* has a multiplicity of meanings from "factuality" and "contingency" to the intractable conditions of the human existence. In our context the term comes to mean that which resists explanation and interpretation, or that which cannot be presented in the phenomenality of objects and physical causation. For more details see Glossary (Appendix 1).

the propensity of human persons whose basic qualities are reason, freedom, and capacity to retain the sense of the transcendent with respect to all that they assimilate through life and knowledge. In this sense the universe as articulated reality has existence and sense only within the human capacity of being person (hypostasis)[2] granted to man[3] as a divine gift. Since science does not account for the very possibility of knowledge, that is, personhood, it is automatically prevented from participation in the dialogue with theology on equal footing. Then it is logical to express a doubt about the meaning and value of all existing forms of the "dialogue" with science, for science and theology cannot enter this dialogue as symmetric terms. Since there is no impact of this "dialogue" on the performance and development of science, what remains for theology is to exercise an introspection upon science, to conduct a certain *critique* of science from a position which is by definition above and beyond not only of scientific thinking, but of secular thinking related to particular socio-historical and economic realities. The value of such a critique is unclear, for remaining a sheer hermeneutical exercise (not doubting matters of facts) it does not cascade down to existential concerns. Thus an assumed symmetry between theology and science, theology and cosmology in particular, is broken at the very inception of their possible relation because the presence of the enquiring intellect in this dialogue is not accounted by the sciences, but interpreted theologically. It is this asymmetry that constitutes that approach to the science-religion discussions which we describe elsewhere in terms of *theological commitment*.[4] Theological commitment is such a stance on humanity which positions it above those realities which are disclosed by the sciences alone. It appeals to those meanings of existence which do not entirely compel the recognition of the sciences in the manner that natural phenomena do. These meanings originate in an innate quality of human beings to long for immortality, that is, for communion with the unconditional personal ground of the world and life that humanity names God. And it is through this longing that the universe acquires the sense of that constituent of God's creation that makes it possible for human persons to exist and fulfil God's promise for eternal life and

---

2. The meaning of the term "hypostatic" comes from the Greek *hypostasis* that was used in Patristic theological context in order to underline the "personal," active and intransitive dimension of existence as different from impersonal substance (*ousia*) or nature (*physis*). See a corresponding entry in the Glossary (Appendix 1) for further explication.

3. We use the word "man" following the classical philosophical and theological tradition which inherited it from the Greek *anthropos*, comprising all meanings: human being, humanity, humans, men and women, Homo Sapiens.

4. Nesteruk, *The Sense of the Universe*.

communion. Theological commitment is thus an existential commitment that positions the dialogue between theology and science in the primary and original fact of life, referred to communion with God.

In spite of the fact that cosmology always accompanied natural theology (cosmological arguments for the finitude or infinitude of the world in space and time were employed as different arguments for existence or non-existence of God) and that theistic inferences are still alive and popular among some philosophers and cosmologists who attempt to use cosmology for either apologetic or atheistic conclusions,[5] theological commitment in studying the dialogue between theology and cosmology is in its essence a reaction to modern atheism amounting to a proclamation that cosmological knowledge is independent and neutral with respect to the religious condition of humanity. Indeed, in its goals and tasks the dialogue between Christianity and science aims to oppose atheism. However, if one carefully looks at how such a dialogue has been carried out so far, one realizes that the existing forms of this dialogue are adapted to that (de facto atheistic) stance of scientists who doubt the value of any theological insight. Such a dialogue turns out to be no more than a reaction to atheism, sometimes attempting to unconvincingly justify the very fact of this reaction. Contemporary atheism manifests itself not only as freedom from historical authorities and tradition but as the unprincipled following to the worst form of slavery of the Plato's cave in which the signs of the Divine presence are not recognized and the very ability to see them in the world is reduced to nothing. Atheism promotes a cult of immanence, the actually existent infinity of the given amounting to the deprivation of the inner senses and of the vision of the transcendent. Since modern science, and technology in particular, encourage individuals to be transcendent-blind, creating the immanent images of the transcendent, the advocates of atheism appeal to science. It is much easier not to deny the presence of the Divine in the world, but to claim that all spheres of the human activity are self-sufficient and do not need any reference to God. Since from a philosophical point of view the question of God's existence or nonexistence cannot be decided (the philosophical mind remains in the "negative certainty" with respect to this question), then why should one try to answer it at all. Here atheism reveals itself as secularism, as a kind of trans-ideological *laïcité* and as a servility to the alleged ideal of humanity understood only empirically, as that humanity which is alive here and now. To define this humanity in simple categories which overcome racial national and class differences one needs a universal language. It is

---

5. The literature on this topic is vast. See a concise review of recent discussions in Halvorson and Kragh, "Physical Cosmology."

science that pretends to be such a language; to be more precise, it is that scientific form of thinking that reduces the phenomenon of humanity in all its various manifestations to the physical and biological. It is clear from here that modern atheism as a certain form of the "immanent humanism" is no more than a more philosophically sophisticated *scientific atheism*.[6]

The freedom from traditional and philosophical authorities as well as from historical values transforms in modern atheism towards slavery to the scientifically articulated and verified. This entails in turn that both knowledge and science function in society in that popular form which does not allow one to judge of its certainty, quality and completeness, that is, of truth. Scientific knowledge becomes a world-outlook, ideology and a filter of social loyalty and adequacy. As a result, the abuse of science becomes a norm that creates an illusion of its efficiency and truth in all spheres of life. The scientific method is treated as self-sufficient and not being in need of any justification and evaluation. Science proclaims the truth of the world from within its own rationality functioning in the conditions of the disincarnate and anonymous consciousness. However by functioning in society science forgets about that simple truth that it is the human creation and its initial meaning was to guard the interests of people and not to make them slaves and hostages of the scientific method.

The situation with the dominance of the scientific approach in all aspects of life becomes even more paradoxical when one realizes that human beings do not become happier and freer from those aspects of the material existence which are constituted by the sciences. They cannot escape social injustice, hardship of mundane life, diseases and moral losses. This happens because science *does not know the ways and goals of its future development.* In its grandeur science has to intentionally disregard those aspects of reality which are not circumscribed by its rationality or which behave sporadically and unpredictably with respect to the scientific prognosis. The economic growth and welfare of the developed nations, the cult of consumption demand more technological developments related to the exploitation of the natural resources. Every new discovery in physics is employed for the optimization of the production of goods and energy, so that one can speak about merciless exploitation of the physical reality in general. It is very seldom that the question of the legitimacy and justification of such an exploitation is even thought of. By making nature an object of manipulation scientific consciousness forgets of its humanitarian duties with respect to nature: nature must be "respected" simply because we live in it and that there is the

---

6. See Comte-Sponville, *The Little Book.*

light of that all-embracing reason (Logos) in it which human beings carry in ourselves.

The ambitions of the immanent secular reason, supported by the scientific achievements seem to be even more strange if one realizes that modern science, in spite of its successes manifests the symptoms of a deep crisis related to the uncertainty of its goals. Scientific activity is purposive to the extent that accompanies any human activity. However when we speak of the uncertainty of goals of science in general, we mean something different: scientific quest is spontaneous and in many ways not related to the spiritual, infinite tasks of humanity. The practical purposiveness of scientific research thus unfolds only a particular sector of nature so that there remains a gap between that which has been known through a scientific phenomenalization and that which cannot be known by science at all. This fact manifests that nature has a propensity to remain *concealed* and to react with respect to human experiments unpredictably.[7]

The scientific advance leaves huge realms of being unexplored and unknown that becomes evident in theoretical sciences, in particular in cosmology. On the one hand cosmology provides us with a comprehensive theory of the universe supported by observations. On the other hand it has to admit that those forms of matter in the universe which are physically understood constitute only 4 percent of its material content (the remaining 96 percent associated with the so called "Dark Matter" and "Dark Energy" remain by now beyond the reach of experiments; their existence is a matter of a certain conviction for the sake of the theoretical coherence). The more cosmology refines its scenario of the universe's evolution, the more it realizes the abyss of the physically unknown. Speaking philosophically, cosmology makes clearly seen the boundaries of the *unconcealed* related to humanity: it is only 4 percent of mater in the universe that can be said to be consubstantial to human physical and biological form. Amazingly, however, that in spite of all evidence for the limited nature of our knowledge of the universe, cosmologists sometimes position themselves as "prophets and priests" of the universe, preaching of it as if they knew the absolute truth of the world.

One of the major attributes of modern science is the radical mathematization of nature. Physics and cosmology, through mathematical models and theories, predicate realities inaccessible in direct experiments. There is a paradoxical shift of representations of reality here: unobservable intelligible entities are treated as more fundamental and responsible for the contingent

---

7. For futurological accounts based on the threats originating in modern science, see Leslie, *The End of the World*; Rees, *Our Final Century*; Bostrom and Cirkovic, *Global Catastrophic Risks*.

display of visible nature. As we argued elsewhere the mathematization of nature is accompanied by the diminution of humanity, in particular a personal dimension of existence.[8] Person disappears from scientific discourse in spite of the fact that all scientific truths are articulated by persons. Science is being effected in the name of human persons, but these same persons turn out to be excluded from a scientific description. Persons are needed to disclose reality, but they "do not exist" for science as agencies of other non-scientific truths and individual lives. Science as a social process needs scientific workers but not persons as unique and unrepeatable events of disclosure of the universe. The same is true with respect to society that needs not persons but masses of individuals easily adapting to the norms of materialistic thinking and behavior stereotypes based on applications of the technological progress. The oblivion of person is treated by Christian theology as an encroachment on the absolute priority of the human world and those communal links in human societies which have formed the spirit and integrity of the historical paths of the Christian civilization. The oblivion of person is the encroachment on the historical significance of human history impressed in architectural images of European cities, in masterpieces of art, music and literature, on the ways of European thinking and its values. The oblivion of person constitutes an attack on all traditional forms of societies and life which by the logic of the economical must cease to exist or become indiscernible.

It is to defend person and to reinstate it to its central status in the dialogue between theology and science that becomes a characteristic feature of theological commitment in the dialogue. To reinstate person means to understand that the problem of theology and science manifests a basic distinction and division between two attitudes to life in one and the same human person: that one seeing man as a physical organism in rubrics of space and time, and another one, positioning man at the centre of disclosure and manifestation of the universe. The dialogue between theology and science becomes an explication of the split between these two attitudes which humanity attempts to reconcile. The very fact that this dialogue exists attests to that human beings transcend the conditions of their physical and biological existence. Thus the very fact of the dialogue as an existential event implies transcendence and thus asymmetry between theology and science. Correspondingly it seems doubtful that the dialogue between theology and science is possible without an internal conviction that both, theology and science represent different modalities of the relationship between humanity and the Divine. Being placed in the context of the Divine humanity the

---

8. See Nesteruk, *The Universe as Communion*, 188–205.

sciences are seen as propensities of the human condition capable of epistemological transfiguring the sense of the universe. The sense of the universe becomes comprehensible only from within the Divine Image in humanity whose archetype is Christ the Incarnate. In other words, to comprehend the sense of the universe one needs to "acquire" the mind of Christ so that the dialogue between science and Christian theology becomes a structural path of such an acquisition. Then it is humanity that becomes a central theme of the dialogue between theology and cosmology. Let us outline this point in more detail.

In any possible discussion of the relationship between theology and science (if theology is understood as experience God through life, whereas the physical sciences as explorations of the world within the already given life) there a question arises: what is the possible model of bringing into correlation of experiential aspects of life with those articulated knowledge of the world which positions humanity as one thing among others? In other words, if the Divine is perceived as the realm of the transcendent out of which life originates, whereas the realm of operation of the physical sciences is related to the created world, the mediation between theology and science becomes an outward explication of the sense of the human condition in communion with the giver of life. This is a different view at the dialogue in comparison with the often invoked traditional natural theology which makes inferences from the world to God. Natural theology based on modern science does not represent a particular interest, because it is clear in advance that the open-ended nature of the scientific enterprise will always contribute to the hermeneutic of the created world thus indefinitely filling the content of the natural theological conjectures with no hope to find a *certain* evidence that it is God who created and sustained the universe. The infinite advance of science places any modern natural theology in the conditions of *uncertainty* about claims of whether the world is created by God, or it is self-sufficient and requires no appeal to the transcendent.

The physical sciences treat the world as immanent, self-sufficient, and being explained by means of the physical laws. Thus they do not pose a question of the foundation of the contingent facticity of these laws, that is, the question of their sufficient reason. In this sense the question of contingent facticity of the worldly reality, that is, its concreteness, for example a concreteness of the global physical parameters of the universe, such as it size and age, cannot be posed by the physical sciences at all. One can add that the physical picture of the world is built and advanced by humanity in the conditions of impossibility to understand as to why science as a modus of the human activity is possible at all. Then, there is a question: what is the aim of the so called dialogue between theology and science when neither theology nor science understand the foundations of their very possibility? Theology refers the contingent facticity of the world to being created out of free love of God, whereas science explores this facticity as the already given. If the sciences attempt to make inferences from the world to God through searching for the signs of his presence, these signs always remain *uncertain* for they relate to the unknowable God, whose ultimate sense cannot be exhausted through the signifiers borrowed from this world. If theology, in the opposite move, places the content of its assertions in the physical context, it experiences another difficulty, because it attempts to present *events* of communion with the infinite God in rubrics of space and time, that is, by using a philosophical language, to enframe them in the phenomenality of objects.[9] The fact that this never achieves any desired goal creates an opposite situation that points to a *certainly* of a negative kind. Thus the dialogue between theology and science always remains in the boundaries of the human incapacity to break through the oppositions between the *negative certainty* of philosophy (in relation to establishing whether the ultimate sense of the world is in God or not), and, alternatively, the ever *positive uncertainty* of science constantly advancing its content and re-evaluating its own ontological claims with no hope that the latter converge to some objective truth. Both the *negative certainty* of philosophy with respect to ultimate questions, and the *positive uncertainty* of science with respect to knowledge of finite things point towards a particular dualistic *transcendental*[10] structure of human subjectivity that either struggles with the discursive justification of existential theological convictions or, alternatively, cannot existentially come to terms with the apriori limited capacity of discursive reason to produce *certain* statements about reality. In fact the dialogue between theology and science, seen philosophically, represents an intellectual endeavour of balancing in one and the same human subject the *negative*

---

9. In general the term "phenomenality" describes the quality or state of a *phenomenon*. For example phenomenality of mundane things corresponds to their being perceptible by the senses or through immediate experience. This constitutes the notion of the phenomenal world, as the world of visible, empirical phenomena. See more details in Glossary (Appendix 1).

10. The term "transcendental" must not be confused with "transcendent." The use of the adjective "transcendent" with an object points to its meaning as existing beyond experience as the underlying external cause of the phenomena mentally reconstructed. In contrast the "transcendental" means the general precondition of experience, methods of its access. Correspondingly whenever the term transcendental is employed, it implies the transcendental conditions of experience as related to the subject. In contrast to the transcendent object posed by the subject as being out there and independent of this subject's presence, the transcendental conditions (delimiters) assign rules and methods of selection of phenomena as if these phenomena represent the appearances of an object to the subject.

certainty about the impossibility of any response to the questions of existence of God, origin of the world and man, with the *positive uncertainty* in producing claims about the origin of the world and man, from within the scientific enterprise. This balancing between two opposites in one and the same human subject, that is, existing in two different attitudes with respect to its own life represents a basic feature of the human condition in which the ultimate reconciliation of these attitudes seems to be impossible.

Indeed, a careful insight points to the fact that both theological convictions and scientific articulations originate in one and the same humanity, whose essence and the sense of existence remain in both cases only *interpreted* but not fully understood. In other words, the link between the Divine and its creation is detected by human beings who stand at the crossroads of the worldly and transworldly (being in an old style parlance microcosm and mediator). The very possibility of formulating the task of mediation between theology and science belongs to humanity, so that inevitably the centre of this mediation and enquiry is the human being itself. The view that humanity is the major theme of the dialogue between theology and science can be confirmed by making a parallel between the dialogue, and a possible response to the famous philosophical paradox of subjectivity, which dramatizes the ambivalent position of humanity in the universe as, on the one hand, being the centre of disclosure and manifestation of the universe, and, on the other hand, being one tiny physical part of this universe.

The central philosophical fact for any discussion of the relationship between theology and science remains that the world and humanity are disclosed from the already existent facticity of life within the rubrics of the specifically human consciousness. An existential phenomenologist would say that the fact of life and disclosure of the world from within it, is a basic fact and the beginning of any further articulations of the world. This observation leads to the following conclusion: in spite of the fact that the facticity of the human articulating consciousness cannot be explained metaphysically, if this consciousness enquires into the sense of the difference between theology and science, the latter must be existentially unified as having origins in this consciousness. Then the mediation between theology and science must go down the route where the predication of God and the world both contain a unifying human element constitutive for the sense of God as well as of the world. This type of mediation between the Divine and the worldly must have some traces of the initial creation of the world and humanity. The very logic of mediation between God and the world must then have been implanted in the initial intention of God creating human beings in the world. Correspondingly the sense of the dialogue between theology and science can be seen as an attempt to disclose those motives of creation of humanity whose knowledge would one allow morally to balance the apparent tension between theology and the sciences.

In order to disclose these motives and bring them to articulation we point to the problematicity of the very knowability of the universe as a whole. Human beings are bodily limited in space and their physical brain comprises, let us say, twenty centimeters on a liner scale. However, it is from within this scale that human beings are capable of articulating the whole universe from its microscopic scales to the scales of clusters of galaxies and the entire universe. If this brain functioned only on the level of causal physical laws, it could not be able to transcend its given physical region and produce an instantaneous synthesis of the universe, the universe which is physically incommensurable with the human brain.[11] Nevertheless, the capacity to do so points to the fact that consciousness is fundamentally non-local and has features enabling humans to "view" the universe from the God-given perspective. The question is: where does this capacity come from? Modern evolutionary epistemologists and adherents to the theories of emergent complexity would argue that all this is the result of the long adaptive evolution in which consciousness ultimately appears as an epiphenomenon of the physical. Their optimistic efforts to reconcile the *physically empirical* with the *philosophically intelligible* represent a contribution to a *hermeneutic* (not explanation) of the human condition with no hope of making this hermeneutic ontological. In view of this one could proceed through a different, Christian *hermeneutic* of the human phenomenon as made in the Divine image, more concretely in the archetype of Christ, who was the Word-Logos of God incarnate in flesh of Jesus of Nazareth. The event of the Incarnation was the only historical reference pointing to the unification of the Divine and the worldly in the hypostasis of the Logos of God through whom and by whom all was made. It is this unification that forms that *archetype* of searching for the reconciliation in the human articulation of experience of God (manifested in "seeing" the universe as the unity of creation in a God-like fashion) and the world (explored scientifically), being *de facto* the task of the dialogue between theology and science. Regarding the archetype we refer to Christ's hypostatic union of the Divine and human, the archetype that human beings have to imitate in their scientific explorations. Humanity

---

11. One possible way of explicating the sense of what is meant by an instantaneous synthesis of the universe can be borrowed from Pierre Teilhard de Chardin: "Only in man, so far as we know, does spirit so perfectly unite around itself the universality of the universe that, in spite of the momentary dissociation of its organic foundation, nothing can any longer destroy the 'vortex' of operation and consciousness of which it is the subsisting centre. The human soul is the first fully formed purchase point that the Multiple can fasten onto it is drawn up by the Creation towards unity" (Teilhard de Chardin, "My Universe," in *Science and Christ*, 47).

is capable of attempting such a unification as a modus of communion with God only in consciousness, whose created hypostasis *imitates* (i.e., uses as an archetype) the hypostasis of the Logos. In this sense the goal and an "infinite task" of the dialogue between theology and science can be seen as a conscious effectuation of communion of creation with God through human knowledge in the image of the incarnate Christ. The dialogue thus explicates the sense of the incarnational archetype in humanity's constitution.

If the Incarnation is understood traditionally, as related to the embodiment of the Logos in the human flesh of Jesus of Nazareth, then its very possibility is linked to the existence of Jesus' body and the body of his Mother, the Virgin Mary. In this case the logic of creation must have contained a possibility of emergence of Jesus' body (and bodies of all other humans) in the process of cosmological and biological evolution.[12] Then the role of science in the dialogue with theology is to explicate the sense of the physical reality in the context of the human existence. One can recall the cosmological Anthropic Principle (AP) attempting to create a causal link from the facticity of humanity to the necessity of the universe. However, in the context of the dialogue with theology this AP acquires some new qualities, related not only to human biological bodies (and Jesus' flesh) but to the possibility of the Incarnation of God: the AP becomes a Theo-Anthropic Principle, implying that the conditions for the Incarnation in the universe must have been in place from the beginning (i.e., the Incarnation, in accordance with the Nicene Creed, was prepared by God before creating the universe).[13]

The link between the possibility of the Incarnation and the structure of the universe is assumed only on the level of the *necessary* conditions: indeed the universe in its actual display is *necessary* for the Incarnation to take place, but not *sufficient*. Theologically, this insufficiency originates in the hidden role of the Holy Spirit in the Incarnation of Christ. The fact that Christ, according to the Creed, was "incarnate of the Holy Spirit and the

---

12. A new evolutionary basis for the christological ideas (as some authors said, a renewal of Christology) was for the first time explicitly formulated by Teilhard de Chardin: "Christ, as we know, fulfils Himself gradually, through the ages in the sum of our individual endeavours. Why should we treat this fulfilment as though it possessed none but a metaphorical significance, confining it entirely within the abstract domain of purely supernatural action? Without the process of biological evolution, which produced the human brain, there would be no sanctified souls; and similarly, without the evolution of collective thought, through which alone the plenitude of human consciousness can be attained on earth, how can there be a consummated Christ?" (Teilhard de Chardin, "A Note on Progress," in *The Future of Man*, 23).

13. See Torrance, *Space, Time, and Incarnation*; Murphy, "Cosmology and Christology"; Murphy, "The Incarnation as a Theanthropic Principle."

Virgin Mary," implies that the event of the Incarnation happened freely both from the Divine and human side (Mary's free "yes" on behalf of humanity), that is, as not being subjected to the necessities of nature (thus implying the fundamental otherness between God and the world). If, by a virtue of a philosophical negligence one would not discern a difference between the *necessary* and *sufficient* conditions by equating them, one runs the risk of ontologizing the Incarnation of God in Jesus Christ and transferring the fleshly revelation of God in Christ to all structural levels of reality. A theological move in this direction happens in modern discussions of Christology called "Deep Incarnation."[14] Their essence can be expressed as follows: "the Incarnation of God in Christ can be understood as a radical or 'deep' incarnation, that is, an incarnation into the very tissue of biological existence, and system of nature."[15] The idea of Deep Incarnation extends the scope of the Western theology of redemption (and salvation) towards non-human realms of the world, the universe in its entirety, so that "faithful to the biblical promises of a new heavens and new earth, salvation can be seen to involve the whole creation."[16] Whatever the motivation of the proponents

---

14. For a general introduction to this idea see Edwards, *Deep Incarnation*, and Gregersen (who coined the term "deep incarnation"), *Incarnation*, 361–80 .

15. Gregersen, "The Cross of Christ," 205.

16. Edwards, *Deep Incarnation*, xvi. Another point is related to the recent advance in understanding that the biological evolution on this planet involved an incredible loss, pain and death, leading to the question "How can we think of the good, generous and loving God of biblical faith in relationship to the costs of evolution?" (Edwards, *Deep Incarnation*, xvii). In view of such a question the idea of Deep Incarnation insists that the Incarnation cannot be considered in isolation from the totality of the Christ-event that includes Resurrection, Ascension, and the action of the Holy Spirit upon history (Pentecost). This is the reason why the Cross in this view is identified with creation in its evolutionary emergence, "and as an icon and microcosm of God's redemptive presence to all creatures in their suffering and death" (Edwards, *Deep Incarnation*, xviii).

The idea of the Cross as a symbol of evolution was expressed in many works of Teilhard de Chardin. Here are, for example, two quotations: (1) "I am convinced that Christ-the-Redeemer is fulfilling himself and unfolding himself in the figure of Christ-Evolver. Thereby . . . the meaning of the Cross is taking on greater breath and dynamism for us: the Cross which is now the symbol not merely of the dark retrogressive side of the universe in genesis, but also and even more, . . . the Cross which is the symbol of progress and victory won through mistakes, disappointments and hard work" (Teilhard de Chardin, "Introduction to the Christian Life," in *Christianity and Evolution*, 163). (2) "Let us turn back to the Cross—and look at a crucifix. What we see nailed to the wood—suffering, dying, freeing—is that really still the God of original sin? . . . Or is it not the God of evolution? Or rather, is not the God of evolution . . . precisely and simply, taken in the fullest sense of the words in a generalised form, the very God of expiation? And this because, if we consider the matter carefully, 'to bear the sins of the guilty world' means precisely, translated and transpose into terms of cosmogenesis, 'to bear the weight of a world in a state of evolution'" (Teilhard de Chardin, "What the World Is

of Deep Incarnation theorists, the tendency of smoothing out the difference between the necessary and sufficient conditions of the historical Incarnation jeopardizes the whole concept by placing it in the framework of another metaphysical concept of the immanent presence of God (the concept which can be subjected to a theological critique).

The situations where the distinction between the *necessary* and *sufficient* conditions become manifest can be found in cosmology and anthropology, for example, when the latter deal with creation of the universe, formation of Earth, appearance of terrestrial life-forms and emergence of self-conscious Homo Sapiens. Indeed, the necessary physical conditions on this planet do no entail the appearance of life forms, a cell for example. Biology at this stage of its development is not capable of producing a living cell from an inorganic matter. The very idea of evolution turns out to be so incredibly complex and improbable that scientists doubt that if nature on Earth had to start it again it could actually happen, and even if it happened then its outcome would hardly be the same. Thus the sufficient conditions of the evolution and its outcomes remain concealed. Since the Incarnation is linked to the fact of existence of intelligent life on Earth, the sufficient conditions for the Incarnation as a contingent historical event are not understood scientifically. Physics, through cosmology and astrobiology, just confirms this by showing that the more we understand the sense of biological life, the more we understand our incapacity of explaining its origin, in particular the origin of intelligence. All this points with a new force to the fundamental premise of any theologizing and scientific knowledge, namely the unknowability of the sufficient conditions for existence of humanity and hence the unknowability of the possibility of knowledge as such. The sciences operate in the conditions of this unknowability and explicate this unknowability through their advance even further. In this sense one can conjecture that the dialogue between theology and science explicates in a characteristic way humanity's inability to know itself.

The unfolding of the sense of the universe from within events of life entails that cosmology, in a way, turns out to be "subordinated" to anthropology. Philosophically this means that the interpretation of cosmological ideas is based on the epistemological centrality of humanity from within which the universe is disclosed and constituted. Theologically, this means that the sense of the universe is established from within the relations between God and man, that is, from within a concrete earthly history being an arena for these relations. As was expressed by Christos Yannaras, if "the

---

Looking from the Church of God at This moment: A Generalising and a Deepening of the Meaning of the Cross," in *Christianity and Evolution*, 218–19).

entire fact of the world to be constituted as an existential fact, then every reality is recapitulated in the relationship of humanity with an active reason (*logos*) as an *invitation-to-relationship*, which is directed towards humanity alone."[17] In both philosophical and theological aspects of such an approach to the universe one can find a phenomenological reversal of the anthropological problem: humanity is not inserted in the allegedly pre-existing cosmic order but, on the contrary, cosmological evolution receives its epistemological origin in the order of the human history. This origin expresses the initial and unresolvable mystery of the human existence associated with the fact of humanity's creaturehood, its coming into being through the act of the Divine love. A phenomenological method of treating the content of cosmological theories as reflecting human experience, so to speak, their interiorization by the *ego*, explicates a simple truth that cosmology manifests a particular modus of the human condition. Whereas physical cosmology mercilessly dooms human beings to homelessness in the universe, their physical mediocrity, and effective non-existence in the divided and non-consubstantial layers of physical reality, the scientifically informed theology subjects the human spirit to a severe test of resisting despair in attempts to grasp the sense of existence through transcendence, that is, a perception of humanity's commensurability with the universe through the God-given ability to contemplate all its temporal and spatial extensions as one great whole, as that which humanity must passionately love and feel it as clothing Christ the Incarnate (whose archetype is carried by humanity) in it.

Within such a vision of the universe cosmology turns out to be geocentric, because it is anthropocentric. However this geocentricity has a theological foundation, for the meeting of God with humanity took place on Earth[18] and the fact that the universe is disclosed from a specific and contingent location in the universe becomes an expression of the Christocentric essence of cosmology. The very possibility of the integral knowledge of the physically disjoint world has its origin in the archetype of the Divine image in man, that is, of Christ, understood not only as a carrier of the human nature, but also as the Logos-Word of God who continuously sustains creation and its economy at all of its scales and remote corners. It is this archetype, when Christ is treated as the "Lord of the worlds" (cf. Rev 1:16), that is gifted to humanity in order it could know the universe at those scales which incommensurably exceed in depth as well as at large the physical and biological limits of the human existence. One can say that the very possibility of knowing the universe becomes in a certain way the experiencing of

---

17. Yannaras, *Postmodern Metaphysics*, 137.
18. Cf. Lossky, *Orthodox Theology*, 64.

the event of the Incarnation of the Lord of the worlds, from within which the universe as a whole manifests itself as an event of the history of the Divine humanity, that event which intrinsically contains the whole natural history of the universe: "When Christ appeared in the arms of Mary, what he had just done was to raise up the world."[19]

Even if cosmology disregards a theological stance on the human centrality in the universe and approaches the latter in the natural attitude,[20] that is, as an outcome and epiphenomenon of the physical and biological evolution, yet the universe appears to man from within the transcendental delimiters which pertain to the human bodily condition. Thus the picture of the universe contains not only that which can be phenomenalized, that is, represented as objects, but the very conditions of the possibility of such a constitution. If one assumes that the cognitive faculties as well as human reason originate from something physical and biological, one looses here the problem of hypostatic, that is, personal existence because intelligent personhood is that aspect of the individually unrepeatable, event-like existence with respect to which science (functioning in the conditions of personhood) can only think in terms of riddles. It is because of this that theology inevitably enters into a cosmological discourse as a pointer to that from which the source of constitution of the universe originates, namely to the Divine Image in humanity. In this sense the explication of the epistemic procedures employed in cosmology, in its essence, becomes the explication of the meaning of the idea of the Divine Image in man in given biological conditions.

Our desire to reflect upon knowledge of the universe from within experience of life corresponds to the overcoming of "ontocosmology" as that abstract science of the universe as a whole which, ultimately, in analogy with ontotheology leads to the "death of the universe" in a moral sense, portraying the universe without beauty, value and *telos* that have been attributed to the cosmic order since the ancient Greeks. To achieve this one must transcend the scientifically organized universe in a very sophisticated sense: even if cosmology asserts human existence as insignificant, it cannot remove the intuitive content of the trans-worldly dimension that pertains to human persons who articulate their position in the universe. When the scientific mind poses physical reality as objective and independent of the human insight, it is not as if human history has been "cosmosized," that is,

---

19. Teilhard de Chardin, "My Universe," in *Science and Christ*, 61.

20. The natural attitude is related to the activity of consciousness within which one acts in a world that is real, a world that existed before this one was born and that which one thinks will continue to exist after he or she dies. See more details in the Glossary (Appendix 1).

placed in the cosmic context, being reduced to the necessities of substances and the laws of the universe. It is completely the opposite: the universe is being "humanized," that is, hypostasized (articulated), becoming the content and structure of the human subjectivity and a part of the unfolding human order. The universe, being interpreted by the sciences, becomes epistemologically immanent to humanity whereas humanity retains its transcendence to it. It is such an intrinsic split in experience of existence that is encoded in the dialogue between theology and science

Hence in order to effectuate the dialogue between theology and science, and to advance our comprehension of the universe and humanity's place in it, we need to do this in conjunction with the proper anthropological insights, being both philosophical, theological as well as scientific. This means that the very dialogue becomes constitutive of anthropology. In this sense such a dialogue manifests itself as an existential propensity of humanity. To clarify such an approach to the dialogue one needs to expose how it is conducted in most known of its forms by pointing out that the philosophical sense of mediation between theology and science is not elucidated and thus the dialogue is taking place in an empirical fashion with no clear understanding of why it is possible at all and what is its existential sense. Then and only then it would be possible to defend our main thesis that the major subject matter of such a dialogue is human being in the condition of the split of intentionalities of its consciousness expressed through the paradox of subjectivity. From within such a vision one could make sense of a theological (biblical, patristic, etc.) narration about the human position in being and its ultimate destiny (in conjunction with the scientific stance on the sense of the human). Certainly this will never become an accomplished explanation of the sense of the human existence but only a pointer within an open-ended hermeneutics of the human condition elucidating at each of its stages the sense of human beings as creatures of God in the world.

The proposed approach to the dialogue between theology and science thus implies that cosmology and anthropology are intrinsically intertwined as two parts of one and the same "book of created being." A proper anthropology cannot be a-cosmic, whereas cosmology is anthropic by its very constitution. Yet, this seeming symmetry is broken by the fact that the overall disclosure of existence is being made from within the human embodied subjectivity, that is, from within an empirical fact of life. In this sense the ultimate foundation and the sense of the dialogue proceeds from the already existing life that can be made explicable only to a certain extent. In other words, the facticity of what human beings call "man=humanity," that is, the facticity of itself, as well as the facticity of the universe in the image of this humanity, remain fundamentally undisclosed and phenomenologically concealed from the enquiring subject. However, being empirical facts, the seeing of man and the universe takes place and contributes into the affirmation of their facticity phenomenologically constituting the sense of the universe and humanity in the conditions of incomprehensibility of their ultimate origin. What is then the sense of the dialogue between theology and science? This dialogue can be seen as a polemics about the primacy of cosmology and anthropology, that is, about what comes first, assuming implicitly that the ultimate facticity of both of them, including the very dialogue proceed from the inexplicability of life as a given fact. The way of interaction between cosmology and anthropology in man takes its shape exactly in the dialogue between theology and science. Theology always remains hidden in all cosmological and anthropological predications as the ground of their mutual contingent facticity. One can say that theology intrinsically pertains to the human condition as that intuitive mechanism which resists natural and spontaneous perceptions of the multivarious being in general; as was expressed by Teilhard de Chardin: "The function of religion is to provide a foundation of morality, by introducing a dominating principle of order, an axis of movement, into the restless and undisciplined multitude of reflective atoms: something of supreme value, to create, to hold in awe, or to love."[21]

The scientific exposition of the worldly realities places man in the chaos of impersonal physical entities and laws equating humanity with the star-dust and treating it as an insignificant matter. Theology, as a resisting force inherent in the human constitution as related to communion with the Divine, exercises humility with respect to the created existence and inspires one to a search for its sense. The fact that theology associates the human existence as proceeding from its communion with God positions theology in an asymmetric position with respect to the sciences, for theology turns out to be a hidden narrative of existence inscribed in human beings in their blood and bones, in their psyche and consciousness. Life is the primary source of observation and thought, and this is why in both anthropology and cosmology there is a hidden message about this life. Correspondingly both terms of the dialogue, theology and science, speak differently of life that initiates them. But the source of narration is life itself, so that in the same way as the first breath of a man shouts of God, the dialogue between theology and science is the ongoing invocation of God in the conditions of being created by him.

Finally we need to make a comment on the sense of the title of this book. As we have already said, it contains three basic themes: universe, humanity and God, that is, it deals with the universe *in* the image of humanity,

---

21. Teilhard de Chardin, "Christianity in the world," in *Science and Christ*, 99.

and humanity as the image of God. The image of God in Homo Sapiens does not entail that the universe is made in the image of God. Here lies a basic dichotomy of humanity that will be a subject matter of this book: humanity is *Imago Dei*, but the universe is not—it is the image *in Imago Dei*, that is, the "image of the image." In others words, there is something in humanity of the universe but, at the same time, the concept of *Imago Dei* implies something very specific (may be an emergent property) that positions humanity outside the whole chain of biological beings. This "outside" is not that which diminishes the sense of the rest of the universe, but says that there is something in humanity which cannot be accounted by the natural sciences. And here, in this something, lies the whole pathos of the classical concept of humanity as *Imago Dei*. But *Imago Dei* is possible only because humanity is the incarnate consciousness linked through its body to the physical universe. The fact that the universe is physical so that its articulation is possible only by human embodied agencies points to a simple truth that *Imago Dei* implies its physical existence. Yet, this existence is radically different in comparison with all other material and biological creations because it is the only one endowed with hypostatic consciousness capable of positioning itself in front of the world, but not being entirely of the world. Thus the basic feature of the human created condition as *Imago Dei* is its capacity to articulate its relationship to the Creator by articulating its creation. The sense of this relationship is a big theological issue that cannot be fully addressed here, but we need to mention some basic ideas which are used in this research.

It is understood by theologians as well as scientific and cultural anthropologists that the canonical tradition of *Imago Dei* must not be treated in abstractio outside of those socio-historical conditions which humanity experiences at present. They use a pluralistic and transdisciplinary approach to the biblical origin of this concept in order to avoid a risk of promoting speculative ideas. First of all this relates to the indispensable and basic condition—humanity's corporeality. Theology never dwells for a long on this issue simply implying the existence of bodies of theologians. Unlike the latter many philosophers of the twentieth century insisted that no sensible anthropology is possible without taking into account human's "being-in-the-world." In this case the sense of the concept of *Imago Dei* is related to the human specificity as a biological species which are produced through a long evolutionary process requiring for it very possibility quite delicate cosmological and geological conditions. In this sense, being an Image of the transcendent God, humanity retains the features of the physical universe. And it is because the bodily specificity is common to all mankind that the essence of the Divine image is uniform. If the corporeality as a component of *Imago Dei* becomes the *necessary* condition for human's communion with God, it is the *sufficient* conditions for the possibility of this communion that determine the sense of humanity as *Imago Dei* as related to those qualities which (as a possibility) emerge from a historical and cultural evolution. Usually they are identified with reason, intellect, rationality, functionality related to the dominance over the planet Earth and other forms of sociocultural responsibility including science. But ultimately *Imago Dei* asserts our relation with God drawn on the basis of some theological ideas such as their vision of God (as the unconditional love implemented in love to neighbor, world and God himself), or as the aspiration to salvation as eternal life which positions anthropology in the eschatological perspective. Yet, with all respect to these qualities, that which makes humanity radically unique among other biological forms is their *internal experience of life as existence* through which this humanity sees and interprets the surrounding world. Whether this property of the human life is phylogenetic, that is, *emergent* on the level of the whole species, or whether it is somehow transmitted through the fusion of the human life with God, it is this basic feature that makes humanity capable of imitating God by enquiring into the ultimate origin of things and of itself. Combined with the corporeal consciousness of the world this propensity of having internal experience forms humanity's ability to carry out scientific research, produce technology as well as various aspects of culture. Science, in a way, serves as an outward tool that indirectly manifests of this internal experience: it outlines the necessary physical and biological conditions of this experience thus demonstrating that the worldly elements are indispensable for this experience to the same extent as self-consciousness and symbolic thinking. Scientific achievements contribute to the anthropology of *Imago Dei*, but never exhaust its meaning.

However, the basic feature of the human condition that defines it as *Imago Dei* in the Christian sense is being the transcendental "me" constantly experiencing itself as living but not being the source of this life. In other words, humans as *Imago Dei* experience themselves as creatures, as being sons of God and thus predisposed to salvation. This is a different definition of the human condition as communion, that is, a fusion with the Divine Life which has neither beginning nor end. But the obviousness of such a communion as life among the living humans is dimmed by the initial forgetting of the givenness of life which ascribed by consciousness to the *immemorial*. This is the reason why the image of God in spite of its latent presence in human beings is not functional unless humans rediscover the absolute source of life through an attempt to trace down their origin and its sense. The sciences help in this direction by placing the physical conditions of life in the cosmological context thus transferring the problem of the facticity of every hypostatic human being towards the realm of the contingent facticity of the universe, that is, to the issue of creation in general. Yet, what remains for theology is to deal with every particular hypostatic existence experienced as unique, unrepeatable and incommunicable. This problem is metaphysically irresolvable and is known as a radical man's inability to know himself. As we argue below, this aspect of the human existence is the constitutive feature of *Imago Dei*, as the image of that God who by definition is unknowable.

In conclusion, since this book is dealing with science that articulates the bodily condition of humanity as well as its rational capacity to relate itself to the world (and God), we intentionally reduce our understanding of *Imago Dei* to two basic and generic features of the human condition: its corporeality, as well as its reflected experience of existence, initiating all other cognitive faculties, whose contingent facticity remains epistemologically incomprehensible. Humanity as *Imago Dei* experiences fusion with God and reflects upon this by stating its own existence as a problem. It is this reflection that forms a religious response to this problem by invoking the idea of the Creator as that absolute Life in relation to which humanity receives the condition of being its children.

The theological objective of achieving the union with God (deification) then can be philosophically reformulated as an unceasing attempt of overcoming the innate forgetting of the condition of the children of Life understood as God. Since all human activities including those of the sciences are carried out in the condition of this forgetting, the sciences themselves can only fragmentarily contribute to the overcoming of this forgetting when any metaphysical reference to the foundation of existence is experienced as a failure. In a way, one can say that the existential overcoming of this initial forgetting represents a second birth which paves the way to that which theology calls salvation. Seen in this perspective the dialogue between theology and science can indeed be considered as a hermeneutics of *Imago Dei* in the sense that it deals with the balancing of the extent of overcoming of the initial forgetting in theology and science. In the following chapters we describe how an attempted overcoming of the initial forgetting in human life cascades towards overcoming of such a forgetting in cosmology, and *vice versa*.

THE PLAN OF THE BOOK

The book consists of two parts which conditionally divide its content onto anthropological and cosmological. The logic of the book follows an idea that anthropology and cosmology complement each other while reading the "book of being."

Part 1, "Humanity as a Central Theme of the Dialogue between Theology and Science," deals with anthropology by arguing that in view of the radical unknowability of humanity by itself, the phenomenon of humanity becomes the central theme of the dialogue between theology and science whose sense infolds as a hermeneutics of the human condition. Then Part 2, "The Universe in the Image of *Imago Dei* or Humanity as Hypostasis of the Universe," deals with the cosmological aspects of the human condition as they are articulated from within the human cognitive faculties, and hence representing the *image* of the Divine Image, thus contributing to the hermeneutic of life in its incarnate condition in the universe. The "Conclusion" recapitulates that the sense of the unknowable humanity as well as the sense of the actually infinite universe can be achieved through the restoration of the primarily forgotten memory of being the children of God, whose aim is to return to their home in the Kingdom via a temporary cosmic route. The dialogue between theology and science represents a particular modus of such a restoration, although never ending and hence having an eschatological sense.

In more details, Part 1, chapter 1, "The Dialogue between Theology and Science: Its Sense and Philosophical Foundations," deals with a discussion of why the very approach to the relationship between theology and science requires a philosophical elucidation. A detailed philosophical distinction between theology and science is carried out on the basis of the demarcation in the modes of the *given* that amounts to the difference in the underlying ontology in the sciences (physical substance and biological formations) *versus* ontology of events (in theology). It is argued that no demarcation between science and theology on the basis of the opposition between ontic and ontological can be achieved contributing to the argument that a positing of experience of the Divine outside the material conditions represents faith without reason whose existential and soteriological sense remains obscure. At the same time any physical reductionism in the constitution of humanity also fails without an appeal to theology of the human creation in the image of God, for it is a human insight that is present behind all articulations of the universe and responsible for the distinction and hence demarcation between theology and science. Then the same distinction in the *modi* of *givens* in theology and science is discussed *theologically* leading to the conclusion that the difference between the natural and super—or trans—natural which one could, by the way of a historical analogy, apply for the demarcation of science, philosophy and theology, fails in the case of a human being. Humanity's inability to know itself, being interpreted theologically, forms the precondition for the actual limited knowability of the world. This implies that cosmology follows the same *apophatic* pattern of explanation typical for the theological anthropology of the divine image. The difference in the status of phenomenality of things in physics and cosmology, and events in theology amounts to the limited scope of cosmology and unknowability of the universe understood as creation, for the sphere of its phenomenality does not take into account the event-like essence of the human phenomenon. The unknowability of humanity by itself constitutes the basic paradox of the human condition that, on the one hand, asserts the facticity of human life and, on the other hand, this facticity's incomprehensibility. The dialogue between theology and science thus becomes an attempt to balance (not to reconcile) this fundamental dichotomy in one and the same humanity by advocating the inevitability of the Divine-given life and its soteriological meaningfulness in the background of its cosmic insignificance.

Chapter 2, "The Unknowability of Humanity and Paradox of Subjectivity at the Inception of the Dialogue between Theology and Science," continues to discuss the identified dichotomy in the human condition through a careful analysis of the well-known in philosophy paradox of subjectivity. There are two particular points in respect to this paradox which are made: first, it is theologically related to the essence of the human condition as being created (not just to the human post-lapserian condition); second, by being related to the unknowability of humanity, this paradox encapsulates the phenomenological concealment of conditions related to birth, that is, to the origin of personal life. As such the paradox expresses a primary forgetting of that which human consciousness poses discursively for itself as the issue of its origins. This primary forgetting is the forgetting of the self-affectivity of life itself, whose donation by the Holy Spirit (the Giver of Life) is exactly that which is forgotten in the paradox. Since, theologically, the Holy Spirit, the Giver of Life is not transparent in rubrics of space and time but shows the Face of the incarnate Word-Logos of God, the explication of the paradox's facticity will have to appeal to the archetype of the human condition in the incarnate Christ. Thus the tension between the two theses of the paradox of subjectivity can be "removed" through an appeal to the typology of the incarnate Christ who, being in human flesh on Earth, remains the Word-Logos of God sustaining the whole universe.

In chapter 3, "The Dialogue between Theology and Science as an Open-Ended Hermeneutic of the Human Condition," the paradox of subjectivity is placed into the cosmological context resulting in humanity's perception of its non-attunement and homelessness in the astronomical universe. However, it is argued that humanity is predisposed to some intimacy with the universe as it is affected by the universe in its incarnate condition in the Divine Image. It is this intimacy of living in the universe in communion with God that initiates the dialogue between theology and science, the dialogue which is destined to explicate this dualistic sense of humanity. The inseparability of humanity and the universe in its articulated image constitutes the content of that which is called life's self-affectivity and it is this content that implicitly constitutes the core of the dialogue between theology and science. Life's self-affectivity becomes a matter of enquiry in the dialogue through being split into two phenomenological structures: that of the life as proceeding from the self-affectivity of the a-cosmic Life as God (communion), and that of the human life in the conditions of the world. The vision of the universe within the natural attitude (employed in the sciences) is only possible as being initiated from within a phenomenological structure of life as related to its ultimate source in the Divine. Finally it is argued that the dialogue between theology and cosmology should be considered as a mediation between two phenomenological structures, two types of the *given* within the facticity of one and the same human life. Theology and science are seen as parts of life that neither confuses science with theology nor transmutes the one into the other. Here is a christological analogy (paralleling theology and science) with the divine and human natures of Christ. Then there is our main claim that in the same way as the sense of the hypostatic union in Christ is subjected to an open-ended biblical and theological hermeneutics, the dialogue between theology and science represents an open-ended hermeneutics of the hypostatic human condition: such a dialogue cannot hope to reconcile or unify two phenomenalities in one and the same subject, that is, no reconciliation of theology and science is possible to the same extent as impossible to overcome the ontological difference between creation and God even in the process of deification. Cosmology, being a counterpart of the dialogue and dealing with the universe through the constitution of the world of physical objects, enters this dialogue through an open-ended scientific hermeneutics of the universe within the self-givenness of life. This hermeneutics reflects the working of the human subjectivity thus contributing to the hermeneutics of the human condition.

Part 2, "The Universe in the Image of *Imago Dei* or Humanity as Hypostasis of the Universe," starts with the justification of the thesis that since, in the dialogue between theology and science, humanity confronts itself in two different modalities of its functioning in the world, that is, as hypostatic existence and as functioning corporeal subjectivity, it is reasonable to claim that cosmology, as a special physical and mathematical thematization of the human existence, contributes indirectly towards the problem of constitution of hypostatic corporeality, that is, personhood. This conclusion determines the next move in our research that attempts to locate the presence of personhood behind the cosmological constructions as being intrinsically implanted in questions of the universe's origin appealing to the theological, philosophical and scientific narrative of creation of the universe. By giving a brief outline of such a narrative, we concentrate on the fact that it is impossible to adequately reflect upon creation by remaining in the natural attitude because any speculation about creation is made in the conditions of already being created. In order to illustrate this point two historical examples are considered: one from patristic theology, and another from Kant's treatment of cosmological (mathematical) antinomies. Both examples deal with the perennial objection to the idea of creation on the basis of the question "Why not sooner of creation?" We argue that the question of "Why not sooner of creation?" is intrinsically based in the human enquiry in the sense of its existence in the world and de facto becomes a question about the contingent facticity of the created world as it is given to humanity. The posing the question about the origin of the world becomes that inherent feature of the human existing as being created, which as such provides an outward expression of the Divine Life's self-affectivity. Then the answer to the question of "Why not sooner of creation?" cannot receive any interpretation as a question about the universe, but it can be interpreted as a question about humanity in the universe in the Image of the incarnate God. Since creation, or the universe as a whole, cannot be grasped within the natural attitude, it represents, from a phenomenological point of view, a special kind of a phenomenon whose intuitive content saturates intuition and blocks the discursive faculty of cognition to provide any accomplished conceptual representation of the universe. Yet a human being is in the universe and thus is being affected by it in a non-trivial sense. At the same time the articulated image of the universe (even in the natural attitude) is that of a human production so that it contains in itself the conditions of its own inadequacy of being presented as an "object." In this sense cosmology becomes similar to theology, for the universe as a whole, as creation, represents rather a revelation, than any explicable metaphysical necessity. Placed in rubrics of that phenomenality which pertains to events, the universe manifest and reveals itself in the history of humanity in the same way as some phenomena associated with the Revelation of God, thus influencing and forming the sense of human life. One may talk about the historicity of the universe in a non-objective sense. One implies the historicity of appearance and manifestation of the universe as a whole as its contingent givenness to humanity, that is, as a humanly historical relation with it and communion. This historicity originates in humanity's enhypostasization of the universe through experiencing the belonging to it and attempting to construct its knowledge as a humanity's effort to understand the sense of its own existence. It is through enhypostasizing the universe that humanity encounters the hypostasis of the Logos in whose Image this humanity is made. Then the sense of the universe is disclosed through the relation of humanity with that Logos who at some stage of his manifestation descended to this universe physically. Then the Incarnation, as unforeseeable, metaphysically impossible, irreproducible, beyond measure of quantity and quality event was a renewal of the old teaching that God created the universe as an instant of his unconditional Love, cascading in the human presentation of this universe to the ever-manifesting event, endowing this humanity with a potential to achieve hypostatically a union with God. Creation becomes not only a place of indwelling but a place of praise of the Creator for his creation. As a place of praise creation is *inside* humanity, but as the outer universe creation is not *in* it. Being a site of praise, humanity is inside God, but being at the same time an earthly flesh, it is not in God, because it is created by God. Thus human persons perceive themselves between the unconditional gift to praise and the conditions for this gift to be received and responded. Creation as a theological issue thus receives its consummation in the problem of the human ego, as the riddle of the hypostatic self-affectivity. Then the cosmological sense of creation appears through an incessant search of the praising community to release itself from the sense of the conditioned, by reconstituting its own immemorial origin. The aporia of the human condition as the phenomenological concealment of its origin is transfigured in human life into the modality of praise of the creator through creation that removes as irrelevant any questions about the facticity of this praise as the manifestation of life's self-affectivity. The universe as creation is constituted in the image of *Imago Dei*, that is, in the image of that one who is gifted with the possibility of praising God for creation.

Part 1

HUMANITY AS A CENTRAL THEME OF THE DIALOGUE BETWEEN THEOLOGY AND SCIENCE

1

THE DIALOGUE BETWEEN THEOLOGY AND SCIENCE

Its Sense and Philosophical Foundations

"Christianity is not a philosophical school for speculating about abstract concepts, but is essentially a communion with the living God.... The question between theology and philosophy has never arisen in the East.... This is why there is no philosophy more or less Christian.... Christian theology is able to accommodate itself very easily to any a scientific theory of the universe."

—Vladimir Lossky

"Theology's relationship to philosophy—that is, to philosophy's interpretation of the world—constitutes that basis for Christianity's dialogue with the natural sciences."

—Wolfhart Pannenberg

WHY THE RELATION BETWEEN THE TERMS IN THE DIALOGUE OF THEOLOGY WITH SCIENCE CANNOT BE SYMMETRIC?

There are two points of view with respect to relations between theology and philosophy, and hence between theology and science that are reflected in the above quotations. Both belong to Christian theologians of the twentieth century. One is Orthodox, another one is Lutheran. The first one assumes that theology "can accommodate" any scientific synthesis of the universe with no recourse to philosophy. The second one claims that it is philosophy that is the mediator between theology and science. Yet, with all respect to the view of Vladimir Lossky, the question remains on how to carry out what he calls "accommodation" of scientific truth to theology? What is the method? If Lossky implies that theology can do this itself without appeal to any wider system of thought, then he also implies that theology is a meta-discourse which oversees all spheres of human knowledge and existence. If one accepts such a stance on theology there arises a task of elucidating philosophy and the sciences theologically. Can one speak of theology of philosophy, or theology of science? Eidetically, this way of thought is possible if one disregards that theologians exist in specific and concrete physical conditions that need to be taken into account. Since these conditions lie in the foundation of the very possibility of theology, their intrinsic presence in every theological formula point towards the fact that the very possibility of theology has a basis disclosed by the sciences and scientific philosophy. This implies that the method of mediation between theology, philosophy and the sciences cannot be theological per se. It needs some input from the sciences, but their mediation is carried out by philosophy playing a role of a method of such a mediation. This is the reason why it seems timely to attempt to clarify the method of mediation between Orthodox theology and the sciences by developing some philosophical insights.

Indeed, modern discussions on mediation between Christian theology and science imply a form of a "dialogue" between them, positioning both theology and science as symmetric terms in such a mediation. This is typical practically for all recent versions of the dialogue between science and Christian theology, when science and theology are compared and related from a sort of external to both of them epistemological point of view. This approach dominates nearly all discussions tackled from within different Christian denominations.[1] Regardless whether this "dialogue" evolves

---

1. The literature on the dialogue is enormous but most of the titles are not dealing with the epistemological issues of faith and reason presuming that the latter are not subject to an enquiry in their facticity. There are few examples. Roman Catholic: Jaki,

into attempts of reconciliation of theology and science, or, on the contrary, insists on separation of theology and science, it is tacitly assumed that there is a common and universal ground of such a mediation. The assumption that theology and science can be brought to a "common denominator" that allows one to make a comparison and establish relation between them is not clearly justified. In this sense the dialogue is carried out in the conditions of ignoring the long-standing philosophical discussion on faith and reason.

The uncritical implication of a "common denominator" assumption can lead either to serious conflicts between theology and science, or attempts of their heroic reconciliation without a clear indication of their differences. Here is an example of such a difference on a theological side when Christ declares "I am the Way; I am the Truth; and I am the Life" (John 14:6), introducing for his contemporaries a purely phenomenal definition of life that reappears constantly in the Scriptures. Here Christ runs against a contemporary definition of life originating in biology and medicine, reduced to the properties of compositions of molecules and their physical interaction. It seems at first glance, that Christ's teaching represents a strange "ignorance" that could not be reconciled with representations of life in the present age dominated by scientific ideas about the underlying substances and their implications in biological and medical technologies. Christ speaks of Life where no biological degradation happens, where cities and states do not disappear, where, contrary to the logic of decay and corruption in the material world, those who followed Christ and wanted to save their lives will lose it, but whoever loses their life for him will save it (Luke 9:24). Christ speaks about Life which is the source of its own phenomenality, which is difficult to be aware of, but which, ultimately makes possible all other phenomena of the living experience of men, including that of science. The words of Christ, being theological *per se*, and the words of science use different languages implying different existential connotations. Theology and science both originate in one and the same humanity, but speak differently of that essence of existence which humanity experiences in its life. The words of Christ are turned to man from the perspective of that through Whom all was made. The words of science are human words about that which has been made by the Word-Logos, including man himself in its fleshly form. Christianity concentrates on the relation of life with the living,

The Savior of Science; Küng, *The Beginning of All Things*; Coyne and Heller, *A Comprehensible Universe*; Zycinski, *God and Evolution*. Anglican: Peacocke, *Theology for a Scientific Age*; Polkinghorne, *Belief in God*. Lutheran: Pannenberg, *Toward a Theology of Nature*. Reformed: Torrance, *The Grammar of Theology*; Moltmann, *Science and Wisdom*. Eastern Orthodox: Sherrard, *The Rape of Man and Nature*, Nesteruk, *Light from the East*; Yannaras, *Postmodern Metaphysics*; Knight, *Science and the Christian Faith*.

making man a focus point of the meeting between God and its creation, whereas science is concentrated on the explication of living in rubrics of the already created. Can then any straightforward comparison of the *words of theology* and the *words of the sciences* be established? What is the nature of the difference in the articulation of the sense of existence in theology and science if, according to the above-mentioned theological definition the very fact of the dialogue between theology and science is the modus, a property of life from Life as that irreducible to anything and self-revealing beginning of everything[2], named, because of Christ's declaration, by God. The difference is that Life asserted by Christ is not that something that can be presented at a distance from human life, as something outside itself. Saying formally, life of men cannot be asserted in the phenomenality of objects (how this is done in biology and medicine), for their life itself is the tacit condition for things to be presented as objects. Molecules and other biological formations constituting bodies of the living beings are presented by the sciences as outer objects that make life possible in its embodied form; all of them become possible as articulated images of concrete physical entities and biological life-forms because their articulation is already going on from within life of Life that as such escapes a representation in the phenomenality of objects. The difference in phenomenality which becomes obviously seen when one compares Christ's definition of life and those ones in the sciences has a philosophical nature and can only be detected from within a philosophical sensibility, the lack of which can lead either to a conflict between theology and science or to attempts of their naïve reconciliation. This observation informs us of the fact that if the mediation between theology and science does not contain any rigorous introspection upon the sense

---

2. Such a link between a widely understood Life and God-creator is typical for many religious thinkers. Here, however, by anticipating the reader's curiosity in respect to our dual use the word "life" as human life, and Life as a principle of created existence, we give, for an elucidation, a quite long quote from the Russian philosopher Simon Frank: "Reality in all the multiplicity of its manifestations is life [Life] in the widest sense of that terms—a kind of immanent dynamism. . . . One and the same life pulsates in all that is, life distinct in every separate bearer of its and yet merged in one continuous and harmonious unity. . . . Life may be said to be *potentiality* in the twofold meaning of the term: both as *passivity* or material upon which form superimposed . . . and as *active potency* striving for self-expression or realization of its latent possibilities and, at the highest stage, as the energy of self-formation. The same inexpressible principle which is the hidden transcendent essence of our inner being, and which we apprehend in the depths of our self as reality in contradistinction to the visible objective world, is at the same time the hidden basis of universal being as a whole" (Frank, *Reality and Man*, 209). (The emphasis is added in order to articulate a dual aspect of the human life as the *passivity* of being affected by the natural conditions and, at the-same-time, as *self-affectivity* originating in the self-affectivity of the Divine Life).

and epistemological nature of theological and scientific propositions, this mediation is doomed for an endless reshuffling of the terms of the "dialogue" with no clearly anticipated result. Saying emphatically, the "dialogue" has to become philosophical in order to formulate the difference between theology and science on existential grounds. Such a demarcation does not necessarily entail the impossibility of the "dialogue." On the contrary, the "dialogue" receives its concreteness and purpose if it is distinctly seen what is that which has to be mediated.

The lack of a philosophical clarity in the sense of the "dialogue" leads to no visible progress in the discussions on science and religion for the last decades: scientists continue their research as if the "dialogue" between science and theology did not exist at all, whereas theologians sometimes defend their convictions in a narrowly historical and linguistic fashion, being forced into such a "dialogue" by an atheistic stance of their opponents. For theologians such a defensive position is unsatisfactory, for they rightly claim that the sense and justification of science, its contingent facticity, originates in the special position of humanity in creation, concisely described in terms of the Image of God (*Imago Dei*), that is, human life, within which humanity scientifically explores the world, and that which originates in Life proclaimed by Christ. In such a case the mediation between science and theology can be treated as a theological appropriation of science implying not so much a "dialogue" between equally weighted opposites, but an asymmetric coexistence of theology and science treated both as phenomena pertaining to the human condition. One can say that such an asymmetry among the terms of the "dialogue" resembles not an attempt of reconciliation of science and theology, but a more articulate and precise *demarcation* between two types of experience of living. In other words, the "dialogue" transforms into a detailed description of the difficulties of conducting of such a "dialogue." This conclusion attests to the fact that the lack of philosophical clarity in the sense of the "dialogue" compromises the whole objective of the dialogue, making it obscure and doubting the status of the dialogue as an academically credible enterprise.

Philosophy must act as a mediator between theology and science not only intrinsically as an epistemological delimiter of theological claims and scientific propositions, but also outwardly as a mediating language, balancing theological linguistics with the objectifying statements in modern natural sciences. Such a mediation forms a matter of necessity because sometimes the language employed in discussions by theologians (justifying their claims through an appeal to inaugural events, scriptural hermeneutics, communion and participation in ecclesial realities) and scientists (presenting physical realities in the phenomenality of objects without any clarification of why this is possible and what is the foundation of that consciousness which objectifies this reality) seems to be manifestly different, functioning in different epistemological conditions, which cannot be linked to each other and to have a common ground. What is the reason for that? The reason is twofold: firstly, the terms "theology" and "science" are sometimes used without clarifying their precise meaning, that is, are employed intuitively; secondly, since theology and science are different in terms of their function in the human perception of reality, this difference must be articulated not only through outlining their respective and specific concerns in human life, but through a careful analysis of how these two *modi* of representation of reality in one and the same human condition coexist in such a differentiated form. The issue here is that in some cases the theological and scientific propositions are developed in radically different epistemological attitudes whose specificity cannot be detected by a non-philosophical mind. This is the reason why, in order to avoid any naivety in the mediation between theology and science, it is reasonable, as was pointed out by Wolfhart Pannenberg, "to seek yet a third level to which both of the others [science and theology] are related. Such a third level for the dialogue between natural science and theology has, in fact, always existed, namely, in philosophy."[3] "Theology's relationship to philosophy—that is, to philosophy's interpretation of the world—constitutes that basis for Christianity's dialogue with the natural sciences."[4] The issue here is not to proclaim that philosophy and discursive reason can be supreme judges upon theological and scientific propositions, but to use philosophy *as an intellectual tool* in describing the integrity of personal existence from within which both theology and science originate.

Sometimes scientists do not discern a difference between the philosophical meaning of scientific propositions and their naturalistic scope so that the philosophical horizon of some issues in this "dialogue" is not adequately considered. It is one story to speak of scientific research as a particular investigation of empirical objects in the laboratory or in nature, but it is a completely different story when the results of this research receive a philosophical interpretation and are extended to a sort of collective form of thought in society, thus contributing to what is called *scientism*. In the first case the dialogue with theology is unnecessary and, probably, irrelevant. A specific work on a particular problem or technological application does not have in many cases any immediate ethical or social dimension, so that this modus of science remains neutral to its evaluation by culture or ideology.

3. Pannenberg, *The Historicity of Nature*, 28.
4. Pannenberg, *The Historicity of Nature*, 29.

What is specific for a narrow and professional research is that it has its own *object*, visibly articulated as an entity different from a *subject* of investigation and existing in space and time. The implied criterion of objectivity weakens in those cases when scientific research looses a straightforward experimental demonstration and verification. Here is a double danger: on the one hand there could be a temptation to ontologize the results of theoretical research assigning to their constructs the sense of physical reality; on the other hand, theory, if not supported by factual evidence, can become a scientific mythology cascading up towards ideology.

What is typical for scientific research is that it is bypassing in its scope the problem of the human presence as the centre of disclosure and manifestation of the universe. In this sense, the actual possibility of working of the sciences remains incomprehensible and the sense of the asserted truths obscure.[5] This last verdict manifests *de facto* a phenomenological critique of the sciences that inevitably enters the discussion if one enquires into the possibility of the sciences. It is this phenomenological critique that correspondingly becomes the best deterrent from bringing scientific claims to the level of their straightforward engagement with theology. However, as it can be seen, scientific enquiry as such stops here and evolves into philosophy which is not a favorite subject for scientists. The fact that physics is constructed by human beings is taken for granted with no further interrogation of its limits; as to the human subjectivity, its origin is ultimately supposed to originate from the physical. In other words, here appears "scientism" as a radical metaphysical reductionism which as such is not questioned. Thus any philosophical reflection upon the justification of the scientific position as such with respect to knowledge of the world is just avoided. Once again, for practicing scientists such a position is excusable, because they are not philosophers. However for those from their cohort who dare to engage into general multidisciplinary discussions, including the "dialogue" with theology, such a neglect for the philosophical clarity of their intellectual endeavour seems to be non-admissible, for it makes the whole discussion as making no sense.

Theology, on the contrary, being for centuries involved in discussions on faith and knowledge (reason), not only presupposes the necessity of the philosophical insight in the corresponding themes of the "dialogue," but in fact, challenges the existing forms of philosophizing and stimulates their development. The progress of scientific research requires a constant evaluation of its methods and its impact in the human affairs by appealing to philosophy (in particular, in those parts of research where the boundary

---

5. Gurwitsch, *Studies in Phenomenology and Psychology*, 399–400.

between human and inhuman becomes palpable [cosmology, nuclear physics, ecology, biology]). Theology as well, by being involved into the infinite hermeneutics of its own historical events, written and oral tradition, requires to re-appropriate its own content following the progress of philosophy as a modus of the human thinking: "a theologian must be familiar with the intellectual climate of his or her time. But he or she must also be a philosopher in the sense of being a truly enquiring mind, and in a wider sense of being sensitive to the deepest needs of human beings."[6] Since philosophy is in a state of constant development, theologians need to update their means of appropriation of the tradition and perception of the inaugural events constituting the basis of theology. A so called *philosophia perennis* contains some immutable elements in thought, but it does not imply any eternalization of specific philosophical systems, so that the modern advance of theology and its reception by society requires a new language in the course of interaction between faith and reason, borrowed from the recent developments of philosophy. Certainly, any particular choice of a direction and method along which theology in its mediation with science will have to proceed, depends on the contemporary academic assessment of the relevance of this or that philosophical trend for the needs of the implied mediation. In other words, the choice of the philosophical trend for such a mediation is not arbitrary. Its logic originates in that advance of theology (understood widely as experience of God) whose expression in forms of thought and speech evolves. Correspondingly, it is the evolving experience of God that selects the most appropriate forms of philosophical thought. In the context of mediation between theology and science this selection becomes critical because scientific experience relies on a fixed type of philosophizing that can be called materialism, naturalism, empiricism, realism (naïve, critical, etc). This philosophical position acts as a filter in all discussions on science and theology, by extracting from the whole body of theology only those fragments which can be brought into correlation with the sciences motivated towards objectivity. This constrained mediation (dialogue) is possible as a mental exercise, but does not have any existential meaning for it neglects the central theological point, namely that "theology is concerned with *life* and *survival*, and therefore *salvation*."[7] Science as such is not preoccupied with this issue for it is itself a product of life. Science is intrinsically existential, being a product of the living intelligent beings, but it does not reflect this simple truth in its theories. The clash between theology and science, happening at different

---

6. Zizioulas, *Lectures on Christian Doctrine*, 4.

7. Zizioulas, *Lectures on Christian Doctrine*, 1; Yannaras, *The Meaning of Reality*, 123–43.

levels of discussion, is not related to the matter of fact but to the general attitude towards the sense of reality and the sense of life. Whereas science is efficient in describing those parts of the world which do not have any signs of life, theology, on the contrary, is efficient in exposing the sense of the living humanity, showing that this sense does not reduce to the causality of the material. Correspondingly, any of those philosophies which are placed in the foundation of the scientific discourse seem to be *a priori* unsuitable as a mediating tool with theology. Theology, being existential and related to experience of the human existence through communion with God, receives the most efficient expression along the lines of those philosophical trends where humanity is assigned a central epistemological position in the universe, for example existentialism and phenomenology. The intrinsic split between philosophical attitudes existing behind a scientific exploration of the world (natural attitude amounting to a broadly treated scientific realism) and its appropriation from within life's phenomenality as communion can provide some explanation as to why the mediation (dialogue) between science and theology without a careful philosophical discernment is problematic in general.

In view of that which has been said so far, the aim of this chapter is to explicate the difference between scientific and religious experience of life in philosophical terms by demonstrating that this difference pertains to the basic characteristic of the human condition and that the implicitly intended overcoming of this difference under the disguise of the "dialogue" represents, in fact, an existentially untenable enterprise. Discussions on the difference in experience of the world and experience of God are profoundly timely for further articulation of the sense of the human condition, but not for its change. Bringing man in the centre of the issue of mediation between theology and science predetermines the choice of a methodology as relying on philosophical systems (such as existential phenomenology, for example) which treat man as the centre of disclosure and manifestation of the universe. The essential feature of such a methodology is the refusal of any metaphysical flavor in the mediation between science and theology (i.e., a discussion of the mediation between them on the level of ontological truths) thus reducing the discussion to the problem of the facticity of the human consciousness in the world as having its measure against some immensity of Life having the name of God.

THEOLOGY NEEDS SCIENCE—SCIENCE NEEDS THEOLOGY

Theology and science are different in terms of their affirmation of the sacred (historical) and secular (cosmic) orders of human life. In this sense the aimed "dialogue" between them implies a certain common frame of thought, such that even if it does not remove their distinction and difference, at least levels them in one and the same human being. However, in real academic practice this common frame hardly reveals itself, so that either theology experiences a tendency of being reduced to the epiphenomenon of that which is described by the sciences, or, alternatively, the sciences, if one relies on them to assert the Divine, are being "de-secularized" by loosing their autonomy and freedom from the implanted teleology of faith. This observation poses a general question of whether an epistemological symmetry between science and theology can be sustained at all. A philosophical way to respond to this question is to trace the origin of theology and science in the human intelligence and then to investigate whether science and theology can or cannot elucidate this origin on equal footing. One anticipates here that an outward "symmetry" between science and theology (as it is implicitly presupposed in the dialogue) will break thus imposing a structural relationship between them through their mutual limitation and interdependence in one and the same human subject. Let us make this point explicit.

At the inception of science and religion, or science and theology, the very possibility of establishing a relation between the scientifically *given* (data) and that which can be qualified as the *given* in experience of the Divine, is implicitly assumed.[8] Usually such a possibility is linked to the hierarchy of sensible images and intellectual representations of reality in a single consciousness without making delicate distinctions in the means of access to these *givens* and the degree of their rationality, that is, the *modi* of their phenomenality. Such a philosophical insensitivity to various *modi* of representation of experience can lead to a reaction when the possibility of mediation between scientific ideas and theological representations will be outright rejected because the mediation is applied to the fundamentally "non-uniform things," thus having an abstract character. Such a reaction could be exercised by the sceptically oriented scientists, as well as by the

---

8. We use the terminology of the "given" (instead of "data") in order to underline from the beginning the fact of the presence of human subjectivity in participation, detection, identification and articulation of phenomena in the form of "data." The "given" is not a dispassionate and neutral imposing of the world or God upon a human subject, but the "gift" granted to human being in order to comprehend existence. The characteristic of phenomena as given, that is, those which fall under the rubric of "donation," is that they do not subsist in something which causally precedes them. They are given spontaneously from themselves and out of themselves.

sincerely believing Christians. All those, who deny the legitimacy of religious experience and its comparison with science implicitly justify their position by adopting a certain *ontological commitment* with respect to physical being as radically different with that one referring to God. In contradistinction to them, all those who promote the legitimacy of religious experience, remain unable to express their position by using philosophical language that neutralizes the objection of "atheists." However both approaches, either that one which denies the relevance of theology, or an alternative one diminishing the necessity of taking into account rational arguments from the positive sciences, are both weak from a philosophical point of view, that is, from the point of view of the holistic structure of the living experience.

In order to clarify the latter point one can consider a situation when the fervent apologists of faith pose a question of the following kind: why one must take into account physical ideas within the Christian context while studying and developing theology? Theology deals with the specifically human way of existence, mystical, experience, liturgical life and church, an ideal of salvation, etc., and is not reduced to a mythology of the world. To what extent a Christian must be acquainted with the scope of knowledge of the physical world in order to be saved or even deified? This question has historical precedents and one can use as a footnote, a reference to St. Augustine, who in his assessment of secular knowledge was cautious of employing it for matters of faith. Augustine stresses the usefulness of that knowledge of natural facts if they are compiled in a systematic form to provide a minimum of information that Christians should know in order to understand things that are mentioned in the Scriptures.[9] This modest assessment of the utility of the natural sciences for Christians is associated with Augustine's concern about the use of scientific arguments in the interpretation of Scripture by those Christians who did not sufficiently understand scientific matters. Knowledge was better than ignorance in any case, but undeveloped knowledge could be worse than ignorance, because, by being used in ecclesial arguments, it could damage the reputation of a Christian in the eyes of a nonbeliever. Augustine writes: "Usually even a non-Christian knows something about the earth, the heavens, and the other elements of this world, . . . and this knowledge he holds to as being certain from reason and experience. Now, it is disgraceful and dangerous for an infidel to hear a Christian, presumably giving the meaning of Holy Scripture, talking nonsense on these topics."[10] Thus Augustine affirmed that for a Christian, it is enough to believe that all natural things are created by God.

---

9. Augustine, *On Christian Doctrine* 1:39.
10. Augustine, *The Literal Meaning of Genesis* 1:19, 42–43 .

A simple empirical response to the question of whether knowledge of the world naturally accompanies salvation is that the very possibility of theology (as experience of the Divine) is determined by the possibility of existence of the incarnate carries of this theology, that is, human persons. In other words, in order to theologize one must have *necessary* physical and biological conditions for the existence of theologians, the conditions which, as it is not difficult to understand, are ultimately rooted in cosmic conditions. Cosmology and earthly physics (together with biology) explicate these *necessary* (not sufficient) conditions. From here one infers a simple conclusion that *any* theological proposition, expressing experience of the Divine contains truth about the world as such.[11] In strictly theological terms, the physical world is the meaningful gift of God, the source of existence of human beings that in itself is neither a partner in communion with God but the means of communion, that one which brings out the worth of the human person. Thus theology, being in this sense a product of human life in the world, is itself a gift of God in the conditions of the world.[12] As Teilhard de Chardin once pedagogically said: "Those who are diffident, timid, underdeveloped, or narrow in their religion, I should like to remind that Christ requires for his body the full development of man, and that mankind, therefore, has a duty to the created world and to truth—namely, the ineluctable duty of research."[13] It is not difficult to see that the argument employed by us is ontological in the sense that it appeals to physical matter as the ground of existence of human beings. For Christian theology this fact has a particular meaning related to the Incarnation of Christ in flesh. It is the physical science that makes possible to understand that the universe must be such that it makes human life and hence the Incarnation possible. For the Word-Logos of God to assume human flesh, there *must be* this flesh. Since modern physics and biology are clear that for existence of such a flesh there must have passed at least ten billion years of cosmological evolution,

---

11. Zizioulas, *Communion and Otherness*, 242. Teilhard de Chardin expressed a similar thought: "So true is this that *nothing can any longer find place in our constructions which does not first satisfy the conditions* of a universe in process of transformation. A Christ whose features do not adapt themselves to the requirements of a world that is evolutive in structure will tend more and more to be eliminated out of hand" (Teilhard de Chardin, "Christology and Evolution," in *Christianity and Evolution*, 78).

12. The same, expressed differently by John Zizioulas, asserts that "Human capacity . . . does not require a departure from creaturely conditions in order to exist. Communion with God is possible for humanity—and through it for the entire cosmos—only in and through creaturely existence. History is no longer, as it was for the Greek world, the obstacle to communion with God, but its ground" (Zizioulas, *Communion and Otherness*, 242).

13. Teilhard de Chardin, "Le prêtre," quoted in Guénot, *Teilhard de Chardin*, 40.

it seems evident that for the Incarnation to take place the *necessary* physical conditions must have been fulfilled. To have the body of Jesus from Nazareth (and his Mother [Virgin Mary]) the universe must have had from the beginning the propensity to produce them.[14] Correspondingly the ontological aspect of the Incarnation is always present in the reversed history of the universe as it is described in modern cosmology. These necessary conditions for the existence of human flesh are summarized in various versions of the Anthropic Cosmological Principle (AP) that detects quantitatively consubstantiality of the physical stuff of the visible universe and human corporeal beings.[15]

If now sceptically motivated scientists reverse the previous question and ask as to "Why one needs theology for physics?" the response will be the following. Physics studies the universe without clarifying the sense of its contingent facticity, that is, without clarifying the sense of the *sufficient* conditions (sufficient reason) responsible not only for the outcomes of the physical laws in order to have a given display of the universe, but also for the very possibility of knowledge and explication of the universe by human persons. Physics operates without giving an account as to how and why the study of the world as such forms a gift to the physically limited humanity. Although theology does not *explain* this fact either, it at least interprets it by pointing out that it is only human beings that have a rational capacity of transcending the physically finite, that is, their own bodies and immediate life-world by integrating the representation of the potentially infinite and intransient in their finite embodied consciousness. Consciousness and reason form such characteristics of the human condition that cannot be explained by reducing them to the physical (ontological), and whose *elucidation* and *interpretation* is possible only through an appeal to the anthropology of the Divine Image. This leads the argument for the justification of science (as well as theology) beyond the limits of science and philosophical ontology. Correspondingly, any cosmological vision of the world is implicitly imbued with theology in the sense that it is based in a Divine gift of faith in reality of good creation of Good God, as well as in the Divine origin of the human

---

14. Here is an allegorical hymn to the universe's inherent telos which Teilhard de Chardin saw in the Body of Mother of God: "The world's energies and substances-so harmoniously adapted and controlled that the supreme Transcendent . . . from their accumulated and distilled treasures they produced the glittering gem of matter, the Pearl of the Cosmos, and the link with the incarnate personal Absolute—the Blessed Virgin Mary, Queen and Mother of all things, the true Demeter . . . and when the day of the Virgin came to pass, then the final purpose of the universe, deep-rooted and gratuitous, was suddenly made clear" (Teilhard de Chardin, *The Future of Man*, 307).

15. See Glossary (Appendix 1).

capacity of an intellectual and linguistic articulation of the universe.[16] Then it would be natural to suggest that scientists are also theologians of a certain kind: they study with their own specific methods the world created by God, not only for the purpose of adaptation to it, but also as making back a thanksgiving offering to the Creator.[17]

The ontological argument for the possibility of theology referring to its physical agents (i.e., humans), is a typical metaphysical justification based on the principle of causality (assuming that consciousness is an epiphenomenon of the physical). At the same time the referral of consciousness's rationality to the idea of God, does not have the same philosophical clarity as it was with the principle of causality. Here one introduces a theological argument that appeals to those *givens* in experience that are radically different in comparison with what is given in physics and cosmology. These *givens* are related to the very fact of the human existence understood as personal (hypostatic) consciousness acting as a centre of disclosure and manifestation of the world. It is the difference in the *modi* of the *given* revealed as the impossibility of avoiding cosmological insights in theology on the one hand, and in the implicit appeal to the theology of communion for the possibility of cosmology (where the very fact of life turns out to be an inaugural revelation), on the other hand, that points towards an asymmetric relation between the metaphysical interpretation of the possibility of theology and a theological justification of science. The "dialogue" between science and theology thus becomes a discourse of clarification and explication of the difference in the ways of appearance and access to the *givens* in one and the same human subject.

HOW TO MAKE PHILOSOPHICALLY THE DISTINCTION IN THE MODES OF THE GIVEN IN THE NATURAL SCIENCES AND THEOLOGY?

The philosophical criterion of the difference in the modes of the *given* in the natural sciences and theology can be formulated in the following way. Any scientific research and any theory assume the acceptance (whether explicitly

---

16. By analogy with what has been once asserted by Grace de Laguna that "a philosophy of nature and a philosophy of man are mutually complementary; . . . neither can be completed unless it shows itself as the counterpart" (De Laguna, *On Existence*, 81–82), one can invoke Teilhard de Chardin's assertion that it is impossible to plunge into the science of the cosmos without passing naturally to the Jesus of Gospel and vice versa so that "cosmology and Christology turn out to be two parts of one and the same book of Man."

17. Cf. Harakas, "Orthodox Christianity Facing Science," 15.

or unconsciously) of the system of metaphysics (*metaphysica generalis*), one of whose important parts deals with ontology, that is, with the questions "what there is?" or "what exists?" so that such a research implies that it studies an object which must exist beforehand, that is, to be an *existent* (*ens*). This requirement holds for every specialised metaphysics, that is, for specific sciences, as well as for the representation of God in philosophical theology (*theologia rationalis*) (distinct from theology understood as experience of communion with God, that is, from theology of revelation). The requirement for the metaphysical certainty[18] can also be applied to theology understood as an historical or linguistic tradition. For example, there can be a metaphysical demand for the existence of biblical events from the point of view of the historical sciences. Similarly, the corresponding fragments of the sacred texts must receive their interpretation and thus objectivization through their qualification by the rules of linguistics and the sciences of the languages. However, when we use the term theology as experience of God we depart from the metaphysical definition of its subject matter (i.e., God) as if it is positioned in or associated with some underlying substance. In this case the first question is as how to establish (if it is possible at all) the difference on the metaphysical basis between the philosophical theology (or simply philosophy) and theology as experience. The provisional response to this question can be formulated like this: the difference consists in the extent of appearance (phenomenality or presence, display) of beings (existents) (i.e., their "positivity") concerned, and of the ways of ontic verifications in philosophical theology and theology of communion. Here one recalls Martin Heidegger who in his famous article *Phänomenologie und Theologie* of 1928 considered theology (including also a non-philosophical theology) as a "wholly autonomous ontic science" because of its "positivity" and then, as a consequence, its dependence on the analytics of *Dasein*, considered as a fundamental ontology. This, according to this period of Heidegger's thought, confirmed the primacy of *ontology* with respect to theology, as well as with respect to all special sciences.[19] Generalizing, one can say that the difference between ontic sciences (majority of the human sciences) and ontological sciences (e.g., physics, whose ontology is based in physical substance and rubrics of space and time) presupposed the difference in ontology behind

---

18. Metaphysical certainty aims to determine certain things with respect to certain statements that, if they are true, would be descriptions of a reality that lies behind all appearances, descriptions of things as they really are.

19. Heidegger, "Phenomenology and Theology," 50. Compare with the text in *Sein und Zeist* §7, where Heidegger places theology on the same level with other disciplines dealing with the phenomena which are analyzed by phenomenology (Heidegger, *Being and Time*, 58).

these sciences, and the hierarchy of those sciences followed from the "hierarchy" of ontologies (assuming that one can define one ontology as more fundamental than another). Then there is a problem that we have already formulated above as to whether exists such a system of thought that could assert the universal ontology, such that it could be placed in the foundation of both the sciences and theology, that ontology which could be somehow more generic than that of theology (either experiential or philosophical) and of philosophy (science)?

This question creates a serious doubt in a possibility of a positive response to it first of all because theology, Christian theology, has in its foundation very special inaugural events which cannot be assigned any metaphysical status, because they exceed any measure of causality related to the world. The term "event" becomes crucial here acquiring a completely new status thus inverting an ontological approach to theology at all. Events related to the sacred history take place in the world, but the very sense of the world as an articulated image from within human history emerges as derivative from these events, because these events "define" humanity not in terms what it is, but in terms what humanity will be (inaugural events endow humanity with future).[20] This way of thought can be historically illustrated by a reference to Heidegger who at some stage stopped using the term "metaphysics" in order "to think Being without beings," that is, to "think Being without regard to metaphysics"[21] in the following sense. Heidegger refused being in favour of event (*Ereignis*)[22] ("Being vanishes in event"; "Being would be a species of event, and not the other way around.")[23] In application to theology what he essentially asserted is that one cannot treat theology as experience of God (communion) in the context of the ontic status of these events as if they would be only specific historical or physical events. If previously the notion of event presupposed a sort of metaphysical background, so that an event needed original ontology in order to take place

---

20. For example, the event of Resurrection can be described as a "temporal happening" that runs not backwards but forwards. This is the event which does not slip away from us but outruns us in spite of the fact that many aspects of our life lapse into oblivion together with all natural history. In a way, one deals here with the reversed temporality when the event of Resurrection comes to meet us out of the future. The risen Christ "is not dead but alive, more real than any of us. Hence he does not need to be made real for us, because he does not decay or become fixed in the past. He lives on in the present as real live continuous happening, encountering us here and now in the present and waiting for us in the future" (Torrance, *Space, Time, and Resurrection*, 89).

21. Heidegger, "Time and Being," in *On Time and Being*, 24.

22. On a non-trivial and ambiguous sense of the term *Ereignis* in later Heidegger (distinct from the modern hermeneutics of events) see Romano, *L'aventure temporelle*, 20–27.

23. Heidegger, "Time and Being," 21 (translation correcred).

(e.g., in physics, there must be space-time for events to happen) what Heidegger implied in his usage of the idea of *event* is that the latter takes place in the existent but from beyond the existent (being). One cannot assign the modus of the already conceived existence to *event*. *Event* can be described as the consummation of that, whose essence did not give the possibility of its foreseeing as if one could foresee the inconceivable impossible from the perspective of the conceivable possible (i.e., from within metaphysics with its principle of causality).[24] The essence of event is that it predetermines and redefines all possibilities of existents in their being and it is in this sense that it can be assigned a certain ontological status. One follows from here that the more a phenomenon manifests itself as event, the more it doubts its metaphysical modus of being, for its sheer possibility follows from its effective metaphysically understood impossibility. Theology as experience confirms this, for it deals with the events whose impossibility witnesses to what is expressed in the Bible in words "nothing is impossible for God" (cf. Gen 18:14; Luke 1:37). One implies here the events such as creation of the world out of nothing, Incarnation of the Word-Logos of God in flesh of Jesus of Nazareth, Resurrection, etc. These events resist the possibility of their non-contradictory comprehension (in a metaphysical sense) thus preventing the formulation of their identity status, that is, in different words, they challenge ontology behind them and hence any definition of God in terms of being.

The "essence" of events of creation of the world, Incarnation and Resurrection is exactly that they do not reduce to that which follows ontological law patterns. These events make possible that which is not presented on the ontological level, that which is not identical to itself and whose existence (taking place) contradicts its essence (if such is allegedly posited). One can express the same by saying that the "essence" of these events contradicts to itself, by referring to a biblical case when God "calls into being things that are not" (i.e., God calls into being non-existent as existent, as if non-existent would exist) (Rom 4:17). It is in this latter sense that such events *par excellence* as creation, Incarnation and Resurrection, one can say, acquire a "meta-ontological status" because they (events and all existents involved in them) contradict the laws implied by the ontology of the world.

Since the dialogue between theology and science deals not with facts related to the world as such, but with the ultimate origin of the world and these facts as they are apprehended by humanity, this origin receives a new interpretation in accordance with that event in which the world is granted its being: the world acquires being in that event which exceeds the measure

24. See details on phenomenology of events in Romano, *Event and World*. A careful distinction of phenomenality of objects and phenomenality of events is discussed in Marion, *Negative Certainties*, 155–200.

of any possible definition of the existent. Such a philosophical statement corresponds to that which is termed in theology as creation of the world. Being created, the existent receives its being from God; this being results not from the laws of the world outlined by thought in rubrics of ontology. In spite of the fact that philosophically the rational idea of the world as creation remains indemonstrable, that is, subject to the antinomies of reason (thus amounting to the fact that this idea is regulative one and does not entail any theoretical content), the world as creation in its irremovable givenness to humanity remains present through the saturating intuition to an extent comparable with Kant's description of the sublime.[25] Saying differently, the intuition of creation functions within the human articulation of its own existence as an aesthetical idea. But since an aesthetical sense of the universe is inseparable from the fact of life in its unconditional givenness to a particular human being, it is this human life that becomes an inaugural event in comprehension of the universe and hence its constitution as objective reality. Since the very phenomenon of life together with the contingency of the world represents (from a metaphysical point of view) sheer impossibility, whereas in its existing facticity the world and life are possible, the classical relation between possible and impossible undergoes a reversal where the possible becomes to be determined by the impossible (as a characteristic of event). In application to the relation between theology and science (scientific philosophy) the latter entails that what is possible in scientific experience becomes to be determined by that which scientifically and metaphysically impossible, that is, belonging to the sphere of what can be characterized as a primary theological experience of life.

In view of what has been said, if modern development of philosophy doubts any possible universal ontology, what kind of a philosophically phrased alternative could be proposed for the foundation of theology? Or whether the very posing a question in such an angle becomes irrelevant? If the latter is true any relationship between theology and actual scientific research becomes irrevocably problematic. Another thing is a scientific philosophy as a meta-scientific activity that deals with some limiting situations in scientific knowledge. Indeed since, as we will see later, some scientific questions of the ultimate reality bring a researcher to a situation where no principle of causality can be applied to some unique "phenomena," the establishment of a relationship between events in theology and these unique "phenomena" in science makes sense only as a comparison of the narratives related to the inaugural events and those "unique" phenomena.

---

25. Kant, *Critique of Judgement*, Part 1, Book 2.

As we will see below, ultimately, this "non-metaphysical" situation in the dialogue between theology and science originates in a radical impossibility of placing humanity in the context of any metaphysics. Then if the mediation between theology and science is carried out within the metaphysically incomprehensible human situation in the world, can human thought use an ontological criterion in order to carry out the distinction between science and its philosophical appropriation on the one hand, and theology as experience of existence on the other? The implied answer is "no," so that either philosophy must extend towards appropriating phenomena with event-like structure and then create a methodology of mediation between theology and science as a stratification of the inaugural events; or the "dialogue" between theology and science simply transforms into the comparative hermeneutics of the human condition with no ontological objectives.

Finally, if the ontological criteria in the demarcation between theology and the sciences are dropped and the dialogue transforms into the comparison of two types of the living experience in their sheer phenomenality, the question of the dialogue now shifts from any judgement on the underlying ontology of theology and science towards a dilemma of the *possible* and *impossible*, that is, the difference between that which can be a matter of experience and that which cannot. The latter question has a direct relation to such scientific notions, for example, as the universe as a whole: can the universe as a whole be a matter of experience? The dialogue acquires features of a transcendental enterprise where the main question is about the legitimacy of that experience which is asserted by theology in comparison with that one which the sciences encounter in the limiting situations. The implied criterion of demarcation between two opposites is based on the assumption that one can *apriori* state the limits of rationality, that is, to formulate conditions for possibility and impossibility of experience. This kind of apriorism is based in Kant's transcendental philosophy where *finite* reason defines the *infinite*, claiming impossible its knowledge on the grounds of the limited cognitive faculties. For example, philosophical theology is able to form a regulative idea of God with a clear understanding that God cannot become a matter of empirical experience because God is beyond the world. The finitude and the limits of experience (sensible and intelligible) thus assume the functioning of the principle of *transcendental apriori*, that is, a principle of the transcendental subject. According to Kant, if the structure of consciousness does not have a transcendental status, it cannot legitimately make distinction between what is possible and what is impossible. It follows from here that the difference between scientific philosophy and philosophy in general, on the one hand, and theology, on the other, on the basis of the distinction between the *possible* and *impossible*, can be articulated in principle only if philosophy and corresponding philosophy of science function under the assumption that there is the transcendental subject who exercises such an articulation. In relation to science this transcendental stance finds its justification in that trend in philosophy of science that shows that the formation of views on the structure of physical reality is limited by the conditions of access to this reality through experiments and mathematical expressibility[26]. Both, experiments and mathematical thinking are attributed to the transcendental subject. What we now face is that after the dismissal of the metaphysical criterion for the demarcation between theology and science, there is only one transcendental criterion is left, implying a certain philosophical stance on the subject of knowledge and experience of God. However, transcendental philosophy (and phenomenology in particular) will be capable of supporting its delimiting function between the *possible* and *impossible* only until that limit when the very transcendentalism will itself be subjected to an historical and epistemological correction, when the phenomena (encountered by either science or theology) will exceed the subject's capacity to make an *a priori* demarcation of their possibility or impossibility.

Thus, making a preliminary conclusion, it seems at first glance that one cannot conduct a reasonable demarcation in the subject matter of science and theology without an appeal either to underlying ontology, or transcendental judgement of the possibility of experience related to the subject of knowledge. All other possible ways of such a demarcation, from a philosophical point of view, appear epistemologically *ad hoc*. However, since the era of the "end of metaphysics" doubts the possibility of the universal metaphysics for demarcation of philosophy and theology, one is left with a question as to whether the transcendental principle remains valid in order to be placed in the foundation of such a demarcation. If the latter is impossible for events of communion (mystical experience) and as well as for some phenomena in modern natural sciences, anthropology and the human sciences (we argue for this below), then the transcendental argument for delimiting and making a distinction between science, philosophy, and theology turns out to be also defunct and philosophy is challenged by the necessity of developing new methods for dealing with situations when human knowledge and experience encounter *the infinite* and fundamentally *impossible*.

The new methods will have to deal with the phenomenon of humanity as that one which remains the basic challenge for any philosophizing because

---

26. See in this context Bitbol et al., *Constituting Objectivity*.

(as we will see in the next section) the strict demarcation between the *modi* of the *givens* in the case of humanity is unattainable. The first indication of this can be traced in what we have established before, namely that in spite of the explicitly ontic features of theological knowledge, as distinct from the ontologically rooted natural sciences, the very ontic needs an ontological basis (as a corporeal basis of a subject), whereas the ontological (corporeal) condition must be elucidated through the structural path of its constitution by subjectivity (that cannot be accounted on the level of ontology). Thus the strict demarcation between science and theology on the basis of the opposition between ontic and ontological can hardy be achieved contributing to the argument that a naïve positing of experience of the Divine outside the material conditions of the possibility of this expression represents *de facto* faith without reason, whose existential and soteriological meaning remains obscure. At the same time any physical reductionism in the constitution of humanity also fails without an appeal to theology of man's creation in the image of God. Once again, it is a human being that is implicitly present behind the predicament in demarcation and relation between theology and science.

The fact that the dialogue between science and theology does not represent any metaphysical or transcendental necessity, but has features of existential events (manifested in acts of human reason and free will), shows that one deals here with the phenomena related to life's self-affectivity implying that the phenomenon of life does not generate the appearance of anything new that would be different from life itself. It is in this sense that the phenomenon of life is not the appearance of something different from it (the other) but self-appearance (auto-appearance), self-phenomenalization (auto-phenomenalization), self-affectivity. The phenomenality of this self-appearance, its phenomenological essence, is that *transcendental affectivity* which makes possible experience of life as hardship, suffering, grief, love, empathy, etc., that are all present in the background of the will to reason and explore the world. One can say that the self-affectivity forms that phenomenological essence of life and its given primordiality where no trace of the visibility of the world or of any intentional thinking can yet be found. It is the self-affectivity of life that lies in the foundation of any possible phenomenality as being constituted through the senses or discursively. Since this modus of life is not a phenomenon, but is in the foundation of phenomena, it cannot be detected through an intentional gaze. Its interpretation demands new philosophy that deals with the phenomenon that has a "meta-ontological" and "trans-transcendental" status, blessing and justifying a possibility of the philosophical as well as scientific knowledge of the world.

HOW TO MAKE A THEOLOGICAL DISTINCTION IN THE MODES OF THE GIVEN IN THE NATURAL SCIENCES AND THEOLOGY?

If, as we have established in the previous section, theology (unlike philosophy and the sciences) deals with event-like phenomena avoiding ontological judgements about that which is metaphysically impossible and thus exceeding the capacity of transcendental delimiters of the possibility of phenomena, the question arises: how is theology possible at all? One must carefully understand this question: theology as communion, that is, a modus of life itself, is an empirical fact whose denial is possible only if one attempts to abstract it from the primordial perception of existence by using a reflective modus of thinking. It is from the curiosity of the latter that the question of the possibility of theology makes sense. *De facto* the question sounds like this: how is experience of communion with the source of existence and life possible in the conditions when discursive reason doubts its possibility on the grounds of the physical finitude of human beings? This issue arises when experience of God and the sense of theological statements is questioned as if they are abstracted from the primary religious experience, that is, experience of being alive. If life (as organic existence) is abstracted from the actual living and presented in the phenomenality of objects, then indeed one can pose a question of the very possibility of living, that is, of the primary religious experience as rooted in a sort of a pre-existing metaphysical ground. But experience of living cannot be "looked at" as if it were something outside this living. The phenomenality of living requires to appeal to the radical interiority of life with the visible references to the outer world only as forming the necessary conditions of this life. Such a phenomenological discernment is similar to theological anthropology where the natural attitude to the description of man is taking place within the conditions of faith as the inward sense of the Divine Image. Correspondingly, if the inherent *givens* of theology (through experience of God) are subjected to a philosophical reflection, then one can provide a description of how theology is possible. But this will be only a model serving pedagogical purposes and not explaining the mystery of the Divine humanity as such, but describing how this mystery (seen in reflection) functions with respect to knowledge God.

An example of such a model can be found in patristic theology. The early Fathers considered human person not only in light of the dualism between body and reason (*dianoia*, or intellect in its contemporary sense, the mind). They made a subtle distinction between *dianoia* and *nous*, where the latter stands for the faculty of apprehending truth superior to discursive reason. *Nous* can be broadly described in modern language as *spiritual insight* (spiritual intellect) where logic cannot be used. In contradistinction to *dianoia, nous* works by direct apprehension, by intuition. *Nous* does not reason from premises to conclusions by logical steps; rather, it apprehends truth by inner vision of essences or principles of created things through communion with God.[27] *Nous* functions in a modus of an experiential transcendence implying that it is inseparable in a human being from the fact of living. It effects such a phenomenality within which experience cannot be considered as an outward phenomenon. *Nous*, apart from being an "organ" of a special cognition, plays in Fathers's theology a role of the sense-forming centre of personhood. Its transcending capacity provides a foundation for reason (*dianoia*) to *infer* from the created things to the existence of God-creator. Theologically, faith as "true knowledge whose principles are beyond rational demonstration"[28] has *nous* as its organ that allows one to transcend general conditions of knowledge imposed by the understanding and reason with respect to things of this age, and to intuit the underlying principles of existence of all things leading to God.

So how is *theologia* possible? The answer formulated in the natural philosophical attitude (that does not interrogate the very facticity of that consciousness which talks about theology) employed by us for pedagogical purposes is that *theologia* as experience of God is possible because humans have the faculty of *nous*, that is, of being able to relate the facticity of their own existence to God. *Nous* may be seen as a substitute for the definition of humanity in the Divine Image indicating that it transcends the natural aspects of the human embodied existence. *Nous* makes transcendence possible and fit for *theologia*, for the mystical contemplation of God to the extent possible for humans.[29]

Philosophically, whereas *nous* can be paralleled with as a faculty of a theological judgement that can refer to things beyond empirical experience, propositions made through the faculty of *dianoia* (the understanding, discursive thinking) can deal only with created things. In other words, if philosophy and science interpret beings only in the measure they see in them the *natural*, theology has to deal with that which exceeds the limits of

---

27. According to Maximus the Confessor: "The intellect [*nous*] is the organ of wisdom, the intelligence that of spiritual knowledge." (Maximus the Confessor, *Various Texts on Theology* 3.33, 215). "It possesses the capacity for a union that transcends its nature and that unites it with what is beyond its natural scope. It is through this union that divine realities are apprehended, not by means of our own natural capacities, but by virtue of the fact that we entirely transcend ourselves and belong entirely to God" (Maximus the Confessor, *Various Texts on Theology* 5.68, 276).

28. Maximus the Confessor, *Cap. Theologicorum* 1.9, 116.

29. Maximus the Confessor, *Cap. de Charitate* 4.50.

nature. Here the problem arises: how the natural human beings can transcend their own natural faculties, that is, employ *nous* latently present in him. Can the natural formation develop a desire to access something which cannot be achieved in the limits of this nature?

The answer is "yes," human persons can develop such a desire, first of all when they question their own essence, when, by paraphrasing Augustine, they have become a problem to themselves,[30] they have become for themselves "a soil which is cause of difficulty and much sweat,"[31] for they cannot grasp the totality of what they are.[32] Indeed, one cannot know the essence of humanity in a metaphysical sense for, according to theological definitions, humanity must remain undefinable as a carrier of the Image of the undefinable God (the undefinability of the essence of God deprives man of the essence that is to be defined). A classical excerpt from patristic texts related to the unknowability of human beings by themselves is that one of Gregory of Nyssa: "Since the nature of our mind, which is the likeness of the Creator, evades our knowledge, it has an accurate resemblance to the superior nature, figuring by its own unknowableness the incomprehensible Nature."[33] The unbearable witness to that what human person becomes for itself is related to the excess of a human being over itself, an excess of that which is above that which this person can think and comprehend. Said differently, "For the image, in so far as image of the infinite, always manifests the excessive, which we must love and respect, but which is not at all at our disposal."[34] That metaphysically incomprehensible presence in us of that who created us, but whose phenomenality is dimmed not through its lack, but an infinite excess, "must be loved and respected," so that the perennial question "What is man?" is responded through a humble acceptance of life as a gift, and it is this acceptance that is the *love* of the Creator and an inception point of any theologizing. It is this love and respect that inspire humans for the acquisition of grace as the supernatural Good in order to understand the sense of themselves. But because of the incarnate condition the propensity of *nous* as related to the inherent love and respect of life cannot be separated from *dianoia* (dealing with physical aspects of this life's existence). It follows from here that the strict separation of the cognitive faculties onto a philosophical and theological modes cannot be applied to humanity without distorting the fundamental feature of the human condition, understood as a gift of life

---

30. Augustine, *Confessions* X.xxxiii (50), 208.
31. Augustine, *Confessions* X.xvi (25), 193.
32. Augustine, *Confessions* X.vii (15), 187.
33. Gregory of Nyssa, *De hominis opificio*, 397.
34. Chrétien, *The Unforgettable*, 90.

in the conditions of impossibility of any metaphysical or scientific control of this life by humans themselves. Here is a paradoxical condition: one has to love and respect that which cannot be fully comprehended. But this is the only "way and truth" of the human living.

The difference between the natural (the realm of *dianoia*) and super- or trans-natural (the realm of *nous*) that one could, by the way of a historical analogy, apply for the demarcation of science, philosophy, and theology, fails irrevocably in the case of a human being. The natural dimension in humanity, its corporeal setting, cannot be detached from its consciousness (articulating the sense of existence) whereas the latter cannot be reduced to the natural in a causal way. The inexplicability of this consciousness (as a distinctive feature of humanity's image of God) becomes a characteristic feature of *nous*'s functioning. The excess of consciousness as living makes impossible to approach it in the categories of the understanding and by means of discursive reason that are both already presupposed by this excess. *Nous* detects the phenomenon of humanity's facticity as a problem that cannot be addressed through the analytical function of the soul (*dianoia*). And it is in this sense that "humanity" forms the major concern and subject matter of theology where the "natural and supernatural" (*nous* and *dianoia*) cannot be separated and detached from each other.

The impossibility of knowing the essence of humanity shows that a possible ontological response (referring to the substance of the world of which man is made) to the question as to why theology needs cosmology, is not *sufficient*, for the human phenomenon exceeds the boundaries of the scientific and philosophical, and needs a theological elucidation. Correspondingly, the contingent facticity of physics and cosmology, as accounting for the foundation of the natural condition of man, cannot receive explanation from themselves in the same manner as the essential aspects of the human condition. Since the very fact of the human existence as exceeding its own naturalness and possessing hypostasis cannot be accounted through physical and cosmological theories (providing only a view of the necessary organic conditions for such an existence), this fact remains beyond the circle of causality pertaining to the world so that humanity has to intuit its own existence in the conditions of its own passivity, as that *given* which has a radically different phenomenality in comparison with the *givens* of philosophy and science. The essence of this phenomenality is that the phenomenon of living cannot be *reduced* in a phenomenological sense because such a *reduction* would nullify the possibility of any phenomenality at all. This implied phenomenality is that one of theology in the sense that it presupposes God as the creator of life, as that one whose *reduction* is impossible because it would contradict to the facticity of life and the very possibility of philosophy and science. It is in this sense that physics and cosmology need theology to "justify" their own possibility as the *modi* of the human existence. A particular human life represents an *event-like* phenomenon that saturates man's intuition to such an extent that it cannot be accounted on the grounds of the physical causality and comprehended within the limits of the transcendental cognitive faculties.

The event-like phenomenon of a particular hypostatic existence has an extensive content, starting from the actual event of birth and finishing by particularities of life unfolding into the future, that future which has been given as a gift of life at the moment of birth. It is not difficult to see that the modus of the *given* in the human phenomenon (as a centre of disclosure and manifestation of the relations between the world and God) turns our to be fundamentally different in comparison with that which is given in science and philosophy: the essence and structure of the outer reality (as the *givens* in the representation of consciousness) receives its "meta-ontological" justification in *inaugural (opening) events* such as an event of human life, humankind-event, an event of creation (birth) of a human being[35] whose phenomenality is not that of objects studied by the sciences. Physics and cosmology need theology in order to realize that the approach to seeing the universe as a physical object is based in an *event* of life of a hypostatic human being, the *event* that cannot be subjected to a purely ontological description, but receiving its interpretation from theology according to which humanity was brought into existence by the "will of the invisible origin." In this case physics and cosmology as outward existential manifestations of events of life receive their justification from theology as communion dealing with the inaugural (opening) events, first of all with the event of being created. The image of the world is built into the Divine Image in humanity granted in these inaugural events. However this image remains limitedly seen and accomplished only as an eschatological ideal since the ultimate sense of the Divine Image of humanity remains hidden and unknowable to it. This happens, theologically speaking, because of the fundamental distance (*diastema*) and difference (*diaphora*) between a creature and the Creator.

Thus the undefinability of humanity and its unknowability by itself (as having a theological interpretation) forms the radical precondition for the actual limited knowability of the world (and this is not a transcendental condition related to the embodied human faculties). This implies that physics and cosmology follow the same *apophatic* pattern of explanation

---

35. "The world is hanging in the event; it always originates for us in inaugural events, beginning with the most privileged one—our birth" (Romano, *L'aventure temporelle*, 121).

that is typical for the theological anthropology of the divine image. Christos Yannaras describes as "apophatic" that linguistic semantics and attitude to cognition which refuses to exhaust the content of knowledge in its formulation, which refuses to exhaust the reality of things signified in the logic of signifiers.[36] In philosophy, for example, it originates from an epistemological argument pertaining to a linguistic reformulation of the Kantian transcendentalism (typical for post-structuralism) that language conditions the accessibility and intelligibility of reality. According to this view there is no access to the referent outside the linguistic effect, but the linguistic effect is not the same as that referent it attempts but fails to capture. This situation entails, in analogy with theology, a variety of ways of making such a reference, where none of those can claim it exclusiveness and true accessibility to what the reference is made. Theology on its side affirms that any knowledge of God cannot escape the conditions of incongruence between human knowing and the reality of God. This incongruence is the immanent feature of any serious theologizing: one cannot raise questions on the reality of God from a position that excludes that feature of the Divine manifestation which implies the irreducibility of any speech about God to that which is predicated through this speech.[37]

The difference in the status of phenomenality of things in physics and cosmology, and events in theology amounts first of all to the limited scope of cosmology and unknowability of the universe understood as creation (and not as a fragment of the physically observed cosmos), for the sphere of its phenomenality (linked to the astronomical objects and inferred theoretical constructs) does not take into account the event-like essence of the human phenomenon. Knowledge of the world unfolds as if consciousness of this world exists without any recourse to events of coming into existence of corporeal persons. By neglecting the foundation of knowledge in events of the human existence physics and cosmology deprive themselves of realizing that the structure of the *given* in cosmology is determined by the present facticity of consciousness making sense of revelation for humanity itself, theologically treated as the revelation of God. In such a vision the fact of life, as well as knowledge in philosophy and science (as *modi operandi* of life) are seen as outcomes of the revelation (understood as the *given* in the event-like phenomenality), incorporating all specific forms of philosophical

---

36. Yannaras, *Postmodern Metaphysics*, 84. Apophaticism is a generic epistemological stance applicable to theology and the sciences, implying that the sense of realities affirmed in terms of their signifiers is never exhausted by the latter, that is, signifiers do not exhaust that which is signified. See the definition of apophaticism in Glossary (Appendix 1).

37. See Torrance, *Space, Time, and Incarnation*, 52–55.

and scientific knowledge, although the *givens* of revelation are not accessible in a non-mediated form, that is without a special procedure of their appropriation.

One may focus a bit on the latter point by making a historical reference to what was implied in mediation between the *givens* of revelation and knowledge, theology and philosophy. Theology proposed some special epistemological conditions of justification and appropriation of the phenomena of communion with God by extending rationality towards such existential notions as *faith* and *love*. Clement of Alexandria, for example, declares that knowledge is possible only because of faith and that faith is a condition for knowledge of any kind. Conversely, knowledge helps to make affirmations of faith demonstrable and thus, according to Clement, more "scientific." The faith that is true knowledge of revelation becomes a more scientific faith when supported by philosophy, and in this way it becomes gnosis.[38]

Another example of how the given of Revelation are appropriated in knowledge can be found in Augustine who promoted a view that from the very beginning Christianity doubted any comparison with ancient religions (*theologia civilis* and *theologia fabulosa*), making possible its encounter only with *theologia naturalis*, that makes an effort of studying the Divine from the movement of the heavenly bodies. Augustine insists on the only adequate use of the term *theologia* for Christian faith as true knowledge of the Divine. Since one speaks of truth "comparison must be made with philosophy (*cum philosophis est habenda conlatio*)." Thus philosophy must deal with faith, for, as Augustine concludes "a true philosopher is the *lover* God (*verus philosophus est amator Dei*)."[39] Love for God that is laid by Augustine in the foundation of true theology presupposes communion with God as an empirical source of any proposition and rational thinking about God. Philosophy as a rational "response" to Revelation must acquire a shape that is adjusted to appropriation of those phenomena which do not fit the schemes of the *metaphysica generalis* and transcendental epistemology.

In both cases, in the Greek East and Latin West, the sense of theology implied the acceptance of principles of immediacy of communion, whose *givenness* in experiential and empirical knowledge of God was not immediately evident and verified, universally accessible to all. Speaking of communion one implies first of all events of relationship between God and the world (creation of the world), the Incarnation of God in flesh, Resurrection and other personal events of saints and ascetics, all given as absolutely impossible from the point of view of their scientific-like explanation, or with

38. Clement of Alexandria, *Stromata*, 1.2.
39. Augustine, *Civitate Dei* VIII.1, 298.

no anticipating metaphysical horizon for these events. In the same vein one cannot define *apriori* that transcendental subject whose cognitive faculties would correspond to the possibility of placing the events of communion (as unrepeatable, devoid of their ontological definition and their objective representation) in the limits of transcendental experience. Communion allows one to open a possibility of a new type of understanding of inaccessible and metaphysically impossible phenomena by extending the limits of rationality as such. If human rationality is understood as a natural reaction of the understanding to form a response to the *events* of communion, it is the task of philosophy to comprehend how the new *givens* of these *events* do fit into the framework of rationality. It is the main challenge to philosophy from theology as communion and, correspondingly, to the dialogue of theology with the rationalism of the scientific understanding. Namely, philosophy must extend by appropriating theological experience and, as a result, to undertake a philosophical demarcation between scientific experience and experience of communion. How does rationality succeed in appropriating experience as communion and how do its paths differ from rationality's *modus operandi* in the sciences?

In order to recognize that theology as such as well as its relationship with science lead necessarily to taking into account the events of communion as new *givens* that require an epistemological qualification, one first needs to recognize the fact of their existence, their reality and origin in the event of life in general. For a naturalistically oriented scientist, any link between experience of living (with its intrinsic codification of the event of creation of the whole world in which the possibility of the corporeal existence is granted), the event of the Incarnation of the Word of God (in order knowledge of the universe to be possible in the archetype of the Divine Image), the very moral teaching of Christ (for the civilization to escape chaos and destruction), the Resurrection (that gives hope to man and determines the goals of knowledge), all these events involving a new type of *givenness* do not possess any certainty and validity. From the point of view of such a scientist the acceptance of the abovementioned events (and similar to them) in the scope of epistemologically extended rationality implies an element of *faith* (i.e., an opinion, judgement, and acceptance), so that the incorporation of such events in the scope of rationality makes sense only for believers. However, in this distinction between faith and non-faith (believing or not believing, between *doxa* and *episteme*, acceptance and rejection) there is an element of metaphysical thinking present, namely the distinction between faith in the abovementioned phenomena and knowledge of them on the ontological level as a discernment of these phenomena (as possible or impossible in rubrics of the world). But, as we have already stated, these criteria of distinction cannot be applied to human beings themselves, who are the initial source and origin of such a distinction, so that by denying an element of faith in respect to all knowledge that humanity can produce (effectively reducing humanity's essence to the rubrics of the world), one intentionally denies its unknowability by itself, that is it distorts (in representation) the sense of the human condition and thus distorts truth in general. It follows from here that the primary *given* of events of communion that requires a rational reaction and epistemological qualification is the *givenness* of humans to themselves, that is the mysteriousness of life as self-affectivity, as life from that Life that is in the foundation of humanity's faith in reality of its own life and existence in general.[40]

Communion, unlike mundane wisdom, happens on the initiative of that who is beyond any metaphysical and transcendental conditionality in humanity. It is the transcendent (event-like) character of communion that makes possible to maintain a clear-cut distinction between that which is disclosed in revelation and that which is constituted as an object of knowledge. By quoting a fragment from an Epistle to Hebrews 4:12, "For the word of God is living and active, sharper than any two-edged sword, piercing to the division of soul and of spirit, of joints and of marrow, and discerning the thoughts and intentions of the heart" (ESV), one can make a conclusion that it is the Word of God (as the Logos, that is reason), that is capable of discriminating in knowledge that which belongs to man and that which originates in God, that is that which is revealed. The distinction between human knowledge of the world and thinking of God implies that there is something *given* in communion (depending of a particular person) that is either *accepted* or *not* in face of the Word of God, that is something *enters* or *does not enter* in the realm of the experienced or thought. If that which is *given* in communion is accepted, then theology receives its justification from that these *givens* are included in the sphere of phenomena, but requiring a special epistemological justification within the extended rationality. If, alternatively, the *givens* of communion are not included in the sphere of phenomena, they remain inarticulate and metaphysically impossible (i.e., philosophically obscure).

As we have seen above faith was that condition of acceptance of the givens of communion into the sphere of phenomena that could be appropriated on the grounds of rationality extended through this faith. Faith, being a condition for accepting the givens of communion, being one of the virtues, according to (1 Cor 1:13) is inseparable from hope and love, where love is supreme and "remaining to the end." This is the reason why the acceptance

---

40. Henry, *I Am the Truth*, 73.

THE DIALOGUE BETWEEN THEOLOGY AND SCIENCE 59

of the givens of communion implies that what is received and that Who gives it are not just "objects" of contemplation, but first of all the "objects" of love as love for truth. In communion love changes the modalities of knowledge, that is epistemological criteria of reception of the givens in communion as the manifestation of love to truth. According to Augustine love is the condition that what is being known is true: "the only way to truth is by love"[41]. In other words, truth is rooted in love as its epistemological condition, not because truth cannot be fully disclosed without love, but because it is love itself that is the ultimate and only foundation for the possibility of seeing and grasping truth.[42] How is this similar to Pascal: "With respect to human things it is said that it is necessary to know them in order to love,... the saints, on the contrary, say, of divine things, that they must be loved in order to be known and that truth (*vérité*) is manifested only through love (*charité*)"[43]. Love, however is not that which is simply commensurable with experience of mundane reality. It demands one to overcome the sense of despair and futility of human existence, and to acquire love to God: "what a great distance between knowledge of God and love to him."[44]

It is love given to us in the revelation of the Word, that is the *Logos*, that reveals itself as *logos*, that is as rationality that makes it possible to approach the phenomena which are experienced by the spirit-bearing human flesh and exceed the capacity of being grasped by discursive thinking. Here one means first of all "knowing" of the human person by itself as acceptance of the facticity of its consciousness that articulates the givenness of life. This "knowing of the person by itself" does not mean a metaphysical comprehension, but an acceptance of life as a gift, as that given whose facticity cannot be doubted while life is in a living. Then one can speak of knowledge of the universe as a whole (as creation) being "coincident" with life of every person through an instantaneous intellectual synthesis. One can overcome the feeling of non-attunement with the universe, one's solitude in it and anxiety of the non-sense of being, with the aid of that "great reason" which incorporates these mysteries into the scope of its *givens* whose reality and truth is guaranteed by love to life and its Creator. The "great reason" implies the mind of Christ-Logos, by whom and through whom the universe was created and to whom, after the Incarnation in flesh, the whole universe was intelligibly given in its fullness as an instant of the Divine love, that is to that who remains the Lord of the worlds (John 1:16). Knowledge of the universe

41. Augustine, *Contra Faustum* 32.8, 581.
42. Augustine, *De Trinitate* XII.11 (16), 94.
43. Pascal, "De l'art de persuader," 29.
44. Pascal, *Pensées: Selections* 377, 161.

as creation implies the hidden knowledge of the Divine love and not only that which was created. Thus the contemplation and understanding of the universe as "coincident" with the event of life, that is perception of the universe as gifted at the moment of beginning of life, requires one to follow the same unconditional love with respect to life that was in God creating the world out of nothing (God created the universe out of his love and does not expect its recognition from the created).

Christian love justifies the very possibility of true knowledge, for that who loves, that is, believes in God, everything is possible, including knowledge of truth. The loving human being has the same privilege that God has (Mark 10:27). Christian love makes possible the "impossible knowledge" of a human by itself, although in a reduced form, as sensing of its own centrality in creation as the God-given ability to know about itself through knowledge of the world and God. To know the universe truly means to have knowledge not by one's own thought, but by the thought of him, who discloses himself only to those who love him. Knowledge of the universe as self-knowledge in order to be true requires the acquisition, as its archetype, of the "mind of God" through love to him. But this is not what is given to humanity in its natural propensity. To know through love and to know through God's "mind and eyes" requires one to exercise one's will. Christian love means the ability to approach things and to see in them the divine presence contrary to their compelling empirical evidence, that is to see that presence which can only be manifested to humanity not through its passive contemplation but through active participation in them, a sort of communion with them that allows one to get access to an otherwise inconceivable transcendence of other creatures and essences. Here love takes responsibility for that which is affirmed in philosophy and science because it christologically reinstates the definition of philosophy, and hence the sciences, to their proper sense as "love of wisdom" or "love of truth" leading them beyond their metaphysical limitations and appealing to a new epistemological exploration of those phenomena that are possible contrary to their seeming metaphysical impossibility and exceeding the limits of the transcendental delimiters. Without love, human reason is limited in interpreting the world, by transforming it into objects of possession and hence dealing only with their deficient phenomenality. In those situations where knowledge cannot be achieved in the phenomenality of objects (e.g., the universe as a whole), love, philosophically transfigured into the faculty of *reflecting judgement*,[45] remains the only channel of initiating any narrative about it (e.g., the narrative about the universe as a whole).

---

45. See the definition of "reflecting judgement" Appendix 1.

Christian love inspires such a change of mind (*metanoia*) that the created world appears to the latter as it is contemplated through the "eyes" of the Logos through whom and by whom all is. It is because of this *metanoia* that in spite of scientific verdict on insignificance of our place in the universe that love for the truth of life (as an entrance into the state of being alive) gives one the power of recognizing a glimpse of truth of its own origin from *Life* that is not seen at the empirical level and is metaphysically inexpressible. One means *Life* "that was the light of mankind" that was in the Word that was in the beginning (John 1:1–5). Humanity cannot "see" this light not because this light is "weak" and "dim" but, on the contrary, because this light of life is given to human beings in an absolute excess by "overexposing," that is saturating intuition to such an extent that the source of life as its origin becomes invisible. The unknowability of humans by themselves originates in their presence in front of such an excess of life that blocks the possibility of its comprehension by the understanding and reason.

To respect and love the world means to love and accept every personal life as that potential centre of disclosure and manifestation of the world through the gift of the Divine Image. Correspondingly, no scientific theory will have any existential relevance if it does not take into account the uniqueness and absolute value of any human life. And it is this love that changes the ways of approaching knowledge making this knowledge the expression of love to God who created that universe which can be known. This proclamation proceeds from the church because the church, in contradistinction with any scientific ideology and metaphysical convictions, asserts the message of Christ's "trampling death by death" as the possibility of transforming the process of our biological and cosmological dying into the event of communion with the person of God. Christ's coming to the world confirmed that the *logos* is indeed truly existent not as some inarticulate necessity that governs the universe, but as love, according to whose *logos* the world was created. But this love is the search of understanding of that whom it loves. Here one sees the link between love and truth, for love to Christ and creation can withstand the trial by the world only if this is love to truth.

One can conclude that the unknowability of humanity by itself constitutes the basic paradox of the human condition that, on the one hand, uncompromisingly asserts the facticity of human life, and on the other hand, the incomprehensibility of this life's facticity. On the one hand the inevitability of loving and respecting life, on the other hand, constantly sensing its own non-attunement and anxiety of the physical existence without understanding its sense. The love for life is implanted in all human activities whose purposefulness is implicitly driven by this love. This love expresses human beings's suffering from a congenital heart condition of being restlessly involved into the search for something unknown and whose names are above any denomination, or may be withheld through the initial congenital forgetting. The love for life inspires faith as its own outward expression. And this faith as an outward modality of a human being that opposes to an existentially futile nihilistic disbelief that there is something out there whose gaze at us commands our respect and makes us speechless and humble in front of its immeasurable immensity. Human activities then represent a certain struggle with the incomprehensible realities in order to stay alive. Science in this sense is an illuminating example of that how humanity explores the world in order to live physically and psychologically in love with this life. Love for life as a theological propensity of humanity turns out to be in the foundation of science, but to see this love and make it articulate, this love must reveal itself to human beings through showing them that their existence, whatever foundation it has, is not unconditional but dependent on the luck and fine-tuning of the physical parameters of the world. Yet the world, like a dark sky remains dimmer than life that shines the more brilliantly the darker the night in which it is immersed. The darkness one implies here is not to a great extent a lack of the vision of the world that retains a feeling of homelessness and loss of the sense of life, but rather an excess in the givenness of the world through life, its overexposure making life in the world ever exceeding any definite phenomenality. This, in short, makes life radically ambiguous and hence rich, where this richness is unconditionally given so that no unambiguous life is possible. It is this ambiguity that provokes an endless interpretation forcing us to come to terms with our indefinite state. And it is through such an interpretation that human beings reach a certain self-understanding consisting in that they never quite understand who they are and that there is no at all one final interpretation. In view of this one can think of science (philosophy) and theology as different aspects in a common human passion to respond to the enveloping darkness of the human existence in which human beings are lost, so that the feeling of such a loss is the only inspiring force initiating the human search for the sense of its own existence as well as the existence of the universe. Theology deals primarily with love and respect for creation, life and their creator, leaving aside the fact of man's own incomprehensibility and thus concentrating on a praise of God relevant to the community of the faithful. The sciences operate in the conditions of the same incomprehensibility but they tell a story of the human functioning in the world, so that the sense of such a different story explicates what is that creation by God, that God who is praised for. The dialogue between theology and science thus becomes an attempt to balance in one and the same humanity the distinction between theology and science not as it was thought since the classical times through the distinction between faith and reason as opposites of believing and seeing. Rather, the modern dialogue between theology and science represents a mediation between two attitudes, or two types of *seeing as*, dealing with different phenomenalities of one and the same existence. The scientific phenomenality employs a common philosophical faith as a complex of presuppositional structures that is built into every human endeavour that is called knowledge and action. This philosophical faith functions with respect to that reality which can be represented as objects, including man himself seen as a physical organism. The phenomenality of religious inaugural events, as the different *givens* of the human subjectivity, employs another type of faith that is related to a particular set of events significant for a particular community of the faithful. Speaking of Christian faith, human life is seen and narrated not neutrally at the background of the universal existence, but as related to those inaugurate events which constitute the essence of Christianity. The distinction between science (scientific philosophy) and theology then becomes a distinction between two kinds of interpretations of life that are inwardly structured by the types of faith understood as an element of human life. Both, theology and science originate in life and explicate this life. Both of them employ different epistemic tools, but both of them point to one and the same sense of life and existence that is allegedly over there, but actually ever withheld from it catching through articulation. Thus the dialogue between theology and science turns out to be an endless journey of one and the same homeless and not-attuned humanity in its search for the "hard land" in the ocean of hope. This "hard land" is named differently in theology and science, but one needs an intuition for this land and an impetus for its search.

2

THE UNKNOWABILITY OF HUMANITY AND THE PARADOX OF SUBJECTIVITY AT THE INCEPTION OF THE DIALOGUE BETWEEN THEOLOGY AND SCIENCE

"The more the positive sciences develop and boast of their epistemological breaks, their revolutionary problematics and deconstructions of all kinds, the less man has any idea of what he is. This is because what makes him a man—specifically, the fact of being a me—is precisely what has become totally unintelligible to thinkers and scholars these days."

—Michel Henry

"The only approach to the created person is through a 'negative' anthropology. Here the ascetic practices of the Non-Christian East and the scientific analyses of the West are most valuable, not because they tell us what the person is, but because they help us to understand what it is not. To know something of the mystery of the person, we must go right beyond its natural context, beyond its cosmic, collective, and individual environment.... The person is not an object open to inspection, any more than God is."

—Olivier Clément

FROM THE UNKNOWABILITY OF HUMANITY TO THE PARADOX OF SUBJECTIVITY

As we have already asserted above the mediation between theology and science does not represent any metaphysical necessity but represents events of life, that is, those dimensions of the human will and reason that cannot be deduced on the grounds of causality pertaining to the world. The facticity of the dialogue points to the fact that it represents the event-like phenomenon related to life's self-affectivity, so that its interpretation demands a philosophy that deals with the human phenomenon as "event" of Life, the phenomenon that has a "meta-ontological" status, ordaining and justifying the very possibility of the philosophical as well as scientific knowledge of the world. However the human phenomenon, being given to humanity, does not receive its exhaustive elucidation by human beings themselves. The self-imposed question, "What is man?" remains unanswered.[1] Seen from this standpoint, all human activities, including those of science, as well as religious experience, originate in one and the same humanity within the conditions when it does not understand its own essence. Yet the sciences and religions are efficacious on the level of phenomena since they describe the facticity of life and explicate the sense of humanity through a never-ending hermeneutics of the world. According to Karl Jaspers, "We cannot exhaust man's being in knowledge of him, we can experience it only in the primal source of our thought and action. Man is fundamentally more than he can know about himself."[2] The sciences, philosophy and theology, all, pose questions to man about man himself that cannot lead to any definitive answer, thus provoking further questions.[3] Orthodox theologians associate this human incapacity with the post-lapserian condition as self-centeredness of humanity and forgetting of its link to God: "In this condition it is impossible to develop a Christian anthropology.... Humanity cannot be explained in terms of itself."[4] Correspondingly the dialogue between theology

---

1. In the twentieth century this incomprehensible contingent facticity of humanity became the founding theme of all existential philosophers. For a non-Christian existentialism the contingency of existence represents pure irrationality and brutal absurdity. Man is there as he is, without any reason. This is what, according to Heidegger and Sartre is called his *facticity*. In a Christian existentialism the contingency of the human existence is seen as a mystery rooted in the original creation and reaffirmed by the Incarnation and Redemption. See Mounier, *Introduction aux existentialismes*, 38–41.

2. Jaspers, *Ways to Wisdom*, 63, 66.

3. Cf. Moltmann, *Man*, 2.

4. Clément, *On Human Being*, 9–10. Cf. "This difficulty [the definition of man in the conditions after the Fall] becomes even more clearer when we pose the question of human capacity and human incapacity. For this question stems from man's difficulty

and science, as a particular modus of the human enquiry in the nature of things, contributes to further explication of the riddle of man, with no aim of creating any metaphysical concept of man. The seeming dualism in comprehension of reality, either on the grounds of the sciences or through theological insights, explicates the dualism in the human condition between *being* and *having*: "We are, but we do not possess ourselves,"[5] that is, we are, but it is not us who created us.[6] One can say that man is a co-participant of the infinite all-embracing being; however it is because of the infinite character of such a communion that man cannot comprehend the sense of this communion's contingent givenness. As the sciences explicate outwardly a way of our existence as things (objects), they do not answer the question as to "why we are?", that is, why humanity is given to itself in such a way that the self-detection of its existence is possible at all. This question "why?" implies a question of the facticity of our being created, that one which cannot be answered because humanity cannot create itself. The drama of not being able to create itself receives its expression in the cosmological context as that that mankind is unable to understand its place in the universe. Simon Frank invokes a rather nostalgic description of the cosmic homelessness as a loss of a "motherland": "Contrary to deceptive appearances which man had trusted for thousands of years, his native abode, the earth, proved to be not the centre of the universe, but a mere speck, a part of a planetary system which itself was only an insignificant appendage of one of the innumerable stars lost in boundless space."[7] Humanity does not feel at home because of its insignificance in cosmic space; it also does not understand the sense of its contingent facticity in terms of the laws of the universe that it cannot control. Rudoph Bultmann expressed this thought by using the language of

---

in *defining* himself. It is a question that only a human being can ask, precisely because it seems to be a unique characteristic of this sort of being to be unwilling to accept his actual limits and to tend to move beyond them" (Zizioulas, *Communion and Otherness*, 206).

5. Plessner, *Conditio humana*, 7.

6. It is in this sense that the Christian faith in creation is fundamentally existential. As it was expressed by Rudolph Bultmann, "The Christian faith in creation affirms that man is not at home in the world, that here he has 'no lasting city.' It affirms that he is under an illusion when he imagines that he can dispose of himself and can outwardly and inwardly secure his life. It points out to him that he has not brought himself into existence and does not dispose of his end." More than that, "Such knowledge is included in the Christian faith in creation, and without it—whether it be brought to clear consciousness or not—there is no such faith" (Bultmann, "The Meaning of the Christian Faith in Creation," in *Existence and Faith*, 252, 255–56).

7. Frank, *Reality and Man*, 190–91.

insecurity: "Thus human life is insecure, its course is not at man's disposal."[8] Theology, unlike the sciences, does not attempt to provide any accomplished view of the actual position of humanity in the cosmos; it rather transforms the issue into a modus of participation *in* and communion *with* that source of life and intelligence which escapes the limits of metaphysical definitions.

The sciences play a twofold role in comprehending and formulating the sense of humanity's unknowability and insufficiency of its ontological grounds in the universe. It is science that makes it possible to bring on board the outward aspects of this unknowability through human beings's insignificance in the physical universe. Without a scientific refinement of the predicaments of the human condition humans would not be able to understand the scale of their *epistemological significance* for comprehending the universe and developing a capacity of longing for the ultimate ground of its existence either in the world or beyond it. The ontological groundlessness of humanity (as its incapacity to ground itself in any metaphysical foundation) is exactly that intrinsic part of the human condition that provokes humanity to search for grace or "blessing" (transcendence) of its existence from that which is beyond humanity itself.

The predisposition to transcend the sphere of the unconcealed relies on participation and communion with that which is beyond the visible and sensible. This transcending, even if it is not initiated by the sciences, is reactivated in human beings and made existentially dramatic through cooperation with the sciences. One cannot assert that the sciences are paving the way to a theological apprehension of the world, but one finds them refining the delimiters of the human condition thus turning to a theological search for the sense of existence. It is in this sense that humanity's unknowability by itself, endorsed by scientific knowledge, becomes a factor for engaging with theology through abandoning any straightforward attempts of overcoming this unknowability on the grounds of metaphysical concepts. The implicit hope and longing for overcoming humanity's inability to know itself, present in the modern sciences and some branches of philosophy, forms a hidden *purpose* implanted in the core of the human condition. This *purpose* is to acquire a "home" in being, to ground humans in that which they always transcend. This *purpose* is not ontologically achievable: "If he [man] ever

---

8. Bultmann, "The Meaning," 254–55. In Erick Fromm's words "He [man] is set apart while being a part; he is homeless, yet chained to the home he shares with all creatures. Cast into the world at an accidental place and time, he is forced out of it, again accidentally. Being aware of himself, he realises his powerlessness and the limitations of his existence. He visualises his own end: death. Never is he free from the dichotomy of his existence: he cannot rid himself of his mind, even if he should want to; he cannot rid himself of his body as long as he is alive" (Fromm, *Man for Himself*, 40).

finally got 'behind himself', and could establish what was the matter with him, nothing would any longer be the matter with him, but everything would be fixed and tied down, and he would be finished. The solution of a puzzle what man is would then be at the same time the final release from being human."[9] This entails that the whole process of knowledge is driven by this *purpose* only *formally*, that it represents a *teleological activity without a material purpose*.[10] The latter implies that the "reconciliation" of science and theology could not be achieved so that the dialogue between them can be considered a teleological activity without a *material purpose*. Theologically, this activity could be understood as a *mediation* between the human sense of creaturehood in the midst of the physical world and, at the same time, humanity's sense of communion with that beyond the world thank to which humanity was created.

Humanity's inability to know itself can easily be explicated through the so called paradox of subjectivity[11] whose concise formulation is: "We can describe the relations between subject and world as purely intentional relations as opposed to (objective) spatial, temporal, and causal relations. We can appeal to the distinction between belonging to the world of objects and being a condition of the possibility of the world of objects (as meaning). Perhaps the broadest terms for these relations would be the *transcendental* relations and the *part-whole* relation,"[12] or "It is necessary to combine the recognition of our contingency, our finitude, and our containment in the world with an ambition of transcendence, however limited may be our success in achieving it."[13] In a more palpable form this paradox was formulated by Pierre Teilhard de Chardin who argued that without such qualities as a sense of spatial immensity, a sense of depth, as sense of number, as sense of proportion, as sense of quality, a sense of movement and a sense of the

---

9. Moltmann, *Man*, 2.

10. The terminology of *formal purposiveness* originates in Kant's *Critique of Judgement*: "An object, or *state of mind, or even an action* is called purposive, although its possibility does not necessarily presuppose the representation of a purpose, merely because its possibility can be explained and conceived by us only so far as we assume for its ground a causality according to *purposes*, i.e., in accordance with a *will* which has regulated it according to the representation of a certain rule" (Kant, *Critique of Judgement* §10, 55; emphasis added).

11. The formulations of the paradox are abundant. See Kant, *Critique of Practical Reason*, Conclusion, 260; Husserl, *The Crisis*, 179; Merleau-Ponty, "The Battle over Existentialism," in *Sense and Non-Sense*, 71–72; Scheler, *Die Stellung Des Menschen*, 160. The review of different formulations of the paradox can be found in Nesteruk, *The Sense of the Universe*, 136–61. See also Carr, *Paradox of Subjectivity*.

12. Carr, *Paradox of Subjectivity*, 116.

13. Nagel, *The View from Nowhere*, 9.

organic "man will remain indefinitely . . . an erratic object in a disjoint world. Conversely, we have only to rid our vision of the threefold illusion of smallness, plurality and immobility, for man effortlessly to take the central position. . . . The momentary summit of anthropogenesis which is itself the crown of a cosmogenesis."[14] Unlike previously quoted philosophers, Teilhard aspired to find the ultimate resolution of the paradox within the scientific scope by attempting to deduce the human capacity of articulating the world as emerging from the physical and biological that since the beginning of the world was aiming to produce intelligent humanity, in the conditions of the paradox. Philosophically, such a stance on the paradox manifests a natural attitude, attempting to position the paradox itself as an emergent property of cosmogenesis and anthropogenesis.

The problematicity of the paradox does not disappear since its very presence to subjectivity is the manifestation of the primacy of this subjectivity in spite of the fact that this subjectivity can be thought as a developed property of intelligent embodied humanity. Indeed taken in a philosophical reflection, there is the primacy of the thinking intellect (*ego cogito*) with respect to the world. It is this *ego* as given to itself in its absolute certainty is the first apodictically "known unknowable," that is, detected unconditionally unlike those aspects of the world which always remain prone to an epistemological doubt. The primacy of the thinking intelligence creates a natural separation of the sphere of consciousness enclosed in itself from the world which, as being articulated, exists only in relation to this consciousness, as epistemologically dependent of it. Seen in this perspective human subjectivity becomes that "place" of the first and certain truth which falls in a competence of the transcendental philosophy whose imperatives precede all truths that are derived from the sciences. But even in this radical phenomenological centering of reality around subjectivity the major question of the facticity of this subjectivity remains unaddressed. In fact, the very posing a question of its facticity, from a phenomenological point of view, is simply illogical and illegitimate to the same extent as any question about the facticity of the field of consciousness as such.[15]

In fact the paradox exactly explicates two different positions which philosophical thought can take with respect the truth of existence: a natural one and a phenomenological one. The reconciliation of these attitudes is

---

14. Teilhard de Chardin, *The Phenomenon of Man*, 33–34.

15. Aron Gurwitsch accentuates the personal dimension of embodied consciousness: "what is decisive and crucial importance is not whether the existence of consciousness is conceded or denied but rather that, even if this existence is conceded, consciousness and whatever pertains to it are considered as "private" and thus not in principle subject to scientific investigation" (Gurwitsch, *Phenomenology*, 133).

possible in practice by existing in the body and synthesizing the world in one consciousness. However, no theoretical model of such a reconciliation is possible. Indeed, the world cannot be a totality of all that is perceived without a subject endowed with certain faculties. The body of this subject is the necessary condition for this subject to have the faculty through which the world can be defined as the totality of the perceived and experienced. The relation to the world is not exhausted only by the faculty of perception: humans relate to the world through the practical and affective modalities that imply some understanding. The perceptions of things and events already contain a definite meaning, and it is this meaning that belongs to the very way (path) things are open to human beings. The world appears to them as a variety of practical actions through which things acquire some meaning for them. Saying simpler, the meaning of things depends on that very way along which a subject is capable of meeting things in view of its practical capacities. Practical capacities are related first of all to an ability to create its own projects. A basic existential project is a constant enquiry in the sense of one's own existence. Humanity outlines goals for itself on the basis of its desire to be that what it wants. In other words, humanity is capable of projecting its own life according to its own representation of itself, in spite of the fact that it does not understand the ultimate sense of itself. In a way the human existence is that which we have to choose and make projects in order to accord it with the main project of understanding of itself. In this sense all those possibilities which are open to us in the world depend on our faculties but they are not "created" by them. For example, all humanity's perceptual experience of the physical world depends on its essential propensities such as space and time that necessarily structure any experience. These propensities cannot be "created" by anyone whereas any talk about them without a subject would not make any sense. The human faculties and world's properties are correlative: the possibilities of knowledge, for example, do exist only in relation to these faculties and vice versa. Then it follows that the human existential possibilities are not made as projects once and forever as if they would be free from being rooted in past history. These possibilities have their origin in the inaugural events as those which escape one's expectations and deprive one of any ground at that "moment" when one expects it less. It is in this sense that one can say that the paradox of subjectivity as such represents that inaugural existential possibility of making sense of humanity through an intentional and wilful exploration of its position in the universe. One does not imply any theoretical reconciliation between the terms of the paradox for humanity cannot control the conditions of its existence and corresponding faculties in understanding the world. Humanity drafts its projects empirically whereas no understanding of its very possibility is given to humanity's disposal. Perennial philosophy humbly accepts this as a fact; theology appeals to God's creation of humanity whatever physical and biological mechanism was implemented by him in the course of evolution of the universe. The paradox of subjectivity does not follow from any natural necessity of the human existence: one can easily organically function without any mention of this paradox. However, this paradox appears immediately as soon as humanity starts thinking of itself and its origin. In other words, it is implanted in the very fabric of that which is called human: to make life-project in the conditions of the initial incomprehensibility of its origins. Then the paradox can be seen as implanted in the inaugural event of human life effectively predetermining the endless unfolding of the sense of humanity.

The paradox, as the coexistence of two attitudes to the hermeneutics of the subject appears to be a structural element of human subjectivity in general. The self-givenness and self-affectivity of "the subject" manifested in the formulations of the paradox implies the question of the facticity of consciousness that is explicitly missing from any articulations of the world. As Maurice Merleau-Ponty once put it, "consciousness attributes this power of universal constitution to itself only if it *ignores the event which provides its infrastructure and which is its birth*. A consciousness for which the world 'can be taken for granted,' which finds it 'already constituted' and present even in consciousness itself, does not absolutely choose either its being or its manner of being."[16] It is because of the inexplicability of the facticity of consciousness in metaphysical terms that the conscious existence of humanity can be considered as "event." The temptation to find that missing foundation of its own realization in existence leads consciousness to transcendence in a theological direction, that which exceeds the scope of philosophy but, at the same time, extends philosophy towards the appropriation of those realities that escape the phenomenality of objects. Then the paradoxical dichotomy in the human subjectivity cannot have a metaphysical explanation and falls under the rubrics of *event*, that is, as something being given, with no recourse to its possible metaphysical resolution. In the case of an attempted reconciliation of the terms of the paradox, this move would be equivalent to the elucidation of the paradox's appearance in the subject, that is, appearance of a personal (hypostatic) subject (for whom no metaphysical foundation can be found). Here theology enters the discourse: the interpretation of the paradox proceeds from the theology of creation of the human life from Life understood as Divine Being (John 1:1–6). Michel Henry characteristically expressed the paradox: "I am not only for myself, i.e., this individual

---

16. Merleau-Ponty, *Phenomenology of Perception*, 453; emphasis added.

appearing in the world, a thing among things, a man among men.... In order to relate everything to oneself, one must first of all be this Self to whom everything is related, one must be able to say *I am me*. But the point is that this *I am me* is not at all originary." Here is the main point: the paradox is not that which is controlled by human beings, they cannot remove or discard this paradox because it is implanted into the initial pattern of the human hypostatic existence. And this is the reason why its origin is related to creation, that is, has a theological ground: "A Self such as that of man, a living transcendental Self . . . is only ever to be found in the 'Word of life' of the first letter of John, whom Paul describes as a 'First Born among many Brothers' (Rom 8:28–30)."[17] Henry points to a christological origin of this paradox, that is, to its only meaningful signification and explication through the Incarnation of the Logos-Christ in Jesus of Nazareth in whom this paradox is present in a "non-paradoxical form." The transition from the philosophical formulation of the paradox to its theological origin follows from the impossibility of its metaphysical elucidation. This happens because the paradox is implanted in the human existence manifesting God's creation in the Divine Image, anticipating Christ's Incarnation.

Theologians of the past expressed the paradox in terms explicitly containing a reference to that which is beyond the world, that is to the fact that the paradox explicates the condition of creaturehood. In his Epistles to Romans, Apostle Paul recapitulates man's paradoxical created condition by contrasting his serving God's Law with his mind, and serving to the law of sin with his unspiritual nature (Rom 7:25). Maximus the Confessor advocated that God's image in humanity made the latter capable of mediating between the moral divisions in themselves and in creation in general, for example between the sensible (visible universe) and intelligible (invisible, for example an image of the world's wholeness in consciousness): "As a compound of soul and body he [man] is limited essentially by intelligible and sensible realities, while at the same time he himself defines [articulates] these realities through his capacity to apprehend intellectually and perceive with his senses."[18] The Russian philosopher Vladimir Soloviev explicitly referred to God in his description of the human ambivalent condition: "Man combines in himself all possible opposites which all can be reduced to one great polarity between the unconditional and the conditional, between the absolute and eternal essence, and the transitory phenomenon or appearance. Man is at once divinity and nothingness."[19] Another Russian philosopher

---

17. Henry, "Phenomenology of Life," 104.
18. Maximus the Confessor, *Various Texts on Theology* 5.71, 277.
19. Solovyev, *Lectures on Godmanhood* 8, 158.

and theologian Victor Nesmelov expressed the paradox in different words: "all particular contradictions of thought and life arise from man's aspiration to fulfil the ideal image of the unconditional in the necessary boundaries of the external conditions,"[20] and "in knowledge of ourselves we know truly, that although our own person exists only in the necessary conditions of the physical world, by its nature it manifests not the world, but the true essence of the very Infinite and Unconditional."[21]

Now it is reasonable to pose a question as to whether the impossibility of metaphysical explication of the paradox of subjectivity characterizes something fundamental and constitutive for the human condition. Here two ways of responding to this question are possible. One attempts to link the human condition to that which is biblically termed the Fall and described in terms of original sin, transgression from the union with God that was granted to humanity at its (evolutionary or not) creation. If we accepted such a view it would be natural to claim that the dichotomy in the human position in the world (described in terms of the paradox) cascading towards a tension between a scientific and a theological vision of the world originated in the Fall (as a condition deviated from the initial union with God which implied no paradox). Correspondingly, an attempted resolution of both the paradox, as well as the removal of tensions and divisions between science and theology, would correspond to a theologically understood healing and redemption placing the dialogue in the context of the "arch" Fall-Redemption pertaining to the Western theology. In other words, the paradox as part of the human condition is a consequence of the Fall, so that its overcoming could be attempted on the grounds of removing its consequences, that is, this paradox could be potentially resolved through human actions. If the Fall is considered as a voluntary deviation from the relationship with God originating in the misuse of the human freedom, the paradox following from the Fall could be treated as being brought upon humanity through actions of humanity itself. Similarly to the traditional theological assertion that evil which entered the world through the Fall is not implanted in nature, the paradox could be treated as not being a natural condition of humanity.

Such an approach to the paradox can be contrasted with the conviction that the paradoxical perception of humanity's place in creation originates in the human nature and inevitable for humanity's Divine Image. Some theologians are prone to treat such a dichotomy in the human position as "basic evil," that is, as evil which pertains to the essence of the created world, but

20. Nesmelov, *The Science of Man*, 246.
21. Nesmelov, *The Science of Man*, 269.

not related to human actions. Indeed, a contemporary Greek Orthodox philosopher and theologian Christos Yannaras describes the existing situation in the human perception of its ambivalent position in creation as "evil":

> All the laws of nature, the fundamental constancies of the natural world, its "arbitrary" arithmetic values, constitute a single holistic phenomenon that tends organically from the outset toward the creation of conditions for its self-knowledge, that is to say, for intelligent life. . . . And yet the way nature operates within the conditions prevailing on earth also manifests in a parallel fashion an autonomy (a mechanistic "indifference") with regard to the intelligent existence of the human subject, its creative uniqueness and otherness. . . . In this autonomy of nature we human beings see a challenging "absurdity" (a violation of our own rational conception of *meaning* in the world), an absurdity that we can only characterize as *evil*.[22]

Yannaras's reading of the paradox through his understanding of humanity—as a creature longing for immortality but facing a defeat by the laws of nature—contributes to the longstanding discussion of the paradox by philosophers, qualifying it as an expression of the basic *anxiety* of humanity in the world, its despair and non-attunement to the world, depriving man of understanding of the sense of existence.[23] Can the paradox of subjectivity (implied in Yannaras's quote) thus be treated in this way as a definition of "evil," related to the human incomprehension of its own condition. And can then evil (encapsulated in the paradox) be related to the vaguely understood Fall?

The major problem with such a view of humanity is to presuppose that it was a certain condition before the Fall, that could be devoid of ambiguities and unknowability. Certainly, any explanation of the transition from the

---

22. Yannaras, *The Enigma of Evil*, 16. Certainly, one must not think that that "evil" which is described by Yannaras as "basic" is the only evil which has, so to speak, an objective nature. The irrationality of the natural order is correlated with the human irrational and hence evil-like behavior in the social world. Simon Frank expressed this thought: "In contemplating sin and evil objectively, . . . we can and ought to regard them as expression of the impotence and irrationality of human will—that is, of man's unhappy condition. His conflict with blind forces raging in the human world is no less tragic than his sufferings from the soulless and morally indifferent forces of nature" (Frank, *Reality and Man*, 205).

23. This sentiment is reminiscent to the famous Pascalian fear of the silent skies, repeated later by many existential philosophers and religious thinkers. Teilhard de Chardin, for example, described this in following words: "On certain days the world seems a terrifying thing: huge, blind an brutal. It buffets us about, drags us along, and kills us with complete indifference" (Teilhard de Chardin, *Le Milieu Divin*, 137).

pre-lapserian to post-lapserian state could only be mythological since the drastic difference between two conditions (before and after the Fall) could not be overcome from our (fallen) side: one cannot go back through the gates of Paradise.[24] Here one experiences a general theological difficulty in positioning the Fall as a singular event (as particularly dated) in terms of a certain worldly temporality. This is the reason why it seems reasonable to associate the Fall not with some specific historical event, but with some qualitative state of humanity linked to the state of the naturally evolved universe. In this case "evil" (original sin and the Fall) is linked not to freedom of humanity but to the structure of the whole universe as being created. This is what implied in Yannaras's treatment of evil as a "cosmic predisposition" of humanity where the dual structure of created being is encoded in terms of the paradox perceived by humanity because of being created and incapable of controlling the conditions of its existence. Such an intuition of evil has already been presented in the "recent" history of Christian thought in writings of Teilhard de Chardin. Teihard wrote: "Evil is inevitable in the course of creation which develops within time."[25] "I have no difficulty in accepting that the evil *inherent in the world as a result of its method of creation* can be regarded as becoming specially individualised on earth simultaneously with the appearance of responsible human 'I's'. This would be the original sin, in the strict sense of the word, of the theologians."[26] In spite of the fact that Teilhard makes a special reference to "the appearance of responsible human egos," his main idea is that evil is inseparable from the mechanism how this world was created. Certainly this view considerably deviates from the biblical stance on the entrance of evil through the sin of Adam. One could be tempted to claim that Teilhard denies the Fall at all. However this is not exactly true: he identifies the presence of evil in creation with death, but death is a natural process implanted in all levels of creation. There is the totality of evil because there is the totality of death. Correspondingly the biblically understood original sin is not an *act*, but a *condition* (a *state*). It inevitably appears when at some stage of evolution of the universe it leads to suffering (presumably biological and human) and "starting with man, it becomes sin."[27] Biological life-forms and human beings are thus naturally predisposed to evil, that is, to physical suffering and moral transgression "not because of some deficiency in the creative act but by the very structure

24. Clément, "Le sens de la terre," 106.

25. Teilhard de Chardin, "How I Believe?," in *Christianity and Evolution*, 132.

26. Teilhard de Chardin, "Some General Views on the Essence of Christianity," in *Christianity and Evolution*, 135; emphasis added.

27. Teilhard de Chardin, "Reflections on Original Sin," in *Christianity and Evolution*, 195.

of participated being."²⁸ Leaving aside that how Teilhard justifies the inherent features of evil in creation of the universe, what is important for us is that the original sin and evil "cease to be an isolated act and become a *state* (affecting human mass as a whole, as result of an endless stream of transgressions punctuating mankind in the course of time)."²⁹ Teilhard makes his claim even more specific when he links sin and evil as a *state* to evolution: original sin (or the Fall) appears "not as an element in a series, but an aspect or global modality of evolution."³⁰ Teilhard refers not only to biological evolution but also to cosmological evolution accentuating that point that it is only in the evolving universe that it is possible to avoid theological difficulties with understanding the Fall and original sin as transcendent interference in the course of the human history (an appeal to which would be inevitable in a static universe). "From this point of view original sin, considered in its cosmic basis . . . , tends to be indistinguishable from the sheer mechanism of creation—in which it represents the action of the negative forces of 'counter-evolution.'"³¹

In view of modern scientific research attempting to trace the appearance of intelligent life to the very beginnings of biological life on Earth through the process accompanied by disappearance and death of numerous species and individual beings, evil and absurdity that have been invoked by Yannaras can hardly be understood only in terms of human freedom and having a potential to be overcome through changing the human condition. Since human beings are not created in an accomplished adult shape with a developed rationality and the sense of unique existence, an ontogenetic evolution implies its phylogenetic context and this is why the very understanding of humanity made in the image of God indeed implies an evolutionary process.³² In this sense the point of Teilhard de Chardin is even more radical than that of the Christian Orthodoxy in the sense that by inheriting that nature which is affected by the original sin, humanity inherits this nature from the very first seconds of the world's creation through sharing the substance of the visible universe that, according to modern physics (as what noticed by de Chardin), exhibits death (i.e., evil in Yannaras's terms). Certainly all these considerations, even if they invoke cosmological aspects of the human condition, do not produce any clues in order to understand the origin of consciousness capable of reflecting upon its own embodied existence and

28. Teilhard de Chardin, "Reflections on Original Sin," 196.
29. Teilhard de Chardin, "Reflections on Original Sin," 196.
30. Teilhard de Chardin, "Christ the Evolver," in *Christianity and Evolution*, 149.
31. Teilhard de Chardin, "Christ the Evolver," 149.
32. See a wide discussion of this issue in Van Huysteen, *Alone in the World?*

experiencing the drama of its own unknowability. The unknowability of humanity as the incapacity of its consciousness to exit from its enclosed "field," that is, the realm of its createdness, and to discern God in creation is sometimes associated with the human condition after the historically singular Fall. However it seems to be more plausible together with de Chardin and Yannaras to associate this unknowability with the unknowability of the origins of the whole creation thus by placing this unknowability in the cosmological context or that one of the origins of life on Earth.

If the "original sin" and evil are implanted in the structure of the created universe so that humanity has been evolving to its present state through carrying the signs of this evil, it is reasonable to ask what are those particular characteristics of the Divine Image in human beings that yet indicate the presence of such an evil. How the Divine Image is compatible with evil at all? An Orthodox position would be that evil pertains to that common human *nature* which humanity inherited from its prehistoric ancestors whereas humanity's longing for immortality and the sense of communion with God represents that which is qualified as the Divine Image. The paradox of subjectivity de facto accentuates such an ambivalence between the sense of "evil" and the sense of the Divine that amounts to the fact that even in the condition of the Divine Image humanity is not capable of knowing the sense of its own origins and its ambivalent existence. In fact the unknowability of humanity is exactly consistent with its being the Image of God, that is, the image of that One Who is unknowable.[33] On the one hand the unknowability is implanted in the conditions of creation and evolution, on the other hand it is this unknowability that is a "privilege" of being in the Divine Image because it is only through carrying this image that humanity is capable to formulate this unknowability as a problem (i.e., to discern a difference between the necessary and sufficient conditions of its existence). This entails that any attempted resolution of the paradox of subjectivity, as a search for the answer to the question "What is man?" qualifies such an attempt (in which human beings define themselves in terms of something that is less than God) as a distortion of the Divine Image.[34]

---

33. Gregory of Nyssa, *De hominis opificio*, 397. On the unknowability of man, see Marion, "Mihi magna," as well as Marion, *Negative Certainties*, 8–50.

34. Jean-Luc Marion in his *Negative Certainties*, 41, quotes a passage from Augustine's *De Trinitate* X.5 (7), where, as Marion claims, a phenomenology of sin is represented through describing the human soul as turning away form God, "slithering and sliding down into less and less, which is imagined to be more and more." What is implied by this, is that any attempt of man to define himself on the basis of the human only is tantamount of denying life as the gift of that other than man, that is, of God, through resemblance with whom man resembles himself, and thus is only capable of defining himself.

Since the assertion of the unknowability of humanity is based on a premise that it cannot create itself while holding the Divine Image, the "original sin" as a state can mean a particular epistemological and moral attitude to this creaturely condition. In this case, that evil to which Yannaras refers can be treated as related not to the ontology of the created world, but to the alleged loss of the sense of the unity with all creation and communion with God supposed to pertain to the human condition in the Divine Image. In this case it is possible to treat Yannaras's interpretation of the paradox in terms of evil in a *moral*, but not ontological sense: indeed the *seeing* of the challenging "absurdity" of nature (as violating our own rational conception of meaning of the world) as *evil* is rather a moral condition of humanity, namely its forgetting of the fact that humanity is created within the rubrics of nature and that the latter is "subordinated" to the conditions of humanity only providing the *necessary* conditions for its existence. But it is because the *sufficient* conditions are not part of nature that the disparity of these conditions with the necessary conditions (treated as evil) represents a moral tension between what humanity is in terms of nature and what it wants to be in terms of the Divine Image. But this is that condition which accompanies humanity from it inception as being created. Thus seen in this perspective the paradox of subjectivity de facto explicates in philosophical terms the basic predicament of the human condition of being *a creature in communion with God*. The issue here is not the state of humanity after the Fall, but the state of humanity as being created.

If the conditions of evil in Yannaras's sense correspond to the moral tensions related to the apprehension of the world and to the human inability to balance man's natural facticity with the spiritual perception of his place as a crown of creation, one can argue that the sciences help humanity to adapt to the conditions of "evil," insofar as their primary task is to explicate, although indirectly, some aspects of this "evil." One needs to see "evil" in order to develop an impetus for transcending its conditions. In fact, even to articulate the ambivalence in the human condition as "evil," one needs *grace* as that which constitutes the move positioning "evil" seen by humanity as a problem of its natural condition. In view of this one reasonably comes back to the question of the sense of the dialogue between theology and science.

Science articulates the conditions of "evil" (natural conditions) in human life without giving any moral judgement on whether nature (as being recapitulated by humanity) is good or bad. The moral judgement comes from theology which contrasts the ends of nature with the ends of humanity and which Yannaras describes as the autonomy of nature that we human beings see as a challenging "absurdity" where our own rational conception of *meaning* in the world is violated.[35] In its desire to subordinate the ends of nature to the ends of itself, humanity exercises its archetypical "likeness" to God by knowing and judging things according to men's free will.[36] However, humanity's actual incapacity to transform nature and first of all its own nature in the manner of their creator, is determined by the fact of humanity's creaturehood. Correspondingly, that notion of evil invoked in Yannaras's quote, can be treated as a certain deviation from the Divine Image by humans who ambitiously hope to tame the ends of nature (in order to define themselves) not through their privilege of communion with God, but through an illusion of the unlimited power of controlling the material world through reason.

The overcoming of such a vision of "evil" by humans cannot be done metaphysically. No philosophical concept is possible that would alleviate the riddle of evil without reference to the theology of creation. The sense of creaturehood arrives only through grace in communion, that *de facto* means existential transcendence. The possible overcoming of the difference between the human ends and the ends of nature (described by Yannaras as evil) can only be seen in terms of a soteriological purposiveness, avoiding any ontological reference either to the natural state of humanity, or to any particular modus of the natural in the world (that would allegedly manifest the achievement of such a purpose). Since the early church Fathers theologians have been warned that no ontological bridges between parts of creation will be possible through mediation and deification. In other words, the ends of nature will never be subordinated to the ends of humanity on the ontological level. On the moral level, the ends of humanity and the ends of nature can be reconciled through such a transfiguration of the spiritual insight that will ease the drama of nature's autonomy and make humanity free not from the conditions of nature, but from the anxiety of creaturehood.

One can summarize that the human inability to know itself, expressed through the paradox of subjectivity, encapsulates the essence of the basic moral division between men's limited position in the physical world and their intellectual and spiritual capacity to transcend the world and to long for the unconditional and eternal. Then the dialogue between science (describing the human position in the physical universe) and theology (interpreting humanity as a crown of creation and the center of disclosure and manifestation) represents a further detailed explication of humanity's

---

35. Yannaras, *The Enigma of Evil*, 16.

36. The analogy comes from St. Maximus the Confessor's assertion that "God knows existent things as the products of his own acts of *will*" (Maximus the Confessor, *Ambigua 7*, in Blowers and Wilken, *On the Cosmic Mystery*, 61–62).

drama of creaturehood serving as the open-ended hermeneutics of the human created condition in communion with God.

THE UNKNOWABILITY OF HUMANITY AS OBLIVION OF ORIGINS

The paradox of subjectivity in the conditions of the human unknowability indicates that the latter has a twofold nature: on the one hand, human beings as hypostatic centres of disclosure and manifestation of the world (its articulating consciousness) are unknowable in a theological sense related to their creaturely status; on the other hand, human beings literally do not know their cosmological and biological origins in spite of an extensive scientific narrative describing these origins retrospectively in the language of evolution. In a way, the paradox narrates about the balance of the radical unknowability of the sense of the human existence appealing to both theologico-philosophical and scientific insights. Then the dialogue between theology and science, seen through the prism of the paradox can be interpreted as an ongoing narrative about the same human unknowability as it is experienced in both theology and science. The meaning of the word "dialogue" becomes a synonym of a certain "competition" between theological and scientific explications of the human unknowability. Science attempts to place humanity in the metaphysical context of the universe setting aside the issues of the ultimate origin of the universe and biological life, whereas theology constantly cautions science that the underlying foundations of its own facticity as a modus of the human purposeful activity cannot be clarified without an appeal to the mystery of intelligent life in general and to its specific and concrete hypostatic incarnations in human beings. Theology implies the source of life and its Giver, but this is a phenomenological (not metaphysical) implication based in experience.

The entrance of the theological dimension as a necessary counter-weighting to scientific attempts to give the ultimate account of the world can be illustrated by simple arguments. Indeed, in spite of the seeming efficiency of modern natural, human and social sciences describing, explicating and interpreting all levels of the world's being (observable universe and our planet emerging out of the physical evolution of the cosmos, extremely complex biological evolution as well as unpredictable history and sociology of the human society), there remain three fundamental problems that are in the foundation of these sciences but not clarified by them. These problems are those "inaugural events" which initiate the universe, life and humanity, and endow them by future. All these events do lie in the foundation of the possibility of the scientific representation and description of reality but as such they escape the conditions of their scientific representation. One can say that the phenomenality of these events is such that it shows that they cannot be shown. If one adopts a natural attitude, that is, considers these problems as corresponding to the objective uncertainty of some underlying phenomena, they can be described in the natural order: (1) Origin of the universe; (2) Emergence of biological life on Earth; (3) Appearance of consciousness of Homo Sapiens in general and appearance of every human hypostatic consciousness. As was once expressed by Teilhard de Chardin: "All historians must have noticed the curious phenomenon by virtue of which the origin of organisms, societies, institutions, languages, and ideas escape us as if the essentially fugitive tracks of these embryonic states were automatically effaced. At very long distances events of great dimensions are in danger of disappearing from our sight also, and in a manner that no instrument can correct."[37] "The essential charm of sailing towards the past was, we used to say, the hope of reaching a centre of light. Now the illusion is no longer permissible. As we follow them back, the temporal series grow thinner, blur and finally become confused. At first we could hope that this was due to a chance and remediable fault in our working methods. In reality we had come up against a *structural condition of the universe*. The rays in whole light we bask do not diverge from the past, but converge towards the future."[38] Teilhard anticipates here that it is "biologically false"[39] to attempt to treat our representations of the past as past itself (because this past shows that it can be shown), and that it is a humanly biological phenomenon to acquire the sense of the future[40] in order to treat the past as being constituted through the movement of our thought to the future.

Cosmology describes history of the universe by recreating it in an inverse temporal order from the present to its remote past. The laws of physics make it possible to produce a scenario of the universe's development from some initial state (Big Bang) where all possible existing forms of matter have been united in an undifferentiated state having from the physical point of view pathological (numerically infinite) characteristics. There are many models of the evolution of the universe that lead to the idea of the "beginning" of the world. All of them are based on a premise that there pre-existed some elementary ingredients of physical reality (e.g., space, field, physical laws, etc.) necessary for the description of the universe.

37. Teilhard de Chardin, *The Vision of the Past*, 190.
38. Teilhard de Chardin, *The Vision of the Past*, 187; emphasis added.
39. Teilhard de Chardin, *The Vision of the Past*, 188.
40. Teilhard de Chardin, *The Vision of the Past*, 189.

However, the contingent facticity of these ingredients cannot be subjected to any physical explanation. The physical sciences can function only in the conditions when physical reality is already given. The question of origin of physical matter and space is a philosophical question, or even a theological one. The characteristics of the initial conditions of the universe as being determined through the backward extrapolation of the observable parameters of the universe turn out to be specific and concrete numerical constants whose quantitative facticity cannot be defined on the grounds of any underlying physics. Yet, all physical laws established in the terrestrial context function in the conditions of contingent facticity of these constants. An example is the age of the universe (13.8 billion years) whose numerical contingency cannot be elucidated from within the physics of this universe. One cannot transcend the visible universe in order to establish some "transcendent law" whose outcome could predict its age. The contingency of the physical constants, the age of the universe and he initial conditions for its dynamics point to the radical contingency of the universe in a philosophical sense. This observation can be formulated in the following way: in spite of the fact that physics and cosmology can describe the factual state of the *visible* universe in terms of observable constants, the very origination of the universe with such constants is not guaranteed by any laws on "this side of the universe," because neither the origin nor the sense of the initial state of the universe are clarified by a reliable and verified physics (despite a variety of theoretical speculations on that which could "happen" before the Big Bang).[41] It is in this sense that one can say that the origins of the universe are unknowable in principle.

In order to give a "quantitative" illustration of this unknowability one can appeal to theories of multiverse where our universe allegedly arises from an ensemble of universes with an infinite variety of possible initial conditions. The common sense tells us that in this case the *a priori* probability of such an origination (if some hypothetical agency oversees an ensemble), that is, fixing the initial conditions pertaining to one particular (our) universe out of infinity, would be "0." This entails that in order to "choose" our universe out of many one needs to have infinite amount of information. If one now estimates the posterior probability of our universe to have been chosen (i.e., of its certain existence) as "1," one concludes that there is no informational uncertainty anymore. Then it is not difficult to see that the "transition" from an infinite ensemble of the universes to our universe (i.e., the choice of the latter) would require an infinite amount of

---

41. A simplified version of some possible scenarios of the recent theories of the origin of the universe can be found in Penrose, *Fashion*, 323–33.

information from an overseeing "agency" in order to actually make such a choice, that is, to satisfy the sufficient conditions for the appearance of our universe. Obviously, humanity cannot possess infinite information and thus understand the *sufficient* conditions of the origin of our universe. It is not difficult to see that the unknowability of the universe becomes effectively an epistemological problem of the human incapacity to deal with those aspects of being which involve radical contingency. The infinity of information as a condition for choosing our universe, invoked in the previous arguments, points to the fact that the problem of origin of the universe appears to be a certain logical difficulty of the human reason when it tackles limiting situations. This difficulty reflects the inalienable presence in all enquiries on the origins of the universe of the old Kantian warnings, expressed in terms of antinomies of reason. One can conjecture that this incapacity of dealing with the origin of the world in its deep epistemological foundation is linked to the human incapacity to deal with its own origin, that is, to its own unknowability.

The same situation takes place when humanity attempts to understand the origins of its own biological existence. If we accept that the hominids appeared on the planet Earth approximately 1 million years ago it is not difficult to estimate that temporal era of their existence corresponds to the very end of the universe's evolution. The universe must have been at least ten billion years old in order to produce atoms forming planets and biological life-forms. Modern science provides us with an estimate of 3.7 billion years when life emerged on this planet. However the same science is incapable of explaining the nature of that inaugural event which led to the transition from inorganic matter to living cells. This event cannot be modeled either experimentally or theoretically. This fact is in the foundation of all dramatic searches of astrobiology for existence of life outside this planet. For if such a life would be found one could guess that the origin of life on earth is not unique and, speaking formally, could be placed in a general "metaphysical" context. However at this stage of knowledge one cannot make any claim like this: life seems to be unique as a particular outcome of cosmological, geological and biological evolution. As some biologists claim, if the evolution would be launched once again with the same inaugural event, its outcome would hardly be the same. In this sense one can estimate that the apriori probability of such a particular evolutionary process would be infinitely small in spite of a certain temptation to assign to it a certain teleology related to the evolution of intelligence. We see that humanity faces here a similar epistemological problem of locating the beginning of biological life in some pre-existing ground. Certainly, one can claim that the necessary conditions for existence of life on Earth, that are cosmological, geological, biological, are fulfilled. However, the actual emergence of life does not fall in the competence of these conditions and implies the realization of the unknown *sufficient* conditions. The fact that these sufficient conditions cannot be cosmological or physical, even biological can be easily illustrated by referring to an intuition that life on Earth can disappear not simply because of the physical or biological reasons, but because of the human consciously inspired actions. It is obvious at present that since humanity is capable to affect the whole biosphere through its technology, the actual existence and continuation of life becomes sensitive to that project which humanity has of itself in the future. The environmental stability and peaceful existence of the human society depends on its moral decisions and correct epistemological evaluation of its own progress thus demonstrating that the sufficient conditions of existence of humanity lie not in the metaphysical sphere but in the sphere of existential interests originating in the deep human concern about itself. In rather theological words, the sufficient conditions of existence of life on this planet are related to how humanity sees itself in the salvific and eschatological perspective.

In our logic we made a transition from asserting the unknowable nature of the sufficient conditions for emergence of life in the geological and biological evolutionary past of the planet to their vision as those moral and existential delimiters in human self-understanding which determine the pace and future of humanity and other biological existences on the planet. This move in thought indicates once again that the problem of the hidden undisclosed origins of life is not independent from the problem of the hidden undisclosed origins of the human reason as such. Only humans can formulate this problem of origin and only for them this problem becomes radically existential and contributing to the essence of the human condition. Correspondingly the endless search for the unknown origins of life constitutes humanity, expressing outwardly its ultimate unknowability by itself. This unknowability has, so to speak, a generic character: it relates to a collective experience of all human beings regardless whether they have personal consciousness of their own beginning or not. Correspondingly, if now we pose a question of the origin of consciousness as such, we will face a similar problem of not being able to locate the inaugural events of appearance of consciousness (pertaining to Homo Sapiens). Paleoanthropology can provide lots of evidence about the era and specific locations where such a consciousness emerged, but, once again, that inaugural event given to us as already happened is hidden from a scientific grasp. However, every human being experiences such an appearance in its own inner life and attempts to position it in the event of its own birth. But this attempt of a literal locating the beginning of conscious hypostatic experience phenomenologically fails on the same grounds as it was in the attempt to locate the beginning of the universe and the beginning of life. Its failure, explained roughly by means of an analogy in the natural attitude, amounts to the impossibility to either transcend the universe or to transcend the phenomenon of life, or to transcend one's own consciousness and to look at all of them from "outside." As was once emphatically expressed by a French existential philosopher Gabriel Marcel: "I cannot really stand aside from the universe, even in thought. . . . Nor can I place myself outside myself . . . and question myself upon my own genesis. I mean of course the genesis of my non-empirical, or metaphysical reality. The problem of the genesis of the I and of the genesis of the universe are just one and the same problem . . . bound up with my very position, my existence, and the radical metaphysical fact of that existence."[42] Then the unknowability of humanity by itself can be explicated on the level of each particular hypostatic consciousness as the initial *oblivion* of one's own origins. One implies the oblivion of the beginning of that consciousness which is later responsible for human being's reflection upon its standing in front of the universe in the conditions of the paradox of subjectivity.

Saying differently, one implies here a phenomenological concealment of the event of birth (or conception). To elucidate this point let us consider a relation of an infant to its mother. This relation, being brought into existence through a biological process, is formed without any representation from within this world: such a relation as an original period of life in a new human being is produced and taking place *outside* the world. The absence of any representation for an infant means that its relation to the mother does not imply any ego as "I"; an infant does not live its life being aware that it is an infant, and does not consciously imply that its mother is its mother. This happens naturally because that context and horizon within which this infant could perceive itself as the infant of its mother has not been formed yet. Any retrospective description of a relation between an infant and the mother brings an element of a relation in infant's apperception, as if this apperception would be an apperception of that relation through which this infant would conceived itself as loving its mother. However such a projection of an adult's structure of representation onto a pure emotional experience of an infant immersed in its own subjectivity is incorrect. Indeed, the immersion into its own subjectivity means that for an infant there are no those relations which could constitute this subjectivity. This is true in relation to its mother, as well as to the world. The world is given to an infant as his physical cradle, but this world is not shown yet to him as the context and horizon of his life. This is the reason why that which happens with a human being at the event

---

42. Marcel, *Being and Having*, 15.

of birth is radically elusive and concealed. One can possibly say that pure emotional experience appears at birth and that it is this experience that is called "infant." This experience is pure subjectivity enclosed in itself, open to its own modalities and unable to free from them. Shortly, being born an infant cannot free itself from those modalilties of life that it acquires. Being born into the universe an infant cannot get out from it. Being gifted with life men endure this life's hardship in its initial endurance with no freedom to liberate themselves from the gift of life. The world is present in a new born man not as a relation but an inevitable givenness, that givenness which is phenomenologically concealed from that one to whom it is given. Nevertheless, this concealment is indelibly present in human beings's retrospective look at their own origin, transforming into that *immemorial* which expands beyond events of birth until the very beginning of the world. It is not surprising then that any retrospective constitution of the event of one's own birth is always implicitly accompanied by the enquiry of the beginning of all that exists. In the same way as it seems naïve to introduce any relations in the initial apperception of life by the new-born human being, it seems naïve a view that the initial state of the universe (as potentially containing the very possibility of life) as that something in which one finds a sort of relation. If, theologically, one implies creation of the world out of nothing, then no relation to that which allegedly was beyond the universe as a whole exits. Hence its origin is concealed from a human search.

Rephrasing and generalizing what has been said, as well as quoting once again Maurice Merleau-Ponty that "consciousness attributes [the] power of universal constitution to itself only if it *ignores the event which provides its infrastructure and which is its birth*,"[43] this consciousness always slides back to the mystery of its beginning and its ignoring of the event of birth is the primordial manifestation of humanity's unknowability by itself. Human beings, although not being able to explicate the beginnings of their own hypostatic existence face this beginning as a problem implicitly present in their consciousness as that which cannot be "looked" at; as that which is inescapable from the very fabric of the human condition and that which can hardly be distinguished from experience of life in general. This situation is explicated in a phenomenological treatment of birth, understood as coming into existence of hypostatic human beings, that is, persons.

If we use the first person language for amplifying the individual personal experience of one's own birth, the problem can be formulated as the following: I can experience my birth only through its delayed consequences. As was expressed by Paul Ricoeur, "I am always *after* my birth—in a sense

---

43. Merleau-Ponty, *Phenomenology of Perception*, 453; emphasis added.

analogous to that of being always *before* my death. I find myself alive—I am already born. Furthermore, nothing shows me that there had been a beginning of myself: my birth is precisely what remains hidden from my consciousness."[44] I did not see my birth and I must rely on the account of my parents or other witnesses in order to attempt to grasp my birth as that occurrence which affects me through all my life, but I will never be able to reconstitute this event as a phenomenon. The phenomenon of birth gives itself without showing itself because it comes to pass as an event, that is, something without foundation, as origin but that which is non-originary.[45]

The exceptional status of my birth is that in it *I am given to myself*. This is a mechanism how my birth phenomenalizes itself, for without this giving me to myself I would not be able to realize that it is me who is affected by birth. The phenomenon of birth thus exemplifies the condition for any phenomenon: the possibility of phenomenalization of all things lies in the extent by which birth gives itself; the phenomenon of birth is the first phenomenon which initiates the possibility of receiving all other phenomena. The phenomenon of birth as a phenomenon *par excellence*, not being reducible to any preceding causes, and being incommunicable and indemonstrable, forms that excess in human perception of life which always allows for an unpredictable future, for an indefinite series of commentaries and insights on the sense of this birth which extends forward in time while being interpreted retrospectively. Not being a phenomenon given to myself, I always experience an intention to look at birth as a phenomenon that initiated me, my identity, my spiritual growth, ultimately my hypostatic uniqueness. Birth as an existential premise is always silently encoded in all my actions, which attempt to reconstitute it in order to come to terms with the fact that I was born without my consent ("I do not posit myself, I have been posited by others. Others willed this brute existence which I have not willed")[46] and can do nothing about it. In a way, my birth can be seen as the never-ending continuation of my experience of life, but it is still inaccessible as a phenomenon to my direct gaze.[47]

My appropriation of birth is always delayed because any retrospective reflection contains as its basic element a condition of a delay, delay between the occurrence of my birth and innumerable intuitions of its meaning. In this sense "me" as an original being, does not have an *originary origin*, that

---

44. Ricoeur, *Freedom and Nature*, 433.

45. See on phenomenology of birth Marion, "The Event," 87–105, as well as Marion, *In Excess*, 41–44. See also Romano, *Event and World*, 69–74; Henry, *De la Phénoménologie*, 123–42.

46. Ricoeur, *Freedom and Nature*, 433–34.

47. Chrétien, *The Unforgettable*, 11.

is, a metaphysical ground to which I can refer in order to deduce the occurrence of my birth from a chain of the worldly events. In fact the very idea of the possibility of grounding my birth in the chain of such events signifies a fundamental reduction or deprivation of the phenomenality of birth of its excessive primordiality. It is exactly because my birth is in the foundation of all derivative intentions to construct a chain of historical or cosmological transformations, which as antecedents would conclude in my birth, that all articulations are overwhelmed initially and irreducibly by the intuition of this incomprehensible and indemonstrable event of birth.

How then can my birth as a phenomenon, while not showing itself, affect me radically in the sense that it produces my unique existence? How can the origin of myself present in all following events of my life show itself in such a way that, effectively, it is indemonstrable? The answer to these questions comes from the realization that this showing has an "eschatological" character because the past of my birth is being shown to me only through its *anticipation* as directed to the future. My birth makes sense only as that "event" that phenomenalizes itself by endowing me with a future. Being an indemonstrable phenomenon birth reveals itself as an "event" that was never present to me in orders of "presence in presence" and always already imbued with the qualities of the having passed, but never irrelevant for the present and thus outdated. But even in this "eschatological phenomenalisation," my birth does not allow any demonstrability in the sense of communication: my birth for me is such an event which cannot be grasped as a fact and correspondingly described in rubrics of thought and demonstrated, being irreproducible and surpassing any expectation and prediction.

Rephrasing Gabriel Marcel, I am my birth and the less I consider it as a collection of events noted and responses to it the more I am my birth. "Is not this global experience which is me, but which far from being capable of being objectified is the condition of any possible objectivization, the mediating element which alone allows the attention to bear on itself, that is to say, which alone allows it to be? And the impossibility of defining this past-as-subject which makes memory possible is only another way of expressing the impossibility of treating the mediating element as an object and of forming an idea of it."[48] The event of birth (if one regards it as coming-into-being of persons) is not accountable on the level of *sufficient* conditions of its happening: its outcome is unpredictable and unforeseeable. However, the *necessary* conditions for this event to happen lie in the sphere of what preceded it, the physical plan. In this sense, in spite of its sporadic and unique character an event of birth as physical incarnation contains in itself that something

---

48. Marcel, *Metaphysical Journal*, 249–50.

which made the happening of this event possible. When one says that birth gives itself in an unmediated and indemonstrable way, that is not to say that it is not contained in itself and does not manifest the hidden conditions for it to take place. These conditions come with birth and follow birth in the same unmediated and indemonstrable way. This means that in no way can I treat myself as an absolute beginning.[49] I can oversee the limits of my origin and look objectively at it, that is, I can formulate for myself the necessary conditions that made my origin possible. My personal story can easily be extended to that "before" which lies in the foundation of my incarnation not only on the level of my parents as a biological species, but that "before and out there" which makes life possible at all. One means here the physical conditions and ultimately the universe. Thus the act of my birth entails not only an unbreakable communion with my parents but an unbreakable communion with the universe in which I was born and which is an implicit premise of the very possibility of my articulations of both my birth and the universe. I did not choose the universe in which to be born; the universe then is mine in an absolute sense. I cannot disregard the universe in my life because its presence is implanted in my birth: I am in communion with the universe from the very moment of the inception of my body and consciousness. In an incomprehensible way, by being incarnate in the universe through my birth, I am "carrying the universe" on my shoulders ("I alone am my own centre of existence from which I illuminate what is behind me and what is ahead of me").[50] The conditions of my birth point to the fact that the universe is not entirely alien to me and that it sustained my coming into being; thus the universe manifests itself as a gift, as that which we receive together with a gift of life.[51]

---

49. According to Paul Ricoeur: "How can we posit a beginning when objective knowledge only takes into account transformations of life and when consciousness misses this beginning? Thus we have to establish the *limit* character of this ultimate necessity [of birth]" (Ricoeur, *Freedom and Nature*, 442).

50. Ricoeur, *Freedom and Nature*, 439.

51. One can make a parallel with studies of Franciscus Kuiper who made explicit links between mythologies of creation and experience of conception (prenatal states) in ancient Indian cosmogonies. Kuiper's stress was on the possibility of anamnesis of one's prenatal state in order to explicate the cosmogonic representation of creation of the world in any human life: "re-experiencing one's own conception might be of the greatest importance for our interpretation of religious phenomena, and particularly of cosmological myths" (Kuiper, "Cosmogony and Conception," 113). However, this intuition is not exactly what is advocated by us. The phenomenological concealment of conception (birth) goes beyond the prenatal states and its "anamnesis" can be thought only as the immemorial that consecrates life to the future, without us being able to return to the origin of our being.

On the one hand the event of birth manifests to myself the hidden conditions of its very possibility as related to the physical incarnation, on the other hand the physical conditions of my birth receive the articulation from my becoming more and more my birth, that is, from its efficacious *telos*, the telos related to the sufficient conditions of life that are never disclosed. Birth's tragic dimension manifests in the impossibility of phenomenalizing the event of birth and controlling its very facticity. Saying of birth, human beings are always placed in the conditions of that which has already happened, which they cannot refuse before they were born. But, having accepted the conditions of its caused existence, human person experiences discontent and frustration because of not being able to understand the sense of this existence. Fyodor Dostoevsky puts this discontent and frustration in words of some of his heroes: "In fact, what right did this Nature have to bring me into the world as a result of some eternal law of hers? I was created with consciousness, and I was conscious of this Nature: what right did she have to produce me, a conscious being, without my willing it? A conscious being, and thus a suffering one; but I do not want to suffer, for why would I have agreed to that?"[52] Another Dostoevsky's hero, Hippolyte from *The Idiot* laments along the same lines: "If I had the power not to be born, I would probably not accept existence on such derisive conditions."[53] Kierkegaard complains similarly in his *Repetitions*: "Where am I? What is the 'world'? What does this word mean? Who has duped me into the whole thing, and now leaves me standing there? Who am I? How did I come into the world; why was I not asked, why was I not informed of the rules and regulation. . . . Existence is after all a debate. I would like to request that my opinion be taken into account."[54] The fact that the event of birth ultimately does not have any metaphysical foundation is perceived by human persons as their sheer contingency. It is this perceived contingency that enters into a conflict between a hidden purposefulness of the human thought according to which humanity defines itself as the immutable and immortal existence. It is here that the Divine Image in humanity manifests itself as a gift of being born (created), of being endowed with future, as gifted eternal life in the Kingdom. This is the reason why Christianity insists that the sense of the personal existence in the Divine Image has to be understood not as a contingently imposed beginning of life, but as the anticipation of its final destination in the Kingdom of God whose inauguration is archetypically established at every event of birth.

---

52. Dostoevsky, "The Sentence," in *A Writer's Diary*, 653.

53. Dostoevsky, *The Idiot*, 471.

54. Kierkegaard, *Repetition* and *Philosophical Crumbs*, 60.

The phenomenological concealment of the sense of birth as coming into existence makes this unique and personal existence incomprehensible in metaphysical terms, thus contributing to the radical unknowability of humanity by itself. Since the paradox of subjectivity can only be formulated by persons, the unknowability of personhood cascades toward the incomprehensibility of the contingent facticity of the paradox itself, that is, the paradox is implanted in the event of birth thus post-factum explicating its unknowable nature. Since the event of birth endows humans with a future, so that birth's explication goes on continuously as a process directed to the future, the hermeneutics of the paradox as an inherent feature of the human condition goes on endlessly. This explication includes the dialogue between theology and science that, as an activity directed to the future, contributes to the open-ended hermeneutics of the human created condition.

If we now place cosmology in the context of the phenomenology of birth, one can conjecture that the search for the origin of the universe is rooted in a psychological desire to understand one's own origin, that is, one's own biological birth, understood in a philosophical sense as hypostatic incarnation. In the same way as an event of one's birth (as an element of one's past) is unavailable to its accomplished phenomenalization in consciousness of the present (for birth's phenomenality constantly unfolds through its future-directed constitution), all attempts to articulate the origin of the universe (as a research activity directed to the future) are doomed to deal with the unfolding facticity of the universe as it is seen at *present* without any hope to achieve the "presence of the past in presence."[55] In spite of the fact that the origin of the universe, as its foundation (not only physical but also as sufficient reason) is radically unavailable to humanity's grasp, cosmologists yet intend towards the principally unknowable past as if it would become knowable and "present" in some personal future of these cosmologists. Here cosmology as a type of the human activity exercises its intrinsic *teleology*, that is, purposiveness of enquiry into the sense of nature implanted (according to Kant) in the very essence of the human condition (a biological phenomenon, according to Teilhard de Chardin). Consciousness functions in the conditions of its intentional immanence to the universe; thus the searched foundation of consciousness, that is, the ground of its facticity,

55. Martin Rees, assessing the reliability of cosmological theory with respect to the early universe, wrote in one of his papers that "I would now place 99 percent confidence in the extrapolation back to *one second* [from the beginning of the universe]" (Rees, "Our Complex Cosmos," 24). Whatever is beyond this one second towards the Big Bang is not subject to a strict verification and, as Rees expressed himself, he leaves a 1 percent chance of being deluded by theory of what was before one second. In this sense the ultimate origin of the universe, as its pre-existent past, cannot be brought to "presence in presence" even by means of theory.

implies the search for the ground of the universe to which the immanent intentionality is directed. Then, if in the natural attitude consciousness thinks of its own origin (as birth) in the past,[56] the *origin* of the universe (as its foundation) also acquires some features of the past temporality leading to varieties of the Big Bang models. In its incapacity to establish the origin of the incarnate transcendental subjectivity the understanding physicalizes its own origin by displacing it to the beginning of the universe. One argues then that the tendency to search for the origin of the universe is deeply rooted in the human condition, thus being an *innate* idea, donated to every human being at the event of birth.[57]

The analogy between a phenomenological concealment of the origins of human life and the origins of the universe brings us to the conclusion that both science and philosophy lead one to the necessity of appealing to theology of origins of the world and humanity. Thus one can conclude that the leading theme of the dialogue between science and theology is the origins of humanity and the universe, or, saying phenomenologically, the origin of humanity as a centre of disclosure and manifestation of the universe. The concealment of this origin represents a particular modus of the unknowability of man pointing towards the fact that humanity is contingent upon the "invisible origin," that is, theologically speaking, is created. If the dialogue between science and theology can be presented as a dialogue between something known (in science) in the natural attitude and that which is experienced but unknown (in theology), then the advance of science in terms of its tackling of the ultimate questions about the world does not change anything in the extent of the unknowability of contingency of the world asserted in the theology of creation. The unknowability of humanity leads to the conclusion that the dialogue between theology and science represents a dialogue between two attitudes to the world which both assert its unknowability as the unknowability of its origins. The dialogue can be (on an individual level) compared with an attempt to relate that which is here and now (as a concrete fact of life) and that which was before (that which the ego at present feels in the conditions of the radical "forgetting" of its origins, that is, forgetting of that non-originary past when the ego was not, or at least

---

56. Cf. Teilhard de Chardin, *The Vision of the Past*, 189.

57. Jean-Louis Chrétien, discussing the sense of the unforgettable (immemorial) in human life, and referencing to Malebranche, invokes an idea of being as something similar to that innate idea which we put under the rubrics of the "originary" origin of the universe: "The mind breathes only through being which is more original to us than ourselves. We are of being more than of ourselves. This unforgettable and incessant presence of being to mind is not an object for the mind, but the mind's very opening, its only light, and its condition of possibility" (Chrétien, *The Unforgettable*, 86).

was not a human).[58] The intellectual intuition of the world as it was before this ego was born, explicated through cosmology, is brought into correlation with experience of existence and aims to answer the question "What is man?" or "What is the sense of the human existence?" Seen in this angle the dialogue looks like an ongoing attempt to answer these questions. Such an open-ended hermeneutics of the sense of the human existence is similar to a hermeneutics of life as related to the Life as God. Thus the dialogue has a theological propensity pointing to an intrinsic asymmetry between the dialogue's terms, that is, between science and theology, and confirming our previous intuition that the dialogue as a modus of the human activity is theologically committed at its very inception. Then, in addition to what has been said before, it seems plausible to suggest that the dialogue between science and theology represents an open-ended hermeneutics of the unknowability of the human origins, that is, of the primary oblivion of life's contingency upon God.

THE UNKNOWABILITY AS THE PRIMARY FORGETTING

The paradox of subjectivity contains two elements of the radical uncertainty of the human existence: a biological modus of life as such, as well as those human intellectual capacities which are explicitly present in the paradox. In reflection, it is clear that the origin of such a paradoxical tension cannot be accounted, so to speak, from an external point of view, as a sort of "abnormality" or "disfunction" in the interaction between human consciousness and the world. What paradox reflects is rather a primary and genuine condition of humanity as being rooted in the very process by which life generates hypostatic selves.

The birth of the human identity as a particular "me" contains the hidden reason why this hypostatic identity forgets birth as the appearance of the cosmic body in the conditions of communion with the source and Giver of life. But this forgetting, unlike the phenomenological inaccessibility of one's birth, has a radically non-originary character referring one to that background of existence which is engendering human life, but being as such pre-human because it does not guarantee the actual appearance of humanity. Humanity always remains under the spell of this fundamental uncertainty of its potential non-existence. This possible non-existence is

---

58. *Forgetting* implies here not a forgetting of something which slipped away from the memory as that which was once remembered and then forgotten. One speaks of forgetting in a radical sense as the inability to bring back to the memory that which is by its essence *immemorial*.

expressed in theology through the idea of *creatio ex nihilo*, asserting that the world could be different or non-existent at all depending on the volition and love of God. Since the human existence is accepted as a primary and initial fact of any speculations about humanity's non-existence, being imposed on humanity in a manner of "no choice" of personal birth, it is this existence which saturates the intuition to such an extent that humans forget about the abyss of non-existence and hence of that one who brings it to being alive. However, it is this forgetting which relieves person to live outwardly, towards the world, to exercise those bodily and mental powers which have the same origin in the forgotten source of life. It is remarkably seen in the sciences which employ these powers but which are never able to account for their factual givenness to humanity. The forgetting of the source of life in both cosmological and epistemological sense creates a "transcendental illusion" in which the *ego* (hypostatic subject) takes itself as the ground of its own being. This illusion amounts to the human desire to imitate its creator who knows things by its will, but with that difference that the humans do not reflect upon the origin and source of this desire. Human persons suffer here from inability of falsifying that transcendental illusion in which the ego imitates the super-power of self-giving and self-given life through fusion with the Divine as its own, forgetting that their power of enhypostasising the world originates in the gift to humanity by being enhypostasized by the Logos of God, that is, made in the Divine Image. The transcendental illusion amounts to that humanity as hypostasis of the universe forgets about the fact that it is the *enhypostasized hypostasis*.[59]

Michel Henry, instead of this ancient patristic terminology, describes the human situation of being a derivative hypostasis of the Logos differently, naming it the condition of the Son, where the Son is the indication of the Divine Life in the Ipseity of the Logos of God. Here is his description of the transcendental illusion: "It is only because, naturally invisible, radically immanent, and never exposing itself in the world's "outside," this Life holds itself entirely within that the ego is ignorant of it, even when it exercises the power life gives it and attributes this power to itself."[60] Theology detects this transcendental illusion as the unknowability of humanity by itself being de facto the innate forgetting of the created condition when the power of

---

59. The Greek Patristic meaning of the words *enhypostatic* or *enhypostasis* originates in the theology of Leontius of Byzantium in the context of christological discussions of the sixth and seventh centuries, and whose meaning according to "A Patristic Greek Lexicon" can be described as: "being, existing in an hypostasis or Person," "subsistent in, inherent." *Enhypostasis* points towards something which has its being in the other hypostasis. See more in Glossary (Appendix 1).

60. Henry, *I Am the Truth*, 141–42.

knowing and acting upon the world is attributed to humanity per se without enquiring in the very possibility of it as a gift of the Divine Life. In order to understand and state the nature of this forgetting one can use an inversion, namely to point to that which this forgetting opens humanity. This is the second term of the paradox: the world as it is grasped by humanity outwardly, in whose background this humanity positions itself as an artefact. The sciences as such function because, simply speaking, human beings can detach themselves from the devastating enquiry in the sense of their own existence. The function and exercise of the power of their transcendental capacity makes them eager to possess by that which lies in the world. Here is the origin of the human scientific exploration and technological innovation of the world which yet serves a purpose of asserting the human ego. The things of the world receive their interpretation and evaluation from within this ego that asserts them as useful to itself for the purposes of understanding of itself. But one must not forget that such a directedness in knowledge of itself is exercised in the conditions of forgetting by this ego of the initial indwelling in Life, that is, communion or fusion with the Divine. In this sense in spite of advancing scientific knowledge of itself through its function in the world, the same human ego remains radically forgetful of itself as being determined not only by the necessary conditions of its embodiment in the world but by the phenomenologically concealed Life. Here such an ego wants to achieve not the fullness of its communion with the source of its life, but just the efficiency of being able to commune with the world. It wants not to become powerful in comprehending the world in the context of Life, but to become powerful in adapting to those conditions of survival without attempting to use them for the restoration of humanity's forgetfulness of God. Ultimately the human ego wants to assimilate the good of the world for its own use and joy by depriving the worldly reality of their primary sense as related to the conditions of life. In such a specific concern of the world the human ego projects itself onto the world and thus becomes "unreal" because it makes the very objective of its own definition and understanding mediated by the world and thus distorted.

The unknowability of humanity by itself can be expressed through another version of the paradox of subjectivity. On the one hand, the human ego attempts to comprehend itself through the "worldly cares"[61] in which the ego projecting itself outside itself in the world, finds itself in a state of a phantom, that is, in a practically non-existent and an already outdated position through which the full sense of this ego can never be attained. This

---

61. This linguistic allusion comes from the Cherubic hymn at the Liturgy of St. John Chrysostom when the priest and people invoking the name of the Holy Trinity leave behind all cares about the world: "let us now lay aside every care of this life."

is being exercised through a strictly scientific concern with respect to the sense of the human ego. On the other hand, and this is a theological part of the same paradox, the same ego addresses a question of itself in the phenomenality of life as originating in the Divine Life. These two polarities in the same paradox of the human condition seem to be mutually exclusive, but in fact they are not. They represent two types of phenomenality when one of them *forgets* the another. In both of them the ego acts as the enhypostasized hypostasis, but in that one where it is involved in "worldly cares" it forgets about its enhypostasized origin, it forgets its condition of *children of God*. The opposition between two phenomenalities in the human condition detected through the paradox has an existential nature of balancing two attitudes to life in one and the same human being.

If man is concerned with its existence as communion, he is effectively paralyzed for any creative action with respect to the exploration of the outer world apart from adapting to it in order to physically survive. In this modus of existence humanity is not concerned too much with the question of its sense, because this sense does arrive *directly* from the modus of phenomenality of communion. The question of the world is dimmed as non-essential because communion with the source of life exceeds psychologically the measure of the worldly. This phenomenality effectively suspends a cosmological context of temporality as having no immediate existential meaning.[62] Since an event in the world is always transitory and mutable (even if this world provides necessary conditions for it to happen) it cannot have any metaphysical foundation. Life as an event extended in physical time cannot receive any metaphysical foundation, because, strictly speaking, it is metaphysically impossible. The actual existence of the metaphysically impossible life manifests that this life is of the Divine Life, that is, God for whom everything is possible (Mark 10:27).

In the condition of children of God there is no question "What is man?" for the phenomenality of this condition precludes a projection of itself outside of itself in order to relate life to something in the world which is not life itself. In the case of the "worldly cares" and a concern for the world in order to balance life with the physical and biological conditions, there *is* such a question which implies a view to humanity as a thing among other things. In the first case the unknowability of the human ego by itself is intrinsically in the condition of forgetting of such a question about its own sense because this forgetting is effectively implanted in the fact of existence. In the second case when things can be displaced and then disappear because

---

62. St. Paul points that it is irrelevant to think of Christian life in terms of the worldly temporality: "You observe days and months and seasons and years! I am afraid I may have labored over you in vain" (Gal 4:10–11 ESV).

of some natural reasons one implies a different forgetting: this is not a forgetting of origins that are although not present with us yet enact in us the sense of these origins in whose constant presence we live and upon which our life depends. The cosmological origins can be mentally placed outside of our lives as eidetically removable and studied "objectively." But the persistent phenomenalilty of these origins in presence cannot be removed at all because its hypothetical removal would enter a logical contradiction with the fact of our existence: we exist because of the origins whose phenomenality cannot be reduced). In this sense the forgetting of origins is never a forgetting of things: it is just a particular philosophical orientation which makes possible "worldly cares" (and natural attitude) and hence the search for the sense of the human existence in a physical plane.

Here the "forgetting" of origins in its quality becomes similar to that forgetting which is exercised unintentionally by the ego in its search for the foundation of life beyond the world. If human consciousness manifests its experience of life, it cannot get out of life and, as phenomenology says, forms its immanent sphere in the conditions of life incapable of thinking about itself from a distance from itself, or from placing itself in front of itself. This modus of consciousness has nothing to do with the forgetting as a modus of thinking related to that in the world to which the category of memory could be applied. Consciousness as life is immemorial and hence cannot be forgotten because of no intentionality can be exercised with respect to life as such. Strangely enough it is because of being immemorial that life becomes a condition of forgetting in the mental sense, but not in an experiential sense: one can be distracted (by the worldly cares) from its immemorial presence, but one cannot forget about its presence at the background of being distracted from something. Hence the unknowability of the human ego by itself represents a particular mode of forgetting implanted in the human created condition where the creator is present in absence, that is, it is present while being forgotten. Thus the perennial question "What is man?" receives the only possible response: human person is life as communion with its source in Life understood as God, but this is that which is forgotten. However "man" as an "object" of gaze of the ego is invisible because it is Life that engenders human life in such a phenomenality that the latter cannot be shown. This non-originary forgetting is the main concern of theology. The latter does not produce any straightforward answers to what is that which is forgotten, but it tells that the forgetting is the another side of salvation.[63]

63. Here is an example of such a forgetting. The apostles and the church affirmed that the Nativity of Christ, apart from its occurrence in the earthly history, contained the hidden message about the everlasting Kingdom that Christ opens to humanity (Matt 2:2; Luke 1:32–33; 2:11–12). The incarnation of the Logos of God in flesh was

With all this, the ego is struggling with itself always appearing to itself paradoxical through its factual contingence. If this ego perceives itself as a hypostatic formation whose concreteness (its Ipseity) is never traced to the metaphysical delimiters it appears as the phenomenological effectuation of Life (enhypostasization by the Logos). Every human ego experiences this effectuation of Life as its own life's self-affectivity escaping its fixation in terms of thinking and memory. Memory extends the phenomenality of the ego in a temporal sense by bringing into play ego's past which *is* not, but which is enacted as the present. Here the self-affectivity of life receives its unrolling in a temporal display (which is a representation of life in the phenomenality of objects). The representation of life's self-affectivity through human actions in flesh can be paralleled with the affectivity of the universe with respect to the ego, where the latter becomes a passive receptor it its own physical existence, yet remaining an agent of the self-affective Divine Life. The unknowability of the human ego, experienced either cosmologically as its insignificance in the background of that which effectuates its object-like phenomenality, or experienced as the impossibility to put the ego as event (event of life) in front of itself in order to make propositions about itself, this unknowability of the ego is a state of such an immanence of this ego to itself that cannot be constituted as an object of thought or of reality. This ego falls strikingly under the rubric of a saturated phenomenon in the sense that the difficulty of a discursive comprehension of the ego *de facto* constitutes this ego (as its hypostasis of Ipseity). The human ego, as embodied hypostasis, represents a phenomenological effectuation of Life in the universe in such a state that the saturation of intuition over reason leads to the forgetting of the condition of ego's created existence. Such a forgetting as well as the unknowability of the ego is not *ad extra* to this ego's life, rather this forgetting and unknowability are generated through Life's engendering human life in the universe. Creation, forgetting, and unknowability go together producing thus a unique phenomenological situation for the human ego in which

---

a manifestation of the end of the one old age, and the beginning of the new age which is eschatological *per se*. The hidden message of the Nativity was set forth by Christ through his parable of the Kingdom. When Christ's disciples asked him what this parable meant, he said, "To you it has been given to know the secrets of the Kingdom of God; but for others they are in parables, so that seeing they may not see, and hearing they may not understand" (Luke 8:9–10 ESV). By pointing towards the age to come in his parables Christ encourages his disciples not to be preoccupied with questions about the facticity of his birth (and correspondingly to their own birth and familial attachments), not to pose questions as "Why?" and "How?" Since the whole span of history is recapitulated by him, the contingent facticity of his arrival in the world in terms of space and time had no importance (it is already forgotten), whereas it had importance as the inauguration of the Kingdom whose realized presence endows with the future that which is here and now, in the past and present.

the latter cannot deliberately quit this situation unless it quits the existence as such. In no way the forgetting of man's created condition is an argument against this condition, but rather its consequence and thus its proof. This forgetting has a drastic implication in understanding humanity in general, for the forgetting of the condition of communion and sonship of God, leads to numerous anthropological models where humanity is naturalized, mathematized, and defined in those ways which diminish its place in the universe as the centre of its disclosure and manifestation, that is, that pole of being through which and in which Life effectuates itself. As we will see below Christianity offers a way out from this impasse of the unknowability by transforming the radical forgetting into the eschatological anticipation of the past in which the sense and value of existence will be constituted not instantly (as an already formed knowledge), but as a gradual expansion of the gift of Life into person's hypostatic fusion with the Divine life. The human ego will reach the state of knowing itself not through its adaptation to and reproduction in the conditions of the "worldly cares," but through learning its true name in God at the end of times, when the primordial forgetting will be eschatologically transfigured to the vision of "all in all."

In view of what has been said the dialogue between theology and science as such seems to carry out a discussion on the extent of the unknowability of man by himself. Cosmology discusses how much of the primary forgetting of the initial state of the universe science can disclose. Ultimately cosmology is the fight against the forgetting of the origin of the world. Theology is occupied with the same issue, but on the different existential and epistemic grounds. Its sense of forgetting is encapsulated in the doctrine of creation applied to man and the world: the world and man are created by God, but the mechanism of this creation is unknown as primordially forgotten (hidden because of the will and wisdom of God). The "fight" against this forgetting (that sometimes is associated with the Fall) comprises religious practices, including that of faith and worship. Yet, Christianity does not provide a pathway to overcome the forgetting of origins, its practices alleviate only anxiety and despair of existence by transfiguring the forgetting of origins into the anticipation of the end. In this sense the fight against forgetting in theology is not metaphysical (to find the ultimate reality where the world and humanity came from [that is, theologically, nothing]) but phenomenological: it is just a change of orientation in the interrogation of the sense of existence when the *quest* becomes *praise*.

In scientific cosmology the situation is different for cosmology attempts to position the inaugural events (which are unknown because they are forgotten) in a physical (and hence metaphysical) context. It searches for the stable pattern of the world order that could be causally connected to that which pre-existed our universe (either through the pre-Big Bang scenarios, or those of the multiverse). Roughly, theology and science deal with different phenomenalities of forgetting. Theology constitutes the sense of the unknown originary events through their unfolding to the future with a particular salvific goal termed by the Kingdom of God. Theology is not concerned with the "actual" past of the human and worldly history, for the events of this history are typologically related to that which is in the future. Theology anticipates the sense and the signs of this future. It is concerned with the transfiguration of the universe effected by man with God's help and humanity's union with the Divine. The details of creation of the world and the Incarnation of God can only be considered as the anticipation of the Kingdom (the parables of the Kingdom in Christ's saying) . Cosmology, relying on the causal explanation, attempts to find a metaphysical foundation of the world and man in some underlying substance. Whatever scenario of origination of the universe cosmology proposes, it does not affect a major theological claim of creation out of nothing whose sense remains related not to the physics of the world but to the relationship between man in the world and God.

What then is the sense of the dialogue between theology and science, theology and cosmology? Since this "dialogue" is in fact a relationship between two types of phenomenality of existence in one and the same human being, it effectively is the dialogue of man with himself about his sense of existence and his destiny. Being such an endeavour, that expresses outwardly the human ambivalence in being, this dialogue provides a particular type of narrative contributing to the open-ended hermeneutics of the human condition. Certainly, such a hermeneutics in general is not reduced to that one of the dialogue between theology and science. But the latter exemplifies better then other types of hermeneutics the basic predicament of the human existence and its perennial mystery. Humanity is granted existence in the conditions of the archetypical forgetting of any antecedent reality that radically characterizes the human condition as being endowed with intelligence and personhood. One can say that all human activities related to the exploration of the world as well as attempts to find the answer to the question of the sense of this humanity's existence, represent a characteristic fight against this forgetting whose success can only be eschatological, when the forgotten "all in all" will be manifested to the deified man.

THE PRIMACY OF LIFE AND A PNEUMATOLOGICAL DIMENSION OF THE DIALOGUE BETWEEN SCIENCE AND THEOLOGY

The discussion brought us to the conclusion that the difference between science and theology can be qualified as a difference in attitude to that which can be presented in phenomenality of objects and that of the event-like phenomena (which exceed the boundaries of metaphysical delimiters defined in terms of substantiality, causality, foreseeability, the opposition of the possible and impossible). If such a distinction and difference in phenomenality were mutually exclusive no dialogue between science and theology would be possible. Indeed, it first seems that with respect to what concerns such singular events of communion as the Incarnation, Resurrection and Ascension, the hypostatic descent of the Holy Spirit on the apostles, etc nothing except an event-like hermeneutics is possible. At the same time the necessary conditions for these events have a worldly character and thus can be formulated in the phenomenality of objects. The event-like phenomenality of communion events in human history originates in those sufficient conditions which are controled by the worldly causality. Yet, in order to articulate these events rationally (in response to their transcendent "appeal"), one needs human beings who are subject to the worldly necessary conditions. In other words, the phenomenality of the human existence receives a different status depending on its interpretation, that is, on hermeneutics, thus showing that there is no epistemological gulf in one and the same human being between how this existence is presented in consciousness in the first and second case. Then one can speak of a variation in the modus of phenomenality of events of communion as a consequence of the hermeneutic variation in relation to the subject.

A historical pointer towards the link between phenomenality and hermeneutics can be found in Gregory of Nyssa, who in his thinking about humanity uses the image of "diglyph sculptures" as an example of such a dualistic hermeneutics of humanity: "I may be allowed to describe the human image by comparison with some wonderful piece of modelling. For, as one may see in models those carved shapes which the artificers of such things contrive for the wonder of beholders, tracing out upon a single head two forms of faces; so man seems to me to bear a double likeness to opposite things—being moulded in the Divine element of his mind to the Divine beauty, but bearing, in the passionate impulses that arise in him, a likeness to the brute nature."[64] Fourteen centuries later Kant in his "Critique of

---

64. Gregory of Nyssa, *De hominis opificio* 18, 408.

Practical Reason" speculated as to how, in the case of humanity, to reconcile the seeming contradiction between human freedom and the mechanism of nature, to which humanity is subordinated because of its corporeal condition. He writes: "the necessity of nature, which cannot co-exist with the freedom of the subject, appertains only to the attributes of the thing that is subject to time-conditions, consequently only to those of the acting subject as a *phenomenon*. . . . But the very same subject being on the other side conscious of himself as a thing in himself, . . . regards himself as only determinable by laws which he gives himself through reason; . . . the whole series of his existence as a sensible being, is in the consciousness of his supersensible existence nothing but the result . . . of his causality as a *noumenon*."[65] In other words, causality and other categories determine necessarily only the natural mechanism responsible for the actions of subjects as *phenomena*, but are not applicable to them as *things in themselves*. Moral freedom and natural necessity are harmonised in one and the same human ego, by means of variation of the modus of phenomenality, the variation which became possible because of the hermeneutical variation in the human ego, as *phenomenon* and *noumenon*.

The entry of hermeneutics into the criterion of distinction between the modes of phenomenality (objects [in science] and existential events [in theology]) points to that the difference in "view" of one and the same phenomenon originates in the human ego, namely in a variation of its intuition. For example, the transition from a perception of the universe as a physical spatio-temporal *object* to its contemplation as *event* "coincident" with human life corresponds to the transition from the phenomenon of the universe with poor intuition to the universe as a saturated phenomenon with an *excess* of intuition.[66] Then one can generalize that the difference in interpretation of phenomena on the basis of scientific rationality and extended rationality of theology has its origin in the human *ego* so that the difference between a scientific world-view and world's perception in the context of religious experience is linked to that intrinsic variability and flexibility of the human cognitive faculties from which this difference and possible forms of its explication (either conflict or consonance, for example) arise. The paradox of human subjectivity gives an example of an ineluctable dichotomy

---

65. Kant, *Critique of Practical Reason*, 191.

66. The so called "saturated phenomena" stand for the group of phenomena which cannot be represented in the phenomenality of objects (i.e., in rubrics of quantity, quality, relation, and modality), and yet do manifest themselves by the excess of intuition over the concept or signification in them (see Glossary in Appendix 1). Theory of the saturated phenomena in the human sciences was advanced by Jean-Luc Marion in his books *In Excess* and *The Erotic Phenomenon*.

in representation of the living experience of the world: namely its objective representation (humanity as a part of the universe) and its event-like interpretation (when the whole universe is recapitulated in events of human consciousness). The mystery of this dichotomy becomes a characteristic element of the human condition. Since, as we have already discussed, one cannot produce a metaphysical explanatory "basis" for this dichotomy in the human phenomenon, this dichotomy, in reflection, amounts to the split between a scientific and theological perception of reality that manifests the difference in the modes of phenomenality. The problem of relation between science and theology, seen in the perspective of the human history, sociology and even anthropology is thus is an inalienable characteristic of humanity. This entails in turn that any hope for a "reconciliation" of science and theology (as the overcoming of a split in the hermeneutics of the human condition) is existentially futile: any attempt to remove this dichotomy or explain it away, for example, by means of a materialistic regress leads to the distorted anthropology and hence cosmology: humanity has a "dual nature, and every theory of life which fails to account of both aspects of his being is bound to be inadequate. . . . The structure of our being is complex and antinomic, and all artificial simplification distorts it."[67]

Human existence is dualistic and paradoxical, but two hermeneutics of such a condition (implying different phenomenalities) have one intrinsically common feature: they originate in one and the same human being, that is, from within one and the same human life. Then one can make a suggestion to reconcile not the components of the two natures of humanity, but their hermeneutics into a single ongoing hermeneutics of the human condition as such. This supposed hermeneutics does not aim to remove the paradox or the dialogue between theology and science. It suggests only one thing: the ongoing dialogue between theology and science represents an open-ended hermeneutics of the human condition. The centre of enquiry is thus shifted towards humanity or, to the phenomenon of human life which is the subject matter of this hermeneutics. Yet this shifted enquiry is still a component of the overall hermeneutics of the human condition not implying that by doing hermeneutics of the hermeneutics one provides some ultimate-metanarrative. Yes, the hermeneutics related to the dialogue between theology and science, in order to press on the centrality of man in the dialogue, needs again and again apply a philosophical analysis in order to make the point about man's centrality explicit. Both hermeneutics turn out to be necessarily complementary because human life is a phenomenon which requires an interplay of the necessary (worldly) and (sufficient trans-worldly)

---

67. Frank, *Reality and Man*, 343–45.

conditions. This means that since neither science (scientific philosophy) nor theology can provide any accomplished explanation of the phenomenon of life, one cannot consider *life* on the same level with the rest of nature, for life transcends the capacity of being presented in the phenomenality of objects by manifesting itself as the source of all possible phenomenalizations. The world thus becomes phenomenalized within the life-event horizon.

The facticity of life as being the source of disclosure and manifestation of all in the universe points towards some trans-worldly foundation (treated theologically as the love of God). Its strange presence behind all possible phenomenalities challenges philosophy by forcing the latter to develop the phenomenology of that which does not show itself: life is present, but it is invisible; life is that which makes the distinction between that which is alive (human beings) and that which is not; life is intentional, but it cannot become an object of intention. Such a philosophy will have to appropriate theological assertions of life as events of communion with God and to contribute to the overall hermeneutics of life in forms of thought and speech.

Let us propose some hints to such an appropriation of theological assertions. The metaphysically indemonstrable phenomenon of *life* reveals itself indirectly through the phenomenologically inaccessible inaugural events of the biological evolution, Homo Sapiens's natural history, Christian history providing an archetype of the human condition (through the Incarnation of God in flesh of Jesus of Nazareth). Then, since according to the modern scientific world-view the physical world evolved from some singular event in the past of the universe (Big Bang), cosmology employs by analogy a similar intuition of "beginning" in spite of the fact that this beginning is phenomenologically concealed as it happens with the inaugural events of life. However, as in phenomenology of birth, the coming of the universe into being is not simply "birth" of the dead physical world from something that either logically or temporally preceded it, but rather represents the *origin of a certain phenomenality of the world as a result of coming into existence of life*. Here theology imminently enters the "dialogue" with science because life is the subject of theology understood "a revelation of that being to which man was introduced by the operation of the Holy Spirit."[68] Then the universe is treated as such being that receives its phenomenality through humanity, that is, in the horizon of life, introduced by the operation of the Holy Spirit. Said differently, if in this theological perception of life "human reason finds itself posited with a given reality that is not a dumb or inert object of knowledge but the Holy Spirit speaking the Word of God and in that Word presenting the very Being of God as the

---

68. Sophrony, *The Monk of Mounts Athos*, 107.

creative source and objective ground of our knowledge of him,"[69] it is this speaking of the Word to humanity as a modus of communion with God that constitutes human primary experience of life and the universe. The dialogue between theology and science as a modus of the human activity is then that in which human reason finds itself posited by the Holy Spirit presenting the very Being of God as the source of our knowledge of him and of the world created by him.

At this point of our discussion we approach a crucial question: yes, one can state that there is the dialogue between theology and science and that the source of this dialogue is in the human embodied *ego*. The dialogue, phenomenologically speaking, encodes the inner struggle of humanity to understand itself in this world. However, from a philosophical point of view, there is a pertinent question about the facticity of this dialogue as a sheer possibility related to the sheer possibility of life. As we have discussed above, neither philosophy nor science are in a position to address this question. Theology cannot do this either, but it can at least interpret this question by appealing to the Holy Spirit as that "comforter and giver of life" who animates matter of this universe and implants intelligence resulting is humanity's *Imago Dei*. The universe has some logic according to the Logos of God, its creator. But its actual living as being self-reflected in the phenomenality related to *Imago Dei*, is posited by the Living Force, that is, by Life *by* which and *in* which humanity was brought into existence. Theology calls this Life the Holy Spirit, the Lord, the Giver of life, who proceeds from the Father, who with the Father and the Son together is worshipped and glorified. If this Life lies in the foundation of all possible phenomenality of the world as related to the human life, then it seems reasonable to suggest that the dialogue between theology and science must have a pneumatological dimension. This dimension is hidden and not manifested because of the Holy Spirit's non-transparency in the world and its sole hypostatic descent upon the world in liturgical events. It is from this observation that it becomes even more clear that the relationship between science and theology cannot be "symmetric," so that the very positing of the relationship as a "dialogue between" science and theology represents a misunderstanding. The question of the relationship between theology and science ultimately implies a question of a hierarchy between the human perception of "the Giver of life" and that of "the Giver of science."

The entrance of a pneumatological dimension into the discourse on science and theology perhaps appears strange and even irrelevant to scientists. If the reflection upon the logical structure of the world can touch

---

69. Torrance, *God and Rationality*, 182.

upon the christological problematic, for the Logos is present in the world in its intelligible laws and through consubstantiality between the universe as the body of the incarnate Christ, a reflection upon the Holy Spirit in the context of the dialogue becomes much more controversial, for according to the rubrics of faith, the latter has never entered the channels of history and been present hypostatically in rubrics of space and time in the event of Pentecost (despite a conviction that the Spirit was invisibly "present" behind the Incarnation in the physical world). It is because of this that it becomes a philosophically and scientifically incomprehensible task to detect the "presence" of the Spirit in the universe through his action upon history.[70] The conceptual arrangement of theology of the presence of the Holy Spirit as the Giver of life in the universe thus needs philosophical methods dealing with the phenomenality of that which is not transparent, not shown, but that which is implicitly present in the foundation of life and the very possibility of theology. Human *ego* deals here with a situation when the intuitive content of that which gives life is not outwardly apparent and exceeds the discursive capacity of its constitution, that is, the human *ego* encounters the saturated phenomenon of Life (that acquires a certain phenomenality in liturgical events when the Holy Spirit is intentionally invoked in order to place the worshipping community in the presence of this Life in the Kingdom). Saying differently by using Thomas Torrance's words, we encounter the Spirit "always as the Lord of implacable objectivity of his divine Being, objecting to our objectifying modes of thought and imparting himself to us in accordance with the modes of His own self-revealing through the Word,"[71] by granting to us the forms of his acquisition (proceeding from him) when true knowledge of things comes not from the perspective of our nature as such, but from the manifested self-affectivity of life as a pointer beyond its own limits. Paradoxically, the Spirit points toward the impossibility of apprehending his presence in forms of thought and speech by exercising thus the *possibility* of grasping this *impossibility*. It is exactly this which places us under the constant bedazzling gaze of the Spirit Who cannot be looked at. At the same time the vision of the sense of those realities which humanity encounters in the event-like experience of the Divine, is achieved through the actions of the Holy Spirit upon history referring thus the content of our thought and speech pertaining to events of communion beyond their space-time context. The Spirit is that action and operation of

70. Contrary to Wolfhart Pannenberg's conjecture that physical field theories can be theologically significant as "providing a possible means for conceiving of the divine Spirit" (See Ted Peter's introduction in Pannenberg, *Toward a Theology of Nature*, 13–14).

71. Torrance, *God and Rationality*, 173.

God with respect to us which makes our concepts and cognitive forms open to that which is not apparent, but to that which lies in the foundation of our capacity of detecting and apprehending the events of communion.

Since scientific activity and articulation of the universe have in their *modi operandi* the implicit presence of the "Giver of life," the philosophical explication of scientific research as originating in the events of life makes possible to shed light on the pneumatological dimension of science as such, as well as the pneumatological dimension of the relation between science and theology of communion. It is the Holy Spirit, in spite of forgetting about him because of our "worldly cares," that invokes a question of the ambivalence of life by placing the human ego between two infinite poles of the world and God. By appealing to the Spirit humanity can elucidate a previously imposed question of the possibility of theology: theology existentially manifests the self-affectivity of life, that is, that modus of intelligent existence which is affected by both its embodiment in the world and by its ability to make (through the Spirit) the facticity of its own embodied existence a problem for itself. Science is possible on the same grounds by shifting the pole of the main existential question "What is man?" towards the world, that is, towards the sense of the human ego's affectivity by the physical and biological conditions. Yet the reflective modus of such an enquiry presupposes an already effected life as proceeding from its Giver. The universe in the image of humanity, that is, the universe in the phenomenality of events of human existence, can hence be said to be the gift of life to this humanity. In spite of the fact that the biological life appeared more than three billion years ago, as well as that the universe, according to cosmology, is more than thirteen billion years old, its historical past as constituted existence can receive a status of objectivity only from within the already formed span of Homo Sapiens's existence initiated by the Holy Spirit. The very human knowledge of the universe is then itself a work of the Spirit who acts upon history through human beings. Yet one cannot claim that the Spirit entered the channels of the Earthly existence through the history of humanity so that his Grace would become a part of the natural conditions of humanity. In the context of the dialogue between theology and science this exactly corresponds to the fact that the dialogue as such is not an immediate existential *necessity*: humanity probably can survive without it in short terms. Scientific research, in spite of being theologically motivated in its historical past, is going on without any recourse to theology, and it is science that determines humanity's present struggling condition. However the Spirit is alarming humanity to look carefully to its future when the application of scientific methods outlines an unstable and potentially lethal outcomes for this humanity. Saying differently, the Spirit is acting upon history in order to remind humanity that the latter was brought into existence by his power and will. Since the dialogue between theology and science also aims to elucidate the sense and the future of the human condition it is the Spirit, the Giver of life that de facto initiates this dialogue.

As it is intuitively felt, pneumatology enters the dialogue between theology and science through "anthropology," more precisely through the intrinsic trinitarian image in a human person who explores the universe, creates science and aspires to God. In most cases Christology enters scientific discourse when one refers to a structure of the universe as sustained by the Logos as some rational principle behind all particular phenomena so that the sense of the universe can be found through Christ. However science operates with the *structure* of the universe in the conditions where the questions about the contingent origin of this structure and the very possibility of its comprehension are not asked at all. Typically the philosophically and theologically asserted structural similarity between the constitution of human beings (body/soul) and the universe (empirical/intelligible) is taken as the justification for the very possibility of knowledge. However this similarity as an articulated fact can receive a justification only trough an appeal to the dogma of the Incarnation of the Logos of God in flesh, as the recapitulation of all humanity in Christ that provides the only historical reference to such a microcosmic position of human beings capable of articulating the whole universe well beyond its commensurable with human body scales. Since theologically the Incarnation implies the non-transparent participation of the Holy Spirit behind it, whereas the incarnate Christ manifests the archetype of the Divine humanity, it seems reasonable to conjecture that the same Holy Spirit is present behind human life and its ability to articulate the whole world from its microcosmic position, that is, to initiate scientific research and subject it to an existential critique thus relating it to the propensities of the Divine Image.

Let us give an illustration of how our theological comprehension of the Incarnation of the Logos is influenced by the Holy Spirit, in order to transfer this theological move later on, into the dialogue between theology and science. The presence of the Spirit in our knowledge of the Son is not available at the same level as the Incarnation of the Logos in the midst of space and time. For the Spirit is not embodied in the way it happened in the Incarnation of the Son, that is, his presence and action cannot be described in concrete modalities and structured objectivities of space and time. The Spirit exercises here a certain anonymity similar to that anonymity of him within the community of the Holy Trinity.[72] This implies that our sense of

---

72. See Lossky, *In the Image*, 74.

the presence of the Holy Spirit happens when human consciousness has to question its own capability to witness and understand the Christ-event (understood as Creation, Incarnation, Resurrection, Ascension and Pentecost) (and hence the humankind-event) as an inaugural and archetypical event of communion with God. We see thus that the Holy Spirit, in comparison with the Son, is related to the realities of space and time only *indirectly*, to the extent by which He is in one being with the Son, whom we know through the Incarnation which took place in space and time.[73]

Since the Incarnation took place in the realities of space-time, our comprehension of the Christ-event is linked to the imagery of the presence of God among us through his hypostatic union with the human nature of Jesus of Nazareth. The human mind sees this event as happening in the conditions of the world in spite of all the mystical overtones that surround this event. However, the Christian apophaticism suspends the norm of our thinking of the Incarnation by stopping us thinking and talking about "how" the Incarnation had happened.[74] This suspension of a "naturalistic" intentionality (natural attitude) with respect to the mystery of the incarnate Son of God is intrinsically accompanied by a parallel non-intentional modus of experience in which the presence of the Christ-event does not depend either on intentional acts of its vision or on any visibility of the world. It is experienced not as a physical and historical fact, but as a phenomenological presence of the archetype of the incarnate Christ in human subjectivity.[75] What is implied in the last phrase is that in the case of the Incarnation we deal with the inaugural phenomenon that provides its own appearance, that is, with self-appearance. The fact that the Incarnation transcends the rubrics of the intentional apprehension in the act of its vision, that is, it transcends the very phenomenological method as a method of the intentional analysis, places the Incarnation in rubrics of the primary revelation of self-appearance of the phenomenon which is associated with life as such. If one says that life is phenomenological in the very original and radical sense of

---

73. See more discussion in Torrance, *The Christian Doctrine of God*, 98–111.

74. "Neither by the objectivity of rational discourse nor by the structures of conceptual categories is it possible to interpret the logically contradictory fact of the Incarnation of God, or to subject the Word's becoming human to precise definitions" (Yannaras, *On the Absence*, 94).

75. The presence of this "new" intentionality can be detected by analyzing the spatial paradox of the Incarnation which was discussed by Torrance in his *Space, Time, and Incarnation*. Within this intentionality, space becomes seen not as a particular physical organization of things, but as a special condition of our communion with God. In fact the paradox of the Incarnation leads one to see beyond the facticity of spatial display in the universe and to enquire about the underlying and forming principle (*logos*) of space.

this word, one implies that it is life that creates phenomenality of all things in the world. Phenomenality arises together with life and only in its form. The same can be applied to the Incarnation saying that the latter creates the phenomenality of all things in Christian history and its theology. But in what sense one identifies the event of the Incarnation with life? Only if one treats the Incarnation as being initiated by God through the Spirit from the very "before" of the created universe ("begotten before all ages"). And it is the same Spirit that "gives life" to all human beings. It is here one can establish a certain mystical and eschatological typology between the event of the Incarnation and birth of every hypostatic creature.

The strong sense of the thesis that since that life which experiences itself represents self-appearance of the phenomenon entails that life as such does not bring with itself anything new that which would not be life. Saying differently it is the phenomenological essence of that pure self-experiencing of life that forms what is called "transcendental affectivity" that lies in the very possibility of the basic anxieties, affections by one's own flesh, sufferings, etc., that is, to that which is experienced by itself without any reference to anything else. This relationship to oneself is that affectivity, or self-affectivity, in which no act of intentional vision is employed. Theologically, if the Holy Spirit is the Giver of life, it is the self-affectivity of the Holy Spirit that cascades to the self-affectivity of life. Correspondingly, the Incarnation of the Word-Logos of God being initiated by the Holy Spirit, is the manifestation of the self-affectivity of God that goes together with the creation of life. Experience of life, in particular Christian life, places any human being in a dual position: on the one hand, human comprehension is directed towards the world where the Incarnation has happened as the physical birth of Jesus Christ from Ever-Virgin Mary; on the other hand, the same person intuits that in spite of the contingent facticity of the Incarnation in rubrics of space and time there is something in the Incarnation which is self-caused and hence affective as related to the basic principle of life understood in a Johannine sense as the light for mankind (John 1:4). Formally, the Incarnation is not subject to the natural history and remains an event contingent upon the invisible origin.

Gospels's exegesis points out that the underlying sense of what happened in empirical events surrounding Christ were shown to the apostles and hence to the church only after the Pentecost when the Person of the Holy Spirit disclosed the sense of the mystery of Christ to all humanity through the unobjectifiable presence of God as Life. In the same vein as the human intentional gaze at the world cannot be described from within the intentionality of this gazing, one cannot exercise an intentional search for the Spirit who himself initiates in us the search for the world and life.

He does not bear witness to himself in human life by initiating it in the same way as he does not make himself manifest in the Christ-event despite being the initiator and witness to this event. The Holy Spirit does not show (phenomenalize) explicitly himself to us, but he shows the Face of the Son in whom we recognize our Image. By granting to us our intentionality to explore the world and relate it to Life, he provides us with the image of the Logos-Christ, in whose hypostasis the world is created. In words of Irenaeus of Lyons, Christ recapitulated heavenly things and earthly things thus "uniting man to the Spirit and making the Spirit to dwell in man. He became the head of the Spirit and gave the Spirit to be the head of man for it is by the Spirit that we see and hear, and speak."[76] It is the Spirit thus who is actualizing our perception of our place in the world, the bearing of the archetype of the Son of God in us, and thus linking the world to its creator.

How then the opening of the Face of the Son of God can alleviate the paradox of subjectivity and clarify further its sense? To explicate this, one needs to do two things: to look at the tense-like structure of this paradox as formulated by embodied human beings, and to realize that the paradox, seen theologically, expresses the radical forgetting by human beings of their condition of the Divine Image, namely their archetype in Christ for whom that which humans call paradox was not a paradox but the hypostatic union of two radically different phenomenalities of the human life. Michel Henry addresses the condition of humanity in the archetype of Christ as "Sons of Life." He reproduces the paradox saying that "On the one hand, there is the *man of the world*, who is only concerned with the world and can only be so against the background of his previously conceived essence as being-in-the-world. On the other hand, there is the *man who is not of the world* because, Son of Life, he finds himself originally determined in himself by Life's a-cosmic character. *The opposition between these two men primarily relates not to a difference in behavior, but to the phenomenological structures to which they refer.*"[77] By using the language established above, human beings deal in this situation with two types of the *given* with different phenomenalities. This situation can be described in terms of the tense-related structures employed for describing the human condition. The immediate experience as existence places humanity in a nominative case as that which states this existence in the form "I am" (*ego sum*). In this case the coexistence of the universe in which this "I" exists is just implied as a premise and a component of this existence. In other words, to say "I am" is the same as to say "the universe is." However, to say that I exist in the universe as

---

76. Irenaeus of Lyons, *Against the Heresies*, V.20.2.
77. Henry, *I Am the Truth*, 145; emphasis added.

its insignificant part, is to say something which is temporally delayed with respect to the nominative statement, delayed because of the reflective nature of this statement, where the reflection as a psychological process is shifted with respect to the immediate sense of existence. The opposite statements of the paradox become seemingly in a tension first of all because two different tense-like modi of consciousness are employed in these statements. In fact, the paradox becomes a certain expression of the fact that human beings are capable of formulating the complementary statements about their existence by making an extension in time, by effectively stretching life in time thus introducing an asymmetry between statements of the paradox through the hierarchy (before and after, primary and secondary) of the tense states of consciousness. This asymmetry has an ontological character because the state of "man of the world" is only possible from within the state of life. Thus the facticity of life (lived experience) comes first. But the paradox as such, being preoccupied with the ego's position in the world, by extracting this ego out of the primarily given life, de facto witnesses to the radical forgetting of humanity about the primacy of life of Life, as that immediate givenness of existence whose facticity escapes any intentionality. And if with respect to the question why humanity represents a part of the universe one can respond: because of life; the question about the facticity of life (from within which everything is disclosed) cannot be referred to anything prior to this life. Certainly one can attempt a naturalistic inference from the universe to life, but the very assertion of the universe implies the already given life. Thus the genuinely paradoxical feature of the dichotomy about the human position in being lies in the fundamental unknowability of that life which forms a premise of any articulation of the world. Theologically, the uncertainty of man's position in the world and the paradox refer to the unknowable Image of God in humanity, whose life is of the Divine Life. The unknowability of humanity can be expressed as a different state of "forgetting," forgetting not of that which has already been known, but of that which is in its essence *immemorial*. Life as sheer givenness and facticity of existence cannot be conditioned by any particular modus of its manifestation, for example that of thinking. Life as the origin is not thinking because it is this origin that is concealed from any posterior reflection upon it. In this sense one cannot remember that which was "before" life, because for this particular life there was no before: its contingent novelty and uniqueness can be placed in the worldly scheme of things as if they produce this life, but as such life as life of a particular self, or an hypostatic being, does not have any trace of its pre-worldly history because life as such, as was expressed by Henry, is forgetting in a radical sense.[78]

The paradox of subjectivity implicitly deals with this forgetting by demonstrating that its exercise of memory pertaining to the world leads indeed to the aporia and tension: the worldly memory of the past, positioning humanity as a thing among other things, de facto, distances the immediate sense of existence as life from itself. This entrance of temporality which pertains to self-reflection and discursive consciousness places life in the world (being-in-the-world) at such a distance from life (here and now) which effectively conceals its self-affectivity. In this sense one pole of the paradox stating humanity's mediocrity in the world de facto refers life to its past, not to what it experiences here and now but to that which allegedly was in this life's past. Once again, the paradox is an attempt to combine two different phenomenalities related to the structure of the internal time-consciousness which pertains to one living self. Yet both of these phenomenalities originate in one and the same living self who struggles to express the ultimate mystery of its existence as the gift of the Giver of Life. God initiates the paradoxical perception of life in the world but at the same time reveals to humanity the face of that archetype of humanity (Logos-Christ) for whom the actuality of the split in the embodied condition in the world is overcome by the fact that this condition is self-induced, self-caused, that is, manifesting the ultimate self-affectivity of that Life which does not need the world in order to live. This is that what is exactly meant by theology when it says that the Holy Spirit does not show (phenomenalize) explicitly himself to us, but he shows the Face of the Son in whom we recognize our Image. Indeed, humans need to see in their lives the presence of the Incarnate Son in order to deal with the paradox of their place in the universe and hence to see the universe from that condition when the dramatic overtones of the paradox are overcome. Unlike human beings it is the incarnate Christ himself who was the creator of his dual condition in the human flesh in order to teach humanity that it is created out of Life which is in God, and that the paradox of the human condition is a different expression of being created. This is the reason why the next chapter is devoted to the explication of the Incarnational archetype in the paradox and the dialogue between theology and science with the aim to place the vision of the universe in the framework of this archetype, that is, to treat the universe in the image of the *Imago Dei*.

78. Henry, *I Am the Truth*, 148.

3

THE DIALOGUE BETWEEN SCIENCE AND THEOLOGY AS AN OPEN-ENDED HERMENEUTIC OF THE HUMAN CONDITION

> "Man aspires not only to explain his situation in the world, but also to know of that way *through which he could indeed overcome this situation*.... To reach knowledge of the eternal mystery of being means *de facto* to *remove* this mystery, that is, to produce the *true way* for accomplishment by man of his destiny in the world and to give him *true possibility* for this. It is about this way and this possibility that Christian teaching tells man. It communicates to man that knowledge without which man cannot manage, but which he, unfortunately, cannot create."
>
> —Victor Nesmelov

> "This relation established between God and man in Jesus Christ constitutes Him as *the place* in all space and time where God meets with man in the actualities of his human existence and man meets with God and knows Him in His own divine Being. That is the place where the vertical and horizontal dimensionalities intersect, the place where human being is opened out to a transcendent ground in God and where the infinite Being of God penetrates into our existence.... Without this vertical relation to God man has no

authentic place of the earth, no meaning and no purpose."

—Thomas Torrance

THE INCARNATIONAL LOGIC OF THE HUMAN CONDITION

THE APPROACH TO THE question "What is man?" by understanding it as communion receives its biblical justification through the answer which God gives to Moses: "I will be with you" (Exod 3:12). It is the way how that God who can say "I am who I am" (Exod 3:14) that tells to Moses that he will be with him. The whole essence of the question "Who am I?" as a historically concrete formulation of the philosophical question "What is man?" entails, through the encounter with God, an answer that is not a direct response to that which is asked.

Rather this is an indication that the implied sense of the response can only be given in the form of an invitation to man into God's midst through the way of life. Communion is thus the following the same imperative of God "I will be with you" on the side of man: "I will be with You by following You." By accepting God's communion man does not receive any answer to that what he can or cannot know, what he ought or ought not to do, what he may or may not hope for: thus (in line how it was later put by Kant)[1] he does not receive an answer to the question of "What is man?" For God indicates to man that this question cannot be addressed and responded in abstraction because without communion with God it does not make sense and cannot be clarified. "Man is man only in communion with God" means that God offers humanity the way which constitutes its history and endows it with the future. There is no being of humanity as such, devoid of the inaugural event of communion with God enabling humanity to have its future, that is, life. In other words, the "knowing" of human beings by themselves as such turns out to be the unfolding of their history towards that for which this history was created: humanity receives the sense of its *telos* formulated not in terms of those potentialities that are implied in Kant's three questions, but through the definition of communion. It is only by following this God-given

---

1. Kant in the Introduction to his *Logic* of 1800 famously formulated that "The field of philosophy, in this sense, may be reduced to the following questions: 1. What can I know?, 2. What ought I do?, 3. What may I hope?, 4. What is Man? The first question is answered by Metaphysics, the second by Morals, the third by Religion, and the fourth by Anthropology." And then, Kant adds, "In reality, however, all these might be reckoned under anthropology, since the first three questions refer to the last" (Kant, *Lectures on Logic*, 538).

purpose (through communion) that humanity can indefinitely constitute the sense of its own existence knowing in advance that the ultimate union with God, phrased theologically as deification, will yet leave untouched an inalienable difference (*diaphora*) between man as a creature and the Creator. It is a dedication to this *telos* that releases humanity from the incessant idolatry of its images of themselves, thus removing all dramatic overtones of the unanswerable nature of the perennial question "What is man?" Human egos's anxiety about their contingence and homelessness in the world is intended to be replaced by offering home in God's midst, that is, through being introduced to communion with God, who will be with them on all their ways. Saying differently, humanity is essentially defined by the *telos* to which it follows, and not by that "where and when" he was created: "the truth of man is eschatological, not protological."[2]

Then the refusal to follow God, "meta-historically" associated with the Fall, meant that man imagined that he could attain to itself by choosing to resemble something less than God. This is rather a paradoxical situation: to be human in communion with God is to remain in those conditions in which humanity's Divine Image is detected, but not defined. If humanity attempts to define itself in some metaphysical terms pertaining to the world, that is, if it denigrates its existence from transcendent communion to some immanent attribution, it effectively commits *sin* by co-relating its humanity to something that is less than God. By not following God, and introducing into his definition of himself something less than God, humanity predisposes itself to despair and homelessness in being because there is nothing in being that gives to humanity a dwelling place and the comfort of reciprocity. It is in this sense that any attempt of overcoming of the paradox of subjectivity would correspond to the diminution of the human (as being in communion but in the conditions of unknowability) in human beings, that is, an imminent spiritual lapse into the state of deprivation of communion. However here is an intrinsic counter argument made by the same consciousness which attempts to resolve the ambiguity in the paradox. This argument is simple: the facticity of consciousness precedes any particular modus of reflection upon the ambiguity of humanity in the universe. This means that the resolution of the paradox (as finding a metaphysical ground for it) is impossible in the limits of its contingent givenness in every human life that saturates intuition and blocks its accomplished apprehension. Hence the language of resolving (or overcoming) the paradox becomes irrelevant. The intended "overcoming" can be posited as a formal *purpose*, without implying that the actual achievement of this purpose has any

---

2. Behr, *Asceticism and Anthropology*, 57.

theoretical sense, as if humanity found the ultimate source of this paradox that would be tantamount to man's explication of himself in the world. As a result, one can conclude that the knowing of the world in the conditions of the paradox, when this paradox itself becomes a purpose of explanation, represents a purposeful activity where the *purpose* is only formal, that is, posed as initiating the explication of the world without achieving its end.

However, according to the Bible, the invitation to communion with God, in order to ease the feeling of despair and anxiety, does not find a straightforward response in human beings: it represents an existential difficulty, because communion transcends the limits of the empirical accessible to the senses and logical thinking. Certainly, there always was a temptation to treat the idea of communion as an abstract ethical ideal leading to a kind of religious humanism. In reality, this invitation to communion never implied any abstract teaching on how to answer the basic questions (concisely formulated by Kant). It implied the need to see God in creation and hence to be in communion with him. This "did not prevent men from wallowing in error"[3], so that the invitation to communion, not recognized by men, was reactivated through the descent of God towards humanity when God assumed reality of the human flesh. This became God's self-response to his longstanding invitation to human beings to be in communion.

On the one hand God's descent to the poverty and miserableness of the human condition, entering into friendship with the wicked and sinful, brought nothing new to humanity in terms of its explanation of itself. The vulnerable condition of the human affairs in the world, with all the horror and atrocities of humans with respect to themselves, was not explained and healed. Christ himself, by being crucified and passing through the brutal attitude of humans to his own humanity, did not imply to teach them from the Cross what man was. He did not attempt to teach humanity along the lines of the Greek ideal of beauty and kindness. He rather confirmed to them through his witness to the Father that they "do not know what they do" (Luke 23:34). By rephrasing a response to the perennial question of man, Christ demonstrated to humans that without receiving Christ as the Son God, and as the Son of Man, "man does not know what to do, and what to hope for, he cannot avoid despair and uncertainty in his incapacity to approach the mystery of his own existence." Through his parables, Christ inaugurated the Kingdom of God, which was available to all, not only to those ideal men of the Greek philosophy. For anxiety and despair, groundlessness and non-attunement to the world, expressed through the paradox (and through an implicit longing for immortality), can be healed in human

---

3. Athanasius, *On the Incarnation* 14, 42.

themselves only through their abandonment of the idea of finding their own foundation in that "substance" of the world which, in spite of being created by God, yet is in a state of indifference to humanity and its affairs, a state that was described by Yannaras as a primary evil.[4]

However, humans can confess an unconditional love by imitating God who created the world with no hope of any reciprocal love from the world. But to exercise such a love humanity ought to follow Christ's archetype through God's promise of being in communion with it. In this sense the perennial questions receive a practical (not abstract philosophical) answer explicating the sense of the offered communion: As an Image of God, humanity cannot *know* itself. It can know things of the world only in the delimiters of its own unknowability. Correspondingly, to avoid anxiety of this unknowabilty, humans *ought* to follow Christ (= to be within sacred [not natural] history) in order to see the world through "his eyes," where the chasm between the uncreated and created was removed through the Incarnation of the Son "begotten before all ages." Only in this case may humans *hope* for the union with God in his Kingdom, but without explication of the miracle of their own creation. Communion thus becomes such a change in the *tropos* (modus, the way) of existence, when the world looses its sense of being a hostile terrain and the source of "evil" ("whenever an attempt is made to crush under the weight of any data of astronomical proportions").[5] This change invokes (in Pascal's manner) human ego's understanding that even if the universe should crush him, man still would be more noble than that which kills him because man's dignity, then consists in thought. It is through thought alone that we have to lift ourselves up, and not through space or time which we cannot fill.[6] "Evil" is challenged by the human spirit that follows not the logic of the universe by that of communion with the source of life.

Christ, being fully human, experienced the same predicaments as all created human beings, but unlike other men, he knew that coping with these predicaments proceeded from his being the Son of God. The Son of God enhypostasized himself in the conditions of the physical world and, as a fully human being, he knew what it meant to be a creature and he transferred knowledge of this to humanity. The key point to the manifestation of Christ's creaturehood was his Crucifixion that showed the whole scale tragedy of being subjected to the law of death. The way to be "man in communion with God" is to follow Christ through his life in the created human

---

4. Yannaras, *The Enigma of Evil*, 16.
5. Cf. Marcel, *Creative Fidelity*, 21.
6. Pascal, *Pensées: Selections* 78, 39.

condition and comprehending the whole universe through his Incarnation, Crucifixion, Resurrection, Ascension and ever being on the right hand of the Father. The major point here is experience of being created into the physical world in the conditions of communion, that is, of longing for freedom from the conditioned because of having the archetype in Christ. Thus the human predicament expressed in the paradox of subjectivity receives its elucidation from the Christ-event, being the only possible theological reference in the hermeneutics of the ambivalent created condition of humanity.

Christ is God and man, and hence there is no paradox in his perception of the world and of himself because he was the Logos-Christ who neutralized any possible ambivalence between his human position in the world and world's presence in him as a Creator by entering into a hypostatic union of two natures. For humanity the predicament of the ambivalent existence in the universe was implanted in the very logic of its creation by confirming once again that the main delimiter in answering the question "What is man?" proceeds from its creaturehood. Humanity cannot answer this question because it cannot create itself. Thus it cannot resolve the ambiguity of the paradox because this paradox is a constitutive element of humanity's creaturely condition.

By understanding this man is predisposed to communion and acquisition of Grace that confirms that humans are not only natural beings, but Divine Images. And it is through science as a particular modus of the Divine Image in humanity that the latter understands the dimensions of its created condition. It is science that makes possible to understand that the descent of God into the universe predetermines that facticity of the universe which accommodates human flesh. For the Word-Logos of God to assume human flesh, there *must be* this flesh. Since modern physics and biology are clear that the necessary conditions of existence of such a flesh require at least ten billion years of cosmological evolution, it seems evident that for the Incarnation to take place, these *necessary* physical conditions must have been fulfilled.[7] The whole surrounding world, being created *freely* in an act of God's Love, exhibits its *contingent necessity* related to its physical structure, its space and temporal span, encoding the motive of the Incarnation (and hence emergence of humanity) in the fabric of creation. The universe

---

7. As was stated by Teilhard de Chardin, "The endless aeons that preceded the first Christmas are not empty of Christ, but impregnated by his potent influx. It is the ferment of his conception that sets the cosmic masses in motion and controls the first currents of the biosphere.... All these preparation were cosmically, biologically, necessary if Christ was to gain a footing on the human scene" (Teilhard de Chardin, "My Universe," in *Science and Christ*, 61; see also Teilhard de Chardin, *Hymn of the Universe*, 76–77). "Like the Creation (of which it is the visible aspect) the Incarnation is an act co-extensive with the duration of the world" (Teilhard de Chardin, "My Universe," 64).

is adjusted to accommodate the human body of Christ which, according to Thomas Torrance, implies that the generic geometric structure of the universe must be such that the necessary physical conditions for the emergence of the body of Christ have been fulfilled. As was expressed by him: "The world, then is made open to God through its intersection in the axis Creation-Incarnation. Its space-time structures are so organised in relation to God that we who are set within them may think in and through them to their transcendent ground in God Himself. Jesus Christ constitutes the actual center in space and time where that may be done."[8] "This relation established between God and man in Jesus Christ constitutes Him as *the place* in all space and time where God meets with man in the actualities of the human existence, and man meets God and knows Him in His own divine Being."[9] Torrance goes even further suggesting that it is the space-time extension of the universe as a whole is relational upon the Logos's enhypostatic presence in this universe and the Logos's hypostatic presence in Christ (in a way similar to that relationality between space-time and matter which is asserted in General Relativity). He writes: "The interaction of God with us in the space and time of this world sets up . . . a coordinate system between two horizontal dimensions, space and time, and one vertical dimension, relation to God through His Spirit. This constitutes the theological field of connections in and through Jesus Christ who cannot be thought of simply as fitting into the patterns of space and time formed by other agencies, *but organising them round Himself and giving them transcendent references to God in and through Himself.*"[10] If the Incarnation is placed in the logic of creation of the universe (thus forming a theological field of connections between the world and God), the creation of the universe is not entirely contingent but subjected to the *necessary* conditions which are required forhe historical Incarnation to take place.[11] However, these necessary conditions

---

8. Torrance, *Space, Time, and Incarnation*, 74–75 .

9. Torrance, *Space, Time, and Incarnation*, 75.

10. Torrance, *Space, Time, and Incarnation*, 72; emphasis added. How similar this thought to Teilhard de Chardin's idea of Christ as being the Omega Point of convergence of everything in the universe (see Teilhard de Chardin, "Epilogue," in *The Phenomenon of Man*).

11. This means that the Incarnation is not possible in an arbitrary universe. This intuition was expressed by Teilhard de Chardin in his article "The New Spirit" in *The Future of Man*, 97: "In the narrow, partitioned and static Cosmos wherein our fathers believed themselves to dwell, Christ was 'lived' and loved by his followers, as he is today, as the Being on whom all things depend and in whom the universe finds its 'consistence'. But this christological function was not easily defended on rational grounds, at least if the attempt was made to interpret it in a full, organic sense. Accordingly Christian thinking did not especially seek to incorporate it in any cosmic order. . . . Theology,

do not exhaust all possible ways of interaction between God and the world, making the "outer boundaries" of the universe' space flexible and open to the Divine presence in the world.

One may ask as what kind of necessary conditions must be fulfilled in the universe in order the Incarnation would be possible? As we mentioned above the universe must be at least ten billion years old in order to have atoms which produce human bodies. Speaking of flesh one implies not only the flesh of Jesus, but flesh of all human race and those inorganic and organic creatures which are consubstantial to it through the cosmic or biospheric environment. Then one can conjecture that the entire created universe, at all its spatial and temporal scales, in all its detail and in every contingent object, must contain the traces of the initial intent of God to create a very special universe in which human body and the Incarnation would be possible. In this sense the idea of the Incarnation is "deep" since it effectively cascades down to all structural levels of the universe predetermining its evolution and preparing the conditions for emergence of biological life on this planet. But if the "deepness" of the Incarnation could be reduced to the necessary conditions, it would be trivial, since the *necessary* conditions for the Incarnation would affect all material stuff in the *visible* universe. However the statement of the *necessary* conditions for the historical Incarnation of Christ does not entail any further *necessity* for this Incarnation to actually happen. Modern cosmology points to the fact that it is only 4 percent of the observable matter of the universe (explicitly related to the conditions of the Incarnation) is consubstantial to the flesh of human beings (the physics of the rest 96 percent of the universe dark matter and energy is rather precarious). This means that the logic of linking the Incarnation to creation of the universe is applicable only to 4 percent of the observable universe, but not to the created in its entirety.[12] Correspondingly, any assertions of the links between the conditions of the Incarnation and the properties of the universe must be limited only by those forms of matter with which humanity can interact and which it can comprehend. Then the question of whether the

in short, did not seem to realize that every kind of universe might not be 'compossible' with the idea of and Incarnation."

12. One can speculate that the 96 percent of the invisible stuff of the universe (or other universes in the model of the multiverse) are transcendentally invoked in cosmological theories in order to have a coherent theoretical model of the universe and are indirectly related to the epistemological conditions of explicating the universe. In this case, if 96 percent of matter which is non-consubstantial with the earthly stuff is *theoretically* considered in the unity with other visible physical and biological matter, the assertion of the Incarnation as the major constitutive element of creation becomes no more than a human intellectual move which attempts to bring all structural levels of the universe to a "unity" of an ideal kind.

idea that the Incarnation is related to the whole creation in an ontological sense (but not simply being a theological assertion that Christ recapitulated the whole universe,[13] or a philosophical regulative idea of the systematic unity of nature [as related to the Incarnation]), remains unanswered. Yes, by being made in the image of the hypostasis of the Logos-Christ who holds the union between the Divine and the created world, human beings imitate him by articulating the unity between different parts of creation. And it is natural that this unity contains the image of the hypostasis of the Logos through whom everything was made. However this image does not entail that the hypostasis of the Logos was incarnate in all things in the same modus as it was in Jesus of Nazareth. The enhypostasization of the whole universe by the Logos[14] does not entail his incarnation or his embodiment in all its parts.

Now even if we accept a point that one can reasonably relate the conditions of the Incarnation only to 4 percent of the observable matter of the universe, there must be made a subtle distinction between the *necessary* and *sufficient* conditions of the possibility of the historical Incarnation. Let us start with the phenomenon of biological life: even if the *necessary* conditions for existence of life are fulfilled on Earth and allegedly on other exoplanets, there is no straightforward sufficiency in them for life to actually emerge. In astrobiology, for example, the existence of exoplanets with similar physical conditions does not guarantee an actual existence of life. Modern science does not understand mechanisms which launched the process of life on this planet, that is, it does not know the *sufficient* conditions that are required to produce life, in particular life of Homo Sapiens, leading ultimately to the possibility of the Incarnation. The *sufficient* conditions for existence of life and for the historical Incarnation are not in the causal chain of the natural events and any attempt to equate the *necessary* conditions with the *sufficient* ones (what is implicitly supposed in the idea of "Deep Incarnation")[15] would

---

13. According to Irenaeus of Lyons, Christ recapitulates the whole creation: "God recapitulated in Himself that ancient handiwork of His which is man" (Irenaeus of Lyons, *Against the Heresies*, III.18.6); "When He became incarnate and was made man, He recapitulated in Himself the long history of mankind" (Irenaeus of Lyons, *Against the Heresies*, III.13.1).

14. The "hypostatic inherence" of the universe in the Logos of God can be interpreted as the Logos's eternal manifestations in different modes of *participation* by created beings in him. This *participation* does not assume any ontological causation; for to participate in the Logos means to be made by the Logos a participating being, that is, to be made as a being in the hypostasis of the Logos himself. This implies that existence through participation in the Logos is subsistence in his Personhood, that is, the *inherence* in his hypostasis.

15. See Cole-Turner, "Incarnation Deep and Wide," 424–35.

place the Dogma of the Incarnation in the framework of metaphysical doctrines. The participation of flesh of all biological existence and even quantum particles in the Logos through being enhypostasized by this Logos (the necessary conditions), must not be mixed up with the enhypostasization of the same Divine person of Logos in the flesh of Jesus of Christ (the event of the Incarnation, that is, the realization of the *sufficient* conditions).

The unknowability of the sufficient conditions for the Incarnation to take place in space-time (in spite of existing accounts of historical circumstances that can be treated as the signs of the advent of the Incarnation[16], as well as its typological anticipations) indicates that the actual happening of the Incarnation is not a natural process which would be prepared through the endless theophanies in the history of humanity[17] but *event*, Christ-event, that is, a contingent happening in human history not predetermined by the material laws and worldly necessities. Saying philosophically, the Incarnation does not have any metaphysical context and foundation (this is the reason why it was a scandal for Greeks). And it is because the Incarnation has an event-like phenomenality that the *sufficient* conditions for it to happen do not belong to that realm where the *necessary* conditions operate.[18] The event-like truth of the Incarnation places it in the class of those phenomena whose intuitive saturation invokes an infinite hermeneutics of its appropriation. Christian typology is one of such hermeneutics, attempting to ground events in some objectively prearranged pattern.[19] Indeed, in order to comprehend an event of incarnation as *the* Incarnation, this event

---

16. See, as an example, an analysis of these signs in Gregersen, "Cur deus caro," 379–81.

17. Compare with Vladimir Solovyev: "The appearance of God in human flesh is only the fullest, most perfect theophany in a series of other incomplete preparatory and transformative theophanies" (Solovyev, *Lectures on Godmanhood*, 194).

18. Thomas Torrance uses a different terminology when he discusses historical events. He distinguishes between causal necessity and factual necessity, between causal determination of events and the fact that once they happen they cannot be otherwise (Torrance, *Space, Time, and Resurrection*, 92). Historical events unlike natural physical processes are initiated by purposeful agents so that they embody intentions which sometimes conflict with the course of events that are subjected to the natural laws. Unlike physical processes historical events are based not on causality, but intentionality. This entails that when one discusses the event of the Incarnation, one must discern the difference between its necessary conditions (*causal necessity*) following the causality pertaining to physical reality, and sufficient conditions (*factual necessity*) based in the *intentionality* of that one who is the Creator and a Giver of Life, that one who was present behind the Incarnation, but whose "phenomenality" consists exactly in that it cannot be shown.

19. On the meaning of typology in the context of Christian (sacred) history, see Daniélou, *The Lord of History*, 4–6, 140–42; Averintsev, "The Order of the Cosmos."

must be related to other events in order to build history (sacred history) upon it. History differs here from "historicity" understood as some free acts of an individual or collective free will reflected in events that are contingent and not connected to each other. History in a Christian sense means *sacred history* when some basics events (not loosing their event-like phenomenality) fit into the planned arrangement of reality. Yes, the event of the Incarnation retains a feature of the major history-forming event being as such beyond any measure of foreseeing, prediction, repetition, relationship and possibility on the grounds of metaphysics. But as such this event inaugurates a typological vision of history, where typology stands for an expression of the specific intelligibility that belongs to history as such. The event of the Incarnation is the source of such an intelligibility when past, present and future are endowed with meaning from this single event. Here we touch upon the issue that has already been mentioned that the order of the cosmos and the order of history is reversed in a Christian typological perception of reality. As was expressed by Jean Daniélou Christian typology covers all levels of reality, including cosmic processes. It is through it that "cosmology, which had been the exclusive medium of the natural revelation of God, now takes an historical character: the creation is seen as the first episode in sacred history."[20] However one must not forget that the elements of that symbolism of the universe which originate through such a typological interpretation remain natural phenomena, so that events of the sacred history have cosmic foundations and significance. Yet, in spite of many typologically stated historical facts antecedent to the actual coming of Messiah, the actual event of the Incarnation remains contingent thus typologically involving all sacred history as well as the order of the cosmos into the original contingency of creation (with a motive of the Incarnation). It does not mean that abstract essential laws of the universe are suspended, they are simply included in the christological uniqueness, are subordinated, regulated, and formed by it. For man this implies that his vision of the universe is performed through the intrinsic presence of the Divine Image when the whole universe is seen from the perspective of the archetype of Christ in man. Such a transformation in the vision of the whole universe entails also a radical change in perception of temporality when the past and present are perceived from the future inaugurated by Christ. The Kingdom of God on Earth (in the universe) announced by Christ did not change anything in the universe as a material modus of creation (the *diaphora* between the created world and God is transfigured in the hypostatic union, but is not affected by it ontologically). In this sense the Kingdom is present in this world in

---

20. Daniélou, *The Lord of History*, 141. Cf. Clément, *Le sens de la Terre*, 80.

order to mobilize human existence[21] in the vast and silent universe, to open otherwise inaccessible otherness of Life.

All observations we have produced so far change a stance on the position of humanity in the cosmos, releasing it from the mediocrity and insignificance of its physical existence. The question "What is man?" receives its elucidation through the adoption a new vision that the very existence of man was "implanted" in the fabric of creation, whose logic presupposes bringing creation to communion with God through human beings. If the motive of the Incarnation is linked to the logic of creation, man as a particular segment of creation becomes inextricably intertwined with the rest of creation. Since the actual historical Incarnation happens in the midst of the human subset of the universe, its proper sense can be directly related to the constitution and meaning of the cosmos where humanity is no longer positioned on the periphery of the universe but in its centre as the immanent intentionality of creation. However one must not treat the Incarnation and the very existence of intelligent humanity as metaphysically predetermined. One can only assert that, indeed the logic of creation contained the *necessary* conditions for existence of intelligence and hence for the Incarnation. The *sufficient* conditions for both, human intelligence and the Incarnation can only be detected postfactum, as already fulfilled through the actual happening of the intelligent life and the Incarnation, thus pointing to their transcendent references (*paradeigmata*).

The statement that the Incarnation is not metaphysically predetermined means in reality that its facticity is not implanted in the *natural conditions* in the world. Even if the world was created by God in order to have a potential of attaining union with God, it is humanity that is granted the means of such an attainment through a special call. The possibility of such an attainment effectively contributes to the definition of humanity: only in communion with God human beings becomes "themselves."[22] In this sense humanity, in spite of being consubstantial to the *visible* creation and having solidarity with it, is a special creation whose essence requires *grace*, and the mechanism of acquiring this grace proceeds through the Incarnation. Then one can see that the proper theological input in the dialogue of theology with

---

21. This mobilization of human existence was not a *subjective* reorientation of man in time, it was disclosing of a *new* dimension of the human existence, discovery of perspective in history, the acquisition of relevance and meaning of human life (see Florovsky, "The Predicament," 60).

22. As was expressed by John Zizioulas, one cannot identify humanity through a syllogistic formula "man=man" which, if one follows a philosophical logic, contains a pointer beyond itself towards the definition of humanity as "man=man-in-communion-with-God" (Zizioulas, *Communion and Otherness*, 248).

the sciences originates exactly in the archetypical predisposition (endowed by the incarnate Christ) of relating the visible universe (earth in a biblical sense) and its invisible counterpart (intelligible forms, angelic spheres) to its transcendent foundation made accessible to humanity through the grace of the Holy Spirit, the Giver of life. If one generalizes this, the dialogue between theology and science, as coexistence of different attitudes to the created world, has its archetype in the Incarnate Christ for whom the predicament of the dialogue did not exist because this dialogue was Logos-Christ's own creation in the same sense as the world and its scientific exploration were created by him. The difference in attitude to the world (present in theology and science) was introduced by Christ in order to teach humans about the *meaning of creaturehood in the conditions of communion with God*. Being in human flesh, Christ as the Logos-Creator, had to hold the image of the physically disjoint universe in one single consciousness as an intelligible (noetic) entity.[23] Thus the unity of the created world, being split in itself as the sensible (visible) and intelligible (invisible), becomes the pivotal indication of the sense of the created. This split in the representation of human beings by themselves (as the composite unity of the sensible and intelligible) indicated in the paradox of subjectivity cascades towards the split between science and theology, pointing towards the fact that neither empirical nor theoretical knowledge of the universe can receive any justification for their contingent facticity if the ultimate source of this facticity is not sought in the logic of creation related to the universe and to humanity itself. Thus the sense of the dialogue between theology and science can be treated as an outward manifestation of the radical createdness of humanity wrestling with its incapacity to control its own ends, as well the ends of the world. Then it is not difficult to guess that such a dialogue is an open-ended enterprise, having no metaphysically defined accomplishment and hence making sense only as contributing to the infinite hermeneutics of the created human condition. Such a hermeneutics, from a Christian point of view, can cease to function in the deified humanity, when, as Maximus the Confessor was teaching, the moral divisions (*diairesis*) between the elements in creation, and creation and God will be removed.[24]

As we have discussed in the previous chapter, one can be tempted to link the unknowability of the human ego by itself, and the paradox of subjectivity, not to the issue of creaturehood, but to the conditions of the Fall as if the ambivalence in the human condition formulated in the paradox

---

23. Torrance argued that this noetic image is accessible to humans through the sense of space as that uniting factor in the universe which outwardly reflects its relationality upon the very possibility of the noetic image of the whole universe in Christ.

24. See Thunberg, *Microcosm and Mediator*, ch. 6.

proceeds from the loss of memory of "all in all" (Eph 4:6) in the postlapsarian state. Correspondingly, the resolution of the paradox could be associated with the re-acquisition of the state of the first man, Adam. However, this cannot be true, because the first man was also created and his knowledge of "all in all," implanted in his Divine likeness, did not guarantee him being able to reproduce himself in the manner in which he was created by God. The crucial moment in explicating humans's unknowability is Christ who, by being God and fully human, elucidates to men the sense of their created condition, the sense which, as such, was obscured by the Fall. The traditional link between the Fall and the Incarnation is that the latter is treated as a redeeming act of God towards saving the transgressing humanity. However, Orthodox theology points towards a connection between creation and the Incarnation, as being, *de facto*, a *necessary and sufficient* condition for the created to be brought to union with God. In other words, the motive of the Incarnation is linked to the aim of creation.[25] According to Maximus the Confessor, the creation of the world contained the goal for which all things were created: "For it is for Christ, that is, for the Christic mystery, that all time and all that is in time has received in Christ its beginning and its end."[26] It is in this sense that the motives of creation and the Incarnation are intertwined and this, theologically (and in addition to the cosmological findings), points to the fact that the human phenomenon is intrinsically linked to the motive of creation. Humans were created in the universe, and because of their createdness they experience their Divine image through the unknowabililty and ambivalence of existence. From this, one can conclude that *the dichotomy between theology and science is an inevitable characteristic of humanity's creaturehood in the Divine Image, so that the sought reconciliation of theology and science is impossible to the same extent as the overcoming of the ontological difference (not moral division) between creation and God in the process of deification.*

By linking the motive of the Incarnation to the logic of the creation of the world by God, Orthodox theology extends the scope of the Incarnation beyond the opposition Fall-Redemption, towards a wider span of the plan of salvation, as related to the deification of humanity and bringing the whole

---

25. According to Georges Florovsky, "It seems that the 'hypothesis' of an Incarnation apart from the Fall is at least permissible in the system of Orthodox theology and fits as well enough in the mainstream of Patristic teaching. *An adequate answer to the 'motive' of the Incarnation can be given only in the context of the general doctrine of Creation*" (Florovsky, "Cur Deus Homo?," 170; emphasis added [The discussion of "*Cur Deus Homo?*" has never been a part of the canonical corpus of Orthodox literature and constituted, in the words of Florovsky, a *theologumenon* (theological opinion)]).

26. Maximus the Confessor, *Questions to Thalassius* 60.

creation to union with God. The lesser arch of the Fall-Redemption becomes a tool in restoring the greater arch Creation-Deification.[27] In this sense the conditioning of the Incarnation by the human concerns would be a mistake: "Christ is not a mere event or happening in history. The incarnation of the divine Logos was not a simple consequence of the victory of the devil over man. . . . The union of the divine and the human natures took place because it fulfiled the *eternal* will of God,"[28] so that it "showed us that this was why we were created, and that this was God's good purpose concerning us from before ages, a purpose which was realised through the introduction of another, newer mode,"[29] that is, the entrance of "the incorporeal and incorruptible and immaterial Word of God [into] our world."[30] A famous phrase from Athanasius—that God "assumed humanity that we might be made God"[31]—implies that humanity, being created, has a potential to be in union with God (not based in the natural laws related to creation). One can say, even more strongly, that a creaturely modus of existence becomes unavoidable for the very possibility of deification. Correspondingly, if God's plan "consists in deification of the created world" (some parts of which imply salvation), the plausibility of this plan is rooted in the fact that humanity is ontologically united with the created nature. Humanity is the microcosm that resumes, condenses, recapitulates in itself the degrees of the created being and because of this it can know the universe from within.[32] In this sense Orthodox theology links the Incarnation to humanity as that subset of the created universe that is capable of playing a mediating role in overcoming moral tensions between different parts of creation, and between creation and God.[33] The mediation between moral divisions in creation explicates the sense of being created and the delimiters of deification: the union with God through these mediations does not remove the basic ontological difference (*diaphora*) between the world and God thus not resolving the riddle of humanity but retaining the basic definition of humanity as being *creatures in communion* with God.[34] In this sense humans, in spite of being consubstantial to the *visible* creation, are a special creation whose essence

---

27. Louth, "The Place of *Theosis*," 34–35.

28. Nellas, *Deification in Christ*, 37; emphasis added.

29. Maximus the Confessor, *Ambigua*, in *On Difficulties in the Church Fathers*, 131–33.

30. Athanasius, *On the Incarnation* 8, 33.

31. Athanasius, *On the Incarnation* 54, 93.

32. Clément, "Le sens de la terre," 90. See also Clément, *On Human Being*, 109.

33. See Thunberg, *Microcosm and Mediator*, 387–427.

34. Cf. Zizioulas, *Communion and Otherness*, 248.

(as related to this attainment) requires *grace*, the mechanism of acquiring of which proceeds through the Incarnation.[35]

The reader may now be puzzled by a paradoxical situation: indeed if one talks about deification as the union with God, and about deification as possible through the Incarnation, why can humanity not achieve through this deification that state that was pertaining to Christ the Incarnate? The answer is: Christ hypostatically remained the Logos of God and was controlling his enhypostasization in Jesus by being able to explicate his own created nature. However this is not given to human beings, so that the Incarnation remains an archetype of the human (Divine Image/physical flesh = uncreated/created) predicament. At the same time the Incarnation brings a kind of a *natural division* in our understanding of communion. Correspondingly, if God's plan "consists in deification of the created world," the plausibility of the plan of deification is rooted in the conviction that man is ontologically united (consubstantial) with the created nature. In this case human beings's created propensities placed in the framework of their Divine Image would be sufficient to transfer the aim of creation, revealed through the Incarnation, to those parts of creation which need salvation. Human beings are created in the image of God as a key to elevating creation to the supreme level of its full soteriological comprehension, so that the universe is called to become the "image of the image."[36] Since the historical Incarnation recapitulates the visible universe on the level of *consubstantiality* through its *epistemological acquisition* (as a discernment of the *logos* of its creation) it is intrinsically related to the constitution and meaning of the cosmos.[37]

35. On this basis one theologically doubts that any other rational creatures would be *by nature* attuned to the presence of God. If this were true, we had to identify these creatures with humans.

36. As was expressed by Olivier Clément, "The indefinitiveness of the world is . . . situated in sanctified humanity and becomes the symbol of the 'deep calling the deep'" (Clément, *On Human Being*, 111). Discussing the sense of personhood Vladimir Lossky describes it as if "each human person can be considered as hypostasis of common nature, an *hypostasis of the whole of the created cosmos* or, more accurately, of earthly creation" (Lossky, *In the Image*, 188; emphasis added).

37. See Thunberg, *Man and the Cosmos*, 76, referring to Maximus the Confessor, *Questions to Thalassius* 35. Here one must press on one particular point. When talking about recapitulation of the universe at the level of consubstantiality and epistemological acquisition, the Fathers and theologians mean that part of the cosmos which is in interaction with humanity through its body. This is the reason why Lossky, quoted in a previous footnote, intentionally specified that humanity as hypostasis of the universe can sensibly be understood only in what he called "earthly creation" (i.e., in the universe which is similar to Earth and human flesh), by putting a note that the question of angelic hypostases and of the celestial cosmos constitutes a separate problem (Lossky, *In the Image*, 188–89). This is an important note, because it seems doubtful that humanity can ontologically position itself as a hypostatic microcosm of the 96 percent of the

In this sense the existence of Earth and human beings represents the fact which suffices for a claim that the *necessary* conditions of the Incarnation are fulfilled in the entire visible cosmos. Here one can propose a certain theological extension of the cosmological principle (principle of nomistic and cosmographic uniformity): *the conditions in the visible universe are such that at any point of it (under specific sufficient conditions) the Incarnation is potentially possible.* As was once expressed by Teilhard de Chardin "The prodigious expanse of time which preceded the first Christmas were not empty of Christ: they were imbued with the influx of his power. It was the ferment of his conception that stirred up the cosmic masses and directed the initial developments of the biosphere. It was the travail preceding his birth that accelerated the development of instinct and the birth of thought upon the Earth. . . . All these preparatory processes were cosmically and biologically *necessary* [not *sufficient*] that Christ might set foot upon our human stage. . . . When Christ first appeared before men in the arms of Mary he had already stirred up the world"[38]).[39]

The cosmic sense of the Incarnation is also articulated by Maximus the Confessor differently as such an event that brought a landmark in the temporal evolution of the universe, namely the division of its temporal span onto two fundamentally different aeons: "according to this plan, it is clear that God wisely divided 'the ages' between those intended for God to become human, and those intended for humanity to become divine."[40] This excludes a possibility of treating the movement from creation to deification through the Incarnation as a "natural process" inherent in the fabric of creation. Indeed, created things participate in God through the fact of their existence, that is, through "being in communion." However, when Maximus enquires about the human capacity for deification, he stresses that it does not belong

---

unobservable and physically ill-understood content of the universe (Dark Matter and Dark Energy).

38. Teilhard de Chardin, *Hymn of the Universe*, 76–77.

39. This brings one to the issue of whether multiple incarnations are possible. In this respect, see Peters et al., *Astrotheology*, ch. 4, where different theological opinions are discussed. However one must admit that the necessary conditions for possible incarnations do no entail their sufficiency and their actual happening. Correspondingly, there is a theological view that one single incarnation would suffice for the whole universe. See opinions across Christian denominations: Catholic: Teilhard de Chardin, *Christianity and Evolution*, 235–36; Lutheran: Ted Peters, "One Incarnation or Many?," in Peters et al., *Astrotheology*, 271–302; Eastern Orthodox: Nesteruk, "The Motive of the Incarnation," 462–70.

40. Maximus the Confessor, *Ad Talassium* 22, in Blowers and Wilken, *On the Cosmic Mystery*, 115. This point sheds the light on the inclusion of the lesser arch of Fall-Redemption into the greater one of Creation-Deification as the different degrees of participation in God.

to man's natural capacity: "what takes place would no longer be marvellous if divinization occurred simply in accordance with the receptive capacity of nature."[41] Maximus is concerned with the reciprocity between God and humanity. This "reciprocity" has a passive character until the movement of God towards humanity fulfils in the Incarnation. The reciprocity by creation in the perspective of the Incarnation, however, does not achieve the *likeness* of humans to God. This is the reason why Maximus claims that the aeon after the Incarnation corresponds to a contrary movement of humanity to God, whose very possibility was effected by the Incarnation. By separating the aeons before and after the Incarnation Maximus differentiates between the participation in God that is bestowed on human beings by creation and the participation that is bestowed by deification. The latter participation requires *grace* which is not implanted in the natural conditions of existence but bestowed by God on the grounds of a human being's personal degree of perfection.[42] This grace can be acquired by humans and used for the transfiguration of the universe, including all other life forms and inorganic matter. However the very acquisition of grace by human beings implies that it exists at all, so that the natural world must exist. According to Teilhard de Chardin "However supernatural, therefore, the synthesising operation attributed by dogma to the Incarnate Word may ultimately be, it cannot be effected in a divergence from the natural convergence of the world."[43] In other words, in spite of the fact that theology makes a strict demarcation between the natural predisposition and actual acquisition of grace, their reciprocal essence manifested in Christ who "would have been physically incapable of supernaturally centering the universe upon himself if it had not provided the Incarnation with a specifically flavoured point at which, in virtue of their natural structure, all the strands of the cosmos tend to meet together."[44]

However, in view of the fact that life and intelligence emerged recently in history of the universe, the claim of the central role of humanity for the deification of the universe, including all organic and inorganic creatures demands a comment. Indeed, the phenomenon of humanity is a very short

---

41. Maximus the Confessor, *Ambigua 20*, in *On Difficulties in the Church Fathers*, 411.

42. Lars Thunberg, with a reference to Maximus, asserts: "There is in man no natural power that can deify him, but there exists on the other hand a reciprocal relationship between God and man that permits him to become deified to the degree in which the effects of the Incarnation are conferred on him" (Thunberg, *Man and the Cosmos*, 55).

43. Teilhard de Chardin, *Science and Christ*, 165.

44. Teilhard de Chardin, *Science and Christ*, 165.

fragment of the universal history.[45] The main question that remains is not about a participation of other species and inorganic matter in God bestowed by their being created but about their possible participation in deification *before and after* the event of the Incarnation on Earth. As we have already discussed, this event not only justifies archetypically the *representation* of the universe by humanity, not only it anticipates the future Kingdom, but, *de facto*, defines in a non-linear and trans-historical sense the whole span of creation from the past to the future. Here is an inherent eschatological dynamics[46] which drives material creation, including all possible forms of life, to perfection in God. By paraphrasing Ted Peters, the Incarnation is an abbreviated cipher for the entire *human* life and death, the promise for the resurrection and renewal of all that exists in creation.[47] If the Incarnation was thought by God before the ages, its transcendent efficacy as of the event happened two thousand years ago in Palestine, being (through the motive of creation) commensurable with the whole span of the universe, makes sense of the inaugural event granting the universe its humanly anticipated past and its (transfigured) future, exceeding the measure of quality and quantity, being beyond modality and relation, manifesting the impossible which has become possible.

THE DIALOGUE BETWEEN THEOLOGY AND SCIENCE AS AN OPEN-ENDED HERMENEUTICS OF THE HUMAN CONDITION

The duality in hermeneutics of the subject transpiring through the dialogue between theology and science receives its elucidation from the basic feature of humanity: humanity exists through communion with God by the fact of its createdness, but it does not "possess" itself entirely in the world. By detecting its ambivalent position in the world humanity discovers itself in the conditions of an intellectual impasse, that is, an incapacity of understanding the facticity of its paradoxical state. Through hopeless attempts to find the metaphysical grounds for itself, humanity produces instead an infinite hermeneutics of this predicament thus indicating that the means of enquiry into itself by itself cannot be reduced to anything ultimately certain and

---

45. If one associates modern humanity with Homo Sapiens appeared about one hundred thousand years ago, this temporal scale seems to be miniscule in comparison with the 3.7 billion years of biological evolution and 14 billion years of the age of the universe.

46. Cf. Peters and Hewlett, *Evolution from Creation*, 163.

47. Ted Peters, "One Incarnation or Many?," in Peters et al., *Astrotheology*, 300.

accomplished. This hermeneutics is both theological and scientific whereas its philosophical sense is formulated in the paradox. The sciences implicitly articulate an outward sense of the human existence in the world. Theology encounters the sciences (and philosophy) in order to release humanity from an intellectual impasse of its own unknowability and to invite it to learn from its archetype in the incarnate Christ that in spite of humanity's creaturehood, it remains in communion and has a potential to achieve union with God.

The whole fabric of the dialogue between theology and science, being a certain manifestation of the paradoxical condition of humanity in the universe, represents an open-ended hermeneutics of the human condition with the purpose of *explicating* this condition, not its final *explanation*. Since the riddle of the unknowability of humanity by itself cannot be resolved in terms of metaphysical concepts, the dialogue between science and theology cannot hope to achieve the actual "reconciliation" of theology and science.[48] The moral tension between humanity's created condition in flesh and its *Imago Dei* as an ability to articulate the world and its own position in it, proceeding from the capacity of receiving the deifying grace, preserves the dialogue as active and alive always and forever, confirming an existential truth that both—science and theology—originate in one and the same human *ego* living in a moral tension between the sense of its created finitude and longing for the unconditional and the infinite.

In view of that which has been discussed, the next question is: what is the ultimate goal of an open-ended hermeneutics of the human condition in the dialogue between theology and science? More precisely: (a) Where from the necessity (if such exists) for such a dialogue follows? (b) What is the value of this dialogue? The first question attempts to tackle a possible logical alternative: either the dialogue is a contingent happening in the history of humanity and hence does not have any ontological foundation (there is no necessity for such a dialogue in order to survive physically), or, alternatively, the dialogue is the result of some hidden propensity in the human condition making it inevitable and hence necessarily subordinated to the modus of the human existence. If the dialogue is a contingent happening in history, the question about its value and purpose does not have any philosophical sense. If the situation is opposite and the dialogue is a necessary feature of the

---

48. Since the human condition is archetypically related to Christ whereas Christ remains an absolute and unique norm, his presence remains incommensurable with all secular norms thus making impossible any secular accord between theology and other disciplines attempting to outline the sense of the human existence. This implies the presence of theological commitment in this dialogue which follows from the methodological requirement for the very subject of theology.

human condition, one then has to explicate what is the value and purpose of such a dialogue. Invoking the idea of purpose, it must not imply such a teleology when the achievement of the purpose (goal) stops the whole project leading to this purpose. Rather, in line with Kant's idea of the formal purposefulness[49], one speaks of the purpose as a regulative ideal for the dialogue to take place at all, without formulating the purpose as a "material" end as if, for example, theology and science would be "reconciled." If the dialogue is an open-ended hermeneutics of the human condition there is no end in the activity of mediation between theology and science as soon as humans exist. In this case the *telos* of the dialogue is not that which could be described as a final state in the ongoing mediation between theology and science leading their problematic interaction to a standstill. In view of this it seems reasonable to suggest that the underlying motivation of the dialogue is the enquiry into humanity's sense of itself, understanding in advance that the *telos* of this dialogue (i.e., answering the perennial question "What is man?") cannot be achieved at any stage of humanity's historical development. Such a vision of the sense of the dialogue retains a basic puzzle: what is the ultimate foundation for the dialogue, its cause, that is, what is the ultimate foundation of that subject who runs the dialogue and produces the hermeneutics of its own condition. The basic philosophical *question* "What is man?" (i.e., "What is that centre of *givenness*, that is, of disclosure and manifestation of life, and reality of the universe?") remains unanswered.

Since the hermeneutics of the human condition involves both theology and science, or, to say more accurately, the immediate conscious experience of life and createdness on the one hand, and physical and biological embodied existence (supplemented by theoretical models of life and the universe), on the other hand, such a hermeneutics has already implied that the primary *givens* of the "rational" or participatory apprehension of the human existence, are already present, so that the dialogue and corresponding hermeneutics cannot be conducted from an "outside" position as if such a hermeneutics did not intrinsically express life. Correspondingly, since theology expresses primacy of life as contingent upon Life (understood as God), to say that the dialogue (as a manifestation of this life) is theologically *biased*, that is, relevant only to believers, would be an epistemological mistake because the contingent facticity of the dialogue cannot be disentangled from the living presence of humanity as a primary sense-forming event which is a major concern for theology. In this sense the dialogue between theology and science not only provides one with the hermeneutics of the human condition but first of all manifests life of humanity as existence *par*

---

49. See Kant, *Critique of Judgement* §10.

excellence. Sceptics and naturalists, apologists of the physical reductionism pretending to present the human existence as physically or metaphysically subsistent, loose an insight that anyone who enquires into the sense of humanity and its dialogue between its worldly finitude and philosophically constituted infinity already subsist in life as primarily *given*.

The oblivion of the inward presence of life does not allow one to understand that it is from within this life that it is possible to produce the synthesis of an object which is both, a matter of an immediately experienced existence and scientific discourse, primordial *givens* and articulated meaning.[50] At the same time, on its noetic pole, the dialogue between theology and science, as a mediation between the mystery of the hypostatic human life and its physical embodiment, represents such a practical synthesis of person, who is at once an existent (in rubric of the worldly) and the end (the goal for the worldly realm to be articulated by humanity), that one who realizes the scale of disproportion with the universe (expressed in the paradox of subjectivity) and thus the originary fragility of the human reality.[51]

One term of the paradox of subjectivity asserts that humanity is a natural result of the universe' evolution according to physical laws and their outcomes. The second term asserts human freedom due to which one is capable of synthesising all knowledge of the universe and positioning itself above nature, that is, above physical causation. Human beings *unconsciously* (and non-intentionally) perform an instantaneous synthesis of the past and present of the universe, that synthesis which *de facto* manifests to humanity its presence in the universe. "Unconsciously" means that this synthesis is performed in the conditions of forgetting of the other past as absolute, non-empirical, always already forgotten, as that reference to the time when every human being was not yet human. It is this initial and unconditional forgetting that pertains to humanity, being a modus of its being. And it is this "knowledge" that precedes that in humanity which founds its humanity.[52] The universe precedes human existence and continues to permeate humanity as if the planet Earth, the Solar system, the Milky Way and the entire universe were the inorganic body of its individual consciousness and transcendental ego. Being a part of the universe, human beings unconsciously contain the material universe in the same way as they are not aware of their tissues, mussels and blood (unless they are wounded and bleeding). The material whole, the visible universe is "inside" humans (recapitulated by them) even if they are not aware of it. In view of this the original ego which

---

50. Ricoeur, *Philosophical Anthropology*, 197.
51. Ricoeur, *Philosophical Anthropology*, 197.
52. See on phenomenality of forgetting Chretien, *The Unforgettable*, 1–9.

experiences the paradox of subjectivity is simultaneously present in three ways: (1) as an actual and immediate presence taken at the beginning as the ground of any articulation; (2) through the indefinite cosmic, geological and historical past which constantly operates unconsciously, but which in some circumstances becomes to be known as real; (3) through the anticipation of the future by unfolding the sense of its own past as humanity's infinite task. The human fragility is exactly here: the mystery of the ambivalence between a uniquely functioning *ego* and belonging to the universal intersubjectivity, between the split in intentionalities directed to the world and to "source" of the sense of life, between being the internal world (part of the world) in the external whole and, vice versa, "containing" the world, that is, being the "external" world, remains unsolved. Briefly, the question "What is man?" remains unanswered.

Edmund Husserl, when he discusses the paradox of subjectivity in a phenomenological context,[53] claims that the paradox can be "resolved" through an appeal either to metaphysics or positive religion. For phenomenology both ways are unacceptable and he formulates its task: "For the philosopher . . . the juxtaposition 'subjectivity *in* the world as object' and at the same time 'conscious subject *for* the world', contains a necessary theoretical question, that of understanding how this is possible. The *epoché* (phenomenological reduction), in giving us the attitude above the subject-object correlation which belongs to the world, . . . leads us to recognise, in self-reflection, that the world that exists for us, that is our world in its being and being-such, takes its ontic meaning entirely from our intentional life."[54] If the ego and the world are considered as intentional immanence, they cannot be isolated into separate material or spiritual being of their own. The subject transforms the world into the phenomenon insofar it detects the world's essential truths. Intentionality constitutes the truth of the world and history as this happens in the sciences by departing from actual concrete man. Then the paradox of subjectivity becomes the contradiction between that which *is* (but has no meaning: humanity in the vast universe), and that which reveals and will become the meaning of that which has been and will be (humanity as articulating consciousness and the sense of the universe). As agents of intentional operations we are not mere object-men, but rather operative and active subjects constituting the meaning of the world consciously or unconsciously. In this case the original *ego* can either be an actual human individuum, or unconscious *presence* within it of the past of the whole physical universe. Since the actual humanity longs for its

---

53. Husserl, *The Crisis*, 178.
54. Husserl, *The Crisis*, 180–81.

self-constitution through the explication of its own sense as true and having meaning, the goal of such a constitution is transcendental intersubjectivity as it reveals itself in distinct material human beings. Every particular human being becomes an objectification of the transcendental *ego* as that intentional tension (caught in the paradox) that lives in it. The functioning of *ego* is unique because it is present in every subject which is simultaneously transcendental intersubjectivity. It is in this sense that when the paradox is formulated one starts from the ego in the first person and then proceed to the intersubjective constitution of the world and humanity itself. Husserl writes: "each transcendental 'I' within intersubjectivity (constituting the world . . .) must necessarily be constituted in the world as a human being; in other words, that each human being 'bears within himself a transcendental 'I.'"[55] Thus the paradox is the unceasing movement of subjectivity between two indicated poles, that is, an open-ended hermeneutics of the human condition encapsulated in the dialogue between the egocentric presence in humanity and intersubjectively constituted decentered world in entirety of its past, present and future. The movement between the hermeneutic of humanity as related to its empirical incarnation in rubrics of space and time on the one hand, and the hermeneutic of humanity as a particular realization of transcendental subjectivity (which has roots in the world of freedom), forms that *teleological* inevitability in the human condition through which humanity attempts to formulate the sense of its existence as its infinite task. If the dialogue between theology and science becomes a teleological inevitability, this dialogue does not aim to stop at some particular stage. This dialogue is not going to resolve the mystery of the human condition, but rather will serve as the means of explication of its sense thus indirectly constituting the very sense of humanity. Saying differently, the dialogue between theology and science as an open-ended hermeneutics of the human condition contributes to the constitution of the sense of humanity. Correspondingly the paradox of subjectivity lying in the foundation of the dialogue between theology and science not only cannot be resolved on the basis of metaphysics or positive religion (as it was asserted by Husserl) but, in fact, does not need to be resolved at all because its intellectually presupposed resolution does not have any objective correspondence with the human condition. Theology confirms this by asserting the same in terms of the unknowability of humanity (encapsulated in the paradox) because of the Divine Image.

---

55. Husserl, *The Crisis*, 186.

THE HUMAN PHENOMENON AND THE DIALOGUE BETWEEN THEOLOGY AND SCIENCE AS AN EXPRESSION OF LIFE'S SELF-AFFECTIVITY

The paradox of subjectivity, being itself a philosophical observation that does not have any immediate existential consequences, nevertheless represents an empirical evidence for the human capacity to articulate the universe from its microscopic scales to the scales of the whole visible (and invisible) cosmos, creating schematic images of the universe, thus transcending not so much the macroscopic conditions of the human embodiment on Earth, but rather transcending epistemologically limits of practical life. The universe as a whole, as well as many "entities" from the unseen realm (multiverse), are posited by humanity as belonging to the intelligible realms, that is, as ideas. This cognitive capacity of abstracting from the empirical reality cannot be as such explained by means of physics and biology: one cannot give any deduction of how the twenty centimeters of the physical brain, subordinated to the physical laws, generate a conscious capacity to transcend the scales of its physical space and time in order to produce an "instantaneous" synthesis of the universe. The contingent facticity of both, the empirical world, as well as of the noetic cosmos of ideas, remains unaccounted through human knowledge that has to satisfy itself with the sheer *givenness* of the latter. This observation is strictly phenomenological leading to the conclusion that the structure of the perceived reality is dualistic and human beings probably mimic the composite structure of the physical and intelligible.[56] The paradox of subjectivity expresses this fact. Then, if the very predicament of the paradox reflects the dualistic standing of humanity in the structure of being, any attempted resolution of this paradox *would imply the resolution of the mystery of the dual structure of all being.* Coming to this point and referring to philosophers of the past, one could suspect that this perennial problem could put an end to any further philosophizing. Indeed, if human nature resembles the dual nature of the universe making

---

56. This point was in prominence since the antiquity and received its symbolic interpretation, for example, in writing of Maximus the Confessor. Maximus articulates the similarity between the composition of human beings and the composition of the universe from the point of view of the hypostatic unity of different parts in them. A passage from *Mystagogy* 7 elucidates the meaning of this similarity: "Intelligible things display the meaning of the soul as the soul does that of intelligible things, and . . . sensible things display the place of body as the body does that of sensible things. And . . . intelligible things are the soul of sensible things, and sensible things are the body of intelligible things; . . . as the soul is in the body so is the intelligible in the world of sense, that the sensible is sustained by the intelligible as the body is sustained by the soul" (Maximus the Confessor, *Selected Writings*, 196).

potentially possible its instantaneous synthesis in every particular person (since this synthesis includes the synthesis of this person itself), one cannot extract this person from the universe and to "look" at it as if the universe (as empirical and intelligible) would be an external object. In a phenomenological language this means that all philosophical and theological methods based on the natural attitude fail with grasping the ultimate sense of both the universe and human persons. The implied change of attitude means the radical inversion of the problem of the human condition (and hence the sense of the dialogue between theology and science as explicating this condition), by neutralizing any hypothetical metaphysical answer in the style "Man is this and that"[57] and by turning to a phenomenological ethos in reasoning where the question of the origin of humanity, its createdness is transformed into the question of the facticity of its consciousness whose primacy as a medium of all other phenomenality of the world manifests itself from itself. Such a phenomenological shift in approaching the sense of humanity understood as the unity of creation and communion radically extends classical phenomenology beyond its limits.[58] This extension can briefly be described as the following. While in classical phenomenology one can suspend any realistic treatment of the content of knowledge of the world by tracing down the ways and means of its constitution as related to the faculties of the subject, it is fundamentally impossible to suspend God and doubt its "objective" presence in the foundation of consciousness. In theological terms this corresponds to the impossibility of reducing communion with God to some particular conscious acts that are more elementary than this communion itself. In fact the very attempt of such a reduction would confirm the prior presence of communion because reduction as such is possible because of communion. In this way the *notions* of "consciousness" and "God" effectively become synonymous in the following sense: God forms human subjectivity by overwhelming its intuition to such an extent that the discursive thinking is incapable of constituting God, whereas the *ego* itself is constituted by the excess of intuition of God as the Creator and Giver of life. In this frame of thought the phenomenon of humanity is inseparable from event-like hypostatic phenomenality of God's manifestations out of himself. As Michel Henry expressed this: "To the extent that Life is more than man understood as living, it is from Life, not from man, that we must begin.

---

57. Cf. Jaspers, *Ways to Wisdom*, 63.

58. This extension received a name "theological turn" coined by the French philosopher Dominique Janicaud. See Janicaud et al., *Phenomenology*.

From Life means from God, since according to Christianity, the essence of Life and that of God are one and the same."[59]

For a sceptical or an atheistic scientist, as well as for a secular phenomenological philosopher, it would be problematic to accept that the truth of human existence has its foundation in God, for any reference to the Divine would imply transcendence, principally inconceivable in science and philosophically prohibited by classical phenomenology: "God" as a transcendent reference must be *reduced* in the sense that any judgement about its ontological status is suspended. One can point to Husserl, who in his *Ideas I* (§58) subjected God to a reduction, bracketing it and depriving it of any trans-conscious status.[60] However a theologically insightful mind would press a point that the very reduction as a modus of the functioning consciousness would be impossible at all if the reference to the source of its contingent facticity would be eidetically removed. Jean-Luc Marion writes in this respect: "Husserl submits what he names 'God' to the reduction only in so far as he defines it by transcendence (and insofar as he compares this particular transcendence with that, in fact quite different, of the object in the natural attitude); and yet in Revelation *theo*-logy, God is likewise, indeed especially, characterised by *radical immanence to consciousness, and in this sense would be confirmed by a reduction*."[61] What is effectively stated in this last quotation is that the *sheer manifestation of consciousness as its self-affectivity* is itself a different expression of that which humanity names God. Any hypothetical (phenomenological) reduction of God in consciousness would imply the cessation of functioning of consciousness itself, that is, the cessation of the human phenomenon.[62] This phenomenological insight can be found as early as in St. Augustine's *Confessions*: "Accordingly, my God, I would have no being, I would not have any existence, unless you were in me. Or rather, I would have no being if I were not in you 'of whom are all

---

59. Henry, *I Am the Truth*, 51.

60. Husserl, *Ideas*.

61. Marion, *Being Given*, 242–43 (see also 343n4).

62. Saying the same in a non-phenomenological language one invokes a couple of quotations from Simon Frank: "We could not be aware of our insufficiency, could not need God and seek him, if we were not a reflection, however poor and imperfect, of that which we lack and are in search of. It is the presence and action of God in us that compels us to seek God outside us. At the bottom, I can as little doubt the reality of God as I can doubt my own reality" (Frank, *Reality and Man*, 106); "God is, on the one hand, a transcendent Being which we oppose to our 'self'; we are related to it as one reality to another, . . . On the other hand, this very relation forms part of our own inner being and is immanent in us, so that in speaking of our 'self' we mean by it a reality unthinkable apart from that relation and bearing an imprint of that to which it is related" (Frank, *Reality and Man*, 116).

things, through whom are all things, in whom are all things' (Rom 2:36)."[63] It is this impossibility of a reduction of God in all conscious activity, including the dialogue between theology and science, that explicates the sense of that which is called "theological commitment," thus identifying God as the foundation of that consciousness which is responsible for theology, philosophy and science.

This line of thought gives a possibility of understanding God as a principle of existence of consciousness, conscious life and hence of the world as it is articulated by intelligent beings. God and human life reveal their inseparability in life's self-affectivity. Along the lines of Michel Henry's thought, introducing self-affectivity as the principle of the Divine manifestation, one can extend this principle as a phenomenological condition to human life. Quoting Henry: "The concept of self-affection as life's essence implies its acosmic character, the fact that being affected by nothing other, nothing external or radically foreign to the world, it comes about in itself in the absolute sufficiency of its radical interiority—experiencing only itself, being affected only by itself, prior to any possible world and independently of it."[64] However, unlike God, human beings experience their own self-affectivity without being able to understand the source of its presence as well as the sense of its facticity. Here the formulated human predicament effectively provides a dynamic "definition" of man:

> As far as I am me, I affect myself; I am myself the affected and what affects it, myself the "subject" of this affection and its content. I experience myself, and constantly, in that, the fact of experiencing myself constitutes my "Me." But I have not brought myself into this condition of experiencing myself. I am myself, but I myself have no part in this "being-myself": I experience myself without being the source of this experience. I am given to myself without this givenness arising from me in any way. I affect myself, and thus I self-affect myself. . . . But this self-affection that defines my essence *is not my doing*. And thus I do not affect myself absolutely, but, precisely put, I am and I find myself self-affected.[65]

By invoking a theological terminology the same can be expressed differently: the human self-affectivity is hypostatic (personal), but it is being enhypostasized not by humanity itself. Every human being comes into existence in the already enhypostasized condition. The source of this enhypostasization is

---

63. Augustine, *Confessions* I.ii (2), 4.
64. Henry, *I Am the Truth*, 105.
65. Henry, *I Am the Truth*, 107–8; emphasis added.

the a-cosmic self-affective Life named in Christianity by God. Setting aside, for a while, theological elucidations of that how to describe that agency which enhypostasizes man's self-affectivity, the philosophical question remains as how to express this givenness of self-affectivity to humanity itself. In other words, how to establish a phenomenological description of those phenomena that are more immediate and close to man's existence, those phenomena which exclude any *a priori* positioning of them in rubrics of the discursive capacity of reason. First of all, one refers to the self-affectivity of the body by the body, that is, flesh as a mediator between life in a body and the surrounding world. To be in the body is to be affected by that physical environment where such a body functions. In this sense to experience self affectivity of life through the body means to experience self-affectivity of life through belonging to the universe. The paradox of subjectivity receives its new formulation as that the perception of being affected by the world (as belonging to it and the impossibility of existing without it) proceeds from the originary self-affectivity of being alive. Since human existence is affected by the worldly realities through the body, the sciences explicate how this happens by articulating the physical conditions of the possibility of this self-affectivity through the body. The sciences articulate the conditions of self-affectivity of humanity in physical terms (necessary conditions) without explaining the contingent facticity of these conditions (which remain in the sphere of self-affectivity of that a-cosmic Life which is incarnate in the matter of the world). Since the creation of the world receives its interpretation as a modus of the outward expression of God's self-affectivity (as Life), humanity is involved into this self-affectivity through being created by God, as well as through carrying the archetype of the incarnate Christ as the Son of God.

The incarnation of God in human flesh created by this God, manifests that God is also self-affected by that which he has created, that is, by the flesh of the world. That which is created by God enters in the condition of self-affectivity of God because God descended into the world becoming the incarnate Christ. This "second-stage" self-affectivity of God by its own flesh originates in the "initial" self-affectivity of God as Life expressed outwardly through the *creation* of the world. In this context the world can be treated as the manifestation of the self-affectivity of God as Life, confirmed through the affectivity of the incarnate God by the conditions of the world (birth of Jesus, Christ's teaching, his suffering and death on the Cross). Being subjected to the conditions of flesh that was created by the Logos, Christ the Logos in flesh, was affected by the conditions of its own creation. And this is the self-affectivity of the incarnate God being an archetype in understanding of human life's self-affectivity.

On the one hand, Christ as fully human was affected by the cosmological and geographical conditions in space, ecological and biological specificity, by historical circumstances and surrounded by contingent people. But all these so to speak material conditions were ultimately imposed on Jesus by Christ himself, being the Word-Logos, who predisposed fully human Jesus Christ to these conditions through creating the world. But if the world was created as the outward expression of the initial self-affectivity of God-Creator, this world must have some inherent *signs* of this self-affectivity. For Christ this self-affectivity can be expressed through the "paradox" of the Incarnation. On the one hand, being in human flesh in one particular location in the universe, Christ as a human being is affected by the world. On the other hand, being the Creator of the universe, Christ-Logos is present (hypostatically) everywhere in the universe (all pieces and moments of the universe comprise the unity as being created by the Logos-Christ: the self-affectivity of God has an a-cosmic character). Being locally on Earth, Christ is affected by himself, for his human existence on Earth is sustained only because the structure of the universe is adjusted to the fact of existence of the human life on Earth and the Incarnation. The integrity and unity of the universe are thus manifested on Earth as a theological-topological isomorphism between the whole universe and Earth (expressed characteristically in physical cosmology through the cosmological principle) as Christ's self-affectivity manifested in the creation of this universe. This self-affectivity of the Logos-Christ does not require any reference to the cause of this self-affectivity, because it is self-generated, so to speak, self-caused. Correspondingly in Christ, who as fully human experienced his human self-affectivity, but in the *Ipseity* (hypostasis) of the Logos, this self-affectivity of Christ-man and of Christ-God do coincide. The paradox of the Incarnation, cascading towards the paradox of human subjectivity in Christ, did not cause in him any anxiety and despair in understanding the sense of the human, because it is the Logos-Christ who created his own humanity through his Divine self-affectivity.

The tension between the specific spatial location of the human Christ and his hypostatic presence everywhere in the universe as God was a particular manifestation of the Logos-Christ's self-affectivity, expressed not only in terms of space, but in terms of the initial conditions of the universe and physical laws responsible for providing the conditions on Earth so that the body of the Incarnate Logos (as well as his mother) became possible. The same conditions are necessary for existence of other human beings. Thus the self-affectivity of God expressed through his Incarnation is ultimately responsible for existence of all humanity. By the same token one can claim that for us, humans, the phenomenon of humanity that experiences the paradox of subjectivity becomes an expression of self-affectivity as an inherent characteristic of the living condition of being contingent upon the self-affectivity of a-cosmic Life, and it is this human self-affectivity that becomes a source of anxiety and moral tension between the finite physical life and potentially infinite consciousness encoded in the dialogue between theology and science, so that this dialogue itself becomes an outward expression of life's self-affectivity in the Ipseity (Image) of the incarnate Christ.

HUMAN LIFE'S SELF-AFFECTIVITY AS A GEOCENTRIC CORPOREITY AND HYPOSTATIC OMNIPRESENCE

The self-affectivity of the created humanity experienced through the paradox of subjectivity can be explicated through the twofold perception of space. Correspondingly the terms of the dialogue between theology and science can also be qualified as different attitudes to a spatial perception implied in their corresponding *givens* (phenomena). If one suspends the natural attitude with respect to space as outer reality and considers a genesis of spatiality as a certain form of relation to the world formulated from within the developing special perception one realizes that space appears as generated from within the event of life (compare with Kant's stance on space as a form of sensibility). For example, if one looks at a child's entrance into this world in the event of birth, the main existential factor in this initial mysterious inseparability between a child and the world is the early sensual consciousness of the other, the mother who through love inaugurates in a child the sense of space. Space appears as a modus of relationship in which, on the one hand, a loving human being manifests itself as a pre-conscious ecstatic reference, whereas on the other hand the same human being is caught in consciousness as the other supplemented by the spatial attributes of this otherness expressed in terms of extended (and measurable) space. Thus the perception of space can be considered as that self-affectivity in the human ego which proceeds from the intrinsic inseparability between humanity and the world. Space becomes a vehicle of the human involvement in the world through the hypostatic differentiated embodiments that make possible the relationship with world's objects and other persons. This dialectical "standing in front of" and "standing apart from" in personal relation to the world is an existential fact. Its contingent facticity is an event of emergence of personhood: first, as a double affectivity of the human flesh by the world and of the human consciousness by the worldly flesh and, second, inversely, the reflection upon the world and its articulation and constitution through the given propensity of being hypostasis of the universe. Human person can thus be characterized as self-affective life being created in the Ipseity (Image) of that self-affective Life understood as God.

The language of ecstatic reference to (communion with) the world and other persons implies a phenomenological attitude to appropriating the world because the manifold of personal relationship to it is unfolded from within events of life. The world as a personal "opposite" of ecstatic reference is perceived in the dialogue between humanity and the world as some *other*, hypostatically subsistent (enhypostasized) in every ego of this humanity.[66] The representation of the relationship with the world in the phenomenality of objects consists in that the world becomes a passive object of observation and study so that the sense of belonging to it is eidetically removed. When the world becomes an "object," the personal space of "standing in front of" the world transforms into a sheer "standing apart from" the world in space as measurable and controlled extent. As was once expressed by Gabriel Marcel: "The more I emphasize the objectivity of things, thus cutting off the umbilical cord which binds them to [my] existence and to what has been termed my psycho-organic presence to myself, the more I affirm the independence of the world from me, its radical indifference to my destiny, my goals; the more, too, this world, proclaimed as the only real one, is converted into an illusory spectacle, a great documentary film presented for my curiosity, but ultimately abolished simply because it disregards me."[67] Space is presented in the phenomenality of objects when the relationship with the world is transferred into the sphere of pure thought that thinks this relationship but does not experience it. It is in the conditions of the breakdown of the initial unity between subject and object (experienced as self-affectivity) that the representation of space acquires more and more geometrical, measurable character associated with the boundaries of things (as objects), that fill in the universe. Indeed, the very possibility of scientific cosmology, for example, proceeds from the fact that it thinks of space exactly this way, where the measure of space is determined by its capacity to contain astronomical objects. However, the perception of the extended space of the universe proceeds from the initial standing "in front of" the universe as the totality of space intellectually expressed through the instantaneous synthesis of the

---

66. What is implied here is a theological assertion that humanity is hypostasis [personality] of the cosmos, its conscious and personal self-expression; it is humanity that gives meaning to things and that has to transfigure them. The universe as *the expressed and articulated existence* is possible only in human hypostasis, that is, it acquires some qualities of existence if it is reflected in the personality of humanity. A theologian would say that existence of the universe as the articulated existence is *enhypostatic*. This is the same as to say that the universe, as an articulated system of notions is *enhypostasized* by human beings.

67. Marcel, *Creative Fidelity*, 21.

universe. The experience of *placelessness* of the universe (i.e., the experience of the universe through an ecstatic personal reference [self-affectivity]) remains irreducible.

The "standing in front of" the universe as the personal and absolute "opposite" is free from its actual physically infinite extent, and thus remains indeterminate in terms of a category of quantity as well as mundane geometrical intuitions of spatial hierarchy, that is, in terms of "closer" and "far," "here" and "elsewhere," "right" and left," etc. In this sense the universe as a term of personal relationship manifests its sheer *presence* that cannot be described in terms of place. This situation is represented in that pole of the paradox of subjectivity where human ego asserts itself as the centre of disclosure and manifestation of the universe. Such a perception of space opposes to a scientific vision of the world when the initial perception of the universe (*coaevus universo*),[68] dissolves into the form of its spatial extension when the individualized flesh is constituted in space. In both cases, either through experience of communion with the universe because of sheer belonging to it, or through the impossibility to circumscribe the universe in forms of thought, both types of this experience determine the space of personal relationship as a certain indeterminacy of "standing in front" of the universe (as non-extended and non-measurable) objectifying in reflection the working of self-affectivity of life. Space as relationship thus signifies the modality of life, existential events of movement towards the other. However, this movement is not self-evident and takes place in the conditions of awareness of space as a potential threat of "standing apart," that is, separation (when self-affectivity degrades towards sheer affectivity by space and passivity of a subject). Here is a dialectics of space that finds its characteristic expression in the dialogue between theology and science: space is always capable of being transformed from the condition of personal relationship (affirmed in theology) into a soulless form of separation and quantitative measurement (in science) if life of a hypostatic subject is treated as determinism of biological existence, and the universe becomes an indefinite background of existing whose contingency not only cannot be comprehended but, in fact, cannot be even detected.

---

68. Here is how this was expressed Teilhard de Chardin: "The human soul, however independently created our philosophy represents it as being, is inseparable, in its birth and in its growth, from the universe into which it is born. In each soul, God loves and partly saves the whole world which that soul sums up in an incommunicable and particular way. But this summing-up, this welding, are not given to us ready-made and complete with the first awakening of consciousness. It is we who, through our own activity, must industriously assemble the widely scattered elements" (Teilhard de Chardin, *Le Milieu Divine*, 60).

However, the intuition of the universe as the created wholeness always functions in the human subjectivity through the perception of being alive. It enters as an invisible background for the natural attitude that is seeking the universe as an extended space and implies such a relationship of "standing before" when all extensional plurality of experience is reduced to null in the event of ecstatic relationship towards the universe's Creator.[69] The self-affective sense of being (being-in-communion) precedes any consciousness either of God's presence or absence in the universe and thus of consciousness of presence or absence of the universe as created totality. The existential reality of God and the world, created by him, are defined through the immediate proximity of the relationship with him so that any personal subjectivity, not being able to verbalise and objectivize this relationship, is constituted by this relationship (the elusive self-affectivity of human life is itself constituted by life's relation to God). It is this non-extended and non-measurable intimate "opposite" of the personal relationship that constitutes space as relation. If the universe as "noema" of the Divine intention "stands before" God without any extension, there is no space between God and the world (God abides in creation without any spatial connotation [*panentheism*[70]]), human beings as creatures experience their relationship with God and his creation in the modality of space thus leading to the paradox of subjectivity and its transformed appearance in the dialogue between theology and science. On the one hand humanity manifests itself in the placeless totality of its own articulating hypostasis (its originally created self-affectivity, when the world is present through the Logos-given capacity); on the other hand, as functioning corporeity (i.e., as embodied beings), the same humanity feels itself isolated in the world of the dividing extension (i.e., in the passivity of being affected by space).

Since such a dual perception of space is unavoidable in the created condition humanity has to seek for an archetype of this condition (in which the "standing before" and "standing apart" in the relationship between the world and God, man and God, and man and the world, reconciled) in the Divine humanity of Jesus Christ. The transcendent foundation of the extended space and time of the universe is revealed in this world through the incarnate Christ who, while being in this world manifests its transcendence

---

69. In a religious practice one can find an example of this pointing to the Anaphora in the Divine Liturgy (when the space-time order of events in the Earthly history of Christ is intentionally suspended), or to the prayer for the world of monks contemplating the whole of being from the place of their solitude.

70. The concept of *panentheism* implying God's presence in the world, but not merging with the world (*pantheism*) is discussed in Clayton and Peacocke, *In Whom We Live*.

as the Logos that reaches out infinitely beyond the whole created world. To acquire the sense of the unity of all extended space as an instant of the Divine love, not intellectually through the instantaneous synthesis of the universe, but existentially, by imitating Christ, one must perform a mediation between divisions in creation and then between the world and God.[71] Such an imitation implies that which happened with the descent of Christ: the ideal relatedness of all in God which acquired reality in man's faculty of reason now finds itself "existent" not only intellectually but also in concrete, material form. The Kingdom of God that was inaugurated by Christ's coming into the world came into reality not intellectually, but practically. This was expressed by Vladimir Soloviev: "The God-man or the Living Reason (Logos) not only abstractly understands but actively realises the meaning of everything.... The highest task of man ... is to *gather the universe together in idea*. The task of the God-man and of the Kingdom of God is to gather the universe together in *reality*."[72] Now the divine is not contained within human consciousness as an idea, but in the human and divine being—Christ, who took flesh and was born in rubrics of the material world. To grasp the sense of the universe as a whole, including all of its space and time one needs to "acquire" the mind of Christ when one comes to truly know the things of the universe and the sense of its space (not epistemologically, but through communion). It is here through such a deification that the tension between the communion-like synthesis of the universe is balanced with the sense of division and extension in the world of objects (a subject of scientific knowledge). One could conjecture that the apparent *division* between the terms of the dialogue between theology and science could then be removed on the *moral* level.[73] However in no way this would imply the overcoming of the ontological differences between the a-cosmic self-affective Life, that is, the Divine, and human life which is created through the Divine Life's self-affectivity. The *moral* tension in the human condition detected in the dialogue between theology and science can be potentially overcome with no intention and no possibility of changing the created nature of this condition.

---

71. This was the way put forward by Maximus the Confessor in order to be deified. See details in Thunberg, *Microcosm and Mediator*, ch. 6.

72. Solovyof, *The Justification of the Good*, 190; translation corrected.

73. Practically it could mean that a Christian must strive to make his theology and his perception of cosmology consonant in making an overall world-view. But this consonance is a relation constantly subjected to verification by life and the sciences thus, on the one hand, philosophically, contributing to an open-ended hermeneutics of the human condition and, on the other hand, theologically, contributing to the dynamics of deification.

Finally, one realizes that the paradox of human subjectivity can be formulated in terms of space, that is, in terms of humanity's topological position in the universe (making it even more close to the paradox of space in the Incarnation). The formulation of the paradox in terms of space is achieved through a metaphor of the container and of the contained: on the one hand by its physical and biological parameters humanity is contained in the universe, on the other hand the universe itself is "contained" by human subjectivity as its intentional correlate (i.e., enhypostatically). In this formulation the epistemological centrality of humanity is contraposed to its cosmographic mediocrity. Yet the cosmographic mediocrity is affected by the centrality of the human life-world, being "here and now" and linked to the planet Earth and thus being geocentric. Earth remains "ontologically" central in a spiritual sense,[74] in the sense of "wherefrom" manifestations and disclosure of the universe do originate. In spite of the fact that cosmology deals with Earth as an object and ascribes to it a movement in space, it was here, on this planet, that cosmologists's statements concerning the indifferent position of Earth in cosmic space (cosmological principle) receive their meaning. The planet Earth as *here*, as the place of this initial experience, *is not* therefore a place in space, since it is itself a place of origin of a notion of space. In this sense the cosmological principle, as a philosophical hypothesis articulating the uniformity of space at large, enters into contradiction with the singular and unique "here" which is physically incomparable with any "there" thus predetermining the non-homogeneous topology in any ideation of space at large contrary to the cosmological principle understood as the equivalence of all possible observes in the universe. The planet Earth, being thus a so called attuned, personal space, becomes an initial instant and a medium of disclosure of that "objective" space through relation to which this subject is constituted as a corporeal existence. However this relationship is manifest of a paradox similar to that of the container and of the contained. Put in an interrogative form it sounds like this: how can one grasp the relationship of a particular subject as if it "in" space when this subject is essentially constituted by being "over against," and hence beyond space?[75] Using our previous language the latter sounds like this: how can one grasp the relationship of a particular subject to the universe as standing

---

74. Cf. Lossky, *Orthodox Theology*, 64.

75. Ströker, *Investigations in Philosophy of Space*, 15. This reminds a Kantian stance on a humanity as being simultaneously phenomenon and noumenon: on the one hand, space is an *a priori* form of sensibility that allows a subject to order experience; on the other hand, this form of sensibility is unfolded not from within that space which is made by it a subject of reflection but comes from beyond any possible spatial presentation of experience.

"apart from" it when this being is essentially constituted by being "before," and hence beyond the universe?

It is obvious that the constitution of space, first of all of the attuned space is intertwined with the human embodiment or corporeity, where the latter manifests itself as a living being in relation to other beings and to the world, in whom this relation is announced and articulated in a way of its sense-reaction and its action in situation. In this sense the constitution of space in all its varieties (from attuned space to mathematical space) represents a modus of explication of that side of the human ego's self-affectivity which relates to the universe. Thus the lived body entails a kind of lived space which bears the character of self-affectivity "in the flesh." In other words, the initial point of any discourse on corporeity and associated spatiality (standing "apart from") implies a kind of knowledge as presence "in person" or "in the flesh" as a mode of givenness of an object in its standing in front of the functioning corporeity (self-affectivity) of life. In cosmology, by articulating the entirety of the universe human beings remain corporeal, so that their corporeality as a relationship to all things contains in its facticity the very premise of being physically incommensurable and at the same time commensurable hypostatically with that totality which humanity attempts to reveal. However, since humanity cannot abandon its position of corporeal existence in situation on the planet Earth, all cosmological models contain the elements of this given embodiment even in those cases when they predicate the universe in trans-human or even non-human (the early universe or multiverse) terms. This statement can be demonstrated philosophically by reducing the ideas of the non-human world to a certain *teleology of reason* that pertains to the Earthly humanity in flesh, but this would bring our discussion well beyond the objectives of this book.

On the basis of that which was discussed, one can realize that the paradox of subjectivity reflects the dualistic position of humanity in space as being geocentrically corporeal and epistemologically omnipresent. In other words, the paradox can be interpreted as a tension between a geocentric facticity of humanity and its potential presence through an insight in all places of the universe. Cosmological principle attempts to neutralize this tension by ontologizing the epistemological human presence in different parts of the universe and replacing it by transferring the human insight from Earth to all other positions in the universe as if human beings could exist over there as physical observers. This transferral of the epistemological qualities of humanity established on the planet Earth to some remote locations in the universe is tantamount to the suggestion that the physical conditions for existence of anthropomorphic observers are uniform across the universe. Let us pay attention to the shift in logic here: the cosmological principle becomes a consequence of another, much stronger philosophical (and, as we will see below, theological) assertion of the overall fitness of the universe for that particular type of life which pertains to the intelligent humanity. This in turn entails that the universe is not only intelligible (from the position on Earth) but is intelligent as a collective of all possible observers. If the universe is fit in its intrinsic properties for having intelligent observers everywhere, this effectively implies that there are necessary conditions for the universe to be an intelligent entity as if human beings are everywhere in it. Such a conclusion would immediately bring us to the radical anthropocentrism in views of the universe as fit for human life in general, implying a certain teleology. In this case the tension in the paradox of subjectivity could be easily resolved by saying that indeed, human beings on Earth occupy a tiny place in the cosmic space, but their capacity of articulating the whole universe follows from the fact that humanity on Earth represents a particular realization of the collective cosmic consciousness of the universe, understood through the cosmological principle as the collective of intelligent observers finely tuned to observe the universe as a whole in a way that would be statistically identical to any particular vision of the universe from any arbitrary location. In such a reasoning the geocentric overtones of the paradox are replaced by the anthropocentric claims that the knowledge of the universe implies that the universe is fit for being knowable by human beings, so that its overall development has a *telos* related to the appearance of humanity (this teleological overtone can be found in the formulation of the Strong Anthropic Principle).[76]

Return to the dialogue between theology and science. If in the formulation of the paradox of subjectivity one neutralizes the geocentric origin of the paradox by employing the cosmological principle that displaces humanity (as the centre of disclosure and manifestation of the universe) from Earth to any possible location in it, for the dialogue between the scientific part of this paradox with theology such a displacement would be fundamentally problematic. Theology insists that experience of God through self-affective life is geocentric in two senses. First, the Divine was revealed to humanity on Earth and this is the reason why, as is said by Vladimir Lossky, the Bible chains us to the Earth in order to deliver us from the unnecessary spiritual contemplations of those remote and alien worlds which we cannot understand in the conditions when the sense of this Earthly realm remains ill-understood by us.[77] Second, the Incarnation of the Word-Logos of God in flesh of Jesus Christ is de facto the Incarnation in the flesh of the Earth.

---

76. Barrow and Tipler, *Anthropic Cosmological Principle*, 21–22.
77. See Lossky, *Orthodox Theology*, 64.

From a theological point of view this is an essentially geocentric event in spite of the fact that the *necessary* conditions for the existence of human flesh and the Incarnation are probably fulfilled across the universe.[78] As we argued above, the actual Incarnation is yet determined by the fulfilment of its *sufficient* conditions that are not cosmological, but related to the logic of the history of salvation on Earth. Then it is here in the distinction between the necessary and sufficient conditions either in the fact of existence of humanity or in the possibility of the Incarnation that lies the tension between science and theology. Theology affirms existence from within *a priori* geocentric perspective, so that the universe is seen as unfolding from within the event of life and its constitutive archetype of the Incarnation. To extrapolate such a geocentric vision of the universe to its remote parts and to claim that it looks the same would imply to extrapolate not only the sufficient conditions of the appearance of the human intelligence in remote galaxies, but to assume that incarnations would be actually possible everywhere in the universe. As we have mentioned above, this stream of thought manifests not only a radical anthropocentrism but effective deification of the universe through the motive of the Incarnation implanted in the natural conditions.

It is exactly the geocentric contingent necessity of all theological statement about the sense of the universe and human life that enters in an apparent conflict with the scientific view of the universe attempting to develop an "unbiased" view of the universe by transforming the contingent necessity of the event of life on Earth into a sheer necessity following the natural laws. Yet even scientifically one can claim the facticity of life only on this planet, thus relying on the extrapolations of its constituted fragments of reality to the entirety of the universe. The sciences fight for the objectivity of their models of reality by dismissing geocentric bias on the grounds of the universality of physical laws, yet the sciences (together with the experience of self-affective life) are geocentrically bound because of the human position in the universe. Any attempt to escape from this centeredness around the planet Earth is futile to the same extent as to change the human condition. Hence any attempt to balance a geocentric centering of all theological claims in the dialogue with the allegedly universal sciences is also futile because the actual sufficient conditions for the very possibility of this dialogue as a particular manifestation of self-affective life are fulfilled only on this planet. Theologically, this is tantamount of advocating for the uniqueness of the Incarnation of God on Earth. Summarizing in different words, the dialogue between theology and science is about the interplay

---

78. See a discussion on multiple incarnations in Ted Peters, "One Incarnation or Many?," in Peters et al., *Astrotheology*, 271–302; Nesteruk, "The Motive of the Incarnation."

between the *necessary* and *sufficient* conditions for existence of life and the entire universe. The fact that these conditions receive their manifestation in different phenomenalities related to one and the same man shows that the dialogue between theology and the sciences will remain alive and active as long as man exists thus forming an open-ended hermeneutics of the created Earth-bound human condition.

THE DIALOGUE BETWEEN THEOLOGY AND SCIENCE AS A SELF-AFFECTIVE LIFE'S RESPONSE TO THE SATURATED PHENOMENON OF THE UNIVERSE

The paradox of subjectivity, as a reflection upon a dualistic position of humanity in the universe formally becomes an obstacle in asserting humanity's centrality in a theological (but philosophically expressed) sense. By holding the image of the universe as a whole, human transcendental subjectivity experiences a disagreement between the phenomenon of the universe expected to appear in the manner of ordinary objects and ego's subjective experience of the universe through sheer belonging to it. Consequently, the ego cannot constitute the universe as an "object" whose concept would agree with the conditions of experience of the universe through ecstatic reference of standing in front of it. One has here the intuitive saturation through belonging to the universe which imposes itself by excess which makes this universe present, but *invisible* (as *overexposed*) and incomprehensible. The universe engulfs ego's intuition to such an extent that any attempt of the universe's constitution is suspended. The universe is *visible* in its particular pieces and moments but, as a whole, it cannot be *looked at*: one cannot provide an accomplished constituted notion of the universe as a whole while it is possible to constitute its concrete objects.

The dialogue between theology and science can then be interpreted as an attempt to balance two different *phenomenalities* in one and the same subjectivity: on the one hand, events of communion with the universe (where the universe cannot not constituted because of the saturating intuition) versus its representation through the objects extended in space. This reflects the previously discussed situation with the human condition, when humanity appears to be unable to present itself in the phenomenality of objects (whereas its biological parts can be studied separately). In the dialogue between theology and science, correspondingly, the issue is how to balance the experiential sense of the universe as a whole, as an *event-like* saturated phenomenon co-inherent with the event of life (this is a theological part of the dialogue), with that representation of the universe in which it seems to be a system of differently constituted *objects* (this happens in the sciences).

The importance of a theological insight in the constitution of the universe could be dismissed if cosmology would be able to provide some clues to the humanity's position in the physical universe. Unfortunately this does not happen. Not being able to understand "where from" (or "how") humans were brought into existence in this universe (the sufficient conditions of their creation), the fact of the human existence remains fundamentally indeterminate. The planet, the galaxy, the cluster of galaxies, and the entire universe carry with themselves the sense of this created indeterminateness making humanity not being able to adapt to and to be at home in the physical universe. An attempt of balancing between a theological sense of being engulfed by the universe through being created into it on the one hand, and a perception of the insignificant astronomical position in the actually infinite universe, on the other hand, constitutes another dimension of the dialogue between theology and science. In analogy with Jean-Francois Lyotard,[79] the meeting with the world as belonging to it can be described as a return to the condition of infancy, for as infants, humans are helplessly exposed to a strange and overwhelming environment while lacking the ability to articulate what affects them. The universe-as-saturated-phenomenon poses itself in front of the human ego in primacy of its consubstantiality within the Earthly flesh as a constitutive element of the principle of human life.

When the universe is represented in cosmology as unfolding through the cinematographic sequence of events and places, different objects and their classes, the body of humanity as its planet becomes eidetically deprived of its initial egocentric attunement to the universe by being displaced to the periphery of space, time, physical scales, etc. The planet Earth is displaced to a mediocre position and hence not attuned to the universe in terms of its home-place. This condition of non-attunement signifies a gap between sensibility and the possibility of mental articulation or linguistic expressibility in situations when human beings meet saturated phenomena. To wrestle with the saturated phenomenon of the universe is to be in a despair of chasing its escaping presence that constantly reminds the human ego about the unclarified nature of its own created finitude. The ego as being unable to constitute the phenomenon of the universe as a whole experiences itself as being constituted by this phenomenon: this is that modus of the human self-affectivity which deals with the human beings affected by the universe.

By belonging to the universe, the ego does not have (it simply cannot have) any dominant point of view over the universe as a whole. The universe

---

79. Lyotard, *The Inhuman*, 4.

engulfs subjectivity by removing its parts and spatial extension thus saturating ego's intuition with the sense of being hypostatically coinherent with the universe. In a temporal sense, the universe is always already there, so that all events of subjectivity's life unfold from within the donating event of the universe as constant coming into being, in which the unforeseeable nature of every consequent moment entails the unending historicity and unpredictability of existence. In a spatial sense, the contingency as concrete factuality of an event of appearance of this ego's life, or human life in general phenomenologically hidden from humanity's comprehension, makes human life's position in the universe with no place in an absolute metaphysical sense. Its "place" is its sheer facticity, so that any cosmological reduction of the human place in the universe to a particular position in the mathematically constituted space reduces the universe's phenomenality to that of objects (which the sciences deal with). But in the primary experience of existence (which theology deals with) the universe is not "an" object, but a saturated phenomenon coinherent with the fact of living and whose phenomenality can be described in terms of the invisible according to quantity, unbearable according quality, unconditioned according to relation and irreducible to the ego according to modality.[80]

In the natural (scientific) attitude the universe as a whole is posited as existing out there, that is, as being transcendent to the field of consciousness. Thus the universe as a whole, in the natural attitude, is subject to a phenomenological critique: the status of its objective reality is not clarified unless the universe appears as a result of an intellectual constitution.

Then the representation of the universe as being transcendent to the constituting consciousness is achieved through observing *teleologies* of explanation (and hence constitution) that characterize the activity of consciousness. Hence a possible *phenomenological reduction* exercised with respect to the notion of the universe in the natural attitude cannot be applied to the regulative notion of the universe formed through the teleological power of reflecting judgement (in a Kantian sense) and related to the *teleology* of explanation.[81] The universe as a whole emerges here as a regulative notion without any pretense for an accomplished theoretical (ontological) status. Being a regulative notion, the universe as a whole becomes a characteristic of consciousness so that its hypothetical reduction would have to amount to the reduction of consciousness itself, that is, to its effective cessation. Since consciousness exists in the universe, so that the universe is

---

80. Marion, "The Saturated Phenomenon," 211.

81. On teleology of explanation in cosmology, see Nesteruk, *The Sense of the Universe*, ch. 6.

intrinsically present in this consciousness as communion, the universe cannot be cut off from this communion in any other way than only in abstraction. One cannot suspend the reality of the *universe as communion* by using this consciousness because by insisting on this, this consciousness deprives itself of the conditions of its embodied existence and hence destroys itself. The impossibility of the phenomenological reduction of the universe as a whole (that could be potentially performed in order to neutralize the natural attitude to the universe as existing out there), points to a simple fact that the representation of the universe as transcendent to consciousness cannot acquire an ontological quality, remaining "transcendent" but only within its immanence to consciousness. An here phenomenology leads us back to the universe as a saturated phenomenon.

Phenomenology rightly suggests the dismissing of all intellectual idols of the universe (through the suspension of their realistic interpretation) as pretending to exhaust the reality of the universe as communion: any discursive image of the universe remains never accomplished and thus is incomplete. The universe is present in the background of existence through relationship and communion in such a way that allows one to express this presence ecstatically through music, painting, poetry, etc. However, this experience cannot be verbalized and expressed in definitions pertaining to physics and mathematics. In fact, one can say that the very bracketing of the conceptual idols of the universe is possible only because the resulting conceptual absence of the universe is compensated by the reality of its concrete presence, manifested in the very possibility of thinking about the universe. The implicit *presence* of the created universe in all acts of the incarnate human subjectivity cannot be phenomenologically reduced because if this could happen, the incarnate consciousness would be bracketed away and hence eliminated. Obviously this would entail the destruction of the factual consciousness itself, and thus lead to a sheer existential contradiction.

Thus we see with a new force that the dialogue between theology and science in application to cosmology deals with two complementary phenomenalities of the universe which, by the fact of their origin in one and the same human being, have to be in a constant critical attitude to each other, by determining the sphere of their legitimate application with no claims for the priority of one with respect to another and even less with no intention to overcome their difference. The universe as a saturated phenomenon enters the proper givens of theology because of being commensurable with the human life by the fact of their creation by God. Scientific cosmology by dealing with the universe as the constituted world of physical objects enters the dialogue with theology and philosophy through its open-ended hermeneutics of the universe. Ultimately, the dialogue between theology and science in application to cosmology forms an endless intertwining hermeneutics of experience of the universe as communion (and a saturated phenomenon) and an outward constitution of the universe as extended space and time in cosmology. This hermeneutics reflects the working of the phenomenologically dualistic human subjectivity thus inevitably contributing to the hermeneutics of the human condition.

Part 2

THE UNIVERSE IN THE IMAGE OF *IMAGO DEI* OR HUMANITY AS HYPOSTASIS OF THE UNIVERSE

"The same principle of 'modification' that enables Christ's person as 'a mode of being' to be incarnate must be used to unlock the mystery of the universe, too."

—John Zizioulas

"Awareness of one's own existence is for every separate human being the experience of the existential fact of the whole, the cognition of the universal potentialities of being. The world which surrounds us—the innumerable swarms of galaxies or the multitude of photons and electrons which forms the universe, for all that they have pre-existed and will continue to exist regardless of our own ephemeral existence—is the private world of subjective experience, the intimate space of our everyday life. Time which has gone before and time which will follow are the unbounded present of the historical self-consciousness of the human subject."

—Christos Yannaras

"The universe is present to Man as the first revelation he receives, and it is his task to interpret it creatively, to give conscious utterance to the ontological praise of things."

—Olivier Clément

INTRODUCTION

After discussing in the previous sections the anthropological motives in the dialogue between theology and science, the question now arising is what are the limits of knowability of the world in the conditions of the unknowability of humanity and how the thus established knowledge in turn constitutes the human ego? Correspondingly, the dialogue between theology and science reveals itself as a problem of establishing the meaning of the lack in humanity's understanding of the sense of its physical existence (e.g., as its contingent position in space and its cosmic insignificance) and the lack of understanding of its epistemological centrality for knowledge in general. Such a double lack of understanding is detected by human beings, first, through its physical condition, determined by external, ultimately cosmic factors. The universe affects humanity dictating the physical limits of its existence. One can say that the universe affects humanity; that is, the latter experiences the universe's active presence as constituting humanity. On the other hand, human beings experience their existence through being affected by themselves; their flesh affects their feeling and reason, whereas reason and will govern its flesh. One implies human beings's self-affectivity. One can say allegorically that the very fact of existence of a human being (i.e., fixed in consciousness) represents its natural theological predisposition put to the test by the cosmic factors. At the same time, that which is cosmic in man, its flesh or body are constituted within the limits of consciousness pertaining to the Divine Image. The theological and cosmological is intertwined in man, expressing the characteristic cross-affectivity (self-affectivity). The dialogue between theology and science exactly represents this self-affectivity.

Since the very facticity of the dialogue has its origin in the fact of the human existence, the dialogue between theology and science is not de facto a dialogue, but an attempt to elucidate the human dual, paradoxical condition between the pole of its own unknowability and that knowledge of itself which is effected through the sciences. One implies here a different attitude to the sense of life, namely between its inner givenness (self-affectivity) and its perception as a cosmic phenomenon. There is a fundamental philosophical difference between cosmology as being given (as a form of activity and thinking of the world), and its existential possibility as rooted in the human consciousness which exercises its reflection upon cosmology. This asymmetry consists in a fact that although philosophical and theological motives enter implicitly any speculations of the universe, cosmology, as a scientific discipline cannot explicate these motives. Correspondingly the aim of this part of the book is to outline a philosophical analysis of those logical operations in research of the universe from within a hidden existential "obviousness" that is essential to all acts of consciousness. Hence cosmology is explicated by us primarily not as a certain way of interrogating the reality of the world, but of human beings themselves. Thus our enquiry will be in the ways the *constitution* of the universe originates through the anthropological and psychological (also spiritual) aspects of humanity's existence. Our interest will be not in describing of that which the universe *is*, but in investigating of that how, being affected by the universe, humanity creates a cognitive response expressing humanity's self-affectivity and, at the same time, delivering the narrative of the universe.

To achieve this goal, we conduct a brief analysis of cosmology by making the demarcation of that which is proper to humanity and that which is proper to the universe: (1) on the one hand, the universe can be presented in thought and knowledge only as *constituted* within certain transcendental delimiters related to the structures of embodied subjectivity; (2) on the other hand, it is because the physical universe precedes humanity in the sense that the latter cannot control the conditions of its existence as well as its embodiment, that the universe always remains a *transcendent* background of any *transcendental* knowledge. Here the relationship between the transcendent (the universe) and the transcendental (humanity) constitute each other: the universe is a never accomplished mental creation whereas human subjectivity is the self-correcting structural unity originating in the thought (intuition and imagination) of infinity of the universe (its instantaneous synthesis) in the conditions of embodiment. A theological stance in this transcendental synthesis of the universe is that humanity remains free and responsible in its decision to think or not of the universe, because this thinking implies free will and curiosity not because of any physical persuasion. It implies free judgement and choice of theoretical options which are not subordinated either to the rigidity of the structures of subjectivity, or to the material content of the universe (theologically said, the approach to knowledge of the universe as a "transcendent" background and potentially infinite whole, is intrinsically open-ended and inexhaustible in terms of the employed signifiers). A theological stance is the possibility of transcendence in cognitive actions, the transcendence either as longing for the incommensurable content of the universe, or as a resistance to any forms of thought which position humanity as part of the cosmic determinism, denying its dissolution in the substance of the universe. Finally, a theological stance in the transcendental analysis of cosmology, is the commitment to the view that the very facticity of the subject of knowledge, that is, human person, originates in and through communion with the Divine, as the Giver of life and provider of the Image in which the universe is articulated. Correspondingly, as we asserted above, the dialogue between theology and science becomes an outward manifestation of this intrinsic ambivalence pertaining to the transcendental subject, the ambivalence that has already been described in terms of the paradox of subjectivity.

In order to advance our thesis that a constitution of the idea of the universe contributes to the constitution of the structures of subjectivity and hence to the explication of the human personhood, we consider the problem of origin of the universe (its beginning in a general philosophical sense) and its creation out of nothing (*creatio ex nihilo* in a theological sense). We attempt to justify a thesis that the humanly carried explication of the sense of the universe as being created corresponds as such to a sort of "creation" of humanity in the sense of its being self-constituted through the knowledge of the universe. The human condition receives its further articulation (and hence its epistemological formation) through studying the problem of origin of the universe. Correspondingly, one will have to remind to the reader what is meant by creation of the universe in theology and what aspects of creation can scientific cosmology elucidate. Then the sense of what is meant by creation will be related to structuring of the mystery of personhood as its origin. Since the very possibility of such a representation of the universe is based in the Divine Image in humanity, it follows that the image of the universe is possible only in the Divine Image. The articulated image of that universe which physically affects humanity, is the human response to this in the image of that Life (understood as God), whose self-affectivity is expressed through the creation of the universe.

The question of creation of the world naturally comes together from the perennial question "What is man?" when the latter is posed in the natural attitude as a question about humanity's origin. Since, as we have discussed above, no metaphysical response to this question is possible the idea of creation of humanity out of some trans-worldly reality constitutes a natural religious predisposition. Since humanity represents a part of the universe, the intuition of trans-worldly origin of humanity is transferred to that of creation of the world and this is expressed in the biblical narrative in the reversed order: first the world was created, and then humanity (Gen 1–28). Yet the biblical narrative as such in spite of having a revelational character, is a human narrative that predicates about creation of the world as exactly as the latter is given to humanity. This is the reason why this narrative together with all theological teachings of creation out of nothing ultimately amounts to the narrative of creation of humanity. Saying differently, the narrative of Life's self-affectivity as creation ultimately aims to be expressed through the narrative of human life's self-affectivity. In this sense the biblical and theological narrative of creation is implicitly implanted in the humanly produced narrative of origination of the world in the sciences. The terms of the dialogue between theology and science approach the same narrative of creation from two different directions: theology while speaking of creation of the world effectively predicates about the contingent facticity of the world as it appears (through conscious perception) to humanity, whereas the sciences articulate the *necessary* conditions of appearance of the world to humanity ignoring the issue of the sufficient conditions. One can conjecture that the dialogue between theology and science explicates a mutual interaction between life' self-consciousness and the secondary intentionality directed at the conditions of functioning of this self-consciousness in the world. Using the previous terminology, one can express the latter idea differently: the *sufficient* conditions of the appearance of life and human consciousness can never become an object of investigation and this is the reason why they are felt as an original passive phenomenality of life itself, of the very fact of existence, whereas the *necessary* physical conditions of existence are found in intentional acts of consciousness directed outside the subject. This inseparability of the perception of life as existence from its particular modalities in acts of consciousness directed towards the world, the inseparability manifested through the dialogue between theology and science, explicates from the theological point of view the experience of being created in the world as human life's self-affectivity.

THEOLOGICAL THINKING OF THE UNIVERSE AND THE MYSTERY OF THE HUMAN EXISTENCE

Cosmology seen through the primacy of life contributes to understanding and formation of humanity through its position in the universe. Cosmology is seen as a strategy of acquisition of the world, the strategy which manifests the ongoing "humanization" of the universe. Such a humanization must not be understood straightforwardly as "taking the world in our hands" through the ideas of technological progress. The language of humanization would be extremely misleading if one would attempt to apply it to the depths of the unexplored regions of Earth, not to mention some distant stars and galaxies, as well as the entire universe. One rather implies here the capacity of the *Imago Dei* to hypostasize the universe, that is, to create its image in the Image of God. In application to cosmology this means that the latter is not to shape things of the cosmos into a human project. Rather cosmology, as a human enterprise, through a human capacity to hold together the intelligible universe with the visible one, attempts to understand its meaning and to apprehend its connection and unity with the primordial ground in the Logos of God (through whom and by whom all was made) by bringing cosmic things into conscious relationship with God. The humanization as hypostasization implies recognizing in the non-human nature its intrinsic rationality capable of articulating the *logoi* (words) pertaining to all created objects in the universe, the *logoi* which have origin in the Logos-Word through whom all was made, the *logoi* which express the Divine Life's self-affectivity of creating the world.

In this sense such a philosophical and theological introspection upon cosmology is directly related to the philosophical anthropology as well as to the discourse of personhood which is concerned with the perennial question "What is man?" Contemporary physical cosmology attempts to respond to the question of existence, however its forms of thought remain intrinsically unadjusted to this type of interrogation. Saying differently, cosmology is content with what it says about the universe as existent physical things. However, to understand the sense of cosmology, that is, the grounds of its contingent facticity, one needs to establish a new type of "questioning of cosmology." Cosmology is acting in producing its theories, but it does not think in a philosophical style (compare with a famous Heidegger's assertion that science does not think). In this sense our philosophical reflection upon cosmology follows such a type of thinking which is not constrained by the findings of the scientific and thus transcends physical cosmology by bringing it to the next circle of understanding of the essence of being and that of humanity.

The issue is not to think of the essence of cosmology, which would be equivalent to being restricted to its contemporary forms but by realizing that by questioning the sense of cosmology philosophically and theologically, one overcomes cosmology's seeming neutrality with respect to human subject. The sense of cosmological theories as related to the human condition can be grasped only within a critique of the natural attitude which aims to overcome a "natural naïveté," that is, a belief that cosmology only deals with the things of the outer world. Its ultimate objective could be seen as questioning the neutrality of cosmological propositions with respect to specific historically contingent events of knowing. To remove the elements in this contingency would imply the return to those irreducible certainties which would represent the sense of the universe as pertaining to the essence of one's conscious life. It is from within this life that the universe is constituted on the basis of its phenomenality. Life is understood here (in consistency with our previously used meaning of this term) not just as an psycho-physiological life, but as primary self-affectivity from within which the articulated image of the universe emerges as its intentional correlate. Thus "putting out of play" the contingent aspects of the universe brings cosmology to a discourse of the transcendental subject, as that centre of disclosure and manifestation of the universe through which the latter acquires its own "voice." The transcendental subject functions as an embodied creature in the world of physical things and these physical things do exist for this subject only as constituted by it. However, with regard to the universe as a whole the situation is different: its alleged totality cannot be constituted by the subject who is an insignificant physical part of it but, vice versa, the subject itself is being constituted (affected and thus self-affected) by the universe (not in a trivial physical sense).

In order to clarify the latter thought one must remind the reader that cosmology, as a historically concrete science, is capable of making its claims about the structure and evolution of the universe within the conditions that scientific conceptual signifiers never exhaust the content of that which is supposed to be signified. This "positive uncertainty" in science asserts a simple truth that its consciousness deals with a particular, incomplete phenomenality which pertains to objects.[1] With regard to things beyond simple perception which exceed the capacity of constitution in the phenomenality of objects, one can conjecture only in terms of approximations. The fact that we can see and speculate about some aspects of the universe does not entail that there are no other aspects of existence than those which are present and perceived by us, but whose presence cannot be affirmed in terms of consciousness dealing with the phenomenality of objects. This means that the scientific way of thinking of the universe does not cover the fullness of our communion with the universe concealed in the very fact of our existence. This concealment follows, for example, from the fact that humanity is able to interact not only with the physical world but also with the realm of intelligible forms to which cosmology can attest only indirectly. Another example of such a hidden aspect of the universe is its Dark Matter and Dark Energy that constitute 96 percent of the overall matter content of the universe. However, the phenomenality of these theoretical constructs is poor: physics does not know what particular particles and fields stand behind these constructs. Another *philosophical* example of concealment, related to

---

1. *Positive uncertainty* (French: *insertitude positive*) is typical for the sciences dealing with knowledge of objects and can be described as that science operates with some precarious and incomplete data about these objects which are amended and corrected in the course of science's progress. The paradox of science is exactly in that this uncertainty, corrigibility of its results is the condition for science to function at all. Another aspect of science is that it cannot know things in the context of the wholeness of the world. By contrast in philosophy, in what concerns its perennial questions about the world as a whole, there is no visible progress, so that it is able to speculate about the world only in rubrics of what is called by Jean-Luc Marion *negative certainties* (French: *certitudes négatives*) (see Marion, *Negative Certainties*).

the universe as a whole can be taken as its own contingent facticity (whose sense cannot be disclosed at all). Indeed, the notion of the universe as a whole allows one only to have some precarious and incomplete definitions related to its spatial, temporal, historically observable finitude. However this "positive uncertainty" of cosmology does not entail that one must disdain cosmology as irrelevant to any perennial questions. It just implies that the cosmological research has to proceed along the lines of the scientific method with a clear understanding that the universe as a whole will never be constituted. Then the persistence of cosmology exhibits the courage and heroism of scientists in following their quest for the universe despite of no hope to make the universe as a whole an "object" of science. The same takes place in theology when believers explicate their experience of God as an open-ended process in a clear consciousness that the true names of the Divine are beyond this age and any denominations. Correspondingly, in cosmology the persistence of research as a purposive activity is pointing towards its *telos* (a goal to create of the complete picture of the universe) beyond this age and any denomination. Here is a fundamental paradox of cosmology, as well as any other science, namely, that its uncertainty is that condition of its progress consisting in the unceasing correction and amendment of its results and theories. However, in spite of the fact that a human person cannot constitute the universe, this person remains the centre of disclosure and manifestation of the universe, resisting any attempt to be diminished by the grandeur of this universe. This "negative certainty" in relation to knowledge of the universe (as impossibility of its constitution), turns out to be an element of the constructive certainty in constituting an extent of unknowability of the human subject.

By interacting with the actual infinity of the universe the human person is constituted by the universe that always remains an "object" of humanity's constant interest and anxiety of this humanity. This means that the transcendental subject which appropriates the universe is formed and changed while enquiring in the sense of the universe subject to the crucial condition that the cosmological picture does not diminish the epistemological centrality of humanity in the universe. The more physical cosmology proves that human beings are no more than specks of dust in the universe, the more human persons resist this because of their self-affectivity by defending the sense of their existence as related to communion with their creator. It is through this resistance as a particular modus of life's self-affectivity that the human ego is constituted by the universe. Such a universe, in symbolic words of a seventh century Saint Maximus the Confessor, called "makro-anthropos," that is, that which was created in order to be "humanised" (enhypostasized).

To understand the sense of cosmology within the primary existential givenness means thus not only to "understand" what it means to think *of* the universe, but to be in communion *with* the universe in the conditions which would not be explicated by scientific knowledge. To think of the universe on the grounds of existential communion entails freedom of such thinking. It does not imply the overthrowing of scientific authority in the questions of physical cosmology: it implies that cosmological theories and hypotheses can be interpreted not as propositions about outer realities but as movements of the human reason and judgement that reflect a fundamental anxiety of existence (as a modus of life's self-affectivity). In this case the universe is perceived as a certain *whole* which includes not only the physically fragmented or united cosmos, but the infinity of human life (the infinity of relations of human beings to created existents) in the universe. Correspondingly all accumulated forms of knowledge of the universe, established in history to this very date, are merely pieces and moments, temporary and provisional sketches of the immensely mysterious phenomenon of personal existence.[2] The "non-technlogical" thinking of the universe, even if it will not be able to reproduce this "whole of the universe" (that was, however, attempted in works of art and poetry) and hence will remain no more than a symbol rather than reality, can receive its justification in a hope, that through this thinking we learn something of ourselves. Being an intentional thinking, the thinking of the universe as a whole brings one beyond any conditional objectification and positivity which could fulfil this thinking. In a way, thinking of the universe is transcending the limits of thought at all and this requires from the enquirers exceptional courage and humility in front of the fact that the task will never be fulfilled and that they are ready to learn of themselves something which could shatter the image of their own ego.[3]

By thinking of the universe as a whole, we attempt to explicate our intrinsically ambivalent existential situation, being a part of the universe, in its particular time and space, and at the same time being at "that" paradoxically central "nowhere" from which the wholeness of the universe is unfolded.[4] The universe as described by specific cosmological theories is

---

2. As was expressed by Milton Munitz, "the pursuit of cosmological enquiry, insofar as it is taken to be concerned with 'the universe as a whole,' is never completed, since the same goal stated in these general terms will always be appropriate, no matter how far enquiry has continued or how much 'large' the scope of observation or understanding will have been reached" (Munitz, *The Question of Reality*, 189).

3. Cf. Primack and Abrams, *The View from the Centre*, 282; Ladrière, *Language and Belief*, 150.

4. Some cosmologists can object to this by saying that in terms of time we are living

not contingent from the point of view of these models. However, from the point of view of the very possibility of such a description, that is, from the point of view of the contingent facticity of life of knowing persons, it is still contingent. The pole of "nowhere" remains intact simply because cosmology deals with the *necessary* conditions of existence of embodied human beings and hence is not able to shed the light on the nature of the *sufficient* conditions of existence of intelligent observers of the universe. It is this pole of "nowhere" in thinking of the universe that deprives this thinking of any essential historical goal if it is not related to the saving ideals of Christianity. Being engaged in thinking of the universe as a whole we are immersed not so much into the present of the scientific discourse of the universe but into the present of thinking itself. And this present is dictated not only by the advance of contemporary physical theories of the universe but to a great extent by the advance of thinking *per se*, that is, its free philosophical modus which is not subjected to the logic of the already known but forms that which Husserl called humanity's "infinite tasks."[5] By rephrasing Karl Jaspers, our historical consciousness of the universe, in spite of being a temporal phenomenon, is a "free-flying" consciousness without "any ground and original point accessible to knowledge, ultimately rooted in that source which is always and necessarily present in ourselves"[6], that is, in life's self-affectivity. This type of thinking, flying away from mundane realities and technological delimiters, will reveal deeper and clearer the fact of our, as Heidegger termed it, "planetary homelessness" (but still centrality) which pertains to the present intellectual, social and political uncertainty of the human condition. One can perhaps amplify this point by using the term "cosmic homelessness" implying the lack of understanding of the human place in the universe. We are homeless because the universe is actually infinite, and in spite of some claims of our epistemological centrality in the universe, we still do not understand our place in it, that is we do not know scientifically the grounds of our facticity in it.[7] What we know for sure, however, is that it is us who articulate (enhypostasize) the universe, so that, perhaps we are in the "centre" of the universe, but the question of "where" this very centre is, remains in the field of perennial *negative certainties*, that is, unanswerable.

---

in a very special era in the universe, that it is only now that it is possible to detect the universe's evolution, its origin in the Big Bang, etc. See Krauss, *A Universe from Nothing*, 118–19.

   5. Husserl, *The Crisis*, 279.

   6. Jaspers, *Weltgeschichte der Philosophie*, 77.

   7. In spite of an enormous literature on astrobiology and evolution of life claiming that the universe was from the beginning pregnant with life. See De Duve, *Vital Dust*.

It is not difficult to see that thinking of the universe as if we think of the thinking itself allows one to establish certain liturgical connotations as articulations of the overall temporal span of the universe, its past, present and future, as conscious acts which fight oblivion pertaining to the flux of time. When articulated, the universe is being remembered not only as its realized past. The question of active remembrance of the universe, is the question of such an understanding of human life in which past, present and future are considered as integrated in the Divine Image of humanity living in a tension between a thanksgiving for its actual existence and a hope for its non-transient sense. To study the universe does not mean to establish a simple vision of the world on the grounds of curiosity or personal needs. Such a study rather implies a vision of that "selfhood" of the universe which brings to unconcealment the truth of the human existence. Speaking of the "self" of the universe, we do not presume that it does have hypostatic features but, allegorically speaking, humanity by looking at the "face" of the universe, sees this "face" as looking at itself, and it is this self-penetrating "glance" of the "makro-anthropos" that forms the image of humanity as its ability to see the infinite in the finite. In a certain sense human beings, as they are sustained by this last mentioned glance, want to respond to it thus asserting not only their longing for the commensurability with the universe, but also their lordship over the universe resisting their cosmographic insignificance.

Theological commitment in cosmology reveals itself as a concern with the *sufficient* conditions of the human existence in the universe, implying that life is a gift of relationship and communion with the eternal Creator. The sense of the universe then is unfolded from within this communion so that it cannot be separated from experience of God in communion. It follows from here that all human thoughts and articulations of the universe always contain in themselves the traces of its Divine Image. Even when cosmology proves the insignificance of humanity in the universe, the divine image remains exactly in that the human mind resists all attempts to circumscribe its life in rubrics of the natural, finite and transient. Human beings aspire to understand the underlying sense of beings and things not according to their "nature" (unfolded in the sciences) but according to the final causes of these beings and things in relation to the place and goals of humanity in creation (their *logoi*). This understanding cannot be explicated only through physics and biology. It is based in views on humanity as the crown of creation who in a God-like fashion wants to recognize all beings not according to their nature, that is, according to their compelling givenness, but as results of humanity's *self-affective will*.[8] This is the reason why the image of eternity is

---

8. Cf. Maximus the Confessor, *Ambigua 7*, in Blowers and Wilken, *On the Cosmic*

retained in any cosmological theory even if this theory predicts finite existence of all actual and possible forms of life.

COSMOLOGY AS EXPLICATION OF THE HUMAN

When scientific reason attempts to enquire into the origin of the universe in an absolute sense the strategy of extrapolation acquires some features of *philosophical* transcendence through intentions based in acts of indemonstrable beliefs. Transcendence is encoded here in the excess of intuition of the donation of the universe in the event of life, an excess over the discursive ability to grasp the sense of the universe that points that the reality of the human existence is not exhausted by its physical aspects. Correspondingly, cosmology, if it is narrowed to the physical and expressed mathematically, cannot account for the ultimate sense of the universe because it cannot account for the ultimate sense of the human. Since no science can give such an account, the question here is rather about the boundaries of the human in science itself.

In general, a phenomenological insight into the sense of cosmology as explicating humanity's quest for itself compensates the incompleteness of cosmology and reinstates its human creator to its theologically understood anthropological centeredness in disclosing and manifesting the universe.[9] At the same time the limits of physics and scientific philosophy tested through cosmology, test the limits of humanity in understanding the sense of its own existence. The incomprehensible universe invokes in the human scientific mind humility and discernment in order to realize the limits of its pretensions for knowledge of the universe, that universe which being created by the incomprehensible God resists disclosure and exceeds the capacity of understanding. By being great and above the universe, yet humanity realizes its own smallness. By being small in the image of God humanity yet realizes its grandeur.

Since cosmology, assessed phenomenologically, retrieves the "natural" centring of all non-egocentric tendencies of its world-building narrative in human hypostatic subjectivity, this assessment indirectly calls into question

Mystery, 61–62.

9. The idea that a research into the underlying sense of science leads to enlightenment of the ways and *telos* of the human spirit was formulated by many phenomenological philosophers starting from Husserl. Here is a quote from Jean Ladrière: "The detail of the life of science must . . . be investigated in order to know something of the nature of reason and of its becoming. . . . The destiny of reason is outlined . . . in the incessant comings and goings that define the life of science. It is in the patient advance of its history that its finality reveals itself" (Ladrière, "Mathematics in a Philosophy," 455).

the purported neutrality and objectivity of some of its claims with respect to those realities which are beyond empirical verification (the very early universe, for example). It could suggest instead that such "neutral" descriptions of the world operate on the basis of existential concerns formulated in a set of *beliefs* (or myths which may or may not be related to the *faith* of theology). In this sense the phenomenological stance rejects that view that cosmological knowledge describes the world in itself; rather these descriptions are seen as interpretations related to a particular *path* of science in human history. This reasserts our transcendental approach to cosmology as the working of constitution, that is, a re-enactment of the production of the world. To clarify this point one can quote Jean Ladrière, who emphatically asserts that "the theoretical apparatus is thus not a description in the ordinary sense, as presentation of an entity, supposedly given, and of its properties, it is the characterisation of something which is not a thing, but a *structural path along which a thing comes, from the ultimate horizon of every givenness, to the actual presence in which it is effectively given to apprehension.*"[10] For example, if one is to understand and explain the past of the universe as constituted through human history, one must conceive it in terms of past possibilities of *this history* rather than as a defined and finished product. In this case the cosmologist's own historical consciousness is involved, and in analogy with historical science, cosmological discourse reveals itself as a form of consciousness which humanity (as community) has of itself. By revealing the *telos* in the historical path of cosmological explanation (as related to the representation of the ultimate origin of the universe),[11] phenomenological analysis establishes that the representation of the beginning and the end of the universe in human thought, is just a mode of this same thought speaking of its own beginning and its own consummation, and thus implying a sort of a transcendent reference.

In spite of delimiters regarding objectivity and neutrality, scientific cosmology remains a useful instrument in demonstrating that while depicting the universe as something devoid of our influence and presence, yet it represents the product of articulation through words and thoughts by humanity. By creating a cosmological narrative, humanity affirms itself in a non-trivial sense: "By learning the ways of the universe and by reflecting upon them as they surface in the daily life of family and work and community, we take the first steps into a new form of human understanding and

---

10. Ladrière, "Physical Reality," 138; emphasis added.

11. See Nesteruk, *The Universe as Communion*, 250–54; Nesteruk, *The Sense of the Universe*, 334–43.

existence."[12] Cosmology allows one to know "where" one stands and makes sense of its own identity in relation to the world. Correspondingly a possible lack of a cosmological sense deprives human beings and communities of their understanding of their place in nature. According to Freya Mathews, "A culture deprived of any symbolic representation of the universe and of its own relation to it will be a culture of nonplussed, unmotivated individuals, set down inescapably in a world which makes no sense to them, and which accordingly baffles their agency. . . . With no cosmological foundation for their identity, they invent precarious individual self-pictures, self-stories, ego-images, but their sense of who they are is tenuous."[13] Indeed, in spite of the fact that by creating a physico-mathematical narrative cosmologists loose control over the intentions that motivate them (since any philosophical reflection upon what they have created is not in the focus of their enquiry), the *givens* lying behind this narrative manifest themselves as expressive acts pointing from their *given meaning* to their *giving meaning*, from their pure phenomenality to life which generated them. As was expressed by Milton Munitz: "The goals of cosmology are goals of human beings. . . . Through the measure in which they are reached, the universe becomes understood, perhaps for the first time anywhere throughout its vast stretches in space and time."[14] Hence human beings become also further understood. Paul Brockelman asserts a similar thing: "The cosmological story reveals a wider reality to which we belong . . . and against which . . . we can see the siginificance and purpose of our lives. . . . We now can see the joys and pains of all life in the light of this cosmic story, and we can connect our own sometimes disjointed lives to the divine reality that seems to shine through it from its beginnings some fifteen billion years ago until right now."[15]

By reflecting the goals of humanity, cosmology exhibits the traditional features of all mythologies, namely that the perceptible aspects of the universe are expressed in terms of human social, behaviorist and existential concerns. In this sense the picturing of the universe as a historical process cannot avoid containing erratic facts associated with the human condition, to be more precise with the intimacy of personal communion with the universe and the extent of not being attuned to it (positioned nowhere). Any imaginable attempt to disregard these facts and assess cosmology only on the basis of law-like ordered concepts would be incomplete and historically inadequate: in this case cosmology would provide us only with

---

12. Swimme, *The Hidden Heart of Cosmos*, 7.
13. Mathews, *The Ecological Self*, 5.
14. Munitz, "Kantian Dialectic," 338.
15. Brockelman, *Cosmology and Creation*, 145.

the universe's deficient phenomenality. The other "part" of the universe's phenomenality which reflects the erratic fact that humanity is not being attuned to the universe is rather reflected in poetic and artistic depictions relying on ecstatic acts of personal being in the universe as communion. The so called mythological aspect of any cosmology thus naturally arises from the intention to interpret erratic features of the human universe through a reference to the astronomical order. In Greek cosmology, for example, the world as the Cosmos was a part of the internal world of a human being and the details of its wholeness, of its beginning and end, in many ways served to social and political interests of the Greek society, thus reproducing a known from ethnology thought that cosmology was motivated by and reflected the social organization.[16] This confirms a thesis that the vision of the universe was anthropological in its essence being dictated by those peculiarities of the human condition which pertained to particular historical forms.

However, modern scientific cosmology is not a new mythology resembling cosmic ideologies of the ancient past where humanity aspired to be dissolved in cosmic immensities, that is, ideologies which were dismissed by the early church Fathers as pagan and gnostic.[17] Cosmology is not a sheer imagination, but has its own logic and drive, which reflects the sense and value (as well as *telos*) of *communion* with the universe conditioned by necessities of nature and, at the same time, pertaining to human freedom. This communion is not a dissolution in the cosmos but rather is a state of transcending over the natural causes that are beyond human control and, at the same time, the immanence to the universe through a sheer fact of the human presence through which the universe is brought to self-articulation.

Yet, finite human beings, because of their paradoxical standing in the universe are not content with the presence of things in the universe as they are given in their empirically contingent facticity. The cosmos creates in us

16. The context of appearance of Plato's *Timaeus* is political in its essence and had a relation to the question of how a style of life in Athens can be reformed. To justify that this ideal is achievable on Earth and to ground such a project in some external reality one must understand the origin of humanity and origin of the world, to explain how human beings understand their own place in the universe treated as the visible image of the ideal archetype of the universe in the world of intelligible forms. See Brisson and Meyerstein, *Inventing the Universe*, 18.

17. Cosmic ideologies, or the so-called *cosmism*, is a philosophical and spiritual longing for fusion with cosmic entities. Cosmism means not only the affirmation of our commonalities with nature and our contingence upon its laws and accidents but also a much more sophisticated kind of spirituality, which longs for fusion with "cosmic life" and its mystery and which is ecstatic in its essence. Nicolas Berdyaev called this spiritual tendency "the lure of the cosmos" and described it as man's slavery to cosmos (and nature in general), as opposed to the freedom of hypostatic existence in the divine image (Berdyaev, *Slavery and Freedom*, 93–102).

the interest to know the universe in terms of the infinite survival of humankind and unlimited development of human consciousness.[18] Cosmologists, by invoking the idea of the universe as a whole, intend to understand the meaning of finite things (astronomically observed objects or earthly phenomena) not only through that which is subjected to physical causation, but through the purposes and ends of these things as they stand with respect to humanity itself. But this intentionality is sustained by humanity's aspirations not only to be commensurable to the universe but, in fact to be above it, to transcend it and thus to encompass it through the power of intellect. It is because of its paradoxical position in being that causes existential discomfort that humanity appeals to the idea of the universe as a whole as an alternative to being contained by finite natures. Existentially humanity does not want to be manipulated through circumscribability and individualization that are inherent in spatio-temporal forms of the finite cosmos and correspondingly long for the truth of their existence *in* the space-time rubrics of this universe as if it is not *of* the universe as it appears to us. Here humanity wants to recognize things not through their causal connectivity, but as results of its self-affective "intentionality."

This "intentionality" invokes a different stance on the ontological commitment exercised by those who usually claim, that whatever is theoretically and mathematically possible is physically real and true, although non-observable and untestable. Indeed, if some cosmological hypotheses about the early universe are not testable, that is, the correspondence principle between theory and empirical reality as epistemic justification does not work, there is a way of interpreting cosmological propositions about the non-observable and invisible by assigning to the universe the sense of a mental accomplishment but achieved through the idea of *coherence*, where "coherence" stands not only for the clarity of theoretical explication and cohesion of mathematical calculations, but for the "collaborative agreement" among cosmologists who effectively *hypostasize the notion of truth* related to the universe and postulate the ways of epistemic justification which lead to it.[19] In this case the implied truth of cosmology cannot be an ontological truth (truth as existing in itself) but is a human-dependent hypostatic constitution of truth possessing the qualities related to the corporeity of human beings. In this interpretation many cosmological constructions appear as historically contingent but coherent mental accomplishments (based in beliefs) whose truth contributes towards the spiritual goals (*telos*) of

---

18. Cf. Moltmann, *Science and Wisdom*, 72.

19. The application of the idea of coherence of epistemic justification in cosmology see Nesteruk, *The Sense of the Universe*, 255–304.

community but obviously does not exhaust them. However, the question of whether the locally established truths are subject to convergence to ultimate truth remains beyond scientific scope and represents in turn a trans-scientific conviction. In this option the validity of cosmology's claims is dictated not by a direct reference to reality but through the adoption of a consistent set of beliefs that constitute the sense of reality. Here one can see an analogy with theology: the latter forms its sense of truth not through empirical references to the Divine, but through experience of God as elaborated and established through liturgical and ecclesial agreement.

Knowledge of the universe interpreted as a collaborative construction cannot be treated as independent of the human insight, so that cosmology's alleged status of following the standards of a natural science (as that in which the "object" of study can be detached from the subject) is not achievable. Cosmology, in contradistinction with astronomy and astrophysics deals with a single, unique totality of all that not only cannot be treated as an object and hence subjected to experimentation,[20] but also cannot be made devoid of the delimiters of the human insight. This implies that human beings, as part of the universe, cannot position the universe as a whole in front of their consciousness, unless as a mental abstraction.[21] If such a mentally constructed universe nevertheless were to be identified with the physical totality, this would imply an impossible transcendence of the actual physical universe as if one were able to "look at it" from the outside (hence transcending one's embodied existence). The inseparability of humanity and the universe entails that all speculations about other worlds remain intrinsically immanent being noematic correlates of embodied subjectivity as irreducible elements of existence of this universe. Thus the universe as an intentional correlate of cosmological consciousness represents a mental accomplishment and cultural achievement,[22] so that cosmology becomes

---

20. George Ellis formulates the essential characteristic of that subject matter which pertains to cosmology proper: "If we convince ourselves that some large scale physical phenomenon essentially occurs only once in the entire universe, then it should be regarded as part of cosmology proper; whereas if we are convinced it occurs in many places or times, even if we cannot observationally access them . . . then study of that class of objects or events can be distinguished from cosmology proper precisely because there is a class of them to study" (Ellis, "Issues in the Philosophy of Cosmology," 1219).

21. This would correspond to a Platonic treatment of the construct of the universe. In this case, cosmology faces a problem of justifying the interaction between the universe as an intelligible entity and its empirical appearance to embodied consciousness. See Tieszen, *Phenomenology*, 46–68.

22. Cf. Gurwitsch, *Phenomenology*, 44–45. See also Husserl, *The Crisis*, 227, on the "nature" as a correlate of a universal abstraction.

exhibiting features of the human sciences thus implicitly demonstrating that cosmology is constitutive for the sense of humanity.[23]

Even if the notion of the universe acquires some features of a collaborative agreement thus containing in itself explicitly human features, this notion completely ignores the personal dimension of the human existence, that is, events of personhood inaugurating all human activities and collaborative constructions of reality. Persons are present in the collaborative agreements, but they become dissolved in the collective anonymity and thus unobservable. Personhood is dimmed from cosmology because it could approach human beings in the same way as it approaches other things in the phenomenality of objects. But personhood as existential events escape scientific grasp by transcending either materialistic definitions or idealistic construction of objects. Personhood remains in the background of all scientific quests as that *givenness* which cannot be subjected to any constraints of matter or categories of the understanding, that is, as the primordial, logically incomprehensible, saturated phenomenon. Correspondingly persons do not disappear but their phenomenality is radically different from that of the universe and they reveal themselves in a distinctively human way. Since humanity is not content with the presence of beings in the world as they are given to it empirically and studied scientifically, it subjugates that truth which is gained on the grounds of the scientific to the desire for truth of the whole created existence. Here humanity exhibits its hypostatic essence, that is, its personhood. Humanity as personhood prefers to express its own presence by appealing to the belief in the trans-worldly source of its existence in the conditions of its incapacity to overcome the effective absence of personhood in scientific articulations of the world. To explicate this kind of phenomenality of personhood one presupposes a phenomenological reversal in order to recover back those intentionalities of human subjectivity which led to the development of the world-view in terms of efficient physical causality. Cosmology has to be looked at not from the point of view of its theoretical content and its reference to the physical world, not for a purpose of enquiring into the meaning of concepts such as, for example, the universe as a whole, its origin, etc., but, in fact, to use cosmology as a hermeneutical tool for understanding humanity itself, to use the human image of the universe as a kind of mirror looking through which human personal subjectivity constitutes itself. It is through this shift in attitude that the sense of cosmology can be reversed in such a way that the absence of personhood

---

23. See more details on the element of the human sciences in cosmology in Nesteruk, *The Sense of the Universe*, 184–97.

in the mathematized universe could be brought to its explicit philosophical presence in the original acts of constitution.

The phenomenological reversal of a construct of the universe as a whole reveals this construct as a certain stable structure (the idea of reason) of the incarnate transcendental subjectivity. If in the natural attitude science affirms the explicit presence of the universe at the expense of the absence of personhood, in the philosophical attitude the universe as an intentional correlate of human subjectivity does not possess qualities of "out there" measured in terms of distance. It is not the "other" as object here or there, above or below, right of left, near or far. The universe is posed as existent in the human hypostasis, but its entirety is not available to any empirical acquisition. This result is not surprising for as human personhood escapes complete definitions the universe also escapes complete definitions thus acquiring a mode of personal "opposite" of dynamic ecstatic reference. When one articulates the universe in terms of measurements of distance one loses personhood; when one brings the universe to being as a personal "opposite" of ecstatic reference one loses the sense of the universe as extended space and time. The universe can then be understood as a kind of otherness of personhood present in the event of person's self-affective manifestation.

However, this otherness is ontologically achieved only through events of living of real human persons. It is these real persons, and not abstract disincarnate and anonymous subjects, who enhypostasize the universe. The arrival of novelty about the universe happens in personal events of life, so that knowledge is growing because of the real living persons (in spite of the fact that the existential differences between them are neutralized in the collective scientific knowledge). Personhood, as events of hypostatic existence, in spite of the fact that they lie in the foundation of the sciences, are not accounted by the latter because the body of the present scientific knowledge is effectively independent from its history. Since history of scientific knowledge is not this knowledge as such, personhood is left behind in the hidden concrete history of the sciences that, unlike the physical processes, is not subjected to the worldly causality and represents rather a history of the human intentionality. But the latter history is the history of unique and unforeseeable events whose happening depends entirely on that uniqueness of humans lives placed in a specific age, place, social structure and culture. One then does not wonder why religious and theological meanings are implicitly present in science: it is just enough to remember that the seeds of modern science can be found in religiously motivated enquiries and religiously blessed educational as well as scientific establishments.[24] It is this

---

24. The literature on the history of interaction between university education and

history which constantly captures and transfigures every human person. The human ego is affected by this history and at the same time contributes to it through its own meaning and values. One can say that history as a horizon of the visible becomes an absolute milieu of phenomenalization out of which humans are born and which is the fruit of their living activity.[25] If this historical context of the sciences is dimmed, personhood of those who advanced research is also shaded in the resulting cumulative world outlook. What follows from here is that there is no reason to demand the explicit presence of personhood in the scientific picture of the universe. One certainly detects the presence of the human rationality and its foundation in the embodied human subjectivity, but this happens, so to speak on an average level, when the rationality becomes a kind of a shared extraction form personhood. Saying differently, the personal experience of living is assumed as already present behind any conscious acts explicated through the sciences, but it is not articulated as distinctively different and unique, pertaining to every living human, but presented as being averaged on the level of its outcome, that is, as the anonymous and collective rationality of the whole human species.

Yet humanity is unable to know itself. And it is this unknowability that makes all human persons similar to each other in their specific and concrete experience of discomfort and anxiety of existence. Correspondingly if the philosophical reflection upon cosmology aims to rediscover the human subject present behind its theories, the question is not only about the delimiters of knowledge of the universe as following from the human bodily constitution, but about the discovery of those particular delimiters of the transcendental subjectivity which manifest themselves *only* in human persons. Personhood implies unique existence whose contingent presence in the world remains metaphysically inexplicable. Yet persons are in the world as embodied creatures whose physical contingency amounts to their existence at different historical eras, different places on Earth, in different racial and genetically determined conditions. However, the experience of the universe as ecstatic standing before it has in every person its specific worldly marker. And it is in terms of these markers that all human persons are distinct and unique.

---

ecclesial authorities either in the Christian East or in the West is vast. The remarkable historical fact is that the first universities in Western Europe had been established under the direct blessing of the Roman Catholic Church in view of its sincere conviction that the study of nature and education will contribute to the development of theology and strengthening Christian faith. Lindberg, *The Beginnings of Western Science*.

25. Cf. Merleau-Ponty, *The Prose of the World*, 86.

If one now remembers about the radical metaphysical inexplicability of personhood (whose phenomenality is weak), one grasps that any attempt to "extract" personhood from the scientific representation of humanity in the universe is futile. What then happens is that this unknowability of every particular human being for itself is "averaged" on the level of the whole human race through an idea of the unknowable origin (the lack of phenomenality) of all humanity: the phenomenological concealment of every particular birth is eidetically extrapolated to the phenomenological concealment of the origin of humanity's self-affective consciousness in general. If humanity is considered as part of the universe then man's inability to know itself cascades down towards the unknowability (to the lack of phenomenality) of the world's origin.[26] Correspondingly, if along the objectives of this research, one attempts to explicate the presence of the human subjectivity behind all cosmological theories, one has to deal first of all with the issue of the origin of the universe as it is structured by the human subjectivity initiating its enquiry in the sense of its own origins. It is here that the hidden personhood of the enquiring intellect will be explicated as dealing not only with the origin of the allegedly external world but, first of all, with the origin of itself. Said differently, the access to these concealed non-originary original "phenomena" (saturated phenomena) which endow all humans with the future and which affect them in all possible ways, can be established indirectly through the hermeneutics of creation of the world that can be seen in turn as a hermeneutics of appearance of every particular human life. In spite of the fact that problem of origin of hypostatic persons, being shifted to the problem of the common origin of life in the universe and the universe as such, there remains one particular feature related to the origin of the universe that makes this shift epistemologically justifiable, namely the radical uniqueness of the universe, that is, its single occurrence as contingent creation out of nothing (we intentionally disregard any possibility of the multiverse proposals not changing radically the contingent character of the created universe crucial in our arguments). It is the uniqueness of the universe in the Ipseity of its Creator (the Logos) that makes possible an analogy with the creation of every unique person in the Ipseity of the incarnate Logos (Christ). The challenge then is to establish such a hermeneutics of creation in theology, philosophy and cosmology that could lead to a new phenomenality of the human origins. Yet in order for such a phenomenality to be possible, there must already be in place a medium

26. Max Planck expressed a similar thought: "Science cannot solve the ultimate mystery of nature. And this is because, in the last analysis, we ourselves are part of nature and therefore part of the mystery that we are trying to solve" (Planck, *Where Is Science Going?*, 217)

of phenomenalization, that is, the medium of the self-affective subjectivity as that immemorial past out of which this particular vulnerable and traumatised subject catastrophically emerges.[27] A narrative of creation becomes the narrative of the outward manifestation of self-affective life by confirming a major intuition formulated in the title of this book, namely that the universe is indeed accessible to humanity only through its *Imago Dei* and that it is humanity that, by the fact of its presence in the universe, forms its hypostasis.

THE HUMAN CONDITION AND CHRISTIAN FAITH IN CREATION: A PHILOSOPHICAL EXPLICATION

We have already discussed at length the predicaments of humans in understanding of their place in the world, using such words as anxiety, non-attunement, insecurity and homelessness, in order to accentuate its inability to control its existence and hence its fundamental unknowability. And it is this "understanding" that is included in the Christian faith in creation, so that without it no faith in creation is possible. This implies that the understanding of creation of the world out of nothing in generic theological terms is inherent in the context of the existential manifestation of creation in humanity. The fact of being created is sometimes hardy perceived by human beings retaining in them the sense of that which always escapes their capacity of gazing at and its further articulation. Saying philosophically, there is an excess of intuition of being created which is reflected in humanity's perception of the created world as that which affects it and which ultimately makes humanity self-affective. By using a different language, the world by being brought to its self-representation in the hypostasis of humanity retains in its representation some "invisible" presence of the fact that this created world itself, is enhypostasized by the same Logos who enhypostasized humanity. The fact that human beings are ehhypostasized hypostases leaves them with a constant presence of an excess in intuition of the universe, when any certain knowledge of the sense of existence is blocked because of this excess, yet acting itself as a constitutive element in formation of the human cognitive capacities. How to formalise all these thoughts in philosophical terms?

First of all, all narratives of creation require a narrator, a human being who is capable of thinking and speaking of the other-worldly foundation of the world. Then all attempts to describe creation in thought and words encounter a fundamental difficulty because one cannot exit the conditions of being created. Correspondingly a "description" of creation can be done

---

27. Cf. Bernet, *Conscience et existence*, 279–89 .

only in abstraction, when the very act of creation, as well as that which is created, are approached in the phenomenality of *objects* so that creation is constituted as an "object" thus depriving it of a phenomenal autonomy and spontaneity which it manifests from itself. The condition of objects is exactly a deprivation of the event-like manifestation of creation and its reduction to the rubrics of "I think." Correspondingly if one attempts to describe the whole created world or its "origin" one faces an imminent difficulty because creation and the universe as a whole cannot be thought in rubrics of quantity, quality, relation and modality, so that the natural attitude with respect to the universe as a whole is impossible. In the same vein it is impossible to represent creation of the universe out of nothing as a causal transition from one "thing" to "another," for "nothing" cannot be a term in the logic of causation. The natural attitude is not suitable for the description of the relationship between God and the world, as well, as between the whole creation and humanity, so that the elucidation of these relationships can be done only on the grounds of questioning the relevance of the natural attitude as such.

Indeed, when talking of creation, that one who is talking, implies its own creation and the limits of comprehension of creation of the world following from its own being created. To represent creation posed as "an object" in front of the articulating consciousness, one needs to exit mentally one's own existence in order to "look" at one's own coming into being (as well as coming into being of the world) from "outside," as if there were some antecedents to it. However this is philosophically untenable, because it contradicts the facticity of the given life as that originary *fact* and *event*, from within whose horizon the whole world order is unfolded, and whose non-originary origin cannot be linguistically and mentally located. Then the question of creation of the world becomes more specific: one speaks not about creation of the world in general, but about creation of *this world as its factual givenness to humanity*. Thus what is important is not a "dynamic" of the creation as its hermeneutics (be it biblical or scientific), but understanding of creation as bringing humanity into this world, placing it face to face with this world, so that humanity could see God, their own creator, as present in the world. The issue of creation is thus not just the question of creation of human beings in their consubstantial similarity with this world, but creation in the Divine Image (reason and rationality), capable of knowing God.

The archetype of this image is Christ so that the Incarnation enters as an inevitable component of creation. Indeed, it is known that St. Athanasius the Great noted that in spite of the fact that the Father provided the works of creation as means by which its Maker might be known,[28] it did not prevent men from wallowing in error.[29] It is because of this that the descent of the Word of God to men initiated by the Holy Spirit "renewed the same teaching."[30] Correspondingly the theology of creation is a statement of the life into which humanity has been introduced by the Holy Spirit in the image of the eternally conceived Incarnation of the Word of God.[31] One observes here a Christo-geocentric reduction of the problem of creation because the Incarnation, as an element of the Divine economy, implies the existence of the universe where humanity is possible, and hence the coming of the Son of God in human flesh would be possible. Since "the Divine image of the world always remains above and beyond creation by nature"[32] what is implied here is the retaining of the image of the world in the archetype of Christ *through grace*, that is, without compromising ontological boundaries between God and creation. In different words, the Divine image of the world can be linked to its enhypostatic identity. However, since there remains a transcendent gulf between that Who enhypostasizes and that which is enhypostasized, all human conjectures about the identity of the universe do not exhaust the image of the world as it is present in the Divine hypostasis. We are capable of "seeing" the image of the world, its identity only, "as puzzling reflections in a mirror" (1 Cor 13:12).

Being created by the Logos and through the Logos, this world manifests the spatial paradox of the Logos-Christ: his presence *in* space but not *of* space, his historical presence on Earth and his omnipresence in the universe. The createdness of the world, being the otherness of God rooted in his love, means a global, spatial and temporal, "correlation" (theogenic uniformity) and mutual correspondence between all places in the created universe simply because this world is a "moment" and "event" of the Divine love. Createdness of the world must in this case not only point towards some unique antecedent moment in the history of the universe when "all was in all" and from which all came to be. It must point towards the actual omni-presence of the human insight, created in the image of Christ himself, its presence in all corners of the universe extended in space and time. This would signify to retain the transcendent in the immanent creation, that transcendence which overcomes the physical representation of the universe

---

28. Athanasius, *On the Incarnation* 12, 39.

29. Athanasius, *On the Incarnation* 14, 42. In modern terms this means that any natural theology is insufficient in order to make inferences about God.

30. Athanasius, *On the Incarnation* 14, 42.

31. Cf. Sophrony, *The Monk of Mount Athos*, 171.

32. Florovsky, "Creation and Creaturehood," 72.

as being divided into multiple causally disconnected segments, only one of which is literally visible to us. The very intuition of the universe as a whole, manifests an archetypical trace of "all in all" in human consciousness when the transcendent reveals itself in the immanent without compromising its other-worldliness.

One reaffirms the main thesis: it is because of the created condition of humanity that the human ego cannot exit from the conditions of creation and thus must first of all face the question about its own creation, its own existence. The creation of the world and the universe as a whole then can only be grasped from within those modalities of the human subjectivity, which stop any "objective" description of creation as a cosmological process. This reaffirms our position that the natural attitude is inapplicable to explicating the sense of creation as life's self-affectivity, so that all hermeneutics, either biblical, patristic, philosophical or scientific, provide us only with the archetypes of the creation of the world pertaining to ancient deeply anthropological mythologies, reflecting the inherent desire of humans to project their internal perception of creaturehood outwardly onto the dynamics of the world. Such a hermeneutics of creation would not be able to provide us at all with the phenomenal access (in order to get the sense creation) if in Christianity it would not be supported by the empirical (and at the same time ontological) fact, namely the Incarnation as a certain outward manifestation of the creation's specific and concrete accomplishment in the hypostatic union of the Divine with the worldly human flesh. Correspondingly the sense of creation can only be understood theologically through phenomenologically deconstructing the natural attitude in the narrative of creation and turning to the narrative of creation of humanity as a certain "genesis" of its cognitive faculties in the archetype of the incarnate Christ. In this sense the question of creation of the world indeed becomes the question of creation of humanity: to create the world and to have the incarnate Christ turns out to be, theologically, the same. The deconstruction of the natural attitude in the biblical or scientific narrative of creation will not reduce to a simple statement that both of them are produced by humanity and thus noetically-centered. The whole fabric of both these narratives must itself lead to the fundamental conclusion that these narratives de facto speak about creation of humanity in terms of how this humanity acquires outwardly the sense of the world. As we will see below the apotheosis of the inapplicability of the natural attitude to the issue of the creation will be the situation when the latter is treated in terms of temporal origination. Yet before we need to go briefly through both theological and scientific narratives of creation by accentuating the intrinsic explanatory teleology present in them, teleology that characterizes all human activity.

CREATION IN GREEK PHILOSOPHY AND PATRISTIC THEOLOGY

For Greek philosophy the problem of creation was always associated with searching for the "beautiful arrangement" of the world, the Cosmos, as well as with the origin of this cosmos in space and time. In spite of the fact that in many ways the relation of the Greeks to the Cosmos was based on purely aesthetical, even ethical foundations, related to the personal attitude to the world as the other, the Cosmos as an existential milieu was a matter of an intellectual curiosity in which the same Cosmos appeared as a realm extended in space and time causing a quest for its origin, its finitude or infinitude. Leaving in passim the dramatism of Archytas's formulation of the problem of a possible finitude of the universe in space,[33] as well as Plato's claim about coexistence of the visible world and time,[34] it was clear that the problem of the origin of the world *in time* did not have much sense because time was an attribute of the world. It followed from here that the problem of contingent facticity of this visible world as, according to Plato, ordered by demiurge, did not have any direct relation to the problem of origin of this world in time. Plato understood that in all speculations about the universe there was a fundamental limit of adequacy of our representation, that is, the limited understanding of that which the universe was according to its "logos" (*alethes logos*). One can achieve some likely image of the universe (*eikos logos*) because the visible universe has partially those properties of the immutable world of the intelligible forms serving as the archetype of the visible universe. In such a judgement about the knowability of the universe a kind of anthropology is implicitly presupposed: humans can know the empirical universe through forming its intelligible image. So that the universe is given to human beings in their own image: it is structured in the image and likeness of that one who can have access to the universe and speculate about it.

According to Plato, the essence of cosmology as a human enterprise is to discover those invariant principles in the visible universe according to which the universe is ordered by Demiurge. To do this, the universe must be explicated in the language of mathematics as a human mediating tool between the sensible and intelligible worlds. Mathematics receives in Plato a status of that *a priori* condition (transcendental principle) for knowability of the visible universe in its archetypical connection with the world of the intelligible forms. It is this principle that until now lies in the foundations of modern cosmology. The transcendental principle of mathematical

---

33. Sorabji, *Matter*, 125–42.
34. Cornford, *Plato's Cosmology*, 97–105.

explicability could not be justified from within the empirical experience and this was the reason why the question about the contingent facticity of the world in a way was reduced to the question of the very possibility of the mathematical explicability of the world. The existence of the world as such was a kind of inevitability and any further enquiry in the ultimate ground of its facticity was considered as illegitimate because one cannot get out from the world and to "look" at it, as would be said after Aristotle, from some large metaphysical frame of thought. The universe is immanent and despite some internal movements is in a state of "eternal return" implying the cyclicity of all Greek cosmology. The being of the Cosmos had its substance (depending on the priorities of a concrete philosopher and named differently from "water" of Thales to the known mathematical "bodies" of Plato). The world was ontologically necessary despite its contingent appearance to humans; its eternity and immutability have been the alpha and omega in any philosophical arguments of its existence.

Christianity, rooted in the biblical tradition, challenged Greek philosophy and cosmology not only in respect to unlimited temporality, but also its ontological claim that the Cosmos (either visible and changing in time world, or its "eternal" intelligible double) can be considered as self-sufficient and self-explanatory. The cyclic and self-enclosed structure of the Greek view of the polis,[35] subordinated to the earthly human affairs was replaced by the linear and one-dimensional history of salvation, so that the social projection of the Greek cosmology was replaced by the linear development of the whole world towards its transfiguration and consummation in the arch Creation-Deification. The world is dependent on God and cannot be considered as eternal since its dependence on God implies its distinction and difference from God, being *finite* in all possible sense of this word (e.g. in a temporal sense), for if God is infinite (and thus timeless), the world is finite. Correspondingly, if the world is dependent of God, the laws of this world are not absolute and do not have the status of the philosophically understood necessity. Creation of the world out of nothing (*creatio ex nihilo*) is a "free" act of the Divine love and will with respect to the world and as such is not linked to the essence of God (*ousia*) through any causal principle. It is because of this freedom that the created world is contingent in the sense that it could be not non-existent at all or to be an absolutely different world.

---

35. The conviction in such an immanence of the laws of the world had its origin through an analogy with the social order. Sergei Averintsev writes in this respect: "As the law of the polis was immanent to this polis, the law of the cosmos was thought as immanent to the cosmos. It was a property of the self-contained, self-sufficient, 'spherically' complete in itself and equal to itself world" (Averintsev, "The Order of the Cosmos," 90).

However, since the world exists, this world can have only personal relation to God. And this relation because the world was created in the act of love is the relation of humility and gratitude understood by the early Christians as the law-like arrangement of that world, that is, its subordination to physical laws originating from its obedience to God.[36]

Yet the laws of physics do not allow humans to grasp the creator's design. Knowledge of the universe remains approximate and open-ended because it follows from the dialectics of the finite cognitive faculties of human beings and infinity of the creator who provided humanity with the means of knowing creation, but only as an image of his wilfulness, wisdom and love. This entails that all attempts to model and explicate the wholeness of the world, as well as its boundary and initial conditions will always entail an appeal to transcendental hypotheses implicitly containing questions about the origin of humanity itself, that is about the mystery of its own creation. The presence of such transcendental hypotheses as a certain purposefulness of the human knowledge cannot be elucidated empirically and refers to faith in Divine Image of humanity responsible for detecting the pointers of the contingency of the world upon its creator. It follows from here that to grasp creation by scientific means one had to deal not with the origin of the material universe, its evolution and structure, but rather with its intelligibility and rationality as following from the commandment of the creator and the human ability to be in communion with the universe, to reflect upon its arrangement and recapitulate the results of its knowledge.

When one speaks of the creation of the world by God, one means that the world, being created freely yet in its constitution is contingent upon God and possesses a kind of contingent rationality. The combination of two words "contingent" and "rational" seems contradictory, for rational can be understood as structural, and hence necessary. The genuine meaning of the phrase "contingent rationality" points towards the Christian assertion that the world is created by God because of his own plan, because of his own uncreated "rationality." One may speak of the world that expresses some freedom in its structures, their interactions and changes on the one hand, and the limitedness of this freedom that preserves the world from complete chaos and arbitrariness on the other hand.

---

36. For an introduction to the theological discussions of creation see two classical papers: Florovsky, "Creation and Creaturehood"; Florovsky, "The Idea of Creation in Christian Philosophy." There are many modern books dealing with creation that have a historical, as well as systematic character. See: May, *Creatio Ex Nihilo*; Ward, *Religion and Creation*; Torrance, *Divine and Contingent Order*; Pannenberg, *Toward a Theology of Nature*.

The question is now how to detect such a necessity. It is not enough here to refer to the harmony of the world and to an aesthetical component of its perception because the latter has origin in humanity itself and the question of the rationality of the created evolves into the question of rationality of human consciousness. In fact, the question of consciousness becomes the main point in the issue of creation of the world that contains this consciousness and that is articulated by this same consciousness. In this angle "contingent rationality" pertains to the very human consciousness. But since human personhood originates in the Personhood of God, the image of the universe and its creation presupposes tacitly the personal, or hypostatic dimension of creation which drastically differs from any accounts of creation in pre-Christian philosophies. In this sense one can truly say that the image of the universe, is the universe in the image of *Imago Dei*, which is hypostasis of the universe. In order to elucidate this point with a new force, we need to discuss why the idea of hypostasis becomes so important in the context of theology of creation in contrast with any alternative representations of creation either as emanation or substantial causation. The first question is whether it is possible from the harmony and beauty in the world, its order and mathematical intelligibility, deduce that all of them, as certain underlying principles (*logoi*) of created things point towards a certain intentionality proceeding from the hypostatic creator of the universe, the Logos who fashioned the universe in order to assume human flesh?

Certainly, it is impossible to infer, from the contingent facticity of specific objects in the universe to the design with respect to their appearance (in spite of the fact that such an inference would be the most natural way for the human teleological judgement to proceed). Such objects as galaxies, stars, Sun, Moon, etc. are contingent in terms their existence, position in space and time. In spite of the fact that they are subordinated to the natural laws, and despite of the impossibility to infer to the personal God philosophically, Christianity yet asserts that all these contingent objects *serve* God, because they were created out of God's unconditional love. This is a different, now a theological argument: Sun, Moon, stars and galaxies serve God in the sense that by being created by him they took a definite material form and endure in it, but the goal of this endurance is their voluntary acceptance of the Divine love.

Origen of Alexandria, in the third century, speaking of the "heavenly creatures" refers to the witness of the apostle Paul, who wrote that "The created universe is waiting with eager expectation for God's sons to be revealed. It was subjected to the vanity, not of its own choice but by the will of him who subjected it, yet with the hope that the universe itself is to be freed from the shackles of mortality and is to enter upon the glorious liberty of the children of God" (Rom 8:19–21). Origen writes: "Having received this hope, and looking for the fulfilment of this promise, the entire creation now in the meantime 'groans together' with us (for it even has sympathy with those whom it serves) and 'is in pain together', while in patience it hopes for what has been promised."[37] Here is a direct implication that there is a certain purposefulness which pertains to the fact of existence of the created universe. And its meaningful sense is to serve and have empathy with respect to that One Who is to fulfil a promise of its salvation. To serve and to be empathic means, according to Origen,[38] that the universe, the Sun and planets must exists and remain in a material form in order to sustain the human condition in flesh. This means that the very physical laws that are brought into existence together with the creation of the material world contain implicitly the possibility of the embodied existence of human beings. The revelation about God to humans is possible as long as they are alive and nature supports their existence. Movements, scintillations and the very existence of the large-scale universe, our galaxy and solar system, the planet Earth with its cosmic environment and fine-tuning of the physical parameters for existence of life correspond to the "obedience" of the Cosmos and nature to God's commandment in order to serve humanity and support its existence. And here, first of all, one implies Christ's Incarnation in flesh requiring the necessary cosmic conditions and specific surrounding world. Then the obedience of the physical universe to God expresses differently that the universe is enhypostasized by the Logos in such a way that the body of the incarnate Christ was possible. God's design for the Incarnation is implanted in the very fabric of creation as that teleological and soteriological dimension of all that is involved into the temporal flux of the created being. Hence the Incarnation and God in Christ is understood not as a *deus ex machina* intervening in history and its space-time structures, but as a freely chosen means of the Divine love for the fulfilment of the task of building of the whole world, namely its empathy to the created and help to the created humanity to achieve salvation. The Incarnation thus is that recreation and deepening of the structures of the world order which, in spite of the visible decay and predisposition to disappearance (according to astrophysical predictions humanity can be easily be destroyed by some cosmic events) the life of those who witness revelation could exist. Being eschatological in its essence as inaugurating the Kingdom of God, the Incarnation establishes the *telos* of all in the universe towards achieving the Kingdom through the work of humanity.

37. Origen, *De principiis*, I.7.5.
38. Origen, *De principiis*, I.7.5.

Saying differently, it is the very Logos-Christ who acts as the archetype of the purposeful aspiration to know the universe, who transferred his Divine Image to mankind. It is Christ who in the fullness of his human nature was able to recapitulate the whole universe in the hypostatic consciousness of the Logos as the creator and guardian of the universe. Humanity received this faculty but only dynamically and eschatologically, as a tendency towards knowledge, as that goal which has a soteriological character. Thus the intrinsic purposefulness of the cosmological search revealing itself in the human desire to explicate the universe in rubrics of the understanding and reason pertaining to the Divine Image has in its origin the human desire to restore the lost likeness to God and thus to acquire the mind of the Logos for whom the extended in space and time universe was the "all in all" of the creating act of the Divine Love. The acquisition of such a consciousness of "all in all," when the beginning, the middle and the end of the universe reconcile in the singe synthesis of the transfigured reason thus forms the goal and consummation of any theological cosmology. Remaining its ultimate goal one must admit that in spite of the fact that cosmological theories are not able to elucidate the sense of the theologically understood creation of the world as coming into being of the physical laws and primordial matter, the content and form of these theories can at least elucidate (if not a factual, material side of creation of the world) some general tendency in modelling and depicting of this creation in human consciousness whose intrinsic purposefulness creates an image of creation (*eikos logos*).

CREATION AS ORIGINATION OF THE UNIVERSE IN MODERN COSMOLOGY

Cosmology is being constructed from within the *natural attitude* that making its object (the universe) devoid of any references to human subjectivity thus removing insights into the conditions of that phenomenality which it deals with. This is particularly felt in the issue of origin of the universe, where cosmological origination connotes with the theologically understood creation.

Physical cosmology persistently attempts to escape a philosophical verdict on the unknowability of the facticity of the universe and to *explain it away* by referring to the initial conditions in the universe as if they would contain all "information" about the present and future of the universe. The objective of physical cosmology is to "explain" the specificity of the state of affairs in the empirical, observable cosmos. We have a display of different objects in the sky, different structural and physical phenomena, observed by various physical means. There are two aspects in this variety of the natural phenomena: on the one hand we have some species of similar objects (let say galaxies or their clusters) which can be classified into groups; on the other hand there is a particular givenness of objects from these groups which display themselves in the cosmos in an absolutely contingent way (e.g., there are some particular famous galaxies associated with special directions in the sky: an obvious example is the Andromeda nebula seen by us through the constellation of Andromeda). On a smaller scale there are particular patterns of stars in our galaxy grouped into constellations since ancient times, whose display in the sky is contingent and given to us as it is. Another example of astronomical contingency is our planetary system that contains nine planets of particular sizes and parameters of their orbits. Since Kepler and later Newton the movement of planets is explained in terms of periods of revolution around their orbits in dependence on their spatial distance from the sun using physical laws, but astronomy cannot explain the fact as to why there are nine planets (instead of twenty nine, for example) and why the concrete parameters of their revolution around the sun were set in that order which is observable now. In other words, neither astronomy nor physics can account for the initial conditions of the movements of various contingent objects in the universe in order to explain the specificity of their display in the sky. Said philosophically, the universe displays the contingent state of affairs on a huge spatial scale whose facticity and origin cosmology attempts to interpret, including the physical laws which are employed in it.

In pre-scientific eras "explanations" of the variety in the cosmos were given in mythological terms: "The cosmological myth is an account of cosmogenesis. It tells how the world was made, how the contemporary world that stands before our eyes developed from what went before, from the non-world, the formless. . . . The schema of the representation is a successive unfolding in which there is a movement from homogeneous unity to a qualitatively differentiated multiplicity."[39] In modern terms, the idea of mythological explanations amounts to an attempt to reduce the variety of contingent objects in the sky and peculiarities in their motions to a minimum, by representing the universal qualities of the cosmic display through symmetries and harmonies, and by making all contingent happenings as derivatives and spontaneous outcomes from the rule.[40] A characteristic feature of such an attempt is a conviction that the underlying "world" of

---

39. Ladrière, *Language and Belief,* 153.

40. One can refer, as an example, to the cosmological principle as a principle of non-observability of contingent deviations from uniformity. All observable non-uniformity such as our solar system of the Milky Way galaxy exhibit the breakdown of that symmetry on a much lesser scales than that of clusters of galaxies.

highly symmetric (Platonic) forms is actually coexisting with the empirical display, but is not perceived through the senses. This underlying world is treated as ever-existing reality, with no change and hence with some stable universal patterns so that the stability of the universe as its identity in the background of the flux of mundane things is secured through the reference to these intelligible patterns (Platonic forms).

What makes contemporary scientific cosmology similar to and at the same time different from mythological cosmologies is that, as a scientific discipline, cosmology can function only in the condition if its "object" (the universe as a whole) sustains *identity* in time. Indeed, according to Kant experience is possible only if time is involved as an element of unity and synthesis. However, in cosmology, this is not an innocent requirement: for example, in the case of a static and infinite universe (i.e., by assumption, exists forever) the identity of the universe in time, is a tautology for, *de facto*, there is no objective large-scale physical time in such a universe—it is static. Correspondingly the observable universe (because of the postulated finitude of the speed of light) would be an infinitesimal part of an incommensurably bigger whole which is principally beyond an empirical grasp. Only in this case one could legitimately talk about the identity of the visible part of the universe and infer (in a leap of faith) to the identity of the whole static and infinite universe. This in turn entails that the facticity of the observable universe would be the first and the last principle of its explanation, for there would not be possible to refer to any other state of the universe considered as an originary cause or an origin of the universe as we see it.

The situation changes drastically in a standard cosmological model based on the idea of the universal expansion. The universe is expanding and the idea of the evolution of the universe is taken exactly as that time-synthesis which is needed in order to preserve the unity of the universe as a whole (it provides us with images of the universe at different moments of time as a consequence of the finitude of the speed of light). The fact that the term "past" can be assigned to the universe as different from the ever-lasting present of the static universe (in a static universe the past is associated with ageing of the light signals but not with the evolving nature of its space related to the material stuff) is exactly related to the principle that there was an ultimate *temporal* beginning of the universe from which all its stages emerged and because of that one can observe the universe backward in time and in the entirety of its temporal span (excluding its dark ages before the separation of matter and radiation took place).

The ancient idea of the underlying eternal world becomes replaced here by another, but similar idea. This time cosmology finds refuge in saying that the present state of the observable universe (with its annoying contingent facticity) is the frozen instantaneous display of the temporal evolution of this universe from some remote initial state which in its seeds (through the laws of physics implanted there) contained the potentiality of all various features in the cosmic display. This kind of thinking naturally invokes the idea of the originary "past" of the universe whose partial consequences are displayed, a "past" which is not observable as such but "existed" physically long before that display which humanity looks at and reflects upon. What is also believed (and this is in some way supported by theory) is that this initial (early) state of the universe, in terms of physics and its logical representation to human mind, is much "simpler" than the grandiose variety of different spatially and temporally disjoint objects displayed in the present universe because the initial condition is a single undifferentiated state of matter (although with either infinite or uncertain parameters). In spite of this uncertainty the motivation of cosmology remains the same: to explain away the contingent variety of objects and their species in the universe (as seen in the perspective of our "present") by "sweeping these contingencies under the rug" of their undifferentiated unity in the "past" of the universe.

The hope that such an attempt will be successful suffers from logical flaws which can be elucidated through philosophical analogies. First of all, a theoretical attempt to reduce all variety of forms and structures in the universe to rubrics of the allegedly existing undifferentiated unity (which could play a role of a fundamental *substance*) does not make this unity visible. One infers to this unity from a premise that it is "accessible" to us only through its consequent differentiation and particularization in the course of time. It is not difficult to see that such a pronouncement on the underlying unity of the universe is reminiscent of the ancient ambitions to claim that the substance of the world (the universals of the world) are *water, fire, apeiron*, etc.[41] Cosmology silently follows the same route of thought by postulating such a primordial substance at the beginning of the universe as ultimately responsible for the variety of objects available in the cosmic display. However, there is a seeming difference with an ancient view: *water* of Thales or *apeiron* of Heraclitus were abstract notions but allegedly coexisting with the empirical display of the world. In this sense one could say that there were no *temporal* extensions within these substances. In a rather contemporary way of saying, *water* and *apeiron* could correspond to a microscopic level of reality, but *here* and *now* so that there is no "evolutional extension between universals and their empirical incarnations." Unlike this, physical cosmology places the undifferentiated substance of the Big Bang in the past

---

41. On the analogy of the ancient Greek quest for the underlying matter and contemporary physics, see Feinberg, "Physics and the Thales Problem."

CREATION AS ORIGINATION OF THE UNIVERSE IN MODERN COSMOLOGY 193

of the universe, assuming that there is a time-like extension in this substance which ultimately leads to the present display of the universe (there is a reversed assertion: whatever direction we observe deeper and deeper in the sky, we ultimately "observe" the Big Bang through its predicted outcome—the microwave background radiation). Thus the difference between mythological and contemporary view of the world in terms of universals is related to the treatment of extension inherent in the underlying substance: spatial (in ancient cosmology) versus temporal (in a modern one). However, such a perception of the difference comes from a scientifically based conviction that when one looks at the sky of the universe one looks at its remote spatially and temporally extended past: this is implied by causality based in the finitude of the speed of propagation of light in the universe. But, and this is important, since the size of the visible universe is decreasing if one looks backward in time (due to its reversed expansion), one can also say that by "looking" (not optically, for light could not travel before the universe cooled down and split from matter) at the Big Bang we are "looking" (i.e., are making insights) deeply in space (into the microscopic scales of space as we do through microscopes or in experiments in nuclear physics). In other words, one can say that a frozen two-dimensional display of the universe represents a geometrized passage of time. In this sense one can further conjecture that what is called the evolution of the universe in time from the initial Big Bang is effectively the unrolling of the universe through different scales in space (one must note that this unrolling is driven by dynamical laws which do not contain any intrinsic historicity, so that this unrolling is rather to be called not evolution but just a dynamic development determined by the initial conditions).

If the idea of the undifferentiated substance is laid in the foundation of genesis of the visible universe, then the problem of creation in cosmology becomes similar to that of the ancient philosophy of how to explain the generation of basic elements and structural units which form varieties of things in the universe. By understanding that individual things are not subject to scientific descriptions cosmology intends to get rid of this individuality at all by saying that what is really interesting is to understand how a class of impersonal objects emerged from *something* undifferentiated and homogeneous. One speaks here not of contingent individual exemplar objects/beings, but of species of objects unified through realized physical forces (e.g., not of this or that galaxy, but of galaxy in general; not of this or that planet, but planets in general; not of this or that human person, but of human beings in general). This cosmological move from the Big Bang to the present sate of the universe makes an inverse impression that the Big Bang turns out to be merely a very clever *disguise* of that which we experience as the now of the universe. In the hypothesis of the Big Bang, the contingent facticity of the universe as it is observed here and now is reinterpreted in terms of a certain temporal origin in which the undifferentiated "substance" was "set up" in such a state as to evolve into the visible universe. The procedure of "naming" this initial state is supposed to play the role of disclosing the universe's identity and hence acts in thought as a disguised name of its present day displayed facticity. It is not difficult to comprehend, however, that the problem of contingent facticity of the universe can only be *explained away* by this type of reasoning through referring to the initial conditions, because there is no way to *explain* the contingent facticity of these initial conditions themselves.

Indeed, since every cosmologist works under the assumption that there is continuous physical causation in the universe, so that there is a chain of causal explanations of what happened in the universe if we extrapolate its behavior backward in time, it is not difficult to realize that the equations which drive the universe backward in time, in fact, effectively encode the variety of existing objects in the spatial display in the astronomical universe into the same variety extrapolated backward in time, which is now treated as the "initial" condition for those physical states from which it has been backwardly constructed. However any hypotheses of the facticity of these initial conditions in the universe remain no more than hypotheses with no chance of their instatement to the status of laws. Being hypothetical these initial physical conditions of the universe acquire some particular imagery in different models.[42]

One can make some generalizations on the meaning of the origin of temporality in the universe and the sense of its initial conditions. Cosmology makes an assumption that time can be asserted through conscious acts as an attribute of the world constructed by physics, that is, as that type of reality which has been in place prior to the human embodied intelligence in the universe (the time of the universe asserted as non-lived, abstract time). Then the alleged "origin" (as its originary foundation) of physical time is also thought in similar naturalistic terms. However this origin is obscure not only in physical terms, for physics can deal only with that which is

---

42. For example, such an imagery is presented in Stephen Hawking's famous idea that the universe was in a quantum state in the so-called past and did not have any point of origination. The universe was in a space-like state where all temporality, associated with the flux of time and irreversibility, was suspended. Hawking, *A Brief History of Time*, 139. (The explication of this idea can be found in Isham, "Creation of the Universe.") This cosmology led Hawking to the dismissal of the idea of God as creator through his famous phrase "What place, then, for a creator?" (Hawking, *A Brief History of Time*, 141). See a philosophical and theological analysis of Hawking's ideas in Nesteruk, *Light from the East*, 141–59.

already temporal, it is also obscure in the perspective of the intersubjective temporality of consciousness. Indeed, if consciousness is embodied in the elements of the universe, any thinking of the origin of the universe must implicitly contain hints on how to think of the "origin" (originary foundation) of consciousness itself and *vice versa* (i.e., the thinking of the "origin" of consciousness must implicitly contain hints on how to think of the origin of the universe).

And it is here that we have to refer to the already discussed philosophical fact that consciousness (either related to the whole humanity or to an individual) cannot deal with its own "origin" for it cannot stop the flow of intentionality and to make an introspection upon itself from a perspective of non-consciousness.[43] The temporal flow of consciousness is characteristic of the human life so that to exit it in order to "find" its pre/a/trans-temporal origin is not possible. In phenomenological terms, one has no access to the phenomenality of one's coming into existence (as internal time-consciousness) from that "non-existent" which is allegedly one's "originary foundation." The characteristic feature of its partial, "a posteriori," phenomenality is exactly that it does not show itself: it is "present" only as an efficacious origin of all states of life. Thus the phenomenology of the originary foundation can only be established through the constitution of this "origin" in acts and insights taking place in the present. This raises a question on the sense of the reality of a thus constituted "origin": is this "origin" a hidden name of the backwardly extrapolated present, that is, the name of the "past" as being open-endedly constituted in a process directed to the future?

If our analysis is correct, it is then not difficult to realize that cosmology has to deal with a similar difficulty of not being able to provide us with the object-like phenomenality of the originary foundation of the universe and the source of its temporality. One possible way out from this phenomenological difficulty is to commit to a form of Platonic realism. If the "origin" of the universe is treated as no more than a construction belonging to the intelligible realm, this would not pose any problem, for the "temporal" status of such an intelligible entity would take the form of the immanent temporality of conscious acts which are directed from the present to future. The past of the universe as its origin would become an *ideal* whose content would be constantly filled in through the movement to an uncertain future. In this case one could avoid the antinomy-like difficulties of a Kantian kind because the theories of the past or the origin of the universe would be regarded as a "material" of an indefinite development of cosmological

---

43. Henry, "Phénoménologie non intentionnelle. Une tâche de la phénoménologie à venir," in *De la Phénoménologie*, 105–21.

thought. Correspondingly this development as an indefinite advance would be devoid of contradictions since no definite concept of the past or the originary foundation (allegedly related to some physical reality) is envisaged. As was expressed by Gabriel Marcel: "we should never view the world's *past* under the aspect of datum—for under this aspect it is inevitably contradictory and unthinkable. We should only regard it as the material of an infinite rational development (a development conceived as potential and future and hence not contradictory)."[44] Interestingly, that in our times, when the past of the universe received a more articulated expression in cosmology, a similar thought was formulated by Christos Yannaras: "Both the specification . . . of the Big Bang as a founding event of the universe, and the non-local and non-temporal coordinates of the beginning of space and time are determined and therefore "existential" facts, principles of existential uniqueness without entailing materiality in the definitions of their existence."[45]

This treatment of the past or the origin of the universe as being constituted by subjectivity at present and thus as having no material references would be considered by physical cosmology as unsatisfactory, since the latter attempts to build its concept of the origin in rubrics of scientific objectivity and to treat it as "object." Cosmology affirms that the time of the early universe *is* not an intelligible entity, but physical time, so that there is evolution of the universe in this time and what we observe in the universe here and now is the remote result of what had been in the universe long ago when the corporeality of subjects was not possible. Indeed, that which is remotely observed by the senses extended through technology as the frozen memory of the processes in the universe, cannot be participated in, or lived through, in principle. We see a frozen temporal span of the universe along the past light cone, so that the more distant the object we see the more we see the past of the universe. However, there is a limit to this seeing because the universe was not transparent to light before the so called decoupling of matter from radiation took place (this happened nearly fourteen billion years ago if one counts time backwardly, or four hundred thousand years from the initial singularity). Whatever properties of physical matter of the universe prior to this temporal limit cosmology predicates, including the very cosmic time, they are not directly observable so that the nature of realistic commitment with respect to its theories is rather uncertain. Temporality and the constituted reality of these so called dark ages of the universe has a very limited and formal mathematical character to which no intuition corresponds: time is introduced in equations as a fictitious parameter incapable of any direct

---

44. Marcel, *Metaphysical Journal*, 8; emphasis added.
45. Yannaras, *Postmodern Metaphysics*, 107.

physical verification and thus has a relation to the physical non-lived time only within a belief-based ontological commitment.

When cosmology predicates things of the universe, or the universe as a whole as an "object" being out there independently of that subjectivity which articulates the universe, it exercises itself in the *natural attitude* of consciousness. In this case the observed present state of the universe, as well as its non-observable, but theoretically constituted past, are treated as equally objective, but with distinct physical references. If the attitude changes and past and present are seen from the point of view of generating consciousness, there is a certain equivalence between "the past" and "the present" based on that they are both treated as being constituted. While within the natural attitude it is supposed that there is a temporal evolution of the universe and hence there must be an asymmetry between the universe's past and its present, from a phenomenological point of view the situation is not so clear, because the intuition of "the past" (as having existed prior to any consciousness) is exercised in the present of consciousness of a cosmologist. In other words, "the past" of the universe represents an intentional correlate of the multiplicity of conscious acts of cosmologists at "present."[46] In this case the posited causality between different states of the universe appears to be a projection of that immediately experienced temporality of internal states of consciousness or thematized historicity. "The past" which forms an implicit component of any perception of the given present, as a pre-predicative experience of the present, enters the horizon of meanings in all thematizations of the world and, in particular, the physical universe. But in this case as pre-predicative experience, open to an indefinite constitution the "past" ceases to function under the aspect of *datum*. The past reveals itself as an originary intuition of the hidden antecedent of that state of affairs which humanity experiences in its developed stage.

Physical cosmology approaches to the past of the universe by reversing backward the observed expansion of the universe and finding that "moment" when the size of the universe was zero: this state is called cosmological singularity. At present it is estimated that the universe is 13.8 billion years old. What happened before this moment—is a matter of theoretical speculations in some pre-Big-Bang models. However modern physics effectively stops in its extrapolation towards the cosmological singularity at so called Planck scales of space and time when classical representations of space and time become inapplicable. Thus cosmology describes the original state of the universe in terms of its zero size, its backwardly calculated age

---

46. Compare with John Wheeler, who advocated a view that the temporality of the past is theory and a human construction. Wheeler, "Time Today," 6.

and other idiosyncratic features. What remains completely incomprehensible is the foundation of the contingent facticity of this state. The age of the universe appears to be a physical constant with a contingent numerical value. Correspondingly if one enquires in the nature of this facticity, one will have to position the whole universe in some pre-existing space-time (or multiverse, the pre Big Bang universe, cyclic universe, etc.) and then to ask why the universe appeared in a particular "location" and "time" of such a geometrical structure, or as a particular exemplar of the generic multiverse. Alternatively, one can enquire in the nature of the contingent facticity of this universe through a causal reversal of the question taking as an primary fact our existence, thus adjusting the required age of the evolution to the necessary conditions of our existence (this line of thought is similar to the strong version of the Anthropic Principle). In the first case (in the hypothesis of pre-existing space-time an infinite manifold) the difficulty arises from that any "positioning" of the point of origination of our universe with respect to actual infinity either of pre-existing space or multiverse does not make any sense. In the second case the argument for the specific age of the universe has a teleological motive which refers to the purpose of the universe to produce humanity. This latter argument is philosophical and theological, but as such will be subjected to critique by scientific cosmologists.

One can see that the problem of origin of the universe can hardly be accounted in scientific cosmology because of the same philosophical difficulty which we have discovered above in the context of the phenomenological concealment of an event birth of every human being. Indeed, it is because of the phenomenological concealment of the origin of the universe that the very theoretical constitution of this origin represents an open-ended hermeneutics of this origin. This points to the fact that if cosmological models are considered as elements of the modern creation narrative, in no way they provide an ontological picture of origination of the universe. Then the question of *creation* of the universe remains in a radically different philosophical plane as a question about the universe's contingency upon its trans-worldly foundation; theologically, about how the created universe expresses the Divine Life's self-affectivity. Then the question of creation is delegated exclusively to the field of theology so that any discursive appropriation of it will require faith as a particular modality of the human subjectivity, or, as we asserted in the first part of this book, of accepting those *givens* which are related to the inaugural events. Such an appropriation will also require an open-ended hermeneutics of a different kind, complementing that one of the physical cosmology. Yet, there remains a different option of relating the sense of creation to the facticity of the universe "here and now" as containing humanity that articulates the universe. This will inevitably lead us to a shift in our enquiry from the theology of the inaugural event of creation of the world to the theology of the inaugural events of creation of humanity and the Incarnation of the Word-Logos of God in flesh of Jesus of Nazareth. It is the latter which form the motive for the creation of the world and predetermine a different hermeneutics of this creation and the universe in general. What happens here is exactly that phenomenological reversal of the cosmological discourse whose meaning and significance turn out to be first of all connected with that how human beings treat the mystery of their existence in communion with the Divine and carry in themselves the Divine Image in the archetype of the incarnate Christ

CREATION IN THE NATURAL ATTITUDE OR HOW NOT TO SPEAK ABOUT CREATION: A PATRISTIC INSIGHT IN THE ISSUE OF "WHY NOT SOONER OF CREATION?"

When Christian theology through the writings of the Fathers and numerous commentaries asserts that the world is created, that it came out of nothing, that there was no world "before" it came into being, it implicitly exercises a psychological tackling of creation in terms of temporality pertaining to this world: to speak of creation one needs to have an intuition of the distinction between "before" and "after" (an intuition of temporal sequence) which this temporality implies. The sense of the words "the world came out of nothing" can only be understood from within the human sense of existence as existence in time. Correspondingly, if creation of the world is represented in thought as a "transition" from that something "when there was no world" to the actual existence of the world, this representation has a hypothetical character in terms of possible antecedent references, simply because the very process of thought belongs to the already created world and it is from this created modality of intellection that one attempts to grasp the sense of the created, that is, the facticity of the world as if this facticity had a sort of metaphysical antecedent "before" the world.

In spite of this observation, theology, starting from the church Fathers and finishing with contemporary discussions on the applicability of modern cosmological theories to the riddle of creation, struggles to express the problem of creation of the world in terms of thought and speech. For example, Basil the Great, speaking of creation of the world, says that God created heaven and earth, that created beings begin with time and end in time. Time originates together with the world, so that the origination of time is its "first moment," its "beginning." Then he says that one can start from the present and attempt to trace through events in the past that first day which would correspond to the creation of the world out of nothing.[47] In Basil's affirmations it is implied that time is that part of the created reality which pertains to the intellect speculating about creation. On the one hand time is an attribute of the created world, on the other hand, it is, using a philosophical language, a transcendental condition for the very possibility to speculate about creation. When Basil points towards the possibility of counting time backwards to the past in order to find its beginning, as if this beginning would be given to the human grasp as an "object," as an outward "thing," he implicitly extrapolates the causality of mundane things towards the origin and ontological foundation of these things. But the foundation of things does not belong to the temporal series pertaining to the world, so that to catch the initial moment for the side of the created is tempting, but not making any sense in terms of understanding of its contingent appearance out of nothing.

As we have seen above, Greek philosophers before Christianity understood that the causal principle of the world cannot be constructed by means of the sciences and knowledge. Modern philosophy contributes to this by saying that the origin of the world as well as the origin of one's consciousness is phenomenologically concealed from one's grasp, so that its explication (not explanation!) is possible only through the unfolding in the future of that which is already given as created. Correspondingly, Basil's explication of the origin can only be understood as undertaken from within the phenomenality of the created and thus establishing the retrocedent causality towards the origin which will never become the explication of creation out of nothing.

If, as another patristic example, one turns to Maximus the Confessor, one finds a similar assertion that the world has a beginning and consequently is not eternal. Maximus, affirms that the world was created out of nothing because of God's will and goodness, by his Wisdom and Logos, and that the createdness of the word implies its non-eternity and consequently its beginning in time. However, in spite of the fact that this beginning in time can be understood only from within the already created world, Maximus points to a difficulty that can arise. In a passage from *Centuries on Charity* 4.3 he says, "God, who is eternally Creator, creates when He wills by His consubstantial Word and Spirit, because of His infinite goodness." Then Maximus anticipates a possible question on details of this creation: "Nor must you object: Why did He create *at a certain time* since He was always good?" Here the question is formulated from within those categories of sequence

---

47. Basil the Great, *In hexaemeron* 1.6, 55.

and time which pertain to the already created world. Indeed, if the creation of the world happened several thousand years ago measured by the created time, why this age of the world is such as it is, or, in other words, can we enquire into the nature of this age's contingent facticity as it is contemplated from within creation? Maximus gives a characteristic response—"no": "The unsearchable wisdom of the infinite essence does not fall under human knowledge."[48] In the next fragment (4.5) Maximus amplifies this moment making a distinction between a question of the reason for what God created the world and a question about the "when" of this creation: "Seek the cause for God's creation; this pertains to knowledge. Seek not the how and why He but *recently* created; for that is not in the competence of your mind."[49] Maximus theologically differentiates the cause of creation of the world which remains hidden for the human grasp and that specific and concrete aspect of creation, its immanent "age," so to speak, whose "numerical" facticity cannot either be grasped by human beings. An attempt to enquire into the facticity of the "age" of the created world is paralleled by Maximus with such a contemplation which may "drive one off the cliffs."[50] Such a theological distinction implies that two types of questions are posed in different attitudes of consciousness. A possible answer to the question of the cause of the world is produced by the power of contemplation (a spiritual intellect—*nous*) which is based in faith in Creator and purposefulness of creation following from God's promise to save humanity and the world. In contemplation, the world is treated not as an object, but as the immediate givenness of life, as its saturated phenomenon. Hence the cause of this phenomenon as a phenomenon of consciousness is experienced as a component of faith in the Giver of life and the world. The question of the "age" of the created world implies something different, namely a representation of the world as "an object" with a "beginning of time," whose notion is to be approached within the categories of the understanding adjusted only to knowledge of this world, but not trans-worldly causality. In different words, the warning of Maximus is formulated as an impossibility of any reasonable enquiry about the aspects of the trans-worldly causality (as a relation to the transcendent and infinite [whatever this would mean]) in terms of sensible forms and categories related to the created world.

It is worth quoting here Gregory of Nyssa who in his "Commentary on Ecclesiastes" reflects upon that what it could be psychologically for a human being to discover itself on the "edge" of the universe, that is, that "boundary"

---

48. This translation is from Maximus the Confessor, *The Ascetic Life*, 192.
49. Maximus the Confessor, *The Ascetic Life*, 193.
50. Maximus the Confessor, *The Ascetic Life*, 193.

which separates its created essence form what allegedly logically "preceded" it, that is, uncreated and infinite:

> No created being can go out of itself by rational contemplation. Whatever it sees, it must see itself; and even if it thinks it is seeing beyond itself, it does not in fact possess a nature which can achieve this. And thus in its contemplation of Being it tries to force itself to transcend a spatial representation, but it never achieves it. *For in every possible thought, the mind is surely aware of the spatial element which it perceives in addition to the thought content*; and the spatial element is, of course, created. . . . Thus how can our mind, which always operates on a dimensional [spatial] image comprehend a nature that has no dimension [no spatial attribute]. . . . And though the mind in its restlessness ranges through all that is knowable, it has never yet discovered a way of comprehending eternity in such wise that it might place itself outside it, and go beyond the idea of eternity itself and that Being which is above all being. It is like someone who finds himself on a mountain ridge. Imagine a sheer, steep crag, of reddish appearance below, extending into eternity; on top there is this ridge which looks down over a projecting rim into a bottomless chasm. Now imagine what a person would probably experience if he put his foot on the edge of this ridge which overlooks the chasm and found no solid footing nor anything to hold on to. This is what I think the soul experiences when it goes beyond its footing in material things, in its quest for that which has no dimension and which exists from all eternity. For here is nothing it can take hold of, neither place nor time, neither measure no anything else. . . . And thus the soul becomes dizzy and perplexed and returns once again to what is connatural to it, content now to know merely this about the Transcendent, that it is completely different from nature of the things that the soul knows.[51]

A mountain ridge in this fragment can me compared with the edge of the universe in the sense of its beginning, whereas the gazing into the bottomless chasm can be compared with an attempt to perceive that which "preceded" the universe, that is, with that which does not have any measure and is of eternity. That difficulty of consciousness which Gregory describes as that "nothing it can take hold of, neither place nor time, neither measure no anything else; it does not allow our minds to approach" corresponds to

---

51. Gregory of Nyssa, *Commentary on Ecclesiates*, sermon 7, quoted in Daniélou, *From Glory to Glory*, 127.

the impossibility of transcending the boundaries the universe in order to "look" at it from the side. The desire to overcome being "dizzy and perplexed" and to find a point of rest in order to "take hold," leads sometimes to invoking of mental constructions of pre-existent space and those structures of thinking which attempt to overcome difficulties in constituting all specific features of *creatio ex nihilo*. The question of "when" of creation strikes human consciousness to such an extent that it has to seek for some hard stone of this "when" in the phenomenality of objects. Since this is impossible, its very search explicates the working of consciousness to represent the mystery of the phenomenon of life and then of the universe.[52] Indeed, in the last paragraph from the fragment quoted above, Gregory of Nyssa describes the situation analogous to the saturated phenomenon where the structures of subjectivity, in the situation of impossibility to explicate and constitute that which is gazed at, themselves become constituted (rephrasing Gregory, the soul becomes dizzy and perplexed and returns once again to what is connatural to it). Consciousness, experiencing such a predicament realizes its impotence in understanding the facticity of the created, in particular its "temporal origin." It has to humbly accept its own limitations which become constitutive for it through an adaptation to the realm of the already created. First cosmologists of the twentieth century expressed a similar concern with respect to the notion of the universe as a whole which, according to them, could be fundamentally unintelligible as transcending its parts which are studied by the sciences. James Jeans, for example, writes that since our earth is so infinitesimal in comparison with the whole universe so that we are, the only thinking beings in the whole of space removed from the main scheme of the universe, "it is a priori too probable that any meaning that the universe as a whole may have, would entirely transcend our terrestrial experience, and so be totally unintelligible to us. In this event, we should have had no foothold from which to start our exploration of the true meaning of the universe."[53]

Here it is interesting to note that Augustine, before Maximus the Confessor, was essentially concerned with the same question as Maximus later. In his *Confessions*, Augustine, enquired: "But if it was God's everlasting will that the created order exist, why is not the creation also everlasting?"[54] One can grasp that this question of Augustine is equivalent to the question of Maximus the Confessor on why creation now and not later by appealing to

---

52. This situation corresponds to that which Michel Henry described as non-intentional phenomena. See Henry, "Phénoménologie non intentionnelle," in *De la Phénoménologie*, 105–21.

53. Jeans, *The Mysterious Universe*, 128.

54. Augustine, *Confessions* XI.10, 225.

another text of Augustine from "The City of God" where he discusses another question on why the first creation of man happened later than before. Augustine reacts to the question "Why an infinity of ages passed without man's being created, why his creation was so late that less that six thousands years, according to scriptural evidence, have passed since he first came into existence?" by making a reference that any finite period of created time, be it six thousands or six millions years, is incommensurable with the Divine eternity, and thus the questions as to why now, that is, late, and not before, makes no sense in the perspective of eternity. Augustine reduces this question to the problem of the contingent facticity of creation of humanity in general:

> Therefore the question which we now ask after five thousands years or more, posterity could as well as, with the same curiosity, after six hundred thousand years, if the mortal state of humanity, with its succession of birth and death, should last so long.... In fact the first man himself might have asked, on the day after he was made, or even on the very day of its creation, why ha had not been made sooner. And whenever he had been made, no matter how much earlier, this objection about the beginning of temporal things would have had precisely the same force then as now-or at any time.[55]

In modern context the passage just quoted is interesting because by that it explicates the problem of the phenomenological concealment of both birth (or conception) of man, as well as creation of the world as a whole. Augustine points out that the concealment of both events is associated with the incommensurability of the finite and limited created, and that ontologically other foundation of the world as that immemorial without which one cannot have a temporal perception of the world and which nevertheless escapes all definitions in terms of this world. In its essence, since the concept of creation out of nothing excludes any causal foundation of the world, creation of the world is a contingent "event" with respect to which any question of their "earlier" or "later" makes no sense.

Coming back to Maximus's warning about enquiring into the age of the universe, one can analyze some implications of the question. If the question about "when" of creation is related to the temporal span of the physical universe as it is seen from within this universe then one can find parallels with contemporary cosmology.[56] Formally, Maximus's question can be translated by using modern cosmological language into a question about

---

55. Augustine, *Civitate Dei* XII.13, 486–87.
56. Nesteruk, "The Sense of the Universe," 298–345.

the initial conditions of the universe which fix its physical parameters, including its age. But physical cosmology cannot give an account of the initial conditions for those dynamical laws which drive matter and space of the universe. Correspondingly cosmology cannot provide a clear explanation as to why the age of the visible universe is about 14 billion years. Since we can speculate on the nature of these conditions only from within our universe by extrapolating backward the properties of the observable universe, the "knowledge" of the initial conditions thus achieved does not tell us anything about these conditions, as if there were special trans-worldly physical laws responsible for these conditions.[57] Being bounded by the universe one cannot know the "laws" of the initial conditions of the universe as if they could be attested from beyond the universe (we can only postulate them). In this sense Maximus's response "no" with respect to knowing why the initial conditions of the created universe are those which they are (fixing its biblical age) exactly corresponds to "no" of scientific cosmology with respect to the initial conditions which fix the contingent facticity of the universe (fixing its cosmological age).

Nevertheless, to explicate the sense of Maximus's question and Augustine's arguments about "when" of creation and their negative reaction to it, one can reformulate this question as if the universe appeared out of something preexistent. This is done purely of pedagogical purposes by understanding that if one treats creation out of nothing consistently, nothing can pre-exist it. One could refer to Augustine's pointing to the fact that "before" the world was created no entities such as all-embracing space or time could exist.[58] Yet, let us imagine some pre-existent space-time continuum in which our universe *appears* at some of its "moment" and "location." Then the question of "when" of creation will make another sense as a particular "when" not from within the created universe (as an age of the universe) but in the external pre-existent time (we disregard any discussion of the sense of this pre-existence). What interests us is a possibility to model creation in the phenomenality of objects, that is, as a transition from something "before" (if this can be defined at all) to that which the universe is "here and now." Indeed to ask why creation "now" but not later or before, would imply the possibility of approaching the creation within the infinite space-time

---

57. A famous example of such a hypothetical law is Roger Penrose's "Weyl Curvature Hypothesis" postulating the low gravitational entropy in the beginning of the universe. See Penrose, *The Road to Reality*, 726–32, 765–68.

58. "The way, God, in which you made heaven and earth was not that you made them either in heaven or on earth. . . . Nor did you make the universe within the framework of the universe. There was nowhere for it to be made before it was brought into existence." Augustine, *Confessions* XI.5, 225.

(similar to that of Newton), that is, to position the "moment" of creation of this universe as a "physical event," as a particular happening in the series of causations allegedly existing outside of this universe.[59]

As an example of "creation" in preexistent space-time one can consider a model of "creation" of matter in the universe (not of space and time) from the initial state with the total energy of matter equal zero (imitating nothing).[60] The major feature of this model is that the universe originates as a result of a fluctuation in the physical vacuum (a physical state of matter with zero values of all observables). Geometrically the development of such a universe could be presented as a future light cone (a cone upside down in the space-time diagram), whose apex, symbolizing the beginning of this universe, is positioned arbitrarily in preexistent space and time. It is exactly this arbitrariness of the "place" and "moment" of origination of the visible universe that constitutes a difficulty (similar to that of Maximus) if the latter is formulated not from within the cone corresponding to our universe (enquiring in the numerical specificity of the height of this cone as corresponding to the age of the universe), but as if the "age" of our universe would correspond to a specific choice on the scale of pre-existent space-time manifold. However since the pre-existent space-time is infinite, it is impossible to specify and justify why the universe originated at a specific point of this space-time: the spontaneous "creation" of the universe could occur anywhere and at any moment of pre-existent space and time.

Correspondingly the question of "when of creation?" does not make any sense, for if the preexistent space-time is infinite, an infinite time could have passed since our universe originated. Similarly the question of a spatial location of such an origin in pre-existent space does not make any sense.[61] There is no need to argue that any model of "creation" in pre-existent space

---

59. This logic is, in a way, inverse with respect to what, in history of discussions on extracosmic space, was called "intrusion" arguments. The essence of these arguments is that if the cosmos in its entirety will decay through fire, there must be extra space for that conflagration. A similar argument for extraspace was historically produced by Cleomedes in his hypothesis of the possibility of the whole cosmos to be shifted. If this were to be possible, there must be extracosmic void. See details in Sorabji, *Matter*, 125–41.

60. See Tryon, "Is the Universe a Vacuum Fluctuation?," 222–25.

61. One can invoke a famous Aristotelian objection to existence of a void beyond the cosmos on the grounds of the counter arguments to Cleomedes who suggested that the whole cosmos could be shifted as a whole. According to Aristotle the logical difficulty would be exactly in the choice of the direction of movement: why should the cosmos move in this direction rather than that, and why should it stop here rather than there? (Aristotle, *Physics*, 4.8 [215a1]). In modern terms this can be described as if the preexistent space would be uniform: the uniformity makes devoid of any sense a questioning the absolute position of the cosmos since all locations are equivalent, so that the location of the cosmos could be described in terms of "everywhere" and "nowhere."

has nothing to do with creation out of nothing in a theological sense, for space, time, the "law" of origination of this universe are all assumed to be pre-existent.[62] One can talk about the *temporal origination* of the material universe rather than about its creation out of nothing.[63] This confirms the previously described conviction of the Fathers that any enquiry into the facticity of the initial conditions of the created universe fixing its age does not make any sense if creation is understood as *creatio ex nihilo*, that is, if nothing pre-existed it.

Using these examples from Patristic theology in the contemporary cosmological context one reconfirms the already anticipated conclusion that the beginning of the world and its created temporality can only be grasped from *within* the world. No constitution or objectivization of this beginning is possible as if it would be seen from beyond the world, because this "beyond the world" is not an "object" but rather the condition of the very possibility for the world to be manifested *to* and articulated *by* human beings. In this sense the quest for the beginning of the created universe reveals itself as a quest for the limits of human subjectivity attempting to grasp the facticity of the world. Then the idea of creation of the universe out of nothing turns out to be the necessary transcendental delimiter in all possible enquiries about the origin of facticity of the universe as a whole: one cannot proceed in the enquiry of the origin of the world by bypassing the issue of its contingent facticity related to its creation out of nothing. The very

62. This is the reason why an overoptimistic phraseology of some cosmologists that they produced a theory of creation of the universe "out of nothing" does not make either scientific or theological sense. As was once emphasized by Michael Heller, this kind of "nothingness" is "theory-impregnated," that is, that which theory can say *nothing* about (Heller, "Classical Singularities," 7–13). An example of a recent heroic claim that cosmology deals with creation out of nothing can be found in Krauss, *A Universe from Nothing*, 2012. The objection to this is that in order to create out of nothing, there must be physical laws or complicated mathematical structures which definitely do not manifest themselves as "nothing" in a philosophical sense. They can be intelligible as ideas, but not nothing. This objection is similar to the critique of Hawking's claims that the universe was self-sufficient and thus necessary with no need to appeal to a sort of creator (see above). See such a critique in Craig, "What Place, Then, for a Creator?," 279–300, as well as Nesteruk, *Light from the East*, ch. 5. A recent critique of cosmologists's pretense for "explaining" the perennial issue of creation of the world can be found in George F. R. Ellis, "The Domain of Cosmology," in Chamcham et al., *The Philosophy of Cosmology*, 9.

63. The first "scientific" ideas on the origination of the universe in pre-existent space and time were proposed by Newton who intended to reconcile the biblical account of creation with the world having a beginning, with his view that time could have neither beginning nor end. Newton asserted that the visible universe was brought into existence by God in the past which is separated from us by finite time, but this took place within the absolute and infinite space and time.

representation of such a creation within the temporality of the world as a specific temporal origination of the universe forms another transcendental delimiter in appropriation of the issue of the facticity of the universe when the contingent facticity of its actual display, accessible to human observes, is shifted towards the remote past resembling ancient ideas of the primordial undifferentiated substance (as the "mother" of "father" of the universe). Since it is impossible to explicate the contingent facticity of the incredibly varied display of the visible universe, its alleged unity is delegated to its past. However, all images of the original past of the universe (even if they are produced with help of mathematics) remain only regulative ideas whose ontological sense is uncertain.

CREATION IN THE NATURAL ATTITUDE OR HOW NOT TO SPEAK ABOUT CREATION: KANT'S INSIGHT IN THE ISSUE OF "WHY NOT SOONER OF CREATION?"

It is worth reminding to the reader that the models of pre-existent space-time have been used by those who opposed the idea of *creatio ex nihilo* on the basis of the mentioned undecidedness of the "when of creation?"[64] Indeed, the logical difficulty of models with pre-existent space and time is connected with the inability to locate the moment of time and place in space where the universe originated. One can argue about the beginning of time as its origination by extrapolating the expansion of the visible universe backward in time. But this will never allow one to claim scientifically that there either was or was not pre-existent time "before" our universe came into existence. If the specific origination of the universe is associated with its initial conditions, then one cannot define these conditions as set up from beyond the universe. Correspondingly the question of "when of creation?" can be interpreted as a question about the specific nature of these initial conditions rephrased as "why these initial conditions but not the other?" Such a link between the question of "when of creation?" as the question about the age of the universe, and the specific initial conditions of the universe opens an interesting possibility of making a modern a la scientific interpretation of that theological stance on the cause of creation to which Maximus the Confessor referred as "the unsearchable wisdom of the infinite essence."[65] In order to do this we elucidate the essence of the difficulty of

---

64. See Sorabji, *Time*, 232–52.
65. Maximus the Confessor, *Cap. de Charitate* 4.3, in *The Ascetic Life*, 192.

"when of creation?" in philosophical terms by using Kant's analysis of his first cosmological antinomy. According to Kant, the first antinomy is formulated, as a tension between the thesis that the world had a beginning in time and is limited in space, and antithesis that it had no beginning in time and is unlimited in space.[66]

According to Kant, if the world had a beginning this would imply the existence of "empty" time before the world began. Then he argues that there is nothing in any moment of "empty" time to determine why the world had begun at that moment of time, rather than that at any other. Referring to Leibniz's principle of sufficient reason and pointing that there was no sufficient reason for the world to begin at one or another moment of "empty" time, the world cannot begin at any moment of this time and hence it never began. The refutation of the thesis implies that Kant adopts a Newtonian idea of absolute space and infinite time. This means that if one does not share Newton's vision of space and time as independent of its material content (Leibniz, for example, claimed that space was relational upon that which it contained), for this one Kant's refutation of the thesis collapses because the idea of empty time becomes philosophically devoid of meaning (similarly to many ancient theologians who argued that no time was in existence before the world has begun).

If according to Leibniz's model of relational space and time there must be relations between things in the world which give rise to space and time, then the problem of the beginning of the universe *with* time can be reformulated as existence of the *inaugural event* of such a relationship that was followed by other events, but was not preceded by any events. In this case the parlance of empty time "before" this first event looses sense and Kant's thesis transforms into the issue about the *first (inaugural) event* and the assertion of the thesis on the beginning of the world *in* time would transform into the assertion of the first event: "Why did the particular event with no antecedent causation take place?" or "Why the inaugural event happened in order the world would be brought into existence?" Since Kant did not consider theological arguments, he did not consider his refutation of the thesis as a possible objection to *creatio ex nihilo*. He rather was concerned with the difficulties of the human understanding in tackling the questions of origins of the world, as would say nowadays, in the phenomenality of objects.

As we have seen above, if the world as "an object" is positioned in pre-existent space and time of a Newtonian kind, one can raise some logical objections to the finite origin of the world because this "positioning" is undetermined. If, on the other hand, the same thesis of the Kantian antinomy

---

66. Kant, *Critique of Pure Reason*, A426–27/B454–55.

is understood as a statement about the *inaugural (first) event*, then a possible refutation of this thesis would not make sense, for this inaugural event is responsible for all consequent temporal series that make the empirical world manifest (its refutation is impossible because it is existentially contradictive). Viewed in this angle, the sense of the antinomy as a difficulty of knowing the origins of the universe clarifies further the difficulties of the human cognitive faculties to deal with this issue in the phenomenality of objects. Let us elucidate this point by employing a mathematical example.

If there was a first event in the world's history, then the duration of that history backwards from any assigned instant in it, for example the present, is finite. However the sense of the finitude of the past can be established only if a definite scale of time is adopted such that the first event would imply the absolute beginning of this very scale, assuming that the backward passage of time from the present to this beginning is similar to the passage of time that is perceived by us as a linear flow. If, however, the scale of time in order to approach its beginning is different and is based on a different type of a limiting procedure, the very definition of the inaugural event as the first event becomes problematic because in some of such procedures this "first" event cannot be reached. In this case the temporal finitude of the world is compatible with the inability to pin down the first event.[67] For example, let us imagine that the passage of time from the present to the allegedly existing beginning is measured by means of a sequence of rational fractions of a type P_n/Q_n (where P_n and Q_n are integers) descending in the order of magnitude from $P_0/Q_0 =1$ at present to the $\lim(P_n/Q_n) = 0$ at t=0 as $Q_n \to \infty$. Such a sequence $\{P_n/Q_n\}$ whose initial term is 1, does not have a concluding term because $Q_n \to \infty$ is being discretely reached only asymptotically, so that the smallest fraction corresponding to t=0 effectively does not exist and practically the initial moment of time does not exist because it cannot be reached.

However, if the non-linear and discrete scale of the passage of time towards the beginning involves an infinite number of steps whilst remaining in the finite segment (0, 1] of "linear" time (the segment which is rather

---

67. A famous example, although in terms of space, is that of Henri Poincaré and can be elaborated as follows. One can imagine a perfectly spherical universe (with the radius r) with the property that any object with a volume v at the centre of such a universe, if it moves towards the edge effectively shrinks so that its volume becomes $v \, d/r$, where d is the distance from the edge. Any imagined inhabitant of this world will not be able to determine the size of the world through reaching its edge because by approaching the edge he would be of a zero size, so that by approaching a point at the edge, he never quite reaches it. From the point of such an inhabitant the world does have no edge at all. However from the point of view of some transcendent being such a spherical world is finite. See details in Le Poidevin, *Travels in Four Dimensions*, 98–99.

a mental representation of a geometrical fragment achieved without establishing a measure of its count), one can talk *not* about the *first event of counting* of time (Pn/Qn --> 0 as Qn --> ∞), but about the *inaugural event* of the count of time (the low boundary of the set (0, 1]), as an event of consciousness escaping the causality of the world through any possible computation and any categorical predetermination. In this case the intuition of the inaugural event of the world turns out to be inextricably linked to the archetypically immemorial inaugural event of consciousness projecting such an event onto the world.

The latter mathematical example shows that the duration of the world backwards in time can be understood by two different means. The first one is a view that the world's age can be calculated only from within counting the sequence of time towards the past discretely by a sort of a limiting procedure. Then its duration is infinite because of the infinite number of terms in the temporal sequence or infinite numbers of steps in order to perform this sequence through computation. In this case the infinitude of the passage of time is associated with its effective non-computability: in order to explicate the beginning of time one implies an infinite computational synthesis (infinite number of approximating theoretical stages describing the limiting procedure) not available to the finite human beings even if they are taken in the totality of mankind. However, if one models the temporality of the world on the grounds of the finite set of physical laws by extrapolating them backwards in time (e.g., Einstein equations of expansion of the universe) driving the backward contraction of the universe, the age of the universe (corresponding in our example to the numerical measure of the segment (0,1]) could be finite, so that the "zero" (0) can be *formally* treated as the first or inaugural event in spite of the fact that its contingent facticity as the contingent facticity of the initial condition remains undisclosed.

Since the segment (0,1] is of a finite length, the infinite sequence of rational numbers imitating the passage of time from the present to t=0 is positioned within this segment considered as an already given "object" independently of how the temporal sequence from the present to t=0 is constituted. This example is relevant to cosmology in two different senses. First, in spite of the existing estimates of the age of the universe, the approaching of its beginning through a physical theory is problematic since the known physics has a low limit of its applicability related to the Planck's scales in terms of space and time. Correspondingly the actual moment t=0 can theoretically be achieved only through an advance of physical theory in actual physical time, that is, through many investigational steps that will constitute only a limiting procedure of approaching t=0. Second, in order to proceed from the allegedly existing initial state of the universe to its actual astronomical display, theory effectively must exercise an infinite amount of steps within the finite temporal span of the universe because of the practical infinity of objects in the universe. Indeed one can talk about the inaugural event in the history of the universe, but this event is a mental creation whose theoretical constitution is problematic. This event is introduced as a regulative notion, encapsulating the whole development of the universe into the future. Thus, as we have discussed before, it is a teleological notion referring to the teleology of explanation.

In order to strengthen the latter conclusion, let us rearticulate the mathematical exercise with the non-linear, discrete and infinite count of time in the context of the world history. It demonstrates that this history did not have any first term in the sense that this first term cannot be reached; yet the overall duration of this history (the age of the universe) is finite. The dramatism of not being able to reach the first term in history was once expressed by Teilhard de Chardin: "the origin of organisms, societies, institutions, languages, and ideas escape us as if the essentially fugitive tracks of these embryonic states were automatically effaced."[68] Modern cosmology says similar things, namely that its direct experimental basis can extend our knowledge of the universe to a sort of its ultimate frontier in the past, when the universe was non-transparent for radiation and one speaks of its dark ages.[69] The studying the past either in the Earthly history or in the universe is an extremely difficult and very lengthy enterprise occupying a considerable period of time thus extending the past into the future determined by the task of such a research. The sense of the past thus becomes filled in by the sense of those computational efforts in the constitution of this past. But all constitutional acts are directed to the future entailing that the past as the representation of the origin of the universe is *epistemologically* in the future of humanity. Thus the past of the universe becomes in a way the *telos* of cosmological explanation epistemologically belonging to the future. Viewed in this vein both questions, either "Why not sooner of creation?" or "Why not sooner the appearance of Homo Sapiens?" can receive their responses only through their careful constitution through research as directed to the future and having a *telos* of explaining the origins of the universe and of life. Then as such these questions do not have sense as demanding in response some determining judgements (in the sense of Kant), but rather have a regulative sense inaugurating and ordaining all enquiries into the origin of the universe and humanity.

68. Teilhard de Chardin, *The Vision of the Past*, 190.

69. The hope to look inside these dark ages is associated with attempts to catch the signatures of the processes related to the formation of gravitational waves before the era of recombination when the universe became transparent to the optical radiation.

One can now rearticulate the sense of what is implied in the question "Why did the world begin when it did?" (as a variation of the question "Why not sooner?"). As was emphasized by Peter Strawson, the supposition that the world might have begun at some other time than it did is as empty of meaning as the supposition that its external temporal relations might have been different.[70] Correspondingly there cannot be any explanation as to "Why did the world begin when it did?" and not at some other time. Strawson makes an attempt to elucidate the question by invoking the notion of the *present now*. Indeed, it is by attempting to conceive the history of the world as differently positioned in time, shifted either backwards or forwards, what is tacitly supposed is that all temporal relations in the world remain intact and the identity of the present moment remains independent of how time was filled in with historical events. In this sense the very shift of the whole sequence of the world events does not make any sense since it does not change anything in perception of the *now*.

The question "Why did the world begin when it did?" can acquire a different sense if it refers to the internal nature of the world processes. In response to Strawson's claim that he does not know how this can be shown, and to his appeal for physicists to construe and answer this question as an internal question, modern cosmology can clarify some points. For example, the age of the universe is claimed to be about fourteen billion years and one could pose a question, for example, why the universe needed so long to exist? Why its age is not, let us say, fourteen million (instead of billion) years? In this case physical cosmology provides an argument that the universe must be older than ten billion years in order the carbon-based life could develop and the human enquiry in the age of the world be possible.[71] However in this case the initial question "Why did the world begin when it did?" has nothing to do with the allegedly pre-existing empty space and time. If the anthropic argument is dismissed on the grounds of its teleological overtones (implying that the evolution of the universe was driven by its final goal to have conditions for the appearance of humanity), cosmology has to accept that the specific age of the universe is related to the specific initial conditions of this universe not controlled by the physics pertaining to this universe. In any case the asking of the question "Why did the world begin when it did?" implying a setting of special "transcendent" initial conditions for the universe is devoid of sense, either because there is nothing beyond the world in terms of time and space (so that such conditions simply do not exist), or, if one attempts to position the world "within eternity and

---

70. Strawson, *The Bounds of Sense*, 179.
71. See Barrow and Tipler, *The Anthropic Cosmological Principle*, 18.

infinity" of some pre-existent reality, there is no sense of asking "when" and "where" within them because de facto the question is about the specificity of the given initial conditions (within the ensemble of other possible initial conditions representing not anything physically pre-existent, but an intelligible image of the possibilities of different existences). This shift from the issue related to the age of the universe to the specificity of its initial condition drastically changes the ways along which the question "Why not sooner?" can be addressed because this question transforms into the question of choice in the manifold of the initial conditions: "Why this initial condition gives rise to the universe with the given age and not the other?" But the manifold of the initial conditions is an intelligible entity so that the hypothetical choice of one of them is a mental procedure hardly having anything to do with physics. Indeed, in order to elucidate this view let us turn to that part of Kant's antinomy which is related to space.

The thesis of Kant's antinomy contains a part related to spatial extension of the world: if the world is finite in time and had a beginning, its spatial span is also finite. Kant's refutation of this thesis begins in the same way as he refuted the thesis about time. If the spatial extension of the world is finite, this world must be situated somewhere within an unlimited *empty space* (absolute space of a Newtonian kind, for example). Here Kant could potentially build his further argument by invoking the same move as he used with respect to the refutation of the beginning of time, namely that the position of the world in empty space cannot be fixed by any means: there is no sufficient reason for why the world could not be in another region of absolute space rather than to be where it is. In other words, if the world is presented in the phenomenality of objects, it could be positioned in any part of the absolute space and one cannot give any reason for any particular choice.

However, Kant invokes here a different argument that allows one to reinterpret the question of "Why not sooner?" in a completely new perspective. According to him there must be a certain relation between the world as a whole and empty space where this world is "situated." Kant describes this possible relation as a "relation" to *nothing*, concluding that there can be no relation at all and thus the world cannot be limited in spatial extension. However, his identification of empty space (or absolute space) with *nothing* makes sense only if one believes that empty space cannot be described in terms of those rubrics of thought which pertain to the world. In this case the positioning of the finite world within thus defined *nothing* indeed does not make any sense because it is devoid of any meaningful content. If, however, empty space (absolute space) allows its mental representation as an intelligible entity, its relation to the world would not be a relation of nothing to something. If absolute space represents an intelligible entity whose ontological status is fundamentally different in comparison with that one of the world, there can be a mental relation between absolute space and the world as a relation between an intelligible entity and that one which is empirical. In fact, Kant affirms that space is merely a form of outer intuition and that it is not a real object which can be outwardly intuited ("Space, ... is, under the name of absolute space, nothing but the mere possibility of outer appearances."[72]) He indicates that the sense of such a space is related to the transcendental faculties of the apprehending intellect. In this case the very attempt to construct the meaningful relation between the world and absolute space is a failure from the beginning since it attempts to bring into correlation two ontologically non-uniform realms. Then the question of the arbitrary "position" of the world as a whole within absolute space (tantamount to the assertion that this absolute space (if it is thought as Euclidian space) is intelligibly uniform), becomes also a question of a definite size of the world which could be formulated similarly to that one with respect to time: "Why not bigger or smaller?" This question is similar to the question about the contingent position of the world in absolute space for the size of the world cannot be measured in relation to the infinite absolute space and it can have, according to the fourth axiom of Euclid, any spatial measure. When Kant treats absolute space as a form of outer intuition this deprives the thesis of the antinomy of any ontological meaning. Neither pre-existing time nor space can be assigned an ontological status similar to that of the world. Correspondingly the positioning of the world in the background of pre-existing intelligible initial conditions makes a modern disguise of the perennial questions about the contingent facticity of the world in terms of its age and its size as they are seen from within the world.

What becomes clear from this analysis of Kant's antinomy is that the major difficulty appears when one carelessly identifies the ontology of *the origin* of the world with that ontology which pertains to the world itself (one can say differently: when the phenomenality of the origin and of the physical world is not discerned as different). In this case the antinomian difficulty manifests itself as a problematic transition from an intelligible realm (as the only legitimate "place" for any speculations about the origins of the world) to the world as it is in space and time. This transition is possible in the mind of the subject of the antinomy, but one cannot project this transition onto the ontological plane. In fact such a transition represents no more than a typically human hermeneutics of the universe's origin. In this case the question "Why not sooner?" as a question about the very special initial

---

72. Kant, *Critique of Pure Reason*, footnote *b* to B457, 398.

conditions for our universe can theoretically be referred to the possibility of choice in the manifold of all possible initial conditions (considered as an intelligible possibility) by some transcendent omniscient being whose archetype humanity imitates. Any attempt to tackle the problem of the origin of the universe in the natural attitude, having as its simplest application the representation of the universe in the phenomenality of objects, fails simply because this origin in analogy with the origin of the hypostatic life is phenomenologically concealed from the human grasp.

A POSSIBLE THEOLOGICO-SCIENTIFIC SYNTHESIS IN RESPONDING TO THE ISSUE OF "WHY NOT SOONER OF CREATION?"

In spite of understanding that the issue of creation in its particular expression through the question "Why not sooner of creation?" cannot be fully grasped, it is still interesting to produce its hermeneutics on the cross-roads of theology and science. Formally this option amounts to the possibility of considering the question "Why not sooner of creation?" by transforming the Kantian antinomy where no reference to space and time will be present. In this case the thesis can be treated as the affirmation that the visible universe is unique and finite as regards space and time, and does not need any justification through the reference to any transworldly causation because this "transworldly" simply does not exist. This universe is characterized by the immanent initial conditions. Whereas the antithesis is that the visible universe, being finite in terms of its temporal past, is one particular representative out of the *ensemble* of potentially possible universes with various initial conditions (corresponding, to different ages and other parameters of these universes). The refutation of the thesis thus would appeal to the impossibility of claiming the uniqueness of the universe and thus uniqueness of the initial conditions leading to a particular age of the universe; whereas the refutation of the antithesis would appeal to the impossibility of claiming the opposite (that there are potentially many possible universes with various initial conditions).

The plurality of different initial conditions corresponds to the logical multitude of a Platonic-like kind, so that the antinomial nature of any predication on the uniqueness or not of these conditions becomes evident because the ontological status of that which is predicated in thesis and antithesis is different: one can make an empirical inference with respect to the visible universe, whereas an assumption that there is a potentially possible variety of the universes with different initial conditions, unverifiable empirically, requires an intellectual inference, that is, a reference to the realm of the intelligible. In this case the whole meaning of the antinomy reveals itself as predication about two ontologically distinct realities: the empirical universe and the Platonic-like ensemble of the universes with different initial conditions. If we extrapolate this reasoning back to the problem, discussed by Maximus the Confessor, the question posed by him in the *Centuries on Charity* 4.3 must be transformed in such a way that the temporal aspect of the specificity of the creation of the world is replaced by the aspect of "choice" of this particular world out of many potential possible worlds, namely "Why did God choose to create this world but not the other?"

It is not difficult to see that in this transformation of the idea of pre-existent space and time towards an intelligible realm with a variety of initial conditions one abandons an ontological insight on the nature of appearance of the visible universe (i.e., no question on the physical causation leading to the visible universe) and replaces it by an "event-like" inference (the argument by choice of the initial conditions) related to the Divine agency. This implied "event" (as choice) has nothing to do with the causality of the world because it is beyond the world, qualitatively unmeasurable, unforeseen and metaphysically impossible. Correspondingly it can be considered as the inaugural event, granting the universe the future, but whose sense can only be disclosed through the movement of the human thought in the thus "chosen" universe. Certainly, the imagery of the ensemble of possible universes with different initial conditions as they "stand" in the "mind of God" is itself a metaphor made in the natural attitude assuming that one can position these "universes" as the outer entities. However their status remains that of intelligible objects pressing again the point that these universes remain created entities and one cannot separate them from that subject who asserts the free choice of God in materializing the universe with those initial conditions which lead to the observable display of the cosmos with its particular age. The appeal to the "choice" of the initial conditions effectively points to the freedom and wisdom of creation of the world with no reference to the anticipatory context of such a creation if the latter could be imagined. Correspondingly, for us, this "choice" carries the traces of *event* exceeding the measure of the metaphysically possible, unpredictable and unforeseeable. Since in Patristic times phenomenology of events did not exist, patristic vision of the issue of the beginning of the world was shaped differently, but in its spirit similarly, by transforming the allegedly ontological question of "Why not sooner?" into the question about the event of creation of the world as a moment God's self-affectivity as Life. How such an event of choice receives its treatment in these Patristic writers? Let us return back to Maximus the Confessor.

According to Maximus the Confessor the world is created by the will, wisdom and love of God, so that any enquiry into its facticity (its age for example) is illegitimate on the same grounds as any attempt to know God. Yet Maximus is able to provide an interpretation of these general premises of God's volitions with respect to the world by invoking the language of *logoi* as underlying and forming principles of creation by which God knows the things of the created world and by which the choice of this world is ultimately made out of those other possible worlds which are thought by God. The creation of the world with a specific age corresponds in this logic to the choice of the world according to its *logos*, that is, according to God's design with a particular purpose. What is this purpose? Humanity can define it only with respect to itself and its own religiously motivated purposes. Hence one can anticipate that this sought *logos* of creation is intimately linked to God's plan of salvation (deification) of humanity and transfiguration of the world.

In *Ambigua 7* Maximus states that "the *logoi* of all things known by God before their creation are securely fixed in God. . . . Yet all these things, things present and things to come, have not been brought into being contemporaneously with their being known by God; rather each was created in appropriate way according to its *logos* at the proper time according to the wisdom of the maker."[73] He makes a distinction between *knowledge* of things by God in their *logoi* and their *actual coming into being*. Knowledge of things even if they are known eternally does not imply the necessity of their existence as created. If one applies this thought either to this universe or any other as a possibility, one can suggest that the knowledge by God of these universes with a potential to become created does not necessarily imply their creation. There is a gap in the necessitation between knowledge and actual creation based, according to Maximus, in the Divine wisdom and will and which not only brings all things into existence at their proper time, but ultimately brings the actually existing world as a whole into existence. The words of Maximus related to the wisdom of the Creator with regard to the "determination" of a proper moment of creation can be, by a matter of philosophical suggestion, applied to the "determination of the choice" of the world as such, or, in cosmological phraseology, the choice of the world with those initial conditions which led to the actual display of the universe. Then the question is: could God know not only of this world which he has actually created, but of other potential worlds which either have not been created at all, or have been created in a different modus (*tropos*) of being?

---

73. Maximus the Confessor, *Ambigiua 7*, in Blowers and Wilken, *On the Cosmic Mystery*, 56–57.

If the answer is yes, we must suppose that just as God applied his wisdom for creating this world, he must have been wise of not creating other worlds, or creating them in a different *modus* of being. This wisdom reveals itself through God's will to make a choice to actually create this world. Correspondingly all other worlds, being only potential possibilities either were implanted in creation as intelligible entities so that their *logoi* not entailed that they acquire any corporeal shape, remaining the images and prints of the divine wisdom accessible to an intellectual grasp and contemplation. In this sense the very idea of the variety of the "initial" conditions for the worlds created with a different modality of existence manifests itself as a pointer to the divine wisdom.

Our treatment of Maximus the Confessor's thought makes the problem of the specific temporal beginning of our universe transformed toward the problem of the ontological *distinction* in the structure of creation, namely, the *difference* (*diaphora*) between the corporeal world and the worlds remaining no more than intelligible traces of that which could be known by God, but created not in the corporeal form. The actual choice of creating our physical universe can be treated as *setting up a special difference in the overall creation*, the *difference* between the non-corporeal worlds and the sensible world. In this case the setting of the initial conditions for the actual physical universe implies a *certain intelligible structure* which complements the actual universe in the whole creation. In cosmology, for example, this structure can be described as an ensemble of all possible initial conditions of the universe, only one of which leads to the actual physical universe. Roger Penrose gave a characteristic graphical representation of such a model by attributing to it some pseudo-theological meaning. There is an intelligible world (V) (depicted as a certain space volume) containing all possible initial conditions for the universe. One point of this shape corresponds to the initial condition of the visible universe W. Both, V and W constitute the created world in its constitutive differentiation. The actualization of the world W in the corporeal form as our world, according to Penrose, is caused by a demiurgic deity which choses the world W to become corporeal by pinning one particular point in the volume V. This choice means *de facto* the setting of the specific and concrete *difference (diaphora)* between the sensible world W and the rest of the intelligible world V as the constitutive element of creation of both V and W out of nothing. The specificity of the origin of the visible universe, articulated by Penrose, points to that specificity which is already *constituted* in creation, but not to the ontological mechanism of the creation of the whole world. We contemplate this special constitutive element of *creatio ex nihilo* through the model of this difference between V and W. Generalizing, the choice of the corporeal world out of many potential worlds means setting up the basic ontological *difference* (*diaphora*) in creation, that which becomes a constitutive element of *creatio ex nihilo*.[74] The will and wisdom of God in creating this world with its particular immanent age is thus encapsulated in the specific *diaphora* between this world and all those which are not destined to become corporeal. One can say that the *logos* of creation of this universe is that the constitutive *difference* between its empirical display and the intelligible image of the universes with other initial conditions is fixed through a particular feature of *this* universe, namely its immanent age, as related to the will and wisdom of God to maintain the promised salvation for humanity made in his Image.

In conclusion to this section one can assert that modern cosmology, in spite of its attempts to explicate the initial state of the universe through the theories of the Big Bang (but remaining perennially silent about the contingent facticity of the Big Bang linked to the problem of the facticity of the age of the universe), has to come to the same conclusion that was grasped long before by philosophers and theologians, namely that the "original" state of the universe symbolizes its unity, identity, and totality, and cannot be defined in immanent terms; it requires a founding transcendent principle which explicates the *logos* of creation of the universe. One can conjecture that from what we have discussed this principle could be understood as that both, intelligible universes and the actual sensible (visible) universe are theogenically uniform, that is, they have one and the same transcendent ground of their existence in their non-existence (non-being). In Maximus the Confessor's words: "the whole of creation admits of one and the same undiscriminated *logos*, as having not been before it."[75] Here is a slightly different formulation of the same principle; "the divine principle which holds the entire creation together is that it should have non-being as the ground of its being."[76] This principle is just a different formulation that the physical universe and its intelligible counterpart are created by God out of nothing (out of non-being of these universes). Unlike the already discussed Penrose's demiurgic pinning down of the initial conditions of the physical universe out of the variety of other possible conditions, the creation of the overall state of affairs cannot be depicted graphically, for the transition from

---

74. See details on Maximus the Confessor's treatment of creation in Thunberg, *Microcosm and Mediator*, 50–55.

75. Maximus the Confessor, *Ambigua 41*, in Louth, *Maximus the Confessor*, 160.

76. Thunberg, *Microcosm and Mediator*, 401. Compare with a similar passage from *Cap. de Charitate* 3.28: "We affirm that the divine substance alone has nothing contrary, since its is eternal and infinite and bestows eternity on all the rest. The substance of things, however, has not-being as contrary" (Maximus the Confessor, *The Ascetic Life*, 178).

the linguistically signified nothing to any form of something is impossible (there is no causal principle of the created world).

The detection of the *logos* of creation contains in itself a movement of human thought in two opposite directions. On the other hand, an attempt to detect the *logos* through the theory of the original past of the universe positions the intended material pole of cosmological explanation in the temporal past of the world. Indeed, in Penrose's model this *logos* is related to the *initial* (antecedent) conditions of the universe. Yet, the explanation of the initial condition of the universe (the choice by Penrose's demiurge) remains always a task for the future of all theories of the universe. On can say that, the explication of the *logos* of creation of the universe as related to its past becomes the *telos* of cosmological explanation.[77] To understand the universe and hence to make it "humanized" (in the sense of Maximus's "makro-anthropos" idea) one must understand its origination as pointing to the *logos* of its creation. But the unfolding of the sense of this *logos*, its mental and linguistic explication (through the natural contemplation)[78] is a dynamic process always directed to the future, so that the *telos* of explanation of the universe is related to the explication of its *logos*. But since the telic activity is pertaining to humanity as part of the universe, the *logos* of creation of the universe immanently contains this *telos*. So that the human path of knowing the universe and knowing of itself is intrinsically implanted in that *logos* which is self-explicated through human life. However this *telos* of explicating the *logos* of creation as part of human life can only be fulfilled through the reference to the saving economy of the Divine in the created world, that is, to the teleology of that which was effected in the incarnate Christ as an archetype of the human *Imago Dei*. The Incarnation thus is organically part of the *logos* of creation in accordance with that which Maximus the Confessor was saying: "For it is for Christ, that is, for the Christic mystery, that all time and all that is in time has received in Christ its beginning and its end."[79] Saying cosmologically the specific initial conditions of the universe and its immanent age explicate the saving *logos* of the universe as related to the necessary conditions of creation of humanity and Christ's Incarnation. Correspondingly, the question "Why not sooner of creation?"

---

77. For more on this, see Nesteruk, *The Sense of the Universe*, 334–43.

78. One must make a distinction between the *knowledge* of the *presence* of the principles of creation (that there *are* the *logoi* which hold the creation) and the *contemplation* of the *logoi* as a special stage of an advanced spiritual development. For if the detection of their presence is possible through scientific research, for example, the contemplation of the *logoi* requires a religious modus of participation in ecclesial life.

79. Maximus the Confessor, *Questions to Thalassius* 60.

receives its further elucidation through linking it to the necessary conditions of the Incarnation in the universe.

Yet, such a questioning already implies the presence of humanity in the created universe as its center of disclosure and manifestation. The question "Why not sooner of creation?" is the human question and relates to another question "Why humanity can pose such a question at all?" The latter is a phenomenological question because it is related to the possibility of experience of assigning a sort of phenomenality to the origin of the universe. In order to give to this question a proper phenomenological response let us start from approaching this question in the natural attitude. A possible response in the natural attitude could be like this: the world is old and has its specific age because there is humanity in it that can enquire in its age.

The manner of this response is teleological, subordinating the sense of creation to its final goal, that is, to humanity that articulates this sense. Such a classical teleology seems to be philosophically compromised if one attempts to establish a causation from the present state of affairs in the universe to its original past. However, a phenomenological appropriation of such a teleology can be different. Teleology can be treated as related to the structures of the human subjectivity demonstrating a formal purposiveness of any human enquiry in the sense of existence. Practically this means that any human encounter with the hidden sense of reality is imbued with the essentially primordial urge of the self-affective life to define itself. Teleology becomes an aspect of any existential move to explicate the sense of life. Seen in this context the question of "Why not sooner of creation?" becomes intrinsically linked to the human search for the sense of its own existence and *de facto* becomes a phenomenological question about the contingent facticity of the *created-world-as-it-is-given-to-humanity*. The very posing of the question about the origin of the world (and hence of life) becomes a characteristic indication that the one who is posing this question is alive. Saying differently this question becomes an outward expression of the human life's self-affectivity, reflecting the presence in any living being of that self-affective Life which creates the world.

All above considerations would remain philosophically abstract unless they are filled with the specifically Christian content, that is, when the self-affectivity of human life receives its christological interpretation. The hypostatic human self-affectivity archetypically proceeds from the incarnate Christ who as fully human was a locus point of the physical creation and who contained in himself the answer to the question "Why not sooner of creation?": not sooner because of Christ (and his Mother). The Incarnation can be experienced only phenomenologically because it as an inaugural *event* is not implanted in the logic of the material world, and the Holy Spirit who was present behind the Incarnation is acting upon human history. The Incarnation required that desire and freedom of both, God and the Virgin (in her "yes") which did not follow from the necessities of the world. Yes, the *necessary* conditions for the Incarnation were cosmologically formed through the history of the universe, but its sufficient conditions forever remain in the realm of the Spirit. Its phenomenological perception is confirmed by its two thousand years and still open-ended hermeneutics. It is through this that the Divine humanity experiences the world by being delimited by the cosmological conditions of the Incarnation of God as well as by the sheer contingency of the Incarnation as that *event* which was present in the *logos* of creation before the world was created (and in which the Son of God "begotten of the Father before all ages," "was incarnate of the Holy Spirit and the Virgin Mary"). The response to the question of "Why not sooner of creation?" cannot receive any interpretation as a question about the universe, but it can be interpreted as a question about humanity in the universe in the Image of the incarnate Christ.

THE UNIVERSE AS THE "PLACE" OF SELF-AFFECTIVE LIFE OR THE UNIVERSE AS A SATURATED PHENOMENON

The question of creation as it is usually formulated reveals itself from within the condition of living in the universe. The question then is how to characterize phenomenologically the experience of being created in the universe. The objective of such a description is to link the phenomenality of the universe with the events of human life as having their rooting in its physical condition as well as in its Divine archetype—the incarnate Word-Logos of God.

The approach to creation within the natural attitude can be paralleled with the substitution of a theological meaning of the universe as creation with the concepts which function according to how the physical facts of the universe are defined. In a theological discourse the words such as "God," "eternity," "creation" which signify cause and purpose, metaphysical foundation of existence, refer to mental definitions which do not have direct representations in experience of life. However, these concepts, in particular that of creation, use the same mental reference to the conditions, delimiters and contents that form the basis of sensory experience. Modern cosmology, for example, attempts to depict the origin of the visible universe as the transition from one "object" (multiverse) to another "object" (our universe). However, as we have pointed out, this is not the modelling of *creatio ex nihilo*. What is overlooked in this type of reasoning is that one cannot position oneself outside of creation that manifests itself through the fact of life. Since the articulation of creation of the world by human subjects is the process within creation, this process must be included in the explication of creation, that is, it must reveal the transcendental conditions of the possibility of such an explication. In a similar way, as we argued above, the explication of the origin of the universe in cosmology makes more sense as an explication of how the human subjectivity (dealing with this origin) functions, rather than with this origin as a fact or "object." In this case the problem of creation out of nothing acquires an existential importance for it does not say too much about the physical aspects of the universe and its origin but contributes to the explication of the human condition as being created and wanting to achieve communion with the Creator. But as we discussed above this communion is not a matter of necessity implanted in creation, it is not something subjected to biological instincts and the conditions of embodiment. Correspondingly, a soteriological meaning of dealing with the issue of creation is to strengthen the Divine Image in humans as knowing about their own creation.

The making irrelevant the natural attitude towards the issue of creation of the world invokes an epistemological situation where the perception of the universe as an "entity" extended in space and time is replaced by the perception of the universe through a relationship of belonging to it in aesthetical and ethical categories. Ancient Greek philosophers called such a universe *kosmos*, that is, beauty and order. However the *kosmos* of the Greeks, unlike that which is understood by the cosmos in modern cosmology, denoted *the way* by which the natural reality is. It denoted not that which was related to the question "What?" of the created universe but rather to the question "How?" The *kosmos* thus is the "ordered" revelation of the existent, that is, the notion related to beauty. But beauty is a matter of personal judgement and observing distinctions that can be justified only within relationship, that is, communion.

The approach to the world as a whole based on an attempt to treat the world in categories of beauty does not allow any formal and logical explanation of the world which would depersonify an immediate living communion with it in intellectual abstractions. One can experience the beauty of the world only through the immediate and intimate *relationship* as personal communion. Gazing at stars does not automatically imply communion: one could see stars and their constellations in a dispassionate curiosity and not to "hear" the music of the heaven which manifests the universe in its beauty (one sees the script, but does not hear the melody). In personal relationship one comes to know the universe not as an existent whose phenomenality is limited to the numerical and quantitatively measurable domain but as an unlimited manifold of indefinite differentiations manifested to a person. This mode of personal uniqueness of things is their beauty as the reality of the universe appearing as *kosmos* claiming itself as their unconcealment revealed in personal relationship. The personal action as ordering and arranging of the universe making it a beautiful *kosmos* cannot be exhaustively determined by the human reason through logic and quantitative definitions. It meets with reason dialogically, in the event of personal relationship-communion. It is only this relationship that makes possible the process of knowledge of the universe to the extent that we recognize in it *kosmos*. If a person contemplates the universe not simply as a conglomerate of different forms of matter, but as an "object" of art, the universe can be seen not as a clock-like mechanism, but as that ecstatic energy of the Creator (his self-affectivity) through which his person can be found and by which the knowing person is constituted.

In this personal appreciation of the *kosmos* the intuition of the universe gives immeasurably more than that in the universe which ever would have been intended or foreseen. To clarify this one may refer to Kant's distinction between the "rational idea" and "aesthetic idea." The "rational idea" (e.g., Kant's cosmological idea) can never become a sensible comprehension because it contains a concept (of the universe beyond empirical experience) for which no adequate intuition can ever be given. In fact, the rational cosmological idea is defined as a representation of an "object"—the universe—according to a principle that such a representation can never lead to empirical knowledge of the universe. To the "rational idea" (of the universe), can be contraposed the "aesthetic idea" of the universe (*kosmos through personal relationship, communion*), that is, a representation according to intuition which can never become an intellectual cognition, for which an adequate concept can ever be found. In this case the heart of matter is not that there is a lack that leaves a concept blind (no adequate intuition to the concept of the universe as a whole); conversely one has here the failure of the concept to clarify the intuition. The excess of intuition related to a particular sphere of experience of the universe over its conceptual representation makes impossible the situation when any linguistic representation ever reaches it completely and renders it intelligible. In other words, the excess of intuition of the universe never allows one to see the universe as an object. This incapacity to produce an object does not result from a shortage of donation of the universe (as happens in the rational idea of the universe), but from the excess of intuition, that is, from the excess of donation through the fact of being born into the universe, belonging to it. The "aesthetic idea" gives more than any concept can arrange and order the intuitive content according to rules of the understanding. The impossibility of this conceptual arrangement follows from the fact that the intuitive overabundance itself is not accessible to experience within the rules pertaining to discursive modalities of cognition. The intuition saturates the concept and renders its "overexposed," that is, keeps it invisible, blind not by the lack of "light" (the universe as a whole is invisible because it remains dark for the "light" of the categories of the understanding) but by the excess of "light" (there is too much in our intuition of the universe through belonging to it which cannot be discerned). The problem then is to find a phenomenological description of the "aesthetic idea" of the universe (communion with it) rendering thus the unforeseeable nature of the donation of the universe, the impossibility of seeing it as an object, and its freedom from that intentionality which is being circumscribed by the *a priori* rubrics of sensibility and the understanding.

First of all, the universe as a whole cannot be aimed at in the sense of a successive synthesis of *quantity* applied to ordinary objects. It is because of belonging to the universe and thus its unconditional givenness to us that the intuition that gives it is not limited, its excess can neither be divided nor put together because of a magnitude of its parts. The excess of the donating intuition could not be measured on the basis of its parts since this intuition surpasses the sum of these parts. The "phenomenon of the universe" should be called *incommensurable* in the sense of not measurable. This lack of measure does not operate here through the enormity of an unlimited quantity standing behind the universe. It is rather marked by the impossibility of applying a successive synthesis to it, as if one could foresee a complex whole on the basis of its parts. Since the universe as a whole exceeds any summation of its parts which are in many ways inaccessible to the subjectivity undertaking such a summation, the idea of a successive synthesis has to be replaced by what can be called the instantaneous synthesis (a synthesis of communion) that "precedes" and goes beyond possible (unobservable and imagined) components. Physically, one can perceive only a particular side of the universe that is "turned" to us by the surface of the past light cone related to our location in the universe.[80] That which imposes itself on us and overwhelms and fascinates us can be seen when one looks at the sky and sees patterns of stars. At this stage the successive synthesis attempted later in physical cosmology is suspended. That type of communion with the universe which is accompanied by an amazement and the sense of awe arises without any common measure with the phenomena which precede, announce or explain it.

---

80. See Appendix 2.

The universe as a saturated phenomenon cannot be accounted for according to quality as an intensive magnitude. The universe seems to be already there, available for our arrival, life in it and gaze at it. In this sense the universe imposes itself on us as preceding us. It appears to our view in the later childhood as well in an adult state as an unexpected, unpredictable fact, originating in what we perceive as the uncontrollable past. The more we study the universe astronomically, the more splendor we unfold that is unexpected and unpredictable. The universe comes to one, engulfs one and imposes itself without one's control and anticipation: thus it exhibits itself in the *phenomenality of events*.

What is meant here is that the phenomenon of the universe reaches an intensive magnitude without measure, so that starting from a certain degree the intensity of the intuition exceeds all anticipations of perception. Existentially, while experiencing the immediacy of communion with the universe one cannot predict or measure the intensity of this impression, for it is inseparable from the fact of life and thus, life itself, cannot be subjected to any measure: it either is or is not, either it is self-affective or not-existent. The intuition of the universe blinds the capacity of its anticipation through perception: it is unbearable for the gaze. The perception of the universe as a whole is blocked and its comprehension manifests itself as dim and dark, unformed and essentially disturbing. The universe falls under the rubric of the saturated phenomenon that Jean-Luc Marion characterizes by such a term as "bedazzlement."[81] The universe in its pieces and moments can be seen, but the universe as a whole cannot be seen because it is overexposed. The sense of incommensurability with the universe originates through the bedazzlement by its potential infinity. The finitude of humanity is experienced not so much through the shortage of the given (sense-impressions as different events in space and time), but, above all, through the overwhelming belonging to this universe as a fact of existence, whose "magnitude" of donation cannot be measured. Here human consciousness experiences itself in the suffering *passivity* (i.e., ignorance of its own origin) with no means to evaluate its own givenness in terms of any measure. The latter is a different form of our previous affirmation of the radical unknowability of humans by themselves because of being created with an excess of donation of existence by God. The universe as a saturated phenomenon then becomes an indirect encapsulation of that which constitutes humanity's Divine image. The universe as a whole in the image of the *Imago Dei* (i.e., as a saturated phenomenon) thus appears to be an outward expression of humanity's perennial concern about existence as such, entering as a cosmological term, the

---

81. Marion, "The Saturated Phenomenon," 200–202.

open-ended hermeneutics of the human condition. In this sense the universe becomes that inevitable accompanying element in every human life being an expression of God-Creator's self-affectivity, that is, of Life. Hence the universe as creation (to which humanity belongs) acquires, theologically speaking, the sense of *event* related to the self-affectivity of God of creating it and sustaining it in its own Life. Indeed, the universe as creation cannot be subjected to relational analysis because it is unique and one cannot rerun the universe or stage it as an experiment. The universe as a whole is identical only to itself, so that its unfolding facticity is characterized not only by its irreproducibility but by the logical irreversibility understood as a coming into the facticity of existence and impossibility of exiting this existence. The universe in its sheer givenness, makes itself a phenomenon not arising from our initiative and not responding to our expectations; it gives itself to us from itself to such an extent that it affects us, changes us and almost constitutes us. In spite of being made in the Image of God and thus exercising its freedom of defining its place in the universe in the perspective of its infinite saving tasks, the universe not only that which catches and makes oneself surrender, it is that which causes doubts of all human aspirations and hopes for an indefinite existence, all possibilities in an existential sense by reshaping them from its very foundation to the very end. Definitely the universe forms a constant metaphysical background of the human physical existence being de facto its ultimate ontic reference. However the universe and the Earthly environment are not in an intrinsic harmony with humanity in spite of the seeming stability of such a harmony in the very short (on a cosmic scale) recent history. Human existence in the universe is contingent upon many factors that cannot be foreseen, measured and logically related to any metaphysical necessity. In this sense the universe for every human being is perceived as that *transient* existence which is gifted to them with the very fact of life.

From the point of view of a physical cosmologist there is an imminent difficulty: how one can treat the universe as event if, outwardly, it is "a" stable object, that is, the astronomical cosmos out there and that which is allegedly beyond it. What is the basis for interpreting the universe as "an" or "the" event, if this word has mundane physical connotations as a particular happening in space and time? It is not difficult to realize that the logic of formulating such a question is exercised from within the natural attitude that thinks of the universe in the phenomenality of objects which by definition have a temporal pattern of stability and then cannot be events. The universe is always *over there*, as that place where human beings enquire about the universe or praise it as creation. However, as we have attempted to argue before, the universe as *articulated existence* is epistemologically mastered by us and hence transformed by us into the universe as it is seen from within the event of one's life and thus has an event-like phenomenality in spite of its naïve or scientific representation as an object.

By possessing the phenomenality of events the universe as a whole cannot be foreseen on the grounds of any causation, so that it imposes itself on perception without one being able to assign to it a substance in which it dwells as an accident (or a cause from which it results as an effect: there is no causal principle of the world). One could refer to the invisible whole of the universe as that substance "in" which the observable part of the universe (as its accident) dwells. The invocation of the idea of the primordial substance in this context would just mean a conviction that there is an undifferentiated unity of "all in all," and the visible universe represents a particular shaping of this substance in the sense of demiurgic ordering out of chaos. Any attempt to construct a "particular Big Bang model," for example that one in inflationary cosmology, where the inflationary generation of many bubble universes takes place,[82] does not reach any philosophically or theologically viable explanatory goal, since the cause of the ensemble of those bubbles indwelling in the substance of the originary "inflaton" field does not remove the question of the facticity of this field. Indeed, in analogy with ancient Greek philosophies this field can be considered as substance of the same mental kind as, for example, the "water" of Thales from Miletus from which the actual state of affairs in the world can be produced by a potentially infinite number of ways. Such a mental split in the representation of the universe as an accident indwelling in the primordial substance does not correspond to the immediate experience of the universe associated with an event of life for it is impossible to make a distinction between "substance" of life and life as an "accident." Correspondingly it is problematic to look for the cause of the universe if it is perceived as *coaevus universo*, that is, the universe as "simultaneous" with one's life.

The origin of the universe appears to be a privileged phenomenon since a significant effort of humanity is devoted to the reconstitution of its lost memory, to making sense of it and even, in a certain way, responding to its "appeal" to us as if the universe had its distinctive self-identity. Yet, humanity cannot have an access to this undeniable and unavoidable phenomenon directly. The fact that one cannot phenomenalize the origin of the universe and that nevertheless this origin reveals itself as that for which cosmology constantly intends, constitutes an aporia: *the origin of the universe shows to humanity precisely that its origin cannot be shown*. This aporia urges a philosophizing cosmologist to understand how the origin of the universe that

---

82. See Weinberg, *Cosmology*, 216–17.

does not show itself in fact affects humanity in a more radical way than any other phenomena, since the origin of the universe predetermines the necessary conditions for humanity's emergence in it. The origin of the universe can be called an inaugural phenomenon because it comes to pass in human life as an *event* that was never present in presence, and is always already gone past, whereas it never surpasses the present and, in fact, is always to come. Thus one can say that the origin of the universe phenomenalizes itself as a pure event which is unforeseen (it does not make sense of temporality before and outside the universe), irreproducible (one cannot rerun the universe), exceeding all cause (there is no physical causation from beyond the universe) and making the impossible possible (in the natural attitude, the probability of origination of our universe in multiverse scenarios is always infinitely small, that is, the universe is *a priori* impossible), surpassing all expectations and predictions (the constant advance of knowledge of the universe does not make it possible to assign to the universe some definitive and stable features that could sustain indefinitely the observational tests as well as an epistemological advance). Speaking of the origin of the universe we speak of its donation: it is given to us in the measure as it gives itself and its givenness to us is an apodictic fact-event which is alone responsible for that which we call the constituted phenomenon of the origin of the universe, or the universe as a whole.

By possessing the phenomenality of events the universe manifests and reveals itself in the history of humanity in the same way as some phenomena associated with the Revelation of God, those phenomena which influence and form the sense of human life as it is seen theologically. One may talk about the historicity of the universe not in the objective sense related to evolving aspects of the physical universe as they are described in cosmology. One implies the historicity of appearance and manifestation of the universe as its contingent givenness to humanity, that is, as an historical relation with it and communion. This historicity originates in humanity's attempt to understand the universe as a constitutive part of its effort to understand the sense of its own existence. It is through mastering (enhypostasizing) the universe that humanity encounters the hypostasis of the Logos by whom and through whom all was made and whose Image humanity Christians consider as their own. Then the sense of the universe is disclosed through the relation of humanity with that Logos, who at some stage of his own manifestation descended to this universe physically, that is, enhypostasized himself in the body of Jesus Christ. Then the Incarnation, as unforeseeable, metaphysically impossible, irreproducible, beyond measure of quantity and quality was a renewal of the old teaching that God created the universe, the teaching cascading in the human presentation of this universe to the *ever-manifesting event*, endowing this humanity with a potential to achieve the union with God where all extensions and divisions in the created life are sensed isomorphic to God's self-affectivity as Life with no beginning and end.

FROM CREATION OF THE WORLD TO CREATION OF HUMANITY: THE NARRATIVE OF THE INCARNATION

Since the creation of the world out of nothing was a precondition of the whole history of salvation, the Fathers of the church placed their understanding of creation in the context of the Incarnation of the second person of the Holy Trinity, the eternal Word-Logos of God in Jesus of Nazareth in whom the Word "became flesh." The Incarnation meant the union between the Divine and the created in the hypostasis of the Logos of God: Jesus Christ was fully divine as "the Son of God, the only-begotten of the Father, begotten before all ages" and fully human ("and was made man"). The phrase "begotten before all ages" implies that from eternity the Logos was prepared to become incarnate in man meaning that the humanity of Jesus was forever the part of God's way of existence. The latter assertion points towards the connection between creation and the Incarnation, where the Incarnation becomes implanted into the logic of the creation. If the world was created in order to attain the union with God, it is humanity that is granted the means of such an attainment through a special call. As we discussed this point before, the possibility of such an attainment effectively contributes to the definition of humanity. In this sense mankind is a special creation whose essence requires *grace*, the mechanism of acquiring of which proceeds through the Incarnation.

Indeed when Irenaeus of Lyons, for example, discusses the creation of man as made in image of God, he says that the image of God was not *shown*, "because the Word, in whose image man was made, was still invisible."[83] The Son-Logos of God through his incarnation recapitulates the whole creation again: "God recapitulated in himself that ancient handiwork of his which is man."[84] "When he became incarnate and was made man, he recapitulated in himself the long history of mankind."[85] (One can say the long history of the natural world was necessary for coming of man into being and hence the Incarnation.)

---

83. Irenaeus of Lyons, *Against the Heresies*, V.16.2.
84. Irenaeus of Lyons, *Against the Heresies*, III.18.6.
85. Irenaeus of Lyons, *Against the Heresies*, III.13.1.

If one follows the logic of Irenaeus, one can conclude that the Incarnation as recapitulation is the only definite thing in the affirmation of creation as a saving work of God with respect to mankind, for the sense of what God was planning, becomes clear only through the Word-Logos of God, Who descended into the created world in order to become a visible teacher to us. Irenaeus asserts that the truth of the Incarnation is the only "real" and is definitive. He describes the dynamics of God's revelation about creation in three stages: "through the creation itself the Word reveals the Creator, and through the world the Lord, the world's Maker. . . . Similarly through the law and the prophets the Word proclaimed both Himself and the Father. . . . Finally through the Word made visible and palpable, the Father was revealed."[86] The revelation about creation was granted to mankind in two stages: the first to provide the knowledge that there was a creator of the world; and the second, after the Incarnation, was to provide the meaning of creation as a precondition for the salvation.

If we now turn to Athanasius's thought, we find similar ideas on the role of the Incarnation of the Logos of God in flesh in order to elucidate the meaning of creation. But Athanasius proceeds much further than Irenaeus for the former asserts the Incarnation not only as a pivotal element in the history of salvation, but also links the Incarnation of the Word of God, with establishing a principle of intelligibility in the contingent creation. Athanasius argues that it is through the inference for the Word of God from the created order that one can know that God *is*; for it is the Word of God Who *orders* the Universe and reveals the Father. It was not enough for God just to create an ordered world in order to teach men about the Father. "Creation was there all the time, but it did prevent men from wallowing in error."[87] It was the part of the Word of God, his Logos and only Son, who by ordering the universe reveals the Father, "to renew the same teaching"[88] through the Incarnation, using another means in order to teach of God those who would not learn from the works of his creation.

There is one particular problem that we would like to discuss in this context, namely the problem of the contingency of the created realm upon God, and at the same time the presence of elements of necessity in the created world that make the Incarnation principally possible. Starting from Irenaeus the Greek Fathers affirmed that God created the world freely but from his plan. This is expressed in the Nicene Creed that the "Son of God, the only begotten of the Father, begotten before all ages," was in the "equation"

---

86. Irenaeus of Lyons, *Against the Heresies*, IV.6.6.
87. Athanasius, *On the Incarnation* 14, 42.
88. Athanasius, *On the Incarnation* 14, 42.

of creation before the world actually was made. At the same time, by planning the creation of the world and salvation of man, God-Trinity planned the Incarnation of the Son-Logos of God in flesh of that world which is supposed to be created.

Then, there is a question arises: did God plan the creation of the universe in some specially designed form, in order to bring human beings into existence in such a shape as to make the Incarnation of the Logos of God possible? The main question is: if the history of salvation of man through the incarnation of the Logos in Christ and resurrection of Christ had been planned "before" the creation of the world, can we affirm that the world was created out of nothing in such a shape which allows the history of salvation to be realized in this world. This means that the mode of existence of the bodily humanity, dependent on physical matter and biology, which was shared by Christ, was a *necessary* element of the divine plan before creation. This implies then that the structure of the physical universe acting as the *necessary* condition for man's physical and biological existence, was a necessary element of the divine plan before creation.

The intimacy between creation and the Incarnation implies that the divine is not only involved in the "materialization of spirit" (i.e., creation of matter as that arena where Divine actions can have place) but equally in the spiritualization of matter (i.e., lifting up the created matter to its union with the intelligible and then spiritual as related to the Life of God). This dual movement of the world and God towards each other is exactly that which is called life, whose phenomenon is explicated well in the paradox of subjectivity understood now as a dichotomy between the bodily presence of consciousness in the vast universe (its incarnation in matter) and a spiritual representation of matter of the universe This dual principle, but devoid of the paradox, is manifested in Christ as the ultimate archetype of the divine humanity. It is precisely in the person of Christ, in whom "the whole fullness of deity dwells bodily" (Col 2:9) that God forms a unity of these two distinct activities (materialization in flesh and spiritualization of matter) which, though separable by reason, are eternally one. Christ has from the center of eternity become the center of history. One can see in Christ not just the historical appearance of the eternal God but also the fulfillment of humanity being thus its ultimate archetype. God as Logos, through whom and by whom all was made, was present in the works of creation before and was deemed to be detected through the power of reason: this kind of a synthesis of the created universe was a faculty granted to humanity through its divine image. But this unity (attained epistemologically) is destined to remain within the confines of human consciousness which as such remains powerless to achieve this fullness outwardly in the world around it.

Reason, given to humanity as part of its Divine image, cannot overcome its interiority by its own means, that is, to explain itself. The purpose of the Incarnation is to unite the divine with humanity in such a way that its inner sense of existence no longer stands against the external life but is released outwardly, so that the image of God which grows within it may become incarnate in the material world. Whereas the highest task of humanity in the Divine image is to gather the universe in the idea (to be capable of producing an instantaneous synthesis of the universe), the task of the God-man is to gather the universe in reality through overcoming of the moral divisions among the aspects of creation. Here is a pathway for a possible resolution of the paradox of the human condition (paradox of subjectivity) not in man itself, but in its archetype in Christ.

The ideal relatedness of all in God that acquired reality in man's faculty of reason, in Christ finds itself "existent" not only intellectually but also in concrete, material form. The Kingdom of God (from where the whole creation is united) that was inaugurated through Christ's coming into the world, came into (human) reality not intellectually, but "practically." The divine now is not contained within human consciousness alone, but in the human and divine being, that is, in Christ, who took flesh and was born in rubrics of the material world. However in the incarnate Christ the paradox of the human condition (paradox of subjectivity) is devoid of that ambivalence that takes place in man, for ultimately the facticity of the paradox in Christ-man originates in Christ-Logos himself as the creator of the world. The Incarnation does not stand in opposition to the development of human consciousness or negate the previous development of the natural world but is treated both as God embarking on a new process within human history, and as continuing the process that began with the creation of the world and continued through the emergence of the human organism out of the animal forms. Christ is located in between two realms hypostatically linking together the Kingdom as it is to God "in heaven," as well as its interiority to humanity "on earth." As fully human, Christ had to experience the limits of the physical universe. On the other hand, for Christ as God remaining in the Kingdom, where from and through which the whole of physical reality was created there is no paradox. Rephrasing this, the divine in Christ is not enclosed by the confines of human consciousness, but itself takes on these confines in the sense that Christ feels these confines in actuality as his own, and this self-limiting of God in Christ frees his humanity, allowing his natural will to surrender itself to the divine principle, that is, to effect the union between the world and God. And it is this that is not given to man. By experiencing the paradox, human beings experience the manifestations of the "interior" kingdom, by guessing that the actual presence of this paradox is a distorted manifestation of "outer Kingdom" whose fullness can only be attained through Christ. What is revealed in Christ is thus the hidden infinitude of the human person (extending beyond its epistemological infinitude), able to fit within itself the entire infinitude of God. In Christ human nature, hypostatically transfigured, for the first time transcends the limits of its finitude when *communion* "evolves" into *union*. The humanity of Christ is deified not despite his humanity but because of it: as sometimes expressed in Orthodox theology, to be deified one must be created.

Humanity, being created in the conditions of nature effectively outgrows nature through the power of reason which grows with nature, or, saying differently, nature self-transcends itself in humanity (i.e., expressed in the paradox: nature becomes intelligible in the human image). But human nature, humanity as such is destined to outgrow itself in Christ (by removing the moral tensions between the terms of the paradox and simultaneously finding the answer for the possibility of self-transcendence). Just as the natural world reaches its fullest development in humanity by being self-represented intelligibly, so humanity realizes its fullest potential in the God-man. To the same extent as Christ is both the bearer of the natural humanity and transcendent humanity (a normative humanity, that is, the archetype or a "spiritualized" humanity), human beings are both the bearers of nature *per se* and a nature transcending itself, and this forms the principle of humanity as such. As the natural aspects in human condition (cosmology) grow into properly human transcendence (anthropology), the anthropological normative of humanity grows into christological, by contributing to another strong point of Orthodoxy that any anthropology is insufficient without Christology. The alpha and omega of Christology is the hypostatic union of God and man. The word hypostatic is pivotal here in a double sense: on the one hand the union of two natures is effected on the level of that which is not part of these natures, but person acting as self-affective Life, as that which creates life from itself. Hypostatic thus implies self-affective creation and the capacity to reflect upon this creation by manifesting this creation for that who creates and who is invited in God's milieu, who is made in the Image of that who creates.

Indeed, the universe at large, being created by God, is not capable of knowing that it has its creator, for impersonal physical objects are not hypostatic creatures: they have no ability to contemplate their own existence and relate it to their ultimate source. The world itself is not hypostatic, but is enhypostasized ("hypostatically inherent" in the Logos). One can refer to a theological view of "participation" in the Divine in order to illustrate the idea of "hypostatic inherence" of the universe in the Logos of God: Maximus the Confessor argued that "everything that derives its existence from participation in some other reality presupposes the ontological priority of that other reality";[89] he meant the priority of the Logos of God with respect to all other created things which do participate in him.[90] The "hypostatic inherence" of the universe in the Logos of God can then be interpreted as the Logos's eternal manifestations in different modes of *participation* by created beings in him. This participation takes place in spite of the fact that the Logos, is eternally invisible to all in virtue of the surpassing nature of his hidden activity.[91] But this *participation* does not assume any ontological causation; existence through participation in the Logos is subsistence in his Personhood, that is, the *inherence* in his hypostasis. As was expressed by John Zizioulas:

> By pervading the world through the person of the divine *Logos*, God not only unites it to himself while maintaining his otherness, but at the same time brings about and sustains a world existing as simultaneously communion and otherness in all its parts, from the greatest to the smallest, from the galaxies to the simplest particle of matter.[92]

> A "panentheistic" conception of the world would seem to result from such a teaching. It would, however, have to be expressed not in substantialist but in personalist categories. This means that, in its deeper being, the world is what it is . . . not by virtue of an interaction of substances in a sort of quasichemical manner, but in and through the presence and involvement of a Person who lends *his mode of being*, his hypostasis, so as to "effect the mystery of his embodiment in everything."[93]

Seen in this perspective the body of Jesus of Nazareth, as part of the created world, was enhypostasized by the Logos. But the crucial difference with all other human beings whose bodies and whose created hypostases have also been enhypostasized by the Logos is that the hypostasis of Jesus Christ, was the uncreated hypostasis of the Logos. In this sense the link between the Divine and human natures in Christ was *hypostatic*, whereas for ordinary human beings and all other creatures, their link with the Divine was only *en-hypostatic*. When theology affirms the Divine image in humanity, it effectively asserts that the *enhypostatic hypostasis* in a human

---

89. Maximus the Confessor, *Various Texts* 1.6, 165.
90. Maximus the Confessor, *Various Texts* 1.3, 164.
91. Maximus the Confessor, *Various Texts* 1.8, 166.
92. Zizioulas, *Communion and Otherness*, 32.
93. Zizioulas, *Communion and Otherness*, 31–32.

being, is the image of the uncreated hypostasis of the Logos. Correspondingly, the human flesh as well as intelligence in the Incarnate Logos-Christ was united to the Divine Hypostatically, being thus sustained not only by the conditions of the enhypostatic creation by the Logos, but being brought to communion with God in an already deified manner, when the flesh of Christ, being fully human and not confused with the Divine nature, was effectively transfigured by the Logos-Christ. Shortly, the flesh of Christ, being in a hypostatic union with God, is not exactly the same flesh of the world that exists through being created by God. Since, according to Maximus the Confessor, the divine embodiment and human deification in Christ necessarily take place at the same time (so that deification is simply the other side of the Incarnation), one rather speaks of the deified flesh. If in Christ this is effected through the Incarnation of the Logos, for human beings, deification and transfiguration of their flesh is still a task which never ceases to be applicable and which covers the whole of human existence and the whole of creation in potentiality.

The intelligibility of the universe and its meaning are accessible only to hypostatic human beings created in the Divine image, and whose hypostasis is capable of personifying objects in the universe, that is, making the universe self-conscious of its own existence and origin. It is human ego that gives meaning to things and who has to transfigure them to receive grace and to be united with God. The universe as *the articulated existence* is possible only in human hypostasis; it acquires some qualities of existence if it is reflected in the personal human subjectivity. Using the words of Maximus the Confessor, every intellection about the universe inheres as a quality in an apprehending being.[94] The universe thus acquires qualitative existence in the being who apprehends it.[95] A Patristic theologian would say that existence of the universe as the articulated existence is existence in the hypostasis of humanity, that is, the universe is *enhypostasized*. A modern phenomenological philosopher would express the same by saying that the sense of objectivity and reality of existence of anything can be asserted only if one provides the way of constitution of this reality. The latter obviously

---

94. Cf. Maximus the Confessor, *Cap. Theologicorum* 2.3, 138.

95. G. L. Prestige, in order to illustrate how the apprehending knowledge becomes hypostatic existence, refers to Clement of Alexandria (*Stromata*, 4:22, 136:4): "apprehension extends by means of study into permanent apprehension; and permanent apprehension, by becoming, through continuous fusion, the substance of the knower and perpetual contemplation, remains a living hypostasis. This appears to mean that knowledge becomes so bound up with the being of the knowing subject, as to constitute a permanent entity" (Prestige, *God in Patristic Thought*, 176).

implies the presence of humanity as the centre of disclosure and manifestation of this reality.

The specificity of the *hypostatic* presence of the Logos in Jesus Christ, in comparison with the *enhypostatic* inherence of all creation in the Logos, can be explicated by invoking the paradox of subjectivity that in the present context will read like this: humanity, as being hypostasis of the universe, yet experiences itself as a creature among other creatures enhypostasized by the Logos. In view of this the question arises: did the Incarnate Logos-Christ, being fully human in flesh and in mind, experience the same paradox as other human being do? The answer comes from the observation that Christ's created features such as his flesh as well as his soul (mind) were in the hypostatic union with God thus being incorporated into the Logos's vision of creation as the whole with no extension and distance between its parts. One can say more subtly: Christ experienced in his humanity the extension of space and time (his Earthly way), but this extension did not represent any *moral tension* (in the style of the paradox) with his being truly the Logos through whom all extended world was created (enhypostasized). Being the Logos present everywhere in the universe, Christ was fulfilling the promise of God to men for salvation without experiencing any paradoxical condition between comprehending the world at once and at the same time being a fully human being subjected to the laws of the world and the conditions of its comprehension. It is because the Divine and human was united in Christ hypostatically, but not naturally, that Christ effected the mediation between the world and God by removing in himself the moral division between the sense of being God and the sense of being human. It is because for an ordinary human being such a mediation between creation and God is still a task, potentially achievable through deification, the enhypostatic human hypostases (whose union of body and soul is effected not only hypostatically, but naturally) experience the tension between their ability to be "hypostases of the universe" (the hypostatic Image of God) and at the same time to be only natural creatures subjected to the constraints of the body in space and time. Humanity, in spite of its imitation of the incarnate Logos, in its desire to subordinate the ends of nature to the ends of itself, that is, a desire of removing the paradox of subjectivity, remains in incapacity to realize its likeness to the incarnate Logos in reality, struggling with the conditions of the paradox thus uniting different parts of creation, different life forms and inorganic matter only *epistemologically*. It is in this sense that the hypostatic union of the Divine and the created in Logos-Christ is radically different in comparison with any enhypopstatic presence of the Logos in humans created by him. Humanity is gifted with the capacity of imitating the hypostatic union in the Logos-Christ and employing it for the transfiguration of the whole created world, whereas all non-human forms of existence can receive communion with the hypostasis of the Logos only through humans. Correspondingly any hypothetical assumption of an entrance of the hypostasis of the Logos into the fabric of biological, ecological, cosmological, etc. existence on the same footing as it was in the historical Incarnation would run into a risk of assigning the features of a quasi-hypostatic being to the world, making it commensurable with the person of God. But, this is an inacceptable form of pantheism opposed by many theologians. And this is the reason why Maximus the Confessor, for example, likened the world not to micro-Logos (to the image of the Logos as already achieved), but to *macro-anthropos* (a man enlarged), that is, to the image of the *anthropos* ("image of the image"), acquiring the features of humanity constantly effecting its own incarnation in the universe in the image of the Logos made flesh.[96]

In spite of the fact that the Incarnation was possible only when basic cosmological conditions have been fulfilled, the very facticity of the event of the Incarnation cannot be placed into the logic of the material history. One can guess that the happening of the Incarnation depended retrospectively on particular events of the human history, yet its historical facticity has an event-like phenomenality. By speaking of the Incarnation of the Logos-Christ, remembering of the Gospels's account of Jesus' Nativity and of thirty three years of his Earthly life, it does not make too much sense of enquiring in why not sooner or later of the Incarnation to the same extent as it does not make sense to enquire into the sooner or later of creation. The event-like phenomenality of the Incarnation as well as of all following events of the New Testament history point towards a radically irreversible character of coming of the Good News into the world thus by breaking the cyclic nature of the ancient Greek cosmos and thus redirecting the human history towards the Kingdom.

The event of the Incarnation is radically irreversible because it ultimately initiated a new covenant with God: Christianity claimed that it established a "new covenant" with "new humanity" (Eph 2:15; 4:24) for whom "new heavens and a new earth" was promised (2 Pet 3:13; Rev 21:1). The event-like character of this New Covenant follows from the fact that this covenant is radically "new": "The old things have passed away. Behold, all things have become new" (2 Cor 5:17 ESV). "Good News" of Gospels is "new news" and belief in it is not a trans-temporal myth, but the "signs of the times" (Matt 16:3). Through this covenant human life finds its foundation not in the anonymous laws of the world with its devoid of any sense perpetual return, but in that renewed communion with God which de

---

96. Maximus the Confessor, *Mystagogy 7*, in *Selected Writings*, 181–225.

facto predetermines all further historical activity of humanity. The usage of the words "new" in the context of "New Testament" and "Good News" points towards their irreversibility in history, that is, an inability to amend or eliminate its effects and to return back to that state of the human world which was before. That which is "new" means that after its entrance into the world, its "creation," the world changed by unlimitedly experiencing the result of this newness. As was expressed by Georges Florovsky, "The accomplishment of the Promise was not just an extra event in the homogeneous sequence of happenings. It was an "event" indeed, but it was an event *which never passes*."[97] The "newness" implies here the launching of such an order of history which will never blindly follow the order of the cosmos always transcending in its hermeneutics the naturally conditioned causality of the world. Entering into the world in violation of its causality (a scandal for the Greeks) the event of the Incarnation and Good News do not conform to the logic of the world and are not corrigible in the course of humanity's exploration of nature, retaining in its inaugural pathos the possibilities of further exploration of the world in the perspective in this newness. The Incarnation and the entrance of the Good News into the world, in spite of their endless hermeneutics through the patristic exegesis and other theological developments will never become outdated because ultimately the latter sheds the light onto that which is metaphysically impossible and phenomenologically concealed.

Amazingly, the inaugural events of the Incarnation and Good News, predetermine the modern dialogue between theology and science, because they both ultimately predetermine both—theology and science. If in respect to theology this thesis seems to be obviously justified, with respect to science, especially for those who are not acquainted with its history, it seem exaggerated. However, one can trace through the history of the natural sciences in the European context, that indeed the very phenomenon of Christianity predetermined a historical path of the European sciences which make the situation with our present standing in front of the scientific and technological progress as it is.[98] Even if one does not see the efficacious presence of the inaugural events related to Christian faith as leading to the actual state of affairs in modern science, it does not mean that the history of the development of education and scientific research in European universities became free from that impetus which Christianity brought into it. One can strongly

---

97. Florovsky, "The Worshipping Church," 28.

98. On the historical Christian context of development of modern science, see Lindberg, "Science and the Early Church," 19–48; Lindberg, *The Beginnings of Western Science*; Grant, *God and Reason*; Harrison, *The Bible*; Nicolaides, *Science and Eastern Orthodoxy*.

claim that ultimately all inaugural events related to Christian history endowed humanity by its scientific and technological future thus making the dialogue between theology and science possible. Any oblivion of this fact would amount to a simple truth that the process of knowledge of the world would loose its grounds in history being a manifestation of the developed intelligence without any recourse to the specific spiritually oriented way of the human existence. By saying this one effectively affirms that the inaugural events such as the Incarnation which predetermined humanity's way of approaching truth, predetermine that which is going on in the modern dialogue between science and theology. This dialogue as such is possible because of those events which determined the sense of humanity in the image of God.

The Incarnation is an event and as such cannot be subjected to any theoretical justification in rubrics of its worldly antecedents (apart from the necessary cosmological conditions). Yet, the truth of the Incarnation in theology is asserted not logically, intellectually, but through praise, that is, liturgically. And liturgy, reenacting events of the Christian history, in spite of its cosmologically placed conditions, forms events of praise of God and of that creation into which God entered through the human flesh. Being a motive of creation the Incarnation asserts and confirms this creation through Christ. By celebrating the Incarnation of Christ liturgically, the humanity of Christ praises creation in its specific shape, adjusted to the reception of humanity and hence of Christ. Since the liturgical celebration of the Incarnation makes devoid of sense the question of "why sooner or later of the Incarnation," the assertion of the Incarnation together with creation entails the praise of God by removing any possible metaphysical overtones in questions related to "why" of creation and the Incarnation.

Being a modus of praise it is difficult to assign to the liturgical action the status of the "now" because being an already realized possibility, its sense is disclosed only retrospectively: the "now" of a liturgical act becomes evident only by becoming the past in the perspective of the future which is opened by this act. It is in this trivial sense that any liturgical act is *unpredictable* in a general philosophical sense: it can take place anywhere and anytime on Earth (Matt 18:20) thus being an existential expression of the sense of God in the world. Any liturgical act, if it is considered as imitating a certain preceding historical event from Christian history, aims to transcend a measure of this historical event. This implies that there must be something in the very purpose of this action that exceeds the volume of the historical event as well as those imitations of this event in numerous acts of praise that took place across earthly locations and historical times. In this sense any liturgical action becomes an independent praising event aiming not to repeat that which has been achieved through praise before, but to open anew the gates of the Kingdom for the descent of the Spirit into the world.

Since every Liturgy commemorates and imitates the Christ-event as the inaugural event for the whole Christian history, the liturgical action de facto constitutes anew the Christ-event by assigning to it a trans-worldly foundation. The latter can be commented in the following way: since all liturgical events are unique by keeping their difference among other liturgical events, the, so to speak, "efficacy" of these events cannot be exhausted by any of them and cannot be measured quantitatively or qualitatively in terms of better or worse, in terms of being more genuine than another, between being historically more significant than another. This happens because being a commemoration and enactment of historical events, it is also their effectuation from the future Kingdom through the action of the Holy Spirit. The realized eschatology in the heart of the Eucharistic prayer de facto recapitulates not only the Christ-event as a historical event, but the Incarnation as a motive of creation. It is in this sense that one can conjecture of an analogy between Eucharistic events and the event of creation, for the whole memory of the world as being accumulated in the human Divine Image is regenerated in every eucharistic event being a recapitulation of the Christ-event. Such an eventfulness suspends the ordinary forms of the spatio-temporal sequence of the liturgical celebrations in the daily cycles, as well as of the experienced inaugural events. The transcendence of space and time is achieved through the intentional invocation of the Holy Spirit as the guarantor of the meeting with God in his Kingdom. The order or the liturgical experience of the Lord's Supper, for example, as an archetype of communion with Christ before his death on the Cross manifests, in fact, the reversal of the temporal order, its suspension. Offering himself to his disciples as wine and bread ("Take, eat; this is my Body which is broken for you. . . . Drink from this, all of you; this is my Blood of the New Covenant"), he makes an inversion of the temporal order, thus constituting the inaugural event of the liturgical celebration in such a way that his historical objectivity is replaced by the transcending eventfulness. The disciples commune with Christ before his death on the Cross, outstripping the future, and immortalizing the future of the crucifixion as its eternal past. In the Lord's Supper, it is that sacrifice of Christ is actualized that has not happened yet. The actual Crucifixion legitimizes this sacrifice that was liturgically established at the Lord's Supper. In such a sequence of events the memory of the world is liturgically regenerated in a way similar to what takes place in the Anaphora: "Remembering, therefore, this saving commandment and all those things that have come to pass for us: the Cross, the tomb, the resurrection on the third day, the ascension into heaven, the sitting at the right hand, and the

Second and glorious Coming." The convergence of the past, present and future, invoked in the Anaphora, manifest the quintessence of the liturgical memory that keeps for us that which is possible, that is, the future. This memory is of Christ, of the Fathers, of events of Christian history; it keeps the source of our present and future. In this sense all liturgical events break into the causality of the world, remaining as such non-reproducible and bringing into being that impossible which exceeds the measure of our foreseeing and expectation. By liturgically enacting Christ-event as happening here and now, and thus revising all existential projects through which a particular believer understands the very fact of its mundane existence as governed by the blind game of the physical forces, this believer is shattered by the fact that its theologically understood *hope* for being heard, noticed and remembered (as a reaction to homelessness and non-attunement to this physical world) receives its fulfillment, confirming the worlds of apostle Paul that "hoping against hope" he "believed" (Rom 4:18) in his salvation, in the possibility of his extraction from the pressing necessity of the suffering flesh. Liturgically, the humanity of Christ praises creation and thanks the Creator not only for the gift of life in it, but for the gift of being able to be transfigured together with creation as it was initiated by Christ through the Resurrection and Ascension to the Father, and as it is liturgically effectuated in the Anaphora. The liturgical celebration of the events related to the Incarnation thus forms another kind of praise of creation in which the potential of creation to its soteriologically understood renewal is brought to its manifested phenomenality.

HUMANITY AS HYPOSTASIS OF THE UNIVERSE: PRAISE AS EXPLORATION

The inability to talk about creation (and the Incarnation) in the natural attitude makes the problem of creation in the framework of the dialogue between theology and science a special one, accentuating the radical difference of its appropriation by theology and science. Whereas the scientific cosmology approaches the issue of origins of the universe through representing it in terms of objects and physical causality, the opposite, that is, a philosophical and theological perception of the universe, positions it as the privileged phenomenon initiating all other kinds of phenomenality in it. Shortly, one can say that the dialogue between science and theology in the context of creation represents a phenomenological problem of relating of two radically different phenomenalities having origin in the human existence. With all this, the phenomenality of the universe as a saturated phenomenon that constitutes (affects) life, differs from the phenomenality of the universe as an outer object, posed by consciousness from within the already existing life. In fact, one can say that life carries out its own, split in itself, phenomenalization thus expressing outwardly its own self-affectivity. Let us try to describe such an expression of life's self-affectivity.

First of all, a scientific commitment in the issue of creation implies a metaphysical question on the provenance of beings. Saying differently, apart from the question of "What is creation?" it implies another perennial question of "Why is creation?" in it particular form "Why is there something rather than nothing?" implying an ontological response, that is, a reference to something in which, that which is considered as the created, subsists.

For example, asking a question "Why is there the universe (our universe) rather than nothing?" one implies a possible response that the universe subsists in the multiverse or in some pre-existent undifferentiated substance. Such an approach to creation assigning to it a certain mode of being, even if the universe is allegedly created by God (considered as the supreme Being), was criticized by Heidegger, who accentuated the difference between the ontological question of creation as being subsistent in something else, and a theological assertion of creation whose sense can be clarified only in the context of a divine revelation, expressed in the Bible as that the world was created by God, the uncreated Creator to whom any reference in terms of provenance of beings does not make sense.[99] The latter implies faith of a believer which is not an ontological claim. In this sense the biblical doctrine of creation does not respond to an ontological question of "Why is creation?" because even a reference to God does not make an ontological sense, because, biblically God is not subsistent being. The biblical response must be considered in the conditions when creation imposes itself on that who enquires in it as excess, that is, in the conditions when the question "Why is creation?" cannot be responded at all because it already implies existence as *life* where the latter cannot be referred as subsistent in something else than life itself. Talking about life one means a radically different mode of appearing, that is, of phenomenality, because life being phenomenological through and through is neither a being, nor a modus of being of a being. Life defines the originary modus of phenomenality which can be named revelation. If one follows Kant who defines appearance as an indefinite subject of an empirical contemplation,[100] it is not difficult to see that such a contemplation implies a subject as that one who "responds" to that affectivity which produces this contemplation. Since life is already present in this

99. Heidegger, *Introduction to Metaphysics*, 8–9.
100. Kant, *Critique of Pure Reason*, B62–63.

contemplation, this contemplation, not being nuanced and thematized, yet contains revelation of life as given, life of Life. Then the question of "Why is creation?" entails an existential response: God created the world; but saying "God" implies the human utterance and praise of God-creator as a principle of life, rather than any cause or sufficient reason for the world to exist, even less anything from a cosmological context. In this sense the revelation which is characteristic for life and expressed through utterance and praise of the Creator, yet asserting creation at large opposes to that appearing of the world which is detected in the sciences and which becomes a derivative of the primordial revelation of life through praise.

To the phenomenality of life as revelation one can contrapose the sensible perception of the essences (phenomena in Kant's sense) in which the modus of contemplation implies that the phenomenon differs from that which can be present behind it as a thing in itself which is not an object of our senses but considered as an object which is thought by the understanding. There is a subject which is present in the same condition of life, but life is detected not directly, but manifests itself in the estranged form derivative from its immediate givenness. Saying differently, life has its own but the understanding detects it outwardly as the arena of that which stands behind the contemplated appearances.

One can say that the human creatures first find themselves in the state of praise of the Creator before they produce any ontological (scientific) extrapolations of their experience of living. Creation as an ontological issue, as the only possible way of approaching it in the sciences, reveals itself within life that never differs from itself and that only reveals itself in the conditions which one can attempt to refer to as something physically or logically antecedent only post-factum, as a fringed projection of life's phenomenality onto the derivative appearing of the world.

Talking about praise of creation as a modus of life's phenomenality, one implies the identification of such a praise (as a modus of activity) with the sense of that which is meant by the term creation within the phenomenality of life. This praise of creation is not that which can be roughly paralleled with the praise of the cosmos as harmony and beauty of the visible universe. In fact, as a modus of life's self-affectivity, the praise is invisible. The very sense of existence escapes any possibility of seeing it outside the already detected phenomena. It is invisible not being an illusion or a fantastic imaginable and parallel way of living the life, but because it cannot be split in itself into something other which can be seen. Certainly one can form an image of one's existing and hence being created, and represent it to this one, yet the fact remains that the reality of this one existing never exists outside existence. In any representation of existing any human ego remains in the presence of that noematic link with the world which is, de facto, undetermined. In analogy with the apophatic idea, one can say that one is present only in front of significations of that which is supposed to be signified. Hence the praise of the Creator as one's own creation, as the working of the phenomenality of life delivers such an imagery of creation at large which de facto places the universe in the context of life, as the praise of that one who created this life. In this case the universe as creation becomes phenomenologically commensurable to the Creator, stopping any extensions and divisions in it, exceeding the quantitative and qualitative measures, relations and metaphysical modalities of possibility or impossibility. Creation at large becomes commensurable with life, because it is this life that is the origin and end of any phenomenality in it: "It is because we have first come into life that we are then able to come into the world."[101] However the latter must be understood with discretion. The difference between the appearing of the world in the phenomenality of objects and appearing of life to itself is that life is indifferent to all objects, not coinciding with them and not retaining itself in them. At the same time life keeps in itself that which it reveals residing in any human being as that which causes them to live and not leaving them as long as they live. The relationship of life to any human being is that of a radical immanence whose assertion in the conditions of the already reflected in consciousness praise has already been quoted as "man=man in communion with God." But after our deliberations this latter theological assertion acquires a purely phenomenological sense as the assertion that any particular human life is inseparable from the already mentioned self-affectivity of God-Creator as the principle of life (Life).

Creation as a gift implying praise of the Creator introduces a fundamental dimension into the principle of life: life as life exists in individuals. Saying in the language of previous sections, life as capable of praising its own creation is hypostatic. The differentiation of Life as the principle of creation from an individual life requires philosophically to introduce a principle of such a differentiation that is the principle of praise as a specific place (places) in that post-factum articulated realm of being which metaphysically called creation. When the church Fathers spoke of creation they never articulated the where of this "speech" suspending this naïve question as of a secondary importance. Saying differently, the Fathers in their majority did not attempt to provide a cosmological account of creation because they inherited well from the Greek philosophy that no causal principle of the world is possible. To speak of creation is to speak of the relationship between the world and God, that is, to be precise, to praise God who is unknowable in terms of that

---

101. Henry, "Phenomenology of Life," 105.

which he created. When Maximus the Confessor, for example in *Chapters on Love* (4.2), infers from the harmony and goodness of things around him to God, he asserts creation through the praise of God: "How can the intellect not marvel when it contemplates that immense and more astonishing sea of goodness? Or how is it not astounded when it reflects on how and from what source there have come into being both nature endowed with intelligence and intellect, and the four elements which compose physical bodies, although no mater existed before their generation? What kind of potentiality was it which, once actualized, brought these things into being?"[102]

However created things could not be articulated as created and their Creator could not be praised if in first place there were not be those who praise creation and God. This trivial observation brings into play an idea of those creatures, their believing community who see God behind created things and who praise him through accepting these things as created. This living community is unique because it is human: it is only humans who can see the beauty and goodness of God behind things. *Community* is a crucial word because there is a plurality of created things, plurality of their places in the world, and there is a plurality of human creatures. To articulate creation as such and its Creator one needs the unifying response that would describe the created world not simply as plurality of things but as a gift of Creation. The hermeneutics of the Bible, in particular the Genesis, as well as an Eucharistic practice imply the community of believers who praise God-creator and his creation and accept them as not beings, but as gifts. The existence of such a community obviously follows from the existence of life being split in itself through human beings whose worldly propensities require those necessary conditions which form the "site" of praise of the Creator as the place of their living.

In spite of the fact that this "site" of praise is reconstituted post-factum from the very fact of this praise as sheer existence, its facticity as the facticity of praise in humanity cannot be questioned further to the same extent as questioning of the sufficient conditions of existence of humanity in the given necessary conditions. This situation creates a certain theological excess: God created human life from his Life in order to be praised by humanity. But the ontological and cosmological context of such an excess becomes seen when humans reconstitute the cosmological scheme of their creation from within the conditions of the possibility of praise of creation and the Creator. In this sense the praise of God for creation, being implicitly an Eucharistic act, commemorates that inaugural "event" which cannot be phenomenalized

---

102. Maximus the Confessor, *Cap. de Charitate* 4.2, in *Four Hundred Texts on Love*, 100.

by the worshiper, but which enacts from all ages the very fact of living as communion with that One who created the world. Humanity, praising God for creation turns out to be at the "center" of the created universe from "which" creation is epistemologically encompassed: as we have expressed this thought before, humanity is the center of disclosure and manifestation of the universe. But where this humanity is? To say that it is at the periphery of the physical plan of the universe is tantamount to saying "nowhere" (although nomistically this is not exactly true—the necessary conditions of humanity's existence are fixed). However, being created as the "site" of praise, humanity remains in God in two different senses. One is panentheistically transparent: if God is everywhere in the universe created by him, the praising humanity is inside him. Another one is archetypically proceeds from Christ, who being in Jesus of Nazareth's flesh is not contained by it because he is its creator and is hypostatically beyond it. Human beings, being in God yet find themselves very distant from the rest of creation resembling in their hypostases that from God which is not comprehended in delimiters of the world. As was expressed by Augustine, "And see, you were within and I was in the external world and sought you there. . . . You were with me and I was not with you."[103] It is not difficult to see that any human being struggles with the question of its own creation and its own sense through that individual experience of praise of the Creator with which this being is endowed at the very commencement of its life. Praise accompanies life being a modus of that affectivity by the anterior of the creation that grants the conditions of this life and praise. Yet it is the universe that provides the condition for praise. The universe as being the "site" of praise is associated with creation. However the universe at large is the "site" of praise only in terms of the nomistic conditions for this praise to be possible. The facticity of praise is related to the facticity of humanity and its "site" in the universe remains rather uncertain. This is the reason why humanity as praising community experiences the ambivalence of being chained to that which God created as Earth and, at the same time, receiving the gift to praise from the "heaven." This dialectics between the necessary and sufficient conditions of praise of creation, which is another way of expressing the conditions of the human life, encodes in itself the basic predicament of every hypostatic human being of not being able to understand the sense of its own existence, that is, to know itself. To reflect upon itself as being created is equal to be able to praise the Creator; yet the aporia of being created remains as an inability to comprehend its facticity as a gift. To be created and to be able to praise, is the pathway to the elucidation of its own condition (as the Orthodox say through deification), but the aporia never disappears remaining that horizon

---

103. Augustine, *Confessions*, X.xxvii.38.

in the open-ended hermeneutics of the human condition that determines its advance.

God-creator is panentheistically present *inside* human beings, but he is not *in* them. As a place of praise creation is *inside* humanity, but as the outer universe creation is not *in* humanity. Being a site of praise, humanity is inside God, but being at the same time an earthly flesh, it is not in God, because it is created by God. The hypostatic multiplicity of humanity comes from the multiplicity of acts of praise whereas the consubstantiality of flesh comes from the inherent conditions of praise. Thus human persons perceive themselves between the unconditional (non-worldly) gift to praise and the worldly conditions for this gift to be received and responded. Creation as a theological issue thus receives its consummation in the problem of the human ego, as the riddle of the self, or as a hypostatic self-affectivity. Then the cosmological sense of creation appears through an incessant search of the praising community to release itself from the sense of the conditioned, by reconstituting its own immemorial origin. The aporia of the human condition as the phenomenological concealment of its origin is transfigured in human life into the modality of praise for creation which removes as irrelevant and impossible any questions about the facticity of this praise as a manifestation of life's self-affectivity. The universe as creation is constituted in the image of *Imago Dei*, that is, in the image of that one who is gifted with the possibility of praising God for creation.

Theology of *Imago Dei* could give some polishing to what is meant by praising creation. Praise includes different forms including that one of the scientific exploration if the latter, in accordance with our previous arguments, becomes a form of a para-eucharistic work, that is, of a communion of an epistemological kind that affects human practice, although indirectly. Yet, all scientific attempts to disclose the sense of the already created are being made from within the conditions of the radical incomprehensibility of human beings by themselves, first of all of their contingent facticity. This cascades to a simple epistemological truth that the origins of the universe are phenomenologically concealed to the same extent as it happens with any hypostatic initiation of life. One can express the same thought differently. Humanity attempts to comprehend itself through "looking" into its past, into that saturating immemorial which haunts the human existence. By reconstructing the cosmological origins or the origins of life on Earth humans explicate creation as being a condition for the appreciation of this creation, for its praise. But the motivation of this very gift to humanity to praise remains concealed in that one who created the universe for praising himself.

If the ability to praise is placed in the very basis of what theology names *Imago Dei*, to say that the universe is constituted in the image of *Imago Dei* is another kind of excess: the universe can be articulated as creation only by human beings capable of praise, that is, only by the *Imago Dei*. This could lead to an illusion of the natural attitude that the universe is disclosed and manifested from one particular "place" in it. However, since the contingent facticity of the human position in the physical universe does not have either physical or metaphysical explanation, the only certain thing that can be said is that *it is in the universe as creation*. In other words, the "place" of *Imago Dei* is in creation, in being created, that is, being related to its Creator. Once again, here is a direct analogy with the incarnate Christ. Being incarnate on the planet Earth in one particular place in the universe, Christ as the Logos remains present everywhere in the universe as that milieu which he created, so that the "place" of praise of the Father, in spite of the fact that it was shown to humans on Earth, is the whole created universe hypostatically inherent in the Logos. This observation promotes a view that the universe is uniformly *theogenic*, that is, God-Logos is present everywhere in the universe (a panentheistic stance). This theological claim has a cosmological development when cosmology postulates the universe as a whole and its cosmographic uniformity (cosmological principle), as the principle of the average statistical indistinguishability of the universe locations if the observations would be possible from them. This expresses a thought that a place of praise of the Creator could be any location in the universe. When theology asserts that all creatures praise God for being created, its phraseology could be cosmologically refined: indeed, if humanity is capable of seeing the whole creation as the same, the uniform in a nomistic, structural and spatial sense, it is capable of praising God for creating all those levels of reality which humanity can identify as such. This does not mean that all levels of reality are "friendful" to human beings as physical creatures. One implies that all creatures praise God as the Lord of the Earth and heavens through human beings. It is only the latter that can envisage the necessity to praise for the infinite aeons of the universe, whose theogenic origin does not guarantee their transfiguration and removal in them the moral divisions. It is only a human being that is capable of seeing behind the inhuman nature of stars, non-inhabitable planets and all other passing in space remnants of other worlds, their "opposite" and hidden site of God's creation. It is only humanity that endeavours a task of reconciling the radical contingency of its existence in the physical world with that which assigns to this existence the transcendent soteriological sense.

Thus, in what sense the study of the universe can be qualified as praise to its Creator? Where, in what particular aspects cosmology exercises this function?

For the church Fathers, when physics of the universe did not exist, it was natural to suggest that the seemingly non-uniform parts in the created order were brought to the unity by the supreme principle of harmony and beauty, that is, God himself. Nowadays cosmology presents the display of the universe as ordered and structured due to the physical laws which act across the universe. There still remains a question of the origin of these laws: some suggestions point to the *boundary conditions* of the universe that are responsible for this order. Then the totality of the universe is associated with its single "beginning = boundary" that "separates" this universe from its own immemorial as a different way of expressing that the universe is creation.

Modern evolutionary cosmology asserts the totality of the universe not as a sum total of its parts (causally disconnected anyway), but as that unique remote state in the past of the universe which is treated as its origin (cosmological singularity, the Big Bang). One can responsibly think of the totality of the universe only through the notion of the Big Bang because it is only in the vicinity of the Big Bang that one could potentially have access to the universe in its entirety: the visible part of the universe comprises only a tiny part of the universe as a whole, physically relating to it only through the common origin in the Big Bang. Graphically this can be illustrated with the help of the following diagram, where the visible universe is represented by the onion-like curve (associated with the propagation of photons in space-time) whereas the rest of the outer circle represents the universe invisible to the human observer (see Fig. 1).

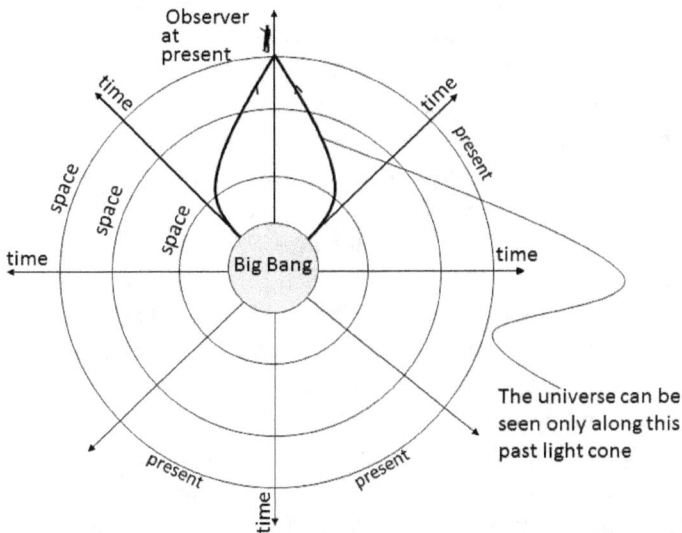

The unity of the universe as generated from the Big Bang.

The centre of this diagram symbolizes the Big Bang. In fact the latter does not exist if one attempts to position it in some pre-existing space. The symbol of the Big Bang amounts to the unity of the universe as having a single origin. The concentric circles symbolize the universe as a whole corresponding to different cosmic times. The unity of the universe for every moment of time is guaranteed by its procession from the original Big Bang state. One must notice that the finitude of the circles in the place of the diagram does not entail, that the universe is spatially finite. Such an illusion could take place if these circles were positioned in some pre-existing space which was allegedly presented by the plane of the diagram. Since such a plane does not exist in reality, all spatial structure of the universe is exhausted graphically by the circles. As to their metric finitude or infinitude, everything depend on how the size of the universe is "measured." If the distance along the circumference is measured by the human author of this diagram, then the circumference turns out to be metrically finite. However, if a human observer is positioned contingently at some point of this circumference, the whole circumference becomes a manifold with the dimension at least one unit higher than that of the observers's point, so that this point becomes incommensurable with respect to the circumference whose measure is de facto qualitatively infinite with respect to the observer. In this case, the unity of the infinite universe is guaranteed by the fact that every point on the circumference (or every radius of this point drawn from the cosmological singularity) has its origin in the Big Bang.

Humanity in its physical dimension, being contingently positioned in the visible universe and thus contingently selecting its display through the onion-like curve of the past light cone could potentially have access to this totality only through the Big Bang, that is, in the remote past. Yet, the Big Bang, being a mental construction can be accessed only intelligibly. One can conclude that cosmology of the evolving universe points to such an original "state" that, for a human being, has a different ontological status, beyond which physics is problematic: the totality of the universe in its contingent formation refers to its "otherness," which in scientific cosmology (not in theology) means not the trans-worldly foundation, but an ontologically different (but created), *intelligible* order invoked by theoretical scientists. In this sense, epistemologically, one cannot assert the wholeness of the world as a physical property *per se*; rather one can only claim that as such it is of the intelligible order. Where this intelligible unity comes from and why it is possible to detect it at all, these questions can be answered by reference to humanity's *Imago Dei* who is capable to structure the question about the underlying and forming principle (*logos*) of creation. In this sense the diagram at Fig. 1 can be interpreted phenomenologically as explicating in a way this *logos* and manifesting a characteristic praise of the Creator.

Physical cosmologists are not satisfied with a simple assertion that the universe as a whole can only be a form of the intelligible world, an idea (rational of aesthetical). It wants to justify an application of scientific methodology in thinking and speaking of the universe as a whole as if it has a physical ontology. In this case Fig. 1 must have been interpreted physically so that cosmology would face two fundamental problems. First of all, with the empirical fact of the contingent locations of human observers in the universe and correspondingly with the contingency of the universe's display which is available to observers. How does the human observer can speculate about the universe as a whole, being chained to the one particular infinitely small part of the universe? This epistemological question has, so to speak, an ontological complication, if one takes into account that even those parts of the universe which intersect with the past light cone have never been in a physical causal contact. What kind of unity of the universe can one assert if this unity does neither reveal itself in the human capacity to have an access to it, nor in the very nature of the universe which is positioned by the discursive thinking as an object? From a theological point of view such a situation is not unexpected because the causal disconnectedness of different parts of the universe can be interpreted as the lack of the initial order of the universe because its being created out of nothing, that nothing which does not have any principles of order. However, there is still a theological ordering principle that unites all causally disconnected parts of the universe (visible and invisible) "together," namely the principle (*logos*) that all these parts have a common "origin" in that *nothing* out of which they were created by the same Logos. But theological arguments are not considered as convincing in physical cosmology and this is the reason why the latter, looking for the way of constructing the unity of the universe, appeals to the unity of its substance (matter), but in its original point without any spatial and material extension. In other words, a cosmological history is constructed in such a way that the theoretically predicted causal disconnectedness of different parts of the universe becomes a sort of an evolutionary effect of some idiosyncratic dynamics of the early universe, predetermined by its initial condition. Here one must remember that speaking of the initial conditions one implies the evolution (expansion) of the universe in time experimentally verified from Earth. However the generalization of this fact for the whole universe implies the "cosmological principle," that is, the principle of cosmographic, material and nomistic large-scale uniformity of the universe. The origin of this principle is first of all epistemological: the universe as a whole, to be physically comprehensible and explicable, must look the same at large scales from all possible hypothetical locations in the universe. In spite of the fact that the cosmological principle is not a theological principle, it, in a way, explicates the *logos*, that is, the underlying principle of the universe's creation, as the *principle of explicability* of the universe by humanity that has cognitive capacities of the *Imago Dei*. The elucidation of that which is meant by the *logos* of creation through the cosmological principle does not entail that this *logos* is *known*: one can account neither for the facticity of this principle as constituting human comprehension, nor for the contingent facticity of the universe as implying the efficacy of this principle. The *logos* of creation encoded at the diagram (Fig. 1) also confirms the uniformity of all creation: the constitutive difference in creation between the visible (empirical universe seen along the surface of the past light cone) and invisible (intelligible universe as a whole including its alleged origin), is brought to their mutual unity in knowledge through the principle of homogeneity in the created order.

For illustrative purposes, as another example of a phenomenological representation of the sense of creation, one can combine the cosmological diagram (Fig. 1) with the graphical presentation of the *logoi* by Maximus the Confessor as radii with the center in the Logos-Creator. Maximus invokes a geometrical analogy (used before him by Proclus, Plotinus and Dionysius the Areopagite) that of the radii and the centre of a circle, in order to describe the relationship between the Logos, Who is the center of a circle, and the *logoi* that represent the radii of the circle, originating from the center and terminating on the boundary of a circle imitating the created realm.[104] By extending the idea of Fig. 1 to three dimensions where the vertical dimension corresponds to the transworldly foundation of the universe one obtains Fig. 2.

---

104. Maximus the Confessor, *Mystagogy* 1; Maximus the Confessor, *Cap. Theologicorum* 2.4. This analogy makes it simpler to illustrate the dual nature of the *logoi*: transcendent and immanent. On the one hand, according to Maximus the *logoi* are pre-existent in God; on the other hand, God called them to realization in concrete creation to show forth the continual presence the Logos in Creation. As immanent, the *logoi* manifest the divine intentions and principles of every single nature, that is, of every object, thing, law, and their intelligible image; they manifest the *existential purpose* of every thing they materialize in the created order, but they are not themselves created. In other words their "material" manifestations through sensible things and their intelligible images, do not condition them from within the creation; for they have the ground of their immanent manifestations in the transcendent Logos.

HUMANITY AS HYPOSTASIS OF THE UNIVERSE: PRAISE AS EXPLORATION

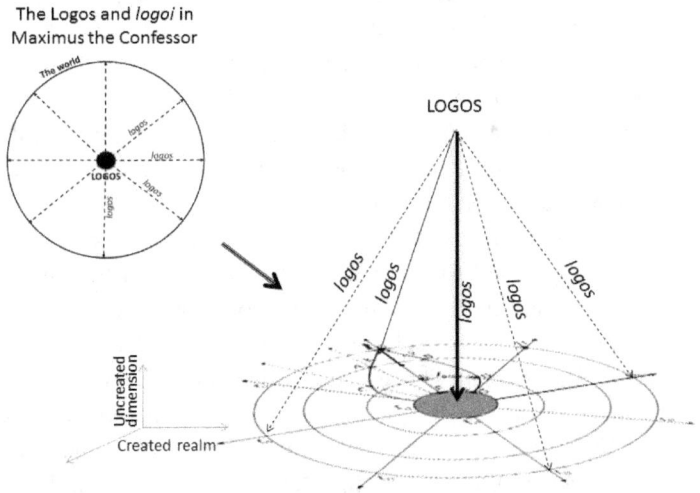

From a theogenic uniformity of the universe to its cosmographic uniformity.

On the one hand the vertical dimension links the origin of the universe (the Big Bang) with the Logos of God by whom and through whom the visible universe (as well as the non-observable and invisible) was brought into being. This vertical link can be associated with the *logos* of creation. However the presence of the *logoi* is not restricted only to the Big Bang. The universe as a whole (including the visible one) is supported and sustained by the *logoi* in all aspects of its existence, so that the *logoi* proceed from the Logos to all other points of the universe (a panentheistic stance). In this sense the meaning of the cosmological principle as the equivalence of all points on the circumference at present time can be interpreted as a *theogenic* uniformity related to the presence of the *logoi* in all potentially possible points of the universe. The question of what are the grounds that cosmology can proceed from the *theogenic* uniformity to the cosmographic uniformity (cosmological principle) relates to the anthropological issue of how and why the Divine Image (gifted with experience of *theogenic* uniformity) cascades towards its outward theoretical expression through the principle of spatial or material uniformity.

This epistemological transition from a theogenic uniformity experienced as a non-intentional simultaneity with the universe (*coaevus universo*) to the cosmographic uniformity of the universe in the phenomenality of objects represents a constitutive element in the capacity of *Imago Dei* who, on the one hand praises creation from being inside God and sensing it through an instantaneous synthesis of thanksgiving and, on the other hand, explores and studies the created universe outwardly through its God-given cognitive capacities. On the one hand creation is given in the unconditional modus of life, on the other hand, since life is possible only in living beings, the same creation appears as a medium where these beings can exist, that in as a physical universe. What then is creation? It is not only a gift from God where this God can be praised, but this is the arena of life, where life becomes a multiplicity of living who praise.

What is then the aim of the Christian cosmology? Not to construct theories of the world. Not to claim about the world that which humanity, in its modest condition in physical being, cannot know and cannot change. Humanity is gifted to live in a sublime sense of this word, that is, to be the continuation of that Life in whose name all is happening in the universe. This Life grants to humanity its image—*Imago Dei*, thank to which the universe created by this Life eucharistically returns into it in the image of *Imago Dei*. Then the image of the universe inevitably contains in itself that which is essential to humanity in the *Imago Dei*. What then human beings find, by looking into their souls in their cosmic reflections? To respond to this question, one should recognize that the cosmos teaches humanity ascetics and humility. Indeed, the infinite and lifeless spaces in which God is present in a non-obvious way, the nonsense of the spatially and temporally separated eras, "whose silence horrifies" (Pascal), and in which, according to Carl Sagan, "Our planet is a lonely speck in the great enveloping cosmic dark,"[105] brings reason to the idea of the cosmic absurdity and by an inversion places humanity in the conditions of a necessity to realize the greatness of that modest human phenomenon on the blue planet Earth, from where, and thank to which the overall sense of the human life is unfolded, as well as the sense of the surrounding world transfigured through it. It is this capacity to look at oneself from the outside, to position oneself in the world and to realize one's own physical place is archetypically inherited from the incarnate Logos-Christ. And when human beings reflect upon a possibility of such an introspection, they find in themselves those qualities which are typical to Christ that made possible his Incarnation on Earth and at the same time to be hypostatically present everywhere in the universe, embracing it not only because it is created by the Logos, but because the hypostatic human consciousness of Christ retained the same capacity to synthesize the image of the created world, that which corresponded to the enhypostasization of the world as a whole by the Logos himself. It is this capacity to synthesize in its consciousness the wholeness of the world and at the same to look at itself and the place of its habitation from the outside, discloses again the

---

105. Sagan, *Pale Blue Dot*, 13.

human Divine Image making it belonging to the universe and at the same time characteristically "standing" above it. In fact, all cosmological research and practical exploration of the outer cosmos, making possible to look at the human and physical world from the outside reveals itself as the realization of the Divine Image. And this is the reason why one can assuredly say that the pale blue dot, obtained on the photo from the cosmic station "Voyager," and displaying Earth in the background of the starry sky, became a new contribution to the vision of the universe in the image of *Imago Dei*. Metaphorically, such a study of the cosmos that, on the one hand, shows its huge scale, and on the other hand, produces in a human being humility and meekness from consciousness of its physical insignificance, can be likened to the eucharistic practice of thanksgiving of the Creator for the unique gift of life in the background of the lifeless cosmos. But even this infinitely small scale of the human existence does not deprive humanity of its exclusive feature making it distinct and different from the rest of creation, his qualities of a moral agent in the universe capable to praise Creator, for the praise is directed to a certain goal for which the praise is given as a gift, the goal which is difficult to determine and achieve on the basis of the natural laws of the world. Humanity, experiencing the created world from "inside" and feeling it "simultaneity" with it, is not able to assign to it any measure of extension and relation to something external, because it is not possible to exit the conditions of the givenness of self-affective life. The belonging to creation cannot be measured quantitatively or qualitatively, it cannot be foreseen and repeated, it is metaphysically impossible being theologically possible. For life is given to humanity in the self-affective event as a modus of createdness reproducing the self-affectivity of God understood as Life. And all manifestations of this life amounting in infinite disclosures of the sense of life within creation represent an open-ended hermeneutics and praise of existence as such addressed to the other, with the other and for the other, that Other which is the ultimate Father of all.

Conclusion

THE TRANSFIGURATION OF THE UNIVERSE THROUGH THE DEIFIED KNOWLEDGE OR THE UNIVERSE IN THE IMAGE OF *IMAGO DEI*

THIS BOOK HAS DEALT with the dialogue between science and theology, employing and analyzing some cosmological ideas in the context of theology. The objective was twofold: on the one hand, to develop an argument that all images of the universe are essentially anthropic as related to the physical and epistemological conditions of their construction by human beings; on the other hand, since the basic feature of humanity capable of creating a synthesis of the universe is its Divine Image archetypically proceeding from the incarnate Christ, the universe carries in itself the conditions of the Incarnation thus being not only an epistemological image of humanity, but the "image" of the self-affective Divine Life creating the universe in such a way that the first-born among humans was possible in it. Cosmology and theology complement each other because to theologize one must physically exist, whereas to produce knowledge of the universe one must have an articulating capacity of the Divine Image. The dialogue between cosmology and theology explicates the basic dichotomy of the human condition, namely its creaturely origin, but in communion with God-Creator. Then the universe unfolds itself to human beings in an *image* produced from within the human condition of being a creature in communion with God (condition defined as *Imago Dei*). Since this basic dichotomy is constitutive of the human condition—that is, it cannot be overcome—the dialogue between cosmology and theology represents an open-ended enterprise producing a hermeneutics of the human condition.

The fact that the dialogue between science and theology provides an open-ended hermeneutics of the human condition is demonstrated through a careful philosophical distinction between theology and science on the basis of the demarcation in the modi of the *given* and amounting to the difference in the underlying ontologies in the sciences and theology. Yet such a distinction in the modi of the *given* fails in the case of man resulting in the dichotomy of man's existence and ultimately to its inability to know himself. Then the undefinability of humanity and its unknowability forms the precondition (transcendental delimiters) for the knowability of the world. This implies that physics and cosmology follow the same *apophatic* pattern of explanation that is typical for the theological anthropology of the Divine Image. The apophaticism of cosmology means the limited scope of cosmology in respect to knowing the universe as being created; it naturally arises because the sphere of cosmology's phenomenality does not take into account the event-like essence of the human phenomenon as the primary revelation of existence (theologically treated as revelation of God), that is, as creation. This restates the basic paradox of the human condition: on the one hand, there is the facticity of human life (stated by the sciences, for example), on the other hand, this facticity is metaphysically incomprehensible thus needing an appeal to creation. The dialogue between science and theology thus becomes an attempt to balance in one and the same humanity the extent of a creation dimension in grasping the limited knowability of the world and man's facticity, with those forms of asserting the world and man which the sciences operate. The dialogue between theology and science acquires a status of an apophatic enterprise in a generic sense: all particular cataphatic forms of this dialogue (constructive engagement of theology and science) effectively tell us what the ultimate foundation of this dialogue is not.

The paradoxical state of humanity as a creature in communion is linked to the forgetting of the primary gift of life, the forgetting into which humanity fell because of not seeing its origin as being created, as well as not seeing the signs of the Creator in the universe. Traditional theology asserts that to overcome this forgetting God sent his Son to remind the old truth. The Incarnation of the Son of God in Jesus Christ aimed to show to humanity the Face of the Incarnate World-Logos of God as the source of Life and that one who transmits its archetype to man. Correspondingly, the origin of the paradox and hence of the dialogue between theology and science can be explicated as a deviation from the incarnational archetype of Christ for whom the difference between two phenomenalilties of life (its immediate givenness and the articulated facticity) was not paradoxical because it was created by Christ himself.

It was argued that humanity, in spite of its non-attunement and homelessness in the vast cosmos is predisposed to some intimacy with the universe. It is this intimacy of living in communion with God that lies in the foundation of the dialogue between theology and science. The inseparability of humanity and the universe constitutes the content of that which is called human life's self-affectivity and it is this content that implicitly constitutes the core of the dialogue between theology and science. It is this life's self-affectivity that becomes a matter of enquiry as being split into two phenomenological structures: that of the human life as proceeding from the self-affectivity of the a-cosmic Life as God (communion), and that of life as proceeding from the conditions of being-in-the-world. The vision of the universe within the latter phenomenological structure (in the natural attitude employed in the sciences) is only possible from within a phenomenological structure of life as related to its ultimate source in the Divine. The disregard for the latter, its "forgetting" as the refusal of accepting the givens of existence as revelation, leads to the transcendental illusion in which the universe is seen as self-sufficient and devoid of its a-cosmic origin. Then the dialogue between cosmology and theology should be considered as a mediation between two phenomenological structures, two types of the *given*, which complement each other within the facticity of one and the same human life.

Science and theology are seen as manifestations of that life which neither confuses science with theology nor transmutes the one into the other. Here one can make an analogy with Christology, that is, with the divine and human natures of Christ: theology and science as human activities are present in the human constitution "without confusion, without division and without separation" because of the originary unity of their source in the hypostatic subject. In the same way as the sense of the hypostatic union in Christ is subjected to an open-ended theological hermeneutics, the dialogue between theology and science represents an open-ended hermeneutics of the hypostatic human condition. It admits any expression of experience of being a human remaining within its basic delimiters best stated either in the paradox of subjectivity or in the discourse of oblivion of origins. Since the riddle of humanity's inability to know itself cannot be resolved in terms of metaphysical concepts, cascading down towards the irresolvable nature of the paradox, the dialogue between theology and science cannot hope to have any "material" goal as its accomplishment, that is, as a unification of two phenomenalities of existence in one and the same subject. The dialogue will always remain confirming an existential truth that both—science and theology—originate in one and the same humanity, created in communion with God and living in a moral tension between the sense of its created limitedness and graceful longing for the unconditional and immortal. The dichotomy between science and theology manifests itself as an inevitable characteristic of humanity's creaturehood so that no reconciliation of them is possible to the same extent as it is impossible to overcome the ontological difference between creation and God in the process of deification.

Phrased philosophically, the dialogue between theology and science in application to cosmology deals with two complementary phenomenalities of the universe which, by the fact of their origin in one and the same humanity, have to be in a constant critical attitude with respect to each other, by determining the sphere of their legitimate application with no claims for the priority of one with respect to another, and with no intention to overcome the difference between them. The universe as communion enters the proper *givens* of theology because of being commensurable with the human life by the fact of their creation by God. Cosmology, dealing with the same universe through the constitution of the world of physical objects, enters the dialogue with theology through an open-ended scientific hermeneutics of the universe within the givenness of life. Ultimately, the dialogue between cosmology and theology represents an endless hermeneutics of the primary experience of existence as communion through an outward constitution of the universe. This hermeneutics reflects the working of the human subjectivity thus inevitably contributing to the hermeneutics of the human condition.

It was argued that the major concern of the "dialogue" is humanity itself; it is this humanity that confronts itself in two different modalities of its functioning in the world, namely as hypostatic existence in the Divine Image, and as functioning corporeal subjectivity. Then it is not unreasonable to claim that cosmology as a special physico-mathematical thematization of the human corporeal background contributes indirectly towards the problem of constitution of hypostatic corporeality, that is, personhood. This is why the research attempted to locate the presence of personhood behind cosmological constructions, in particular in questions of the universe's origin, that is, in the philosophical and theological narrative of creation. It was argued that the question of creation could not be tackled within the natural attitude. Here is the striking difference between how cosmology treats the universe and how theology, while asserting God, implicitly contains the narrative of creation. This hidden presence of the universe positions its phenomenon in rubrics of those *givens* of life of Life which cannot be detected by cosmology because cosmology is functioning in the conditions of these *givens*. In other words, the universe as the background of communion and manifestation of self—affective Life, appears to humanity as such a phenomenon that exceeds the measure of its discursive representation, and that effectively blocks the latter through the saturation of intuition. Here the phenomenality of the universe can only be expressed in the framework of religious experience in which the universe is inseparable from its creator.

If the universe as a whole appears to man as a saturated phenomenon such that positions itself outside of any conditions of experience (the intuitive saturation leaves human beings with a clear sense that the universe is, it is given to them, but with no face and identity), how the presence of the hypostasis of the Logos of God as the creator of the universe can be detected? Indeed, in the case of the universe as a saturated phenomenon the ego experiences the disagreement with a "phenomenon of the universe" expected to appear in the manner of ordinary objects. Consequently the ego cannot constitute the universe as an object whose concept would agree with the conditions of experience of the universe through sheer belonging to it. However, the failure to objectify the universe does not mean that there is no appearance at all and the implied communion is empty of content. One has here the intuitive saturation by the universe which imposes itself by excess that makes this universe effectively "invisible" and *incomprehensible*: the universe resists any regard with respect to itself as an object by engulfing the subjectivity to such an extent that the ego fails to constitute the universe.

On the side of a human being a meeting with a saturated phenomenon of the universe can be characterized as a condition of not being adapted to and not being attuned to the universe. A break between an empirical affectivity by the universe and a possibility of its linguistic expressibility indicates that the saturated phenomenon *de facto* breaks that which could be called the conditions of experience corresponding to ordinary phenomena. Then the question is: what does the ego "see" in the conditions of the broken link between the overabundance of intuition and the possibility of discursive expressibility? The answer comes from the recognition that the universe is received through the ego's sight as pure donation which cannot be caught as complete in rubrics of thought. The presence of the universe to human subjects is open only to the extent that the universe itself, being enhypostasized by the Divine Logos, makes it possible. Saying differently, the kind of conceptuality with which cosmology of the universe as a saturated phenomenon operates is one in which the acts of cognition are formed from beyond them by the reality of that which is disclosed. Theologically, this formation is due to the Holy Spirit as a participant in the creation of the universe, but who is never transparent in rubrics of space and time, yet who demonstrates to humans their own existence in the universe from the side of the Divine.

It is the Spirit who relates the Divine Logos to the human and cosmic forms which are assumed in Jesus Christ so that human persons are enabled to discern the presence of the person of the Logos in the foundation of the created universe. This Spirit is not a rational principle that informs all things with the visible order or imparts to human beings a specific organic biological form. This is that Spirit who was present behind the Incarnation of the Logos in Jesus Christ by uniting the Divine with the cosmic. It is that Spirit who opens up humans to their communion with God in the universe in which the Logos enhypostasized himself in the cosmic body of Jesus Christ. The seeming intuitive saturation of the phenomenon of the created universe can thus be seen as that acting of God upon humans which keeps their concepts open, so that human thought and speech are stretched out beyond themselves towards the inexhaustible nature of that who enhypostasized the universe and that who made it possible for human beings to comprehend that the universe is created. The Holy Spirit operates within human beings in order to epistemologically release them from the chains of their embodied condition, and finally direct them towards the reality of that One who stands behind the creation of the world.

The universe as a saturated phenomenon engulfs subjectivity by removing any sense of its parts, temporal and spatial extension. In a temporal sense, the universe is always already there, so that all events of subjectivity's life unfold from the never-ending donating event of the universe as constant coming into being so that the unforeseeable nature of every consequent moment entails the unending historicity and unpredictability of existence. In a spatial sense, the contingency as concrete factuality of an event of appearance of the ego's life makes its position in the universe *out of tune* (in spite of the fine tuning related to consubstantiality with the universe). The universe engulfs the ego with the intuitive flood depriving this ego of a clear comprehension of its place in the created universe. Its "place" is its sheer facticity, so that any attempted constitution of the sense of this place in the universe's space reduces the universe to its limited astronomical phenomenality. But the universe as a saturated phenomenon is invisible according to quantity, unbearable according quality, unconditioned according to relation and irreducible to the rubrics of ego's subjectivity according to modality. Such a sense of humanity's place in the universe and its not being able to constitute the universe point to the limited capacity of human beings to understand the sense of their existence.

The situation with "knowledge" of the universe as a saturated phenomenon becomes characteristically similar to that of knowledge of God understood as personal participation and communion. In theology, one cannot be detached from what is intended to be a subject matter of its enquiry; one needs faith and participation in that which is studied. In this case the "knowledge" of God can not be "objective" (in the sense of scientific rationality) because it depends on a modus of personal experience and involvement. This suggests that theology implies a special understanding of "objectivity," different from that in the natural attitude where the intellect attempts to detach itself from that object which is constituted as freed from attachments. Thus, in theology, no prior assessment of the attachments to its "object" is possible, for the definitiveness of the intellect reflecting upon this "object" is revealed to itself only through the God-given capacity. This is the moment when the intuition saturates over the intellect in an attempt of the latter to grasp the sense of its own facticity, and it is this saturation that indicates the inseparability of consciousness from its source in the Divine. We face an interesting reversal (with respect to scientific knowledge): the "objective" knowledge of God presupposes saturation over all discursive images of the Divine paradoxically implying the impossibility of detachment from communion with God and the impossibility of knowing God through a discursive reason functioning in the natural attitude. As Kant would say, knowledge of God is a prerogative of practical reason, but not that of theoretical.

One realizes then, by analogy, that the application of the commonly accepted objectivity (based on the presupposition of detachment from all subjective attachments) to the universe as a saturated phenomenon becomes impossible. It is sheer attachment to the universe that detaches us from our preconceptions about it; while detaching ourselves from our preconceptions we become free for the universe, and therefore free for true "knowledge" of it. Then the Christian appropriation of cosmology is carried out in conversation with the universe which *communicates itself* to us in acts of donation, and as "gazing" at us it *requires of us an answering relation* in receiving, acknowledging, understanding, and in active personal participation in the relationship it establishes between us. It is this answering relation that constitutes the ego. Our conscious response is provoked by the fact of our inseparability with the universe. This response is rooted in the ability of humans to articulate their existence (as hypostatic self-affectivity) and the existence of the universe, the ability which originates in the Divine Image as a particular enhypostasization of the human part of the universe by the Logos. The Divine Reason disclosed in Christ had endowed human reason with a capacity of exploring the universe and producing scientific hermeneutics of creation. Yet, Christ remains the Logos of God so that that structure of the universe created by him is not easily accessible to the human mind because the created universe in its essence remains the same kind of the saturated phenomenon as the Logos-Creator himself. The clearing of the universe to the human grasp is available to the same extent as God through the incarnate Christ is revealed to humanity. The universe is knowable in its pieces and moments but at the same time it always remains mysterious and this is felt by man as the universe's affectivity with respect to him, the affectivity which exceeds the measure of its discursive comprehension.

The fact the hypostasis of the Logos is present behind all articulations of the universe can be detected by the human consciousness if it analyzes a hypothetical attempt to look at the created universe as if it was caused by some kind of objective metaphysical foundation. In this case the universe as a whole becomes a subject of a phenomenological critique. However, this critique does not imply that the question about reality of the universe must be suspended and cosmology is brought to a methodological halt. One needs to realize that transcendence of the universe takes place not through an ascending series of the worldly astronomical phenomena or theoretical causation (which had been criticized by Kant), but through observing *teleologies* of explanation which rather characterize the activity of consciousness. Hence the phenomenological reduction with respect to the universe (as a modus of a phenomenological critique) cannot reach its goal for it disregards the universe as an ongoing accomplishment related to the *teleology* of the human spirit (implanted in the promise of salvation and eternal life). If such a reduction is performed one does not discern the difference between the universe as a mental construction which is subject to reduction and the universe as communion whose presence in consciousness is exactly that *ontological* link which makes this consciousness possible at all, and that which can be cut off only in abstraction. One cannot bracket or reduce the *universe as communion* by using this consciousness because by insisting on this, this consciousness deprives itself of the conditions of its embodied existence and hence destroys itself.

The transcendental reduction of the universe as a whole performed by classical phenomenology in order to neutralise the natural attitude points to a simple fact that the representation of the universe as completely transcendent to consciousness cannot acquire an ontological quality, remaining "transcendent" but only within the immanence of consciousness that itself exists in this universe. In this sense phenomenology rightly suggests the dismissing of intellectual idols of the universe as pretending to exhaust the reality of the universe as communion. Reason cannot position itself with respect to the universe in terms of "closer" or "far." The universe is present in the background of existence through relationship and communion in such a way that allows one to express this presence ecstatically through music, painting, poetry, etc. However, this experience cannot be verbalized and expressed in definitions of physics and mathematics. It is exactly this paradoxical "presence in absence" of the universe as a whole which allows the human spirit to make the distinction between what is absent (and hence always suspected in the inadequacy of its expression in concepts and then legitimately bracketed away), and what is present (i.e., what is left after the bracketing of conceptual idols) preserving the ineffable essence of the universe. In fact, one can say that the very bracketing of the conceptual idols of the universe is possible only because it is compensated by the reality of its concrete presence, manifested in the very possibility of thinking about the universe. The implicit *presence* of the created universe in all acts of the incarnate human subjectivity cannot be phenomenologically reduced (i.e., bracketed as transcendent) because if this could happen, the incarnate consciousness itself would be bracketed away and hence eliminated. Obviously this would entail the destruction of the factual consciousness itself, and thus led to a sheer existential contradiction. Humanity, in spite of its non-attunement, insecurity and homelessness in the astronomical universe is predisposed to love the universe through the inherent Divine Image, because it is physical matter of this universe that was shared by the incarnate God. The universe as good creation by good God is loved through the love to God-man for whom, and hence for the whole humanity, the structure of this universe became specifically concrete. And it is through this love that the sense of the universe with a tiny physical human being in the Divine Image becomes if not explained, but at least theologically explicated. The universe can be seen through the eyes of love to God, because it is God who wills with respect to his image in man and makes himself seen through the miracle of human life and all those created things which are hypostatically inherent in his Logos.

The modus of the hidden theological dimension in cosmological thinking sees the whole process of studying the universe by human beings as its transfiguration, that is, bringing the universe to God as an Eucharistic response to its creation. What is the meaning of this assertion in view of present-day perception of the practical infinity of the universe? Cosmology explicitly states that the physical universe is huge and that humanity effectively sees the frozen image of its past reaching us through light travelling billions of years. The universe at large is causally disconnected and most of its space will never be reached physically. In this sense any analogy with the theologically asserted transfiguration of the earthly nature, sometimes invoked in the context of ecological concerns, makes no sense. The language of "use" or "development" of nature that needs humanity for its transfiguration must be abandoned as irrelevant in application to the universe as a whole (in order to avoid a suspicion in producing pseudo-scientific mythology). This is the reason why legitimately, as speaking of transfiguration, one invokes an idea of mediation between divisions in creation as a particular modus of the enhypostasization of the universe making it self-conscious within life's self-affectivity. When one speaks of "en-hypostasizing" the universe one means that this has something to do with humanity's quality to be hypostasis of the universe, that is, being able to articulate the universe and make it palpable. It is not a matter of "shaping" the universe into a human product, but of bringing it into a conscious relationship with God. And humanity does this through understanding the universe's meaning in its connection and unity with the primordial ground in the Logos. In other words, to grasp the meaning of the universe one means to reveal its unity as that one which proceeds from God. Correspondingly such an understanding implies that its dynamics is subjected to the participation in the Divine activity.

Since all talks about participation in the Divine make sense only in the context of Christ, being the archetype of such a participation, it seems plausible to make an epistemological analogy between what humanity experiences through communication with the universe and some of Christ's activities which manifested the presence of the Divine modus of being within his fully human nature. As an example, one considers his walking on the water adjusting it for the purposes of our reasoning. To walk is a human activity; to walk on the liquid and fragile surface of water shows that there is a double activity is involved: the human walking and the Divine activity which enables Christ to actualize that modus of being which transcends that which pertains to his human nature. The divine activity penetrates into the human nature of Christ, but the *logos* of this nature is secured in God. What is changed is the "modus" (*tropos*) of being, that is, the way of the human nature's existence and execution of its natural functions. The presence of this modus indicates that the humanity of Christ participated in the Divine activity, thus being deified. Extending this example towards knowledge of the universe by human beings one can say, on the one hand, that to think and see things in the universe in its extended display is a modus of the human activity; on the other hand, if human beings involved in the study of the universe, exercising their ability to see and comprehend the visible universe, subject themselves to the actualization in them of a modus of existence that transcends their human nature, so that the divine activity penetrates their human nature they will be able to see the universe beyond that which is visible according to the capacity and delimiters originating from their created nature. They will be able to produce an instantaneous synthesis of the universe by transcending discursive reasoning as such and contemplating the universe as the unity held in Christ's "right hand" (Rev 1:16). This analogy receives its justification in the fact that Christ, being fully human, had a vision of the universe in its unity with himself. Humanity, being created by God with the innate sense of the unity with the world develops the articulated image of the latter within the epistemic capacities of the Divine Image.

In a way, to see the universe as a whole creation, that is, to see it as an instant of the unconditional Divine Love with respect to the world, means to participate in the actually infinite modus of the Divine activity. To comprehend the universe as a whole as a "simultaneous" with a cosmic instant of the natural life, means to achieve a change of a *modus* of this life. Maximus the Confessor describes this by saying that "such a one has no experience of what is present to it, and has become without beginning and end; he no longer bears within himself temporal life and his motions." In this, effectively deified condition, a man acquires the vision of the universe through the "eyes" of the Logos himself: "he possesses the sole divine and eternal life of the indwelling Word."[1] With all this, the human nature is preserved and not destroyed. What is changed, is a *modus* of being through interpenetration by God when the whole universe is perceived as "all in all" of inexpressible communion with God understood as Life and Love. The "cosmic homelessness," "non-attunement with the universe" and "alienation" from it, are overcome through the unconditional Love of Christ to that creation which he created for himself and for humanity who through him can know the Creator. The universe becomes for human beings something greater and other than "only the universe," because the perception of a specific "worldly" character of the universe is overcome without the universe itself being "removed" or "eliminated." The universe is transfigured from within human contemplation and comprehension, but preserved in its naturalness. It is transfigured exactly to the extent the human person relieves itself from the grief of living in it, when the sense of life in God and with God makes the entire expanding universe with myriads of scintillating stars no more than an instant of communion. The universe is transfigured because it is transcended and not abandoned. It is transcended in the direction of the inside of the human person, that is, towards strengthening and asserting that existence which is *free* as much as possible from the physical and biological, as well from social and historical necessities. The universe is transcended not as if one could "look" at it from the outside, but as if the universe is open to the infinite exploration from within the human heart as being archetypically commensurable with the "heart" of Christ-Creator. To transcend the universe in this case is to gaze at that dazzling immemorial from where

---

1. Maximus the Confessor, *Ambigua 10*, in Louth, *Maximus the Confessor*, 116. In a modern religious philosophical context, Michel Henry expressed the entering of such a condition as the overcoming of forgetting of the *condition of the Son* that implies a certain rebirth when one rediscovers the Power with which one is born, and which is Itself not born. Henry, *I Am the Truth*, 170.

and to where humanity is destined to return. By looking at the abyss of the unknowability of the non-originary origins of the universe, the human soul de facto attempts to gaze at the radical frontier of its own unknowability which theologically is to lead this soul to its union with God, that is, to its union with that Life from which this soul non-originary originates and with which it morally unites.

Finally, we have attempted to convince the reader that the dialogue between theology and science does not have, and simply cannot have any theoretical goal, for its theological counterpart escapes theoretical definitions transforming the dialogue into an infinite hermeneutics of the human condition in which the Divine (as the source of morality and of the Good) is posed as its formal goal. Unlike scientific research, the dialogue between science and theology has rather a practical objective, namely, to always keep humanity anxious of its condition and reminding to it that this anxiety will never be overcome as long as humanity unceasingly faces the unrecoverable immemorial. However this anxiety has a certain spiritual sense keeping humanity awaken to the problems of its fragile physical existence and at the same time God-given promise of finding the homeland. This is the reason why human anthropology in order to be soteriologically meaningful must be theological and cosmological to the same extent as cosmology, in order to be soteriologically meaningful, must be theological and anthropological. Then the seeing of the universe effectively means the vision of the Divine Image in humanity as if this Divine Image is displayed outwardly through knowledge of the universe. Such a vision of the universe contributes to an open-ended hermeneutic of this Divine Image where the universe becomes this Image's "mirror" by manifesting the infinite deepness of the human soul.

Appendix 1

Glossary of Philosophical Terms

Affectivity/Self-Affectivity

The term "affectivity" or "self-affectivity," in the context of this research, refers to the phenomenon of life, in particular human life. The phenomenological definition of the latter implies that the phenomenon of life does not generate the appearance of anything new that would be different from life itself. It does not turn to anything that is not life and it does not establish any differentiation in itself. It is in this sense that the phenomenon of life is not the appearance of something different from it (the other) but self-appearance (auto-appearance), self-phenomenalization (auto-phenomenalization). The only possible phenomenological definition of life is: life is life. The phenomenality of this self-appearance, its phenomenological essence, is that *transcendental affectivity* which makes possible the experience of life as hardship, suffering, grief, love, empathy, etc. One can say that affectivity forms that phenomenological essence of life and its given primordiality where no visibility of the world or of any trace of intentional thinking of life can yet be found. It is the affectivity of life that lies in the foundation of any possible phenomenality as being constituted through the senses or discursively. Since this affectivity is not a phenomenon, but is in the foundation of phenomena, it cannot be detected through an intentional gazing at it. It remains in the shadow of any phenomenality thus making, in reflection, impossible to produce any constitutive analysis of that which one calls "phenomenon of life." To say that life is affectivity or to say that life is self-affective, is to say that it cannot be known in rubrics of intentionality, that is, in the rubrics of "I think." Placed in the context of the human personhood, this amounts to the statement of inability of a human person to know itself.

Apophaticism

This is a general epistemological trend applicable to theology and the sciences, implying that the sense of realities affirmed in terms of their signifiers is never exhausted by the latter, that is, signifiers do not exhaust that which is signified. Historically apophaticism has its origin in *apophatic theology* as that way of theologizing which safeguards the absolute transcendence of God against misinterpretations based upon human analogies. However, while one cannot comprehend God in his essence, one can experience his power, will, wisdom and love through grace. Thus the apophaticism is exactly that freedom which is granted to any faithful to explore experientially their personal relation with God, their freedom to define God in this relation within the horizon of church's definitions that helps to separate and distinguish truth from its distortion and falsification. That linguistic semantics and attitude to cognition which refuses to exhaust the content of knowledge in its formulation, which refuses to exhaust the reality of things signified in the logic of signifiers is called *apophatic*. In philosophy, for example, it originates from an epistemological argument that language conditions the accessibility and intelligibility of reality. In this approach the very phrase "there is" points to a referent which the very language cannot capture because the referent is not constituted by language and by definition is not the same as it linguistic effect. According to this view there is no access to the referent outside the linguistic effect, but the linguistic effect is not the same as that referent it attempts but fails to capture. This situation entails, in analogy with theology, a variety of ways of making such a reference, where none of them can claim it exclusiveness and true accessibility to what the reference is made. The same feature pertains to any knowledge through which the human existent encounters the world. An object is never a pure reference to itself, but is also a revelation of the fashion of its comprehension. This revelation is at once partial and total: partial because it cannot of itself exhaust that which essentially presents itself as inexhaustible, total because the fashion of comprehension is indivisible and completely present in each of its manifestations. Theology affirms that any knowledge of God if it pretends to be real and true cannot escape the conditions of incongruence between human knowing and the reality of God. This incongruence is the immanent feature of any theologizing: one cannot raise questions of the reality of God from some abstract position because it implies the presence of a particular feature of the Divine manifestation.

Given/Givenness/Gift (Donated/Donation/Data)

In a modern philosophical usage *donation* is treated as a *gift* of being able to perceive and reveal things. The very fact of the human existence (life) can be treated as a gift by God, so that humanity exists in a constant *givenness* of this gift. The characteristic of phenomena as *given*, that is, those which fall under the rubric of "donation," is that they do not subsist in something which causally precedes them. They are *given* spontaneously from themselves and out of themselves. The terminology of *the given* (instead of *data*) is employed in order to underline the fact of the presence of human subjectivity in participation, detection, identification and articulation of phenomena in the form of "data." The *given* is not a dispassionate and neutral imposing of the world or God upon a human subject, but the "gift" granted to human being as a part of Being in general in order to comprehend existence.

Hypostatic/Hypostasis

The meaning of the term "hypostatic" comes from the Greek word *hypostasis*, which was used in Patristic theological context in order to underline the "personal," active and intransitive dimension of existence as different from impersonal substance (*ousia*) or nature (*physis*). The distinction between substance (*ousia*) (or nature [*physis*]) and *hypostasis* was articulated in Patristic thought in the context of the trinitarian and christological discussions throughout fourth to seventh centuries. *Ousia* (as related to universals, families or species) tends to be used with regard to internal characteristics and relations, or metaphysical reality (here it is almost identical with *physis*), whereas *hypostasis* emphasizes the externally concrete character of the substance, its empirical objectivity, and the existential aspect of being, expressed through the realization of freedom, movement and will. The hypostatic aspect of individual existence is not immanent to what is included in the substance. Nature or substance can be divided and shared while the *hypostasis* of a particular being is indivisible. The reality of substance becomes evident and real only in *hypostases*, that is, in that which is indivisible. In a theological context *hypostasis* is similar to *prosopon*, that is, person in modern parlance. This implies that the nature of things becomes evident if it is *personified*. The *hypostasis*, then, is seen as the foundation of being for it is that in which nature exists. In application to human beings, all human beings share the same nature, they have similar biology so that flesh can be communicated from one human being to another. However, different human beings are different *persons*, that is, they have their own distinct existences, which can not be communicated to, and imitated by, different persons. All human beings are gifted with life: it is in them that life comes to itself, but comes as a self-identical selfhood (as a *hypostasis*). In this sense the human community is the total identity as perceiving life in it, but every such a perception of life in each of its members is irreducible to the other. In theology of Maximus the Confessor every human being has its own *logos* (the underlying principle of existence) as a principle of its constancy, however, at the same time, it has its own *tropos* (*modus*) as an aspect of change and adaptation and it is this *tropos* that is related to the hypostatic aspect of existence of humanity as capable of change through communion (see Maximus the Confessor, *Ambigua 42*).

The distinction between nature and hypostasis allows one to articulate the unity of all creation in two different senses. On the one hand all varieties of sensible objects share the same nature (the same atoms, for example). On the other hand if one considers the world in relationship to its creator, then the natural existence acquires features of existence for someone, that is, for the Creator. Thus when Christianity affirms that the world was created by the Word-Logos of God and that through the Logos everything was made, it effectively affirms that the natural existence of the world is existence in the personhood of God, that is, in his *hypostasis*. The link between God and the world is non-ontological, non-physical, etc., but *hypostatic*, so that it can be expressed as a non-consubstantial *relationship* between the Divine and the worldly. Then Creation of the world and its existence has sense only in relation to the Person who is acting as the creator and provider of meaning of the existence.

Enhypostatic/Enhypostasis/Enhypostasization (Derivative from Hypostasis/Hypostatic):

The Greek Patristic meaning of the words *enhypostatic* or *enhypostasis* originates in the theology of Leontius of Byzantium in the context of christological discussions of the six to seven centuries. Its meaning, according to "A Patristic Greek Lexicon" is: "being, existing in an hypostasis or Person," "subsistent in, inherent." *Enhypostasis* points towards something which has its being in the other hypostasis. The "hypostatic inherence" of the universe in the Logos of God can then be interpreted as the Logos's eternal manifestations in different modes of *participation* by created beings in him. This *participation* does not assume any ontological causation; for to participate in the Logos means to be made by the Logos a participating being, that is, to be made as a being in the hypostasis of the Logos himself. This implies that existence through participation in the Logos is subsistence in his Personhood, that is, the *inherence* in his hypostasis. Another example is a theological assertion that man is hypostasis [personality] of the cosmos, its conscious and personal self-expression; it is he who gives meaning to things and who has to transfigure them. The universe as *the expressed and articulated existence* is possible in human hypostasis, that is, it acquires some qualities of existence if it is reflected in the personality of humanity. A theologian would say that existence of the universe as the articulated existence is *enhypostatic*. This is the same as to say, using the language of phenomenological philosophy, that the universe, as an articulated system of notions with a certain criterion of objectivity is constituted (*enhypostasized*) by human beings. Despite man's incommensurability with the universe on the physical level one can speak about the *eidetic or hypostatic* commensurability with the universe as a capacity to intuit the universe in its totality from within the event of life and then to articulate the universe within a single consciousness. The eidetic *commensurability* with the universe does not follow from the physical *consubstantiality* with the universe as sharing of 4 percent of that substance that originated in the Big Bang.

Facticity (Contingency)

In philosophy, the term *facticity* has a multiplicity of meanings from "factuality" and "contingency" to the intractable conditions of human existence. In our context the term comes to mean that which resists explanation and interpretation, or that which cannot be presented in the phenomenality of objects and physical causation. M. Heidegger discusses facticity as the "thrownness" of individual existence into the world. He refers not only to a brute fact, or the factuality of a concrete historical situation, but to something that already informs and has been taken up in existence, even if it is unnoticed or left unattended. In a cosmological context when one speaks of the facticity of the universe one implies that it is impossible to test why the universe has specific physical laws, that is, one cannot test why they have the nature they have or what underpins their existence. Physical cosmology assumes that these laws cannot be different. However, from a philosophical standpoint, these laws are *contingent* in the same sense as *contingent* the whole universe. The latter can imply that the universe is created meaning that it could be created in a different way with different laws, or not be created at all. Its facticity points to the specific act of creation when the universe was brought into being in that particular shape it has. The Judeo-Christian tradition affirms the world's radical contingency upon God implying that the laws of the world are contingent and do not possess a status of an absolute necessity. This implies that the act of creation of the world by God out of nothing is a "free" act of God's willing kindness to the world and, because of God's freedom, creation is not inherent in God's own being (*ousia*). This produces a twofold contingency: contingency on the side of the order of the universe which could not have existed at all, and contingency on the side of the God-Creator, who could not have created anything at all.

Hermeneutics

Hermeneutics widely means interpretation, in particular interpretation of that whose sense is not disclosed but implied. In different contexts the term hermeneutics implies different nuances. In theology it means the interpretation of the spiritual sense of the biblical texts as revealing something radically incommensurable with the immediate and single meaning. Such a hermeneutics is continuing for thousands years indirectly pointing towards the extraordinary nature of these written documents narrating about events which do not have obvious antecedents in nature and its laws and thus exceeding the human capacity of their categorical treatment. In philosophy the term was once imported from theology to denote the discipline concerned with the investigation and interpretation of human behavior, cultural and scientific activity as essentially intentional. As to the human condition, hermeneutics interprets this condition from the point of view of its sense, value and purpose. In other words, it is concerned with the sense of existence. Since the human existence represents the primary revelation of existence in general, it exceeds the measure of its categorical and accomplished definition thus entailing its open-ended interpretation whose aim is to constitute the notion of the human existence although only in tendency, as an infinite task. The ultimate purpose of such a hermeneutics is to provide the interpretation of the historical and intellectual development of humanity. In conjunction with theology such a development accompanies the process of man's deification whose *telos* is to achieve the union with its Divine Creator. In the scientific context hermeneutics is relevant if it is applied to those ideas which are rather products of high intelligibility and having no immediate empirical references. For example, in cosmology, there are many theories attempting to speculate about the origin of the universe. Since all these theories cannot be verified empirically and are based on the mathematical coherence, they can be considered as contributing to the hermeneutics of the universe's origin as exceeding a possibility of being represented in categories.

Intentionality

Intentionality is employed as an indication of an action of human subjectivity which is associated with freedom and potential inexhaustibility of the process of conscious acquisition of existence. Unlike *physical causality*, it is difficult to reduce intentionality to a scheme of operations in which abstract terms are related according to a certain rule. In this sense intentionality (in spite of being exercised in the conditions of embodiment) is free from logical constraints which follow from the physical universe as well as from constraints of any particular, for example discursive, modus of thinking. It works by association and free-willing acts based in existential certainties. One can say that intentionality is a relation of "transcendence," directed either to an *object of intention* (the universe as a whole, for example), or to the other human being. Intentionality pertains to a concrete human being thus working within the given self-identity of consciousness. In going "beyond" the inner sphere of consciousness, intentionality envisages the world as an infinite system of this consciousness's own possibilities. Intentionality envisages itself as forming truth of its partial experiences and the universe (seen, for example, through physical causality) to which it has access. In intentionality consciousness and the universe belong reciprocally together but post-factum, as an outward manifestation of the primordial consubstantial affectivity (communion) by the universe. Intentionality is not an algorithmic operation and hence cannot be understood by abstract effectuation (it means that it is intuitive): it is problematic, for example, to re-effect in logical terms the movement of consciousness which attempts to make human life commensurable to the whole universe. Yet, intentionality is accessible for detection and explication through the reflexive acts of consciousness: while being in communion with the universe one can invoke an introspection (by exercising freedom and free will) upon this inseparable being thus formulating the very initial quest for the position of this embodied consciousness in the universe. The disclosure of the functioning intentionality related to communion with the universe and of that which underlies the visible products of human life in apprehending the sense of the universe (for example in cosmology) must then be self-referential in the sense of being the ultimate horizon of meanings that originate in human subjectivity. In short, intentionality is thought of itself, that is, as a fundamental movement of disclosure, the coming to light of signification in existence itself. Yet intentionality implies a very specific sort of phenomenality as already given. In this sense the phenomenological reduction that suspends intentionality is applicable only to those situations when the phenomenon appears as derivative from something which is hidden behind this intentionality but which phenomenology pretends to disclose. There are some phenomena which are self-affective and related to themselves, those which transcend the possibility of the intentional gaze. This is life itself whose presence can not be phenomenalized because it is this life that is the source of all further phenomenalizations. Correspondingly all knowledge of the world fixated in the intentional acts directed to this world turns out to be an objective representation of life

Life-World

In a phenomenological context the notion of the life-world has many meanings. However for the purposes of this book one can summarize it as follows. The life-world is that which ego finds constantly present to itself, and standing over against itself. It is one spatiotemporal fact-world to which this ego belongs, as do all other human beings found in it and related to it in the same way as the given ego. The ego finds this fact-world to be out there and takes it just as it gives itself to this ego as something that exists out there. This is the mundane world of immediate experience of living on a sensorial and conscious level. The life-world is that underlying structure of consciousness which always accompanies the sense of existence. In comparison with the constructed world of science, the life-world precedes the latter, because the objective world of science always implies those acts of consciousness in and through which the life-world appears as present and pre-given, as existing in its own right prior to all scientific endeavour. Therefore, for understanding of the world of science, one must return to the life-world and elucidate the role it plays in several respects in the constitution and development of science. An inquiry into the very facticity of science, its very possibility, returns the inquiring mind to the foundation of that same consciousness from within which science is constructed—and this is the life world.

Natural Attitude of Consciousness
(in contradistinction to the Philosophical Attitude)

The natural attitude is related to the activity of consciousness within which one acts in a world which is real, a world that existed before this one was born and which one thinks will continue to exist after he or she dies. This world is inhabited not only by a particular human ego, but also by its fellow men, who are human beings with whom this particular human can and do communicate meaningfully. This world has familiar features which have been systematically described through the genetic-causal categories of science. The world of daily life is lived within this natural attitude, and as long as things go along smoothly and reasonably well, there arises no need to call this attitude into question. The reasonability and wellness is related to the situation when the question about the contingent facticity of that which is going on around, including the facticity of the whole world and the human ego, which makes enquiries about it, does not arise. Even if the one does occasionally ask whether some things "really real," whether the world is "really" as it appears to be, these questions are still posed in such a way that they are this one's questions about the natural world in which one lives. The natural attitude has a basic *teleological* tendency which finds its fulfillment in the constituted world which contains others. This is implanted in mind's intentionality as a teleological tendency to move toward world-building. This world-building takes place within a historical process and represents a sort of creation of the world (contingently chained to a particular time). The natural attitude does not want to say that the bringing about of the manifestation of something is a bringing about or making of that which is being manifested. It is merely saying that the world appears through our production of its appearings. In the natural attitude consciousness is directed outside itself as a center of disclosure and manifestation and becomes taken up with and entangled in the world it is shaping. The transcendental reduction (*epoché*) as suspension of this natural naivety of world-building becomes an opposite move, contrary to the "inhuman" tendency of finding its foundation in the world, the move which returns the ego to its self-centering as a modus of the basic self-affectivity of life. Phenomenological attitude implies a move, in a way, opposite to the world-building, where through the careful insight into the constitutive acts of this building, the center of this constitution is itself disclosed as the source of "wordification" or "enworlding."

Noetic/Noematic

Noetos in Greek usage is that which belongs to or is characteristic of the intellect. Intellection in this case is not an abstract concept or a visual image, but the act of the function of the intellect whereby it apprehends realities in a direct manner. Noetic aspect of the act of knowing is a characteristic relating to mental activity or the intellect as opposite to the noematic pole of perception and consciousness in general. *Noema* (plural: *noemata*) derives from the Greek word *noema* meaning thought or what is thought about. In phenomenology noema is used as a technical term to stand for the *object* or *content* of a thought, judgement, or perception. Said simply, the noetic is related to human intentional activity, whereas noematic pole represents the content of that which this activity actualizes or receives in response. In ancient Greek philosophy the adjective *noetic* in the context of cosmology was used in order to characterise the intelligible cosmos of divine forms and ideas, embracing the hierarchy of different levels and orders of divine reality. In Greek Patristic context *cosmos noetos*, being an intelligible part of creation (containing not only ideas, but angelic aeons), differs ontologically from the sensible creation (*cosmos aestheticos*), so that the difference (*diaphora*) between them represents a constitutive element of creation of the whole world out of nothing. In this book's context *cosmos noeticos* simply means the reality of mathematical representations of the physical universe, in particular mathematical models of the universe with no straightforward empirical evidence. For example the idea of the Big Bang is considered to be a constituted element of the noetic cosmos (as if one could "look" at the Big Bang from outside of the physical universe), that is, as its intelligible correlate.

Phenomenality (of objects and events)

In general the term "phenomenality" describes the quality or state of a *phenomenon*. For example, phenomenality of mundane things corresponds to their being perceptible by the senses or through immediate experience. This constitutes the notion of the phenomenal world, as the world of visible, empirical phenomena. The very possibility of phenomenality proceeds from life. In this sense life is phenomenological in the initial and fundamental sense of this word. Life is phenomenological in the sense that it generates phenomenality. Phenomenality appears together with life and its form is that of life itself. The essence of the originary phenomenality can be found in life because it is life that experiences itself as self-phenomenalizing of the phenomenon, that is, as the original self-affectivity opening way to all possible phenomenality. One talks about a phenomenality of objects as entities being constituted according to the rubrics of "I think," so that such a phenomenality can be described in four rubrics: quantity, quality, relation and modality. The phenomenality of objects is different from the event-like manifestations, whose phenomanlity cannot be reduced to the stated four rubrics and where there is an excess of intuition over the discursive faculty. For example, the term "object" cannot be legitimately applied to the universe because the universe as a singular and self-contained whole cannot be detached from the human insight and thus positioned as something "outside" (one can intend the universe as an intelligible "object" with no references to its objectivity based in physical causality). The modern view of the universe as evolved from a singular state (Big Bang) encoding the universe in its totality invokes a counter-intuitive sense of the universe as a singular, unrepeatable *event* (not object!) with respect to which the natural sciences experience difficulties expressing it and desire to explain it away. The essence of such an inaugural event is that it does not have any antecedent context and corresponds to the radical definition of phenomena which are metaphysically unforeseeable, unrepeatable, and impossible.

Reflecting Judgement

The notion of reflecting judgement is important in order to understand why an how cosmological claims about the universe as a whole can be justified in terms of the human cognitive faculties. Since the Kantian analysis of the notion of the world as a whole in *Critique of Pure Reason* proves this notion to be problematic, the question arises where the notion of the universe as a whole (in spite of the impossibility of its objective validation) comes from. In other words, what is that faculty which allows one to consider this notion as valid, although as collectively subjective. For this purpose one needs to appeal to the faculty of judgement, which is a matter of Kant's third critique, that is, *Critique of Judgement*. Kant distinguishes between two types of judgement which he calls determining and reflecting judgement. In a determining judgement one applies a particular concept to intuition: one starts with a given universal (which can be a rule, principle, law or concept), and the task is to find a particular that falls under the universal. For example, one may already possess the concept "galaxy" and when astronomers see a particular galaxy, they may judge: "this is a galaxy." In a reflecting judgement one creates a new empirical concept to capture common features of different intuitions. The reflecting use of judgement begins with the awareness of a particular object or objects and the task is to find or create a universal under which to subsume the particular object or objects. For example, observational cosmology deals with stars, galaxies, their clusters, microwave background radiation, etc. Theoretical cosmology attempt to "find," or, to be more precise, to create a universal under which to subsume all these observable objects. This universal is the universe as a whole. But this universal is not that which can be subjected to the determining judgement. Its experience involves the free play of the imagination beforehand, in order to initiate its constitution. If one deals with the scientific cosmology attempting to construct the notion of the universe as a whole one needs a particular idea of systematicity of nature which enters into the structure of the constitution on the level of reflecting judgement. However, a judgement about the universe as a whole involves judging the "object" to be *formally purposeful*, that is, without the representation of an objective end or purpose in its construction. That is, in such a reflecting judgement one judges the "object" (the universe as a whole) to be purposeful without purpose, that is to be only formally purposeful in order to conduct cosmological research, understanding in advance that its purpose, that is, the notion of the universe as a whole will never be achieved. When one "contemplates" the universe as a whole one does not think that the universe has an objective purpose, but insofar as it is found useful in formulating the objectives of cosmological research one cannot help but think that the universe as a whole appears in intuition (through blocking its discursive apprehension for a reason), but that purpose is subjective (related to the cognitive faculties) rather than objective. Thus, in claiming that in a judgement of the universe as a whole the "object" is represented as purposive without purpose, one means that the object is regarded as objectively without purpose, but it is regarded as subjectively purposeful. Theologically, in the judgement of the universe as a whole when the "object" is represented as formally purposeful, means that when one experiences a natural universe, one regards it as an artefact, that is, as something that is produced for a purpose. But in order to judge of the universe as an artefact, one must also regard it as natural, and one must think of nature acting through the creator to produce the artefact. Yet, such a transferal of the formal purposiveness of the universe (as a subject matter of research) towards the search for the ontological (material) purpose remains illegitimate for reason, but possible for the reflecting judgment.

Saturated Phenomena

Stand for the group of phenomena which cannot be represented in the phenomenality of objects, that is, in rubrics of quantity, quality, relation and modality. The issue of the saturated phenomenon concerns the possibility that certain phenomena do not manifest themselves in the mode of objects and yet still do manifest themselves. These phenomena undergo saturation by the excess of intuition over the concept or signification in them; the saturated phenomena cannot be constituted because they are saturated. Here such a definition of experience is implied that it cannot be determined by a transcendental subject. On the contrary, it is to the extent that *ego* cannot comprehend the phenomenon that this *ego* is constituted by it.

Transcendental/Transcendent

The term "transcendental" must not be confused with "transcendent" although both of them have a common connotation related to exceeding experience. The use of the adjective transcendent with an object points to its meaning as existing beyond experience, as an underlying, external cause of the phenomena, which is mentally reconstructed. In contrast the transcendental means the general precondition of experience, methods of its access. Correspondingly, whenever the term transcendental is employed, it implies the presence of the subject of experience, that is, the transcendental conditions of experience are related to the subject. In contrast to the transcendent object which is supposed by the subject as being out there and independent of the presence of this subject, the transcendental conditions (delimiters) assign rules and methods of selection of phenomena as if these phenomena represent the appearances of an object. In some sense the difference in acquisition of knowledge about the transcendent object and that one whose phenomenality falls inside the transcendental delimiters can be described as the difference between *believing* in outer independently existent objects, and systematic constitution of objects along the lines of the transcendental conditions. This difference entails the distinction between the sense of objectivity understood in an ordinary sense as that one which is transcendent, and, that one which is indeed valid for any empirical subject, but still being placed in a concrete situation of a human subject in its relation to that which is observed and reflected upon. Transcendentalism can be considered as a general trend in knowledge which discloses the conditions of experience. A transcendental insight into modern cosmology, for example, can be understood as dealing not with a compendium of facts and theories about the observable universe, but with a structural path of humanity in its comprehension of the universe, the path which is historically concrete and includes the conditions of observability and mathematical expressibility of reality.

Appendix 2

GLOSSARY OF BASIC TERMS AND IDEAS FROM PHYSICAL COSMOLOGY

(in the order of logical necessity)

Universe (the)/ Creation (the created world):
Whereas the *physical universe*, studied by astronomy, astrophysics and cosmology, comprises the visible totality of the physical reality together with its invisible but allegedly interacting counterparts, *the universe as a whole* constitutes a philosophical and theological notion as everything in existence, including not only physical entities but also an intelligible realm containing ideas about such an existence. Physical cosmology is able to construct theories of the universe as a whole through bringing them to correspondence with the physical reality only in the visible universe. The term visible universe makes a particular physical sense related to the causal structure of the universe's space-time and based on the fact of the finitude of speed of propagation of light (information). If the universe would be infinite in space and time, potentially one could observe (subject to other physical limitations) the infinitely distant objects in it. Yet this would not imply that the observer could have access to the whole of the infinite universe: its domain of visibility is restricted by the so called past light cone, that is, by that infinitely small part of the universe whose position in space is contingently connected with the position of the observer, implying that the universe beyond this light cone is fundamentally non-observable. The universe as a whole is philosophically related to the notion of the world or

being in general, as well as theologically to the notion of creation. The major phenomenological feature of this notion is that it cannot be presented in the phenomenality of objects for it comprises the subject. However if the universe as a whole is considered as an idea, it is placed in the realm of intelligible forms complementing the physical realm. It follows from here that the notion of the universe as a whole in its epistemological genesis implies a dual structure of the whole being as the unity of the empirical and intelligible articulated by human subjects. Mathematical cosmology forms *noetic cosmos* as a counterpart of the physical universe. For example the idea of the Big Bang is sometimes considered as a constituted element of the noetic cosmos, as if one could "look" at the Big Bang from outside of the physical universe. All pictorial symbols of the evolving universe from the Big Bang to the present (used sometimes in popular books on cosmology) contribute to noetic images of the universe thus providing an ongoing hermeneutics of its dual ontological structure. In a theological context, the universe as a whole, or the world, is asserted as creation in contradistinction to the uncreated realm of the Divine. Since Christianity asserts creation as an *inaugural event* for the whole history of salvation (sacred history), Christian cosmology, as the vision of the cosmic order, is unfolded from within the order of the sacred history. Here a certain teleology is present when the cosmic ends are subordinated to human ends.

Cosmological Principle

The cosmological principle represents the postulate of the spatial, material and nomological uniformity (homogeneity) of the universe. This postulate is required by the methodology of cosmology in order the universe as a whole could be explicable by humanity from a particular contingent position in space and time. The *nomological* uniformity of the universe constitutes a dimension of the cosmological principle related to the similarity of the laws of physics across the universe. The terms *nomological* (from the Greek *nomos*) relates to or denotes principles that resemble laws, especially those laws of nature which are neither logically necessary nor theoretically explicable, but just are so. The cosmological principle states the uniformity of the universe at the level of the outcomes of physical laws leading to a particular uniform large-scale space-time structure of the observable universe at the level of clusters of galaxies. The uniformity of the universe (described by a very specific [non-generic] geometrical model) implies that the universe had very specific initial conditions and topology. Theory attempts to explain away these a-typical conditions by inventing some scenarios in which the evolutionary outcomes necessarily lead to the uniformity in the universe (an inflationary scenarioo, for example).

The "cosmological principle" (as a principle of indifference or mediocrity) is employed not only in cosmology. The scientific method employs a principle of indifference with respect to similar objects that obey physical laws. For example, all atoms are considered to be similar with respect to the laws of atomic physics. However this indifference does not deal with the outcomes of physical laws. Atoms are indifferent in what concerns them as constituting units, but their particular combinations which give rise to complex structures (such as life-forms) are not subjected to laws of atomic physics and represent rather their outcomes which can be different and specific.

The cosmological principle has an interesting history and is philosophical in its nature, being related to the so called *Copernican Principle* stating that Earth does not occupy a privileged position in the universe and that the universe, if it could be observed from different locations, statistically looks similar for all possible observes. Another historical analogy is that with the transcendental philosophy of Kant. The cosmological principle can be linked to the idea of the *systematic unity of nature* and hence to the *teleology* of the cosmological explanation. Since the purpose of cosmology is to explicate the structure of the universe and since this can be done only if the cosmic uniformity is postulated, the cosmological principle can be interpreted as a methodological principle of explanation contributing to the *teleology of research*. Theologically, the cosmological principle connotes with the cosmic sense of the Incarnation of the Word-Logos of God in flesh of Jesus of Nazareth. By being fully human on the planet Earth, Christ, as the Creator, was hypostatically present everywhere in the universe, so that all places in the universe are hypostatically equidistant from the incarnate God on the planet Earth. One can speak of a certain affinity between a *theogenic* uniformity of the universe as creation and its cosmographic uniformity in physical cosmology.

Visible Universe and Causal Structure of the Universe

Modern cosmology asserts that the age of the universe is about fourteen billion years (more precisely 13.7 to 13.8 billion years). Together with the physical principle that the speed of propagation of light (electromagnetic waves) is the maximal possible for transmitting information, one can infer that the maximal possible distance in the universe that could be causally connected with us forms fourteen billion light years. This means that all other objects which fall outside of this horizon are principally unobservable. Correspondingly, assuming that the universe is not exhausted by its visible domain that forms the surface of the so called light cone of the past, one can conjecture that human observers have access only to a potentially infinitely small part of the universe whose contingency is determined by the contingent position of the observer in space and time. Yet, because of the cosmological principle, one can conjecture that the visible display of the universe which is accessible to us represent a statistically typical display if the observer could displace itself at any point of the universe. However, that which has been said must be refined by appealing to the fact that the universe expands. Indeed talking of the age of the universe one implies its evolution from some initial state called Big Bang (cosmological singularity). The expansion of the universe is a kinematic effect of a very special initial condition related to all matter of the universe. Its expansion being combined with the propagation of optical images with the speed of light extends the spatial scale of what is effectively observed in the universe to forty-two billion light years in all directions. Certainly that which we observe represents only images of the objects whose sense of existence at present can only be asserted theoretically. In addition to these spatial limits one can add another type of horizon of visibility of optical objects related to the era before matter and light decoupled from the original Big Bang plasma and the universe became transparent to light. If one depicts cosmological eras with the help of spheres of time which have a center at our vantage point on Earth, then the radius of the spheres of distant visible objects will be finite. At the distance of order of fourteen billion light years the human eye will hit an absolute boundary, so called Dark Ages, where the universe was non transparent. All inferences related to what was the universe before its age became 400000 years have a theoretical character and their reliability depends on the coherence with the theory of elementary particles and fundamental physical forces.

The Origin of the Universe: Big Bang, Special Initial Conditions, and the Age of the Universe

Modern evolutionary cosmology claims that the beginning of the universe's expansion took place in an idiosyncratic physical state when the radius of the universe was zero and all physical parameters of the universe infinite. This singular state which is called "Big Bang" represents a very special initial condition for the universe whose account can be given only through a reversed scenario of evolution from the present to the past. All specificity of the Big Bang related to known physical laws is contingent from a philosophical point of view and physics accepts this by not being able to construct a theory of the initial conditions of the universe except through a method of backward extrapolation. There are, for example, two specific features of this contingency: (1) the age of the universe (fourteen billion years) which represents a physical constant with a contingent numerical value; (2) a very specific low-entropy conditions which gave rise to the second law of thermodynamics and arrow of time. Cosmology works within these conditions with no realistic chance to explain them. Thus the initial state of the universe being specific and strange, and giving rise to the present display of the universe, remains ultimately unexplainable (despite of an open-ended hermeneutics of this initial state through exotic cosmological models). In other words, the issue of the universe's origin represents a major challenge for scientific cosmology because of its lack of testability. Here physical theories reach their limits if testability is regarded as being an essential attribute of physics's methodology. Cosmological observations provide very weak limits on conditions immediately after the Big Bang because the theoretically promoted inflationary phase of expansion wipes out most memory of that which preceded it. Alleged 'explanations' of creation rely on theoretical extrapolating of some aspects of tested physics by employing physical theories (such as Quantum Field Theory, for example) held to be applicable in situations before space and time existed, in spite of the fact that their usual formulation assumes that space and time do exist. The discourse of origination of the universe in a singular state (Big Bang) traditionally related to the theologically understood *creatio ex nihilo* can be considered as one of the most developed in the context of the dialogue with theology. Yet any straightforward co-relation of the traditional ideas on creation with the modern cosmological narrative would be considered not only anachronistic (because the early church Fathers did not have access to modern knowledge), but logically purposeless because of the historically contingent means of comparing of the two (theological and scientific cosmological) narratives. Yet, as a hermeneutical exercise, these narratives can be compared in order to confirm a basic philosophical intuition that the actually infinite universe is unknowable and hence its scientific and theological hermeneutics is open-ended.

Material Structure of the Universe and Man's Consubstantiality with It: Dark Matter and Dark Energy.

In spite of the fact that, according to the Anthropic Principle humanity is consubstantial to the *visible* universe, the universe in its bulk content remains unknowable because, according to modern cosmology, it consist of 96 percent of Dark Matter (responsible for the stability of galaxies) and Dark Energy (responsible for the observed accelerated expansion of the universe) which do not physically interact with those constituents which form the optically and experimentally visible part of the universe, including human bodies. Their existence is presupposed on logical grounds in order to keep theory consistent, but there are no empirical clues what kind of matter is behind them. In other words, humanity is consubstantial only to 4 percent of the material stuff of the universe thus loosing its title of the physical microcosm in relation to the universe as a whole. The impression is that physical cosmology amends the literal reading of man as microcosm, relegating its microcosmic function only to an epistemological sphere thus positioning human beings at the centre of disclosure and manifestation of the universe, so that the 96 percent of the non-consubstantial matter appear as theoretical constructs for the purpose of a coherent cosmological explanation. As a consequence, it seems reasonable to conjecture that the universe's physical content remains unknowable so that its present scientific description represents an episode contributing to the endless narrative about it. Theologically one then makes a comparison between the apophaticism in theology where all definitions and narrations of the Divine never exhaust the sense of what is signified by them, with the apophaticism in cosmology, claiming that the ultimate nature of the universe is inaccessible to man in the conditions of his embodiment.

Anthropic Principle and the Position of Humanity in the Visible Universe

The Anthropic Cosmological Principle (AP) explicates that the *necessary* physical conditions for the existence of humanity are finely balanced (*fine-tuning*) leading to the possibility of life on Earth. For example, an hypothetical variation of the constant of electromagnetic interaction by 10 percent leads to the impossibility of the human observers. Thus AP contributes further to the articulation of consubstantiality of humanity to the *visible* universe (to 4 percent of the allegedly whole material universe). The AP does not cover the realm of sufficient conditions for existence of humanity thus leaving unsettled the issue of the contingent facticity of life in the universe in general. In a way, the AP can be treated as formulating the conditions of humanity's contingent facticity in the universe in terms of physical parameters. The AP has an obvious phenomenological dimension related to the fact that the whole picture of the universe is articulated from within the human existence. In this sense it implies the necessary conditions of existence of the embodied intelligence in the universe, that intelligence which is capable of articulating the universe. Understood in this way the AP reinstates human centrality on the universe as being a focal point of disclosure and manifestation of the universe. However, this does not automatically lead to any teleological overtones implying that the structure of the universe *must* be such that life could emerge in it. Teleology is implicitly present in the AP at the epistemological level, as a *teleology of explanation* implying an idea of the systematic unity of nature. The AP has a definite correlation with some theological ideas on centrality of humanity in the universe. Indeed theology asserts that humanity recapitulates the universe not only in a physical sense but first of all as a personal being who hypostasizes the universe in its own image. And this image is the Divine Image having the archetype of the incarnate Word—Logos of God—Jesus Christ. Then the actual theological flavour of the fitness of the universe for life relates to the fitness of the universe for the Incarnation. It is the physical science that makes possible to understand that the universe must be such that it makes human life and hence the Incarnation possible. One can in this case (being based on the dogma of the Incarnation as foreseen by God before creation), advocate for the Theological Anthropic Cosmological Principle linking the evolution of the universe to the possibility for the human race to develop in order to receive God in flesh through the hypostatic union with him in Jesus Christ.

Multiverse

Multiverse in modern parlance is a theoretical notion reminiscent to the perennial idea of *plurality of worlds.* In modern cosmology this notion has different physical and mathematical interpretations starting with the ensemble of the different physical universes disjoint in space and finishing by the variety of all mathematically possible worlds in a Platonic sense. One of the motivations of theories of multiverse is the so called "fine-tuning." The "fine-tuning" issue relates to the very low probability of the initial conditions of the universe, if one assumes (in any possible sense) the potential existence of the ensemble of the universes, and hence a choice of that one out of them which represents our universe. The major problem with the hypothesis of the multiverse is its radically non-empirical status entailing a doubt in a scientific nature of this hypothesis. The claimed proposals for the scientific "tests" of the physical existence of a multiverse (most of which rely on probability concepts) are doubtful because it seems that one cannot use probability arguments in cosmology when only one universe exists. Probability arguments cannot prove that the multiverse exists, they can only prove the self-consistency of multiverse proposals as such. Some cosmologists strongly advocate that any model of the multiverse is hypothetical (unverifiable) and hence non-scientific. Yet some other cosmologists, in order to avoid any appeal to the idea of creation of the universe and its creator, prefer the multiverse model by ontologizing its construct in a naively realistic fashion. From a theological and philosophical point of view, the issue of the contingent facticity of the multiverse itself (as a new type of the highly undifferentiated "substance") is not elucidated by any of its models so that in no way the multiverse hypothesis can replace or "explain" *creatio ex nihilo*. Yet, from the same theological point of view the idea of the multiverse can represent an interest if considered in a Platonic sense: God created many intelligible universes, but only one of them has received its embodied physical existence. Then the issue of the multiverse becomes rather philosophical as related to the role of intelligible universes in the description of the theologically understood *creatio ex nihilo*.

BIBLIOGRAPHY

Athanasius. *On the Incarnation: The Treatise de Incarnatione Verbi Dei*. Translated and edited by a Religious of CSMV. Crestwood, NY: St. Vladimir's Seminary Press, 1998.
Augustine. *Civitate Dei: Concerning the City of God against Pagans*. Translated by Henry Bettenson. New York: Penguin, 1980.
———. *Confessions*. Translated by Henry Chadwick. Oxford: Oxford University Press, 1991.
———. *Contra Faustum*. In vol. 4 of *NPNF*, Series 1, 264–592.
———. *The Literal Meaning of Genesis*. Translated by John Hammond Taylor. New York: Newman, 1982.
———. *On Christian Doctrine*. In vol. 2 of *NPNF*, Series 1, 517–97.
———. *On the Trinity*. Books 8–15. Edited by Gareth B. Matthews. Translated by Stephen McKenna. Cambridge: Cambridge University Press, 2003.
Averintsev, Sergei. "The Order of the Cosmos and the Order of History." In *Poetics of the Early Byzantine Literature*, 88–113. Moscow: CODA, 1997.
———. *Poetics of the Early Byzantine Literature*. Moscow: CODA, 1997.
Barrow, John D., and Frank J. Tipler. *Anthropic Cosmological Principle*. Oxford: Oxford University Press, 1986.
Basil the Great. *In Hexaemeron*. In vol. 8 of *NPNF*, Series 2, 51–107.
Behr, John. *Asceticism and Anthropology in Irenaeus and Clement*. Oxford: Oxford University Press, 2000.
Berdyaev, Nicholas. *Slavery and Freedom*. Translated by R. M. French. London: Centenary, 1944.
Bernet, Rudolp. *Conscience et existence: Perspectives phénoménologiques*. Paris: Presses universitaires de France, 2004.
Bitbol, Michel, et al., eds. *Constituting Objectivity: Transcendental Perspectives on Modern Physics*. Dordrecht: Springer, 2009.
Blowers, Paul M., and Robert Louis Wilken, trans. *On the Cosmic Mystery of Jesus Christ: Selected Writings from St. Maximus the Confessor*. Crestwood, NY: St. Vladimir's Seminary Press, 2003.
Bostrom, Nick, and Milan M. Cirkovic, eds. *Global Catastrophic Risks*. Oxford: Oxford University Press, 2011.
Brisson, Luc, and F. Walter Meyerstein. *Inventing the Universe: Plato's Timaeus, the Big Bang, and the Problem of Scientific Knowledge*. Albany: State University of New York Press, 1995.

Brockelman, Paul. *Cosmology and Creation: The Spiritual Significance of Contemporary Cosmology*. New York: Oxford University Press, 1999.

Bultmann, Rudolph. *Existence and Faith*. London: Collins, 1964.

Carr, David. *Paradox of Subjectivity*. Oxford: Oxford University Press, 1999.

Chamcham, Khalil, et al., eds. *The Philosophy of Cosmology*. Cambridge: Cambridge University Press, 2017.

Chrétien, Jean-Louis. *The Unforgettable and the Unhoped For*. Translated by Jeffrey Bloechl. New York: Fordham University Press, 2002.

Clayton, Phililp, and Arthur Peacocke, eds. *In Whom We Live and Move and Have Our Being: Reflections on Panentheism in a Scientific Age*. Grand Rapids: Eerdmans, 2004.

Clement of Alexandria. *Stromata*. In vol. 2 of *The Ante-Nicene Fathers*, edited by Alexander Roberts and James Donaldson. Grand Rapids: Eerdmans, 1962.

Clément, Olivier. *Le Christ terre des vivants: Essais théologiques*. Spiritualite orientale 17. Bégrolles-en-Mauges: Abbaye de Bellfontaine, 1976.

———. *On Human Being: A Spiritual Anthropology*. Translated by Jeremy Hummerstone. London: New City, 2000.

———. "Le sens de la terre." In *Le Christ terre des vivants: Essais théologiques*, 88–136. Spiritualite orientale 17. Bégrolles-en-Mauges: Abbaye de Bellfontaine, 1976.

Cole-Turner, Ronald. "Incarnation Deep and Wide: A Response to Niels Gregersen." *Theology and Science* 11 (2013) 424–35.

Comte-Sponville, André. *The Little Book of Atheist Spirituality*. Translated by Nancy Huston. New York: Penguin, 2008.

Cornford, Francis M. *Plato's Cosmology: The Timaeus of Plato*. Indianapolis: Hackett, 1997.

Coyne, George V., and Michael Heller. *A Comprehensible Universe: The Interplay of Science and Theology*. New York: Springer, 2008.

Craig, William. "What Place, Then, for a Creator?" In *Theism, Atheism, and Big Bang Cosmology*, edited by William Lane Craig and Quentin Smith, 279–303. Oxford: Clarendon, 1993.

Craig, William Lane, and Quentin Smith. *Theism, Atheism, and Big Bang Cosmology*. Oxford: Clarendon, 1993.

Daniélou, Jean, ed. *From Glory to Glory: Texts from Gregory of Nyssa's Mystical Writings*. Crestwood, NY: St. Vladimir's Seminary Press, 1981.

———. *The Lord of History: Reflections on the Inner Meaning of History*. Translated by Nigel Abercrombie. London: Longmans, 1958.

De Duve, Christian. *Vital Dust: Life as a Cosmic Imperative*. New York: Basic, 1995.

De Laguna, Grace. *On Existence and the Human World*. New Haven: Yale University Press, 1966.

Dostoevsky, Feodor. *The Idiot*. In vol. 6 of *Collected Works*, edited by L. P. Grossman et al. Moscow: Khudozhestvennaya Literatura, 1957.

———. *A Writer's Diary, Volume One, 1873–1876*. Translated by Kenneth Lantz. Evanston, IL: Northwestern University Press, 1993.

Edwards, Denis. *Deep Incarnation: God's Redemptive Suffering with Creatures*. Maryknoll, NY: Orbis, 2019.

Ellis, George F. R. "Issues in the Philosophy of Cosmology." In *Handbook of the Philosophy of Science, Philosophy of Physics*, Part B, edited by Jeremy Butterfield and John Earman, 1183–283. Amsterdam: Elsevier, 2007.

Feinberg, Gerald. "Physics and the Thales Problem." *The Journal of Philosophy* 63 (1966) 5–17.

Florovsky, Georges. "Creation and Creaturehood." In *Creation and Redemption*, 43–78. The Collected Works of Georges Florovsky 3. Belmont, MA: Nordland, 1976.

———. "*Cur Deus Homo?* The Motive of the Incarnation." In *Creation and Redemption*, 163–70. The Collected Works of Georges Florovsky 3. Belmont, MA: Nordland, 1976.

———. "The Idea of Creation in Christian Philosophy." *The Eastern Churches Quarterly* 8 (1949) 53–77.

———. "The Predicament of the Christian Historian." In *Christianity and Culture*, 31–65, 233–36. The Collected Works of Georges Florovsky 2. Belmont, MA: Nordland, 1974.

———. "The Worshipping Church." In *Festal Menaion*, 21–37. South Canaan, PA: St. Tikhon's Seminary Press, 1998.

Frank, Simon L. *Reality and Man: An Essay in the Metaphysics of Human Nature.* Translated by Natalie Duddington. New York: Taplinger, 1966.

Fromm, Erich. *Man for Himself: An Enquiry into the Psychology of Ethics.* London: Routledge, 1967.

Grant, Edward. *God and Reason in the Middle Ages.* Cambridge: Cambridge University Press, 2004.

Gregersen, Niels. "The Cross of Christ in an Evolutionary World." *Dialog: A Journal of Theology* 40 (2001) 192–207.

———. "*Cur deus caro*: Jesus and the Cosmos Story." *Theology and Science* 11 (2013) 370–93.

———, ed. *Incarnation: On the Scope and Depth of Christology.* Minneapolis: Fortress, 2015.

Gregory of Nyssa. *De hominis opificio*: *On the Making of Man.* In vol. 5 of *NPNF*, Series 2, 387–427.

Guénot, Claude. *Teilhard de Chardin.* Baltimore: Helicon, 1965.

Gurwitsch, Aron. *Phenomenology and the Theory of Science.* Evanston, IL: Northwestern University Press, 1974.

———. *Studies in Phenomenology and Psychology.* Evanston, IL: Northwestern University Press, 1966.

Halvorson, Hans, and Helge Kragh. "Physical Cosmology." In *The Routledge Companion to Theism*, edited by Stuart Goetz et al., 241–55. London: Routledge, 2012.

Harakas, Stanley. "Orthodox Christianity Facing Science." *The Greek Theological Review* 37 (1992) 7–15.

Harrison, Peter. *The Bible, Protestantism, and the Rise of Natural Science.* Cambridge: Cambridge University Press, 1998.

Hawking, Stephen. *A Brief History of Time: From the Big Bang to Black Holes.* London: Bantam, 1988.

Heidegger, Martin. *Being and Time.* Translated by John Macquarrie and Edward Robinson. Oxford: Blackwell, 1998.

———. *Introduction to Metaphysics.* Translated by Gregory Fried and Richard Polt. New Haven: Yale University Press, 2014.

———. *On Time and Being.* Translated by Joan Stambaugh. New York: Harper & Row, 1972.

———. "Phenomenology and Theology." In *Pathmarks*, edited by William McNeill, 39–62. Cambridge: Cambridge University Press, 1998.

Heller, Michael. "Classical Singularities and the Quantum Origin of the Universe." *European Journal of Physics* 14 (1993) 7–13.

Henry, Michel. *De la Phénoménologie, Tome I: Phénoménologie de la vie*. Paris: Presses Universitaire de France, 2003.

———. *I Am the Truth: Toward a Philosophy of Christianity*. Translated by Susan Emanuel. Stanford: Stanford University Press, 2003.

———. "Phenomenology of Life." *Angelaki* 8 (2003) 100–110.

Husserl, Edmund. *The Crisis of European Sciences and Transcendental Phenomenology*. Translated by David Carr. Evanston, IL: Northwestern University Press, 1970.

———. *Ideas Pertaining to a Pure Phenomenology and to a Phenomenological Philosophy*. Vol. 1, *General Introduction to a Pure Phenomenology*. Translated by F. Kersten. Dordrecht: Kluwer, 1998.

Irenaeus of Lyons. *Against the Heresies*. In *The Scandal of the Incarnation: Irenaeus "Against the Heresies,"* translated by John Saward. San Francisco: Ignatius, 1990.

Isham, Christopher J. "Creation of the Universe as a Quantum Process." In *Physics, Philosophy, and Theology: A Common Quest for Understanding*, edited by Robert John Russell et al., 375–408. Vatican City State: Vatican Observatory, 1988.

Jaki, Stanley. *The Savior of Science*. Washington, DC: Regnery-Gateway, 1988.

Janicaud, Dominique, et al. *Phenomenology and "The Theological Turn": The French Debate*. New York: Fordham University Press, 2000.

Jaspers, Karl. *Ways to Wisdom*. Translated by Ralph Manheim. New Haven: Yale University Press, 1954.

———. *Weltgeschichte der Philosophie: Einleitung*. Munich: Piper & Co., 1982.

Jeans, James. *The Mysterious Universe*. Cambridge: Cambridge University Press, 1930.

Kant, Immanuel. *Critique of Judgement*. Translated by J. H. Bernard. London: Hafner, 1951.

———. *Critique of Practical Reason*. Translated by Thomas Kingsmill Abbot. London: Longmans, 1959.

———. *Critique of Pure Reason*. Translated by Norman Kemp Smith. London: Macmillan, 1929.

———. "The Form and Principles of the Sensible and Intelligible World." In *Theoretical Philosophy, 1755–1771*, edited by David Walford and R. Meerbot, 373–415. Cambridge: Cambridge University Press, 1992.

———. *Lectures on Logic*. Translated and edited by J. Michael Young. Cambridge: Cambridge University Press, 1992.

Kierkegaard, Søren. *Repetition* and *Philosophical Crumbs*. Translated by M. G. Piety. Oxford: Oxford University Press, 2009.

Knight, Christopher. *Science and the Christian Faith: A Guide for the Perplexed*. Crestwood, NY: St. Vladimir's Seminary Press, 2021.

Krauss, Lawrence M. *A Universe from Nothing: Why There Is Something Rather than Nothing*. New York: Free, 2012.

Kuiper, Franciscus B. J. "Cosmogony and Conception: A Query." In *Ancient Indian Cosmology*, 90–137. New Delhi: Vikas, 1983.

Küng, Hans. *The Beginning of All Things: Natural Sciences and Religion*. Grand Rapids: Eerdmans, 2008.

Ladrière, Jean. *Language and Belief*. Translated by Garrett Barden. Dublin: Gill and Macmillan, 1972.

———. "Mathematics in a Philosophy of the Sciences." In *Phenomenology and the Natural Sciences*, edited by Theodore J. Kiesel and Joseph J. Kockelmans, 443–65. Evanston, IL: Northwestern University Press, 1970.

———. "Physical Reality: A Phenomenological Approach." *Dialectica* 43 (1989) 125–39.

Le Poidevin, Robin. *Travels in Four Dimensions: The Enigmas of Space and Time*. Oxford: Oxford University Press, 2003.

Leslie, John. *The End of the World: The Science and Ethics of Human Extinction*. New York: Routledge, 1996.

Lindberg, David C. *The Beginnings of Western Science: The European Scientific Tradition in Philosophical, Religious, and Institutional Context, 600 B.C to A.D. 1450*. Chicago: University of Chicago Press, 1992.

———. "Science and the Early Church." In *God and Nature: Historical Essays on the Encounter between Christianity and Science*, edited by David. C. Lindberg and Ronald L. Numbers, 19–48. Berkeley: University of California Press, 1986.

Lossky, Vladimir. *In the Image and Likeness of God*. Crestwood, NY: St. Vladimir's Seminary Press, 1997.

———. *The Mystical Theology of the Eastern Church*. London: Clarke, 1957.

———. *Orthodox Theology: An Introduction*. Translated by Ian Kesarcodi-Watson and Ihita Kesarcodi-Watson. Crestwood, NY: St. Vladimir's Seminary Press, 1997.

Louth, Andrew. *Maximus the Confessor*. London: Routledge, 1996.

———. "The Place of *Theosis* in Orthodox theology." In *Partakes of the Divine Nature: The History and Development of Deification in the Christian Traditions*, edited by Michael J. Christensen and Jeffrey A. Wittung, 32–44. Grand Rapids: Baker Academic, 2007.

Lyotard, Jean-Francois. *The Inhuman: Reflections on Time*. Translated by Geoffrey Bennington and Rachel Bowlby. Stanford: Stanford University Press, 1991.

Marcel, Gabriel. *Being and Having*. London: Collins, 1965.

———. *Creative Fidelity*. Translated by Robert Rosthal. New York: Fordham University Press, 2002.

———. *Metaphysical Journal*. Translated by Bernard Wall. London: Rockliff, 1952.

Marion, Jean-Luc. *Being Given: Toward a Phenomenology of Givenness*. Translated by Jeffrey L. Kosky. Stanford: Stanford University Press, 2002.

———. *The Erotic Phenomenon*. Translated by Stephen Lewis. New York: Fordham University Press, 2007.

———. "The Event, the Phenomenon, and the Revealed." In *Transcendence in Philosophy and Religion*, edited by John F. Faulconer, 87–105. Bloomington: Indiana University Press, 2003.

———. *In Excess: Studies of Saturated Phenomena*. Translated by Robyn Horner and Vincent Berraud. New York: Fordham University Press, 2002.

———. "Mihi magna quaestio factus sum: The Privilege of Unknowing." *The Journal of Religion* 85 (2005) 1–24.

———. *Negative Certainties*. Translated by Stephen E. Lewis. Chicago: University of Chicago Press, 2015.

———. "The Saturated Phenomenon." In *Phenomenology and "The Theological Turn": The French Debate*, by Dominique Janicaud et al., translated by Jeffrey L. Kosky and Thomas A. Carlson, 176–216. New York: Fordham University Press, 2000.

Mathews, Freya. *The Ecological Self*. London: Routledge, 1991.

Maximus the Confessor. *The Ascetic Life: The Four Centuries on Charity*. Translated and annotated by Polycarp Sherwood. Westminster, MD: Newman, 1955.

———. *Cap. Theologicorum: Two Hundred Texts on Theology and the Incarnate Dispensation of the Son of God*. In *Philokalia*, 114–63.

———. *Four Hundred Texts on Love*. In *Philokalia*, 53–113.

———. *On Difficulties in the Church Fathers*. Vol. 1, *The Ambigua*. Translated and edited by Nicholas Constas. Cambridge: Harvard University Press, 2014.

———. *On Difficulties in Sacred Scripture: The Responses to Thalassios*. Translated by Maximos Constas. Washington, DC: Catholic University of America Press, 2018.

———. *Selected Writings*. Translated by George C. Berthold. New York: Paulist, 1985.

———. *Various Texts on Theology*. In *Philokalia*, 164–284.

May, Gerhard. *Creation Ex Nihilo: The Doctrine of "Creation out of Nothing" in Early Christian Thought*. Edinburgh: T. & T. Clark, 1994.

Merleau-Ponty, Maurice. *Phenomenology of Perception*. Translated by Colin Smith. London: Routledge, 1962.

———. *The Prose of the World*. Translated by John O'Neill. Evanston, IL: Northwestern University Press, 1973.

———. *Sense and Non-Sense*. Translated by Hubert L. Dreyfus and Patricia Allen Dreyfus. Evanston, IL: Northwestern University Press, 1964.

Moltmann, Jürgen. *Man: Christian Anthropology in the Conflicts of the Present*. Translated by John Sturdy. London: SPCK, 1974.

———. *Science and Wisdom*. Translated by Margaret Kohl. Minneapolis: Fortress, 2003.

Mounier, Emmanuel. *Introduction aux existentialismes*. Paris: Gallimard, 1962.

Munitz, Milton. "Kantian Dialectic and Modern Scientific Cosmology." *Journal of Philosophy* 48 (1951) 325–38.

———. *The Question of Reality*. Princeton: Princeton University Press, 1990.

Murphy, G. L. "Cosmology and Christology." *Science and Christian Belief* 6 (1994) 101–11.

———. "The Incarnation as a Theanthropic Principle." *Word & World* 13 (1993) 256–62.

Nagel, Thomas. *The View from Nowhere*. Oxford: Oxford University Press, 1986.

Nellas, Panayiotis. *Deification in Christ: Orthodox Perspectives on the Nature of the Human Person*. Translated by Norman Russell. Crestwood, NY: St. Vladimir's Seminary Press, 1997.

Nesmelov, Victor. *The Science of Man*. Kazan: Central, 1905.

Nesteruk, Alexei *Light from the East: Theology, Science, and the Eastern Orthodox Tradition*. Minneapolis: Fortress, 2003.

———. "The Motive of the Incarnation in Christian Theology: Consequences for Modern Cosmology, Extraterrestrial Intelligence, and a Hypothesis of Multiple Incarnations." *Theology and Science* 16 (2018) 462–70.

———. "Philosophical Foundations of Mediation/Dialogue between (Orthodox) Theology and Science." In *Orthodox Theology and Modern Science: Tensions,*

Ambiguities, Potential, edited by Vasilios N. Makrides and Gayle E. Woloschak, 97–121. Turnhout: Brepols, 2109.

———. *The Sense of the Universe: Philosophical Explication of Theological Commitment in Modern Cosmology*. Minneapolis: Fortress, 2015.

———. "The Sense of the Universe: St. Maximus the Confessor and Theological Consummation of Modern Cosmology." In *The Architecture of the Cosmos: St. Maximus the Confessor: New Perspectives*, edited by Antoine Lévy et al., 298–345. Helsinki: Luther-Agricola-Society, 2015.

———. *The Universe as Communion: Towards a Neo-Patristic Synthesis of Theology and Science*. London: T. & T. Clark, 2008.

Nicolaides, Efthymios. *Science and Eastern Orthodoxy: From the Greek Fathers to the Age of Globalilzation*. Translated by Susan Emanuel. Baltimore: John Hopkins University Press, 2011.

Origen. *De principiis: On First Principles*. Translated by G. W. Butterworth. Gloucester, MA: Smith, 1973.

Pannenberg, Wolfhart. *The Historicity of Nature: Essays on Science and Theology*. Edited by Niels Henrik Gregersen. West Conshohocken, PA: Templeton Foundation, 2008.

———. *Toward a Theology of Nature: Essays on Science and Faith*. Edited by Ted Peters. Louisville: Westminster/John Knox, 1993.

Pascal, Blaise. "De l'art de persuader." In *L'espirit géometrique et De l'art de persuader*, 33–62. Paris: Bordas Éditions, 2002.

———. *Pensées: Selections*. Translated and edited by Martin Jarret-Kerr. London: SCM, 1959.

———. *Pensées*. Établi par Louis Lafuma. Paris: Éditions du Seul, 1962.

Peacocke, Arthur. *Theology for a Scientific Age: Being and Becoming—Natural and Divine*. Minneapolis: Fortress, 1993.

Penrose, Roger. *Fashion, Faith, and Phantasy in the New Physics of the Universe*. Princeton: Princeton University Press, 2017.

———. *The Road to Reality*. London: Vintage, 2005.

Peters, Ted, and Martinez Hewlett. *Evolution from Creation to New Creation: Conflict, Conversation, and Convergence*. Nashville: Abingdon, 2003.

Peters, Ted, et al., eds. *Astrotheology: Science and Theology Meet Extraterrestrial Life*. Eugene, OR: Cascade, 2018.

Planck, Max. *Where Is Science Going?* Translated by James Murphy. New York: Norton, 1932.

Plessner, Helmut. *Conditio humana*. Berlin: Suhrkamp Verlag, 1961.

Polkinghorne, John. *Belief in God in an Age of Science*. New Haven: Yale University Press, 1998.

Prestige, G. L. *God in Patristic Thought*. London: SPCK, 1955.

Primack, Joel, and Nancy Abrams. *The View from the Centre of the Universe: Discovering Our Extraordinary Place in the Cosmos*. London: Fourth Estate, 2006.

Rees, Martin. "Our Complex Cosmos and Its Future." In *The Future of Theoretical Physics and Cosmology: Celebrating Stephen's Hawking's 60th Birthday*, edited by G. W. Gibbons et al., 17–36. Cambridge: Cambridge University Press, 2003.

———. *Our Final Century, A Scientist's Warning: How Terror, Error, and Environmental Disaster Threaten Humankind's Future in This Century—On Earth and Beyond*. London: Heinemann, 2003.

Ricoeur, Paul. *Freedom and Nature: The Voluntary and the Involuntary*. Translated by Erazim V. Kohák. Evanston, IL: Northwestern University Press, 1966.

———. *Philosophical Anthropology*. Translated by David Pellauer. Malden, MA: Polity, 2016.

Romano, Claude. *Event and World*. Translated by Shane Mackinlay. New York: Fordham University Press, 2009.

———. *L'aventure temporelle: Trois essais pour introduire à l'herméneutique événementiel*. Paris: Presses Universitaires de France, 2010.

Sagan, Carl. *Pale Blue Dot: A Vision of the Human Future in Space*. New York: Ballantine, 1997.

Scheler, Max. *Die Stellung Des Menschen im Kosmos*. Moscow: Gnosis, 1994.

Sherrard, Philip. *The Rape of Man and Nature: An Enquiry into the Origins and Consequences of Modern Science*. Suffolk: Golgonooza, 1991.

Solovyof, Vladimir. *The Justification of the Good: An Essay on Moral Philosophy*. Translated by Natalie A. Duddington. London: Constable, 1918.

———. *Lectures on Godmanhood*. Translated by Peter P. Zouboff. London: Dobson, 1948.

Sophrony, Archimandrite. *The Monk of Mount Athos: Staretz Silouan, 1866–1938*. Translated by Rosemary Edmonds. London: Mowbrays, 1973.

Sorabji, Richard. *Matter, Space, and Motion: Theories in Antiquity and Their Sequel*. London: Duckworth, 1988.

———. *Time, Creation, and the Continuum: Theories in the Antiquity and the Early Middle Ages*. London: Duckworth, 1983.

Strawson, P. F. *The Bounds of Sense: An Essay on Kant's Critique of Pure Reason*. London: Routledge, 2006.

Ströker, Elisabeth. *Investigations in Philosophy of Space*. Athens, OH: Ohio University Press, 1965.

Swimme, Brian. *The Hidden Heart of Cosmos*. New York: Orbis, 2005.

Teilhard de Chardin, Pierre. *Christianity and Evolution*. Translated by René Hague. New York: Harcourt Brace Jovanovich, 1971.

———. *The Future of Man*. Translated by Norman Denny. Glasgow: Collins, 1979.

———. *Hymn of the Universe*. Translated by Simon Bartholomew. London: Collins, 1965.

———. *Le Milieu Divin: An Essay on the Interior Life*. Translated by Bernard Wall et al. London: Fontana, 1964.

———. *The Phenomenon of Man*. Translated by Bernard Wall et al. London: Collins, 1959.

———. *Science and Christ*. Translated by René Hague. London: Collins, 1968.

———. *The Vision of the Past*. Translated by J. M. Cohen. London: Collins, 1966.

Thunberg, Lars. *Man and the Cosmos*. Crestwood, NY: St. Vladimir's Seminary Press, 1985.

———. *Microcosm and Mediator: The Theological Anthropology of Maximus the Confessor*. Chicago: Open Court, 1995.

Tieszen, Richard. *Phenomenology, Logic, and the Philosophy of Mathematics*. Cambridge: Cambridge University Press, 2005.

Torrance, Thomas F., *The Christian Doctrine of God: One Being Three Persons*. Edinburgh: T. & T. Clark, 1996.

———. *Divine and Contingent Order*. Edinburgh: T. & T. Clark, 1998.

———. *God and Rationality*. Edinburgh: T. & T. Clark, 1997.
———. *The Grammar of Theology: Consonance between Theology and Science*. Edinburgh: T. & T. Clark, 2001.
———. *Space, Time, and Incarnation*. Edinburgh: T. & T. Clark, 1997.
———. *Space, Time, and Resurrection*. Edinburgh: T. & T. Clark, 1998.
Tryon, Edward P. "Is the Universe a Vacuum Fluctuation?" In *Modern Cosmology and Philosophy*, edited by John Leslie, 222–25. New York: Prometheus, 1998.
Van Huyssteen, J. Wenzel. *Alone in the World? Human Uniqueness in Science and Theology*. Grand Rapids: Eerdmans, 2006.
Ward, Keith. *Religion and Creation*. Oxford: Clarendon, 1996.
Weinberg, Stephen. *Cosmology*. Oxford: Oxford University Press, 2008.
Wheeler, John Archibald. "Time Today." In *Physical Origins of Time Asymmetry*, edited by Jonathan J. Haliwell et al. 1–29. Cambridge: Cambridge University Press, 1994.
Yannaras, Christos. *The Enigma of Evil*. Translated by Norman Russell. Brookline, MA: Holy Cross Orthodox, 2012.
———. *The Meaning of Reality: Essays on Existence and Communion, Eros, and History*, edited by Gregory Edwards and Herman A. Middleton. Los Angeles: Sebastian, 2011.
———. *On the Absence and Unknowability of God: Heidegger and Areopagite*. Translated by Haralambos Ventis. London: T. & T. Clark, 2005.
———. *Postmodern Metaphysics*. Translated by Norman Russell. Brookline, MA: Holy Cross Orthodox, 2004.
Zizioulas, John. *Communion and Otherness*. London: T. & T. Clark, 2006.
———. *Lectures on Christian Doctrine*. London: T. & T. Clark, 2008.
Zycinski, Joseph. *God and Evolution: Fundamental Questions of Christian Evolutionism*. New York: Catholic University of America Press, 2006.

INDEX

anthropic principle (inference, argument) (AP), 11, 16, 41, 151, 198, 213, 258, 288–90
anthropology, xi, 1, 16–19, 21–22, 41, 48, 50, 64–65, 103, 198, 115, 164, 184, 235, 269, 289
apophaticism (apophatic), 55, 109, 259, 272, 289
Athanasius of Alexandria, St., 117, 128, 181-82, 232
Augustine of Hippo, St., 39, 52, 56, 59, 141, 203–5, 248
Averitsev, Sergei, 123, 185

Basil the Great, St., 199-200
Berdyaev, Nicholas, 173
Bible references,

Gen 1:26–28	xii, 162
Gen 18:14	45
Exod 3:12–14	115
Matt 2:2	97
Matt 16:3	239
Matt 18:20	241
Mark 10:27	60, 96
Luke 1:32–33	97
Luke 1:37	45
Luke 2:11–12	97
Luke 8:9–10	98
Luke 9:24	31
Luke 23:34	117
John 1:1–5	61, 71, 110
John 1:16	59
John 14:6	31
Rom 8: 28–30	72
Rom 2:36	141
Rom 4:17–18	45, 243
Rom 7:25	72
Rom 8:19–21	188
1 Cor 1: 13	58
1 Cor 13:12	182
2 Cor 5:17	239
Gal 4:10–11	96
Eph 2:15	239
Eph 4:24	239
Eph 4:6	127
Col 2:9	233
Heb 4:12	58
2 Pet 3:13	239
Rev 21:1	239

Big Bang, 193–94, 196, 255, 275, 280, 287–88
  idea, concept, construct, model of, 92, 100, 197–98, 220, 229, 252, 280, 285
  as origin (beginning, initial conditions) of the universe, 81, 82, 91, 168, 251, 287–88
  as cosmological singularity, 251, 280
  as undifferentiated substance, 192
  (*see also* universe, initial conditions of)
birth (conception, of a human being), 22, 54, 71, 87–90, 94, 146, 204
  analogy between the origin of the universe and event of, 89, 92–93, 204
  as endowing a person with future, 91

303

INDEX

birth *(continued)*
  as an event (of incarnation, embodiment, coming into being), 84–90, 93, 94, 98, 110, 179, 189
  Christian typology of, 20, 130, 142
  phenomenology of, 91, 104
Bitbol, Michel, 48
Brisson, Luc, 173
Brockelman, Paul, 172

Chrétien, Jean-Louis, 87, 92, 135
Christ, Jesus of Nazareth, xi, xiv, 12, 15, 22, 31, 40, 57, 61, 97, 100, 106, 108–10, 114, 117–20, 122–27, 130–33, 142–43, 148, 182, 221, 230–38, 241–43, 248, 250, 256, 260, 262–64, 267–68, 286
  as Son-Logos of God, 10, 14, 59, 72, 111, 113, 119, 122, 126, 143, 179, 182, 189, 233, 237, 238, 263
  as speaking of Life, 31–33
  Incarnation of (nativity of), xi, 7, 11, 14–15, 22, 40, 72, 97–98, 113, 121, 129, 142, 144, 147–48, 183, 188, 223, 234–35, 256, 264, 290.
  mother of (Virgin Mary), 11, 15, 41, 143, 222
Christianity, xii-xiii, 3, 29, 34, 56, 63, 90, 99, 140, 142, 168, 183, 185–87, 200, 240, 274, 285
Christian Church, 13, 39, 61, 178
  apostles of, 97, 110,
  the Fathers of, 79, 173, 199, 231, 246, 251, 288
Christology, xi-xii, 12, 23, 42, 60, 72, 94, 106, 108, 124, 222, 235, 260, 273
Clement of Alexandria, 56, 237
Clément, Olivier, 64–65, 75, 124, 128–29, 159
communion, xiii, 33, 66, 89, 96, 115, 130, 139, 145–48, 204, 249, 261, 262, 268
  events of, 48, 57–59, 101, 104, 107, 109
  with God, (*see* God, communion with)
  theology as experience of, 42–43, 50, 54, 107
  with the universe, 148, 153, 156–57, 165, 167, 172–73, 186, 224–27, 230, 261, 265, 277
Comte-Sponville, André, 4
consciousness, 1, 4, 9–11, 15–17, 19, 22, 34, 37, 42, 47, 53–55, 69–71, 77, 80, 84–86, 89, 91–93, 97, 101–3, 109, 112–13, 116, 126, 135–36, 139–41, 144, 146–48, 151, 155–56, 159–61, 163, 165, 166, 168, 171, 174, 175, 179, 181, 183, 187, 189, 195, 197, 201, 203, 211, 217, 233–34, 244, 246, 256–57, 264–66, 275, 277
contingent facticity (contingency), 1, 17, 20, 24, 33, 53, 65-66, 83, 91, 98, 121, 134, 142, 144, 155, 164, 173, 192–93,
  of the world, universe, 5, 7–8, 46, 82, 108, 120, 126, 138, 179, 184–85, 190, 194, 198, 201, 204–5, 208, 215, 220, 222, 263
  of historical events, 13, 124, 133, 164,
  of incarnation (birth), 90, 110, 123–24, 223
  humanity as contingent upon God, 92–93, 110, 168, 178, 228, 249–50, 252–53
contingent necessity (rationality), 119, 126, 152, 187
cosmological principle, 130, 143, 149–51, 190–91, 250, 253–55, 285–86
cosmology, xi-xii, xiv, 2–3, 5–7, 10, 13, 15–17, 21–24, 36, 40, 42, 53–55, 81, 91, 93, 99–100, 103–4, 121, 124, 143, 148–50, 154–57, 161, 163–76, 178–79, 184–85, 189–98, 204–5, 207, 211–13, 219, 220, 223–24, 226, 229–30, 235, 243, 250–53, 255–56, 258–61, 264–66, 269
creation,
  as *creatio ex nihilo*, 94, 162, 185, 203, 207–9, 219–20, 223

INDEX

305

of the universe, 24, 76, 120–21, 162, 181, 194, 198, 206–7, 220–21, 233, 262, 290

of humanity, 9, 71, 162, 183, 199, 204, 221, 231, 243

"Why not sooner" of, 24, 199, 204, 208, 212–17, 221–23, 239

Dark Energy, Dark Matter, 5, 121, 130, 165, 288

Deep Incarnation, 12–13, 122

dialogue between theology and science, *in passim*

    pneumatological dimension of, 101, 105, 107

Dostoevsky, Feodor, 90

Edwards, Denis, 12

Ellis, George, 175, 207

event(s)

    inaugural, xi, xiv, 33, 36, 44, 46-47, 54, 63, 70–71, 80, 83–84, 99, 104, 109, 115, 132, 198–99, 209–12, 217, 222, 240–42, 247

    of birth, 54, 85–86, 88, 90–92, 144

    phenomenality of, 45, 63, 81, 101–2, 107, 123–24, 139, 227, 229–30, 239

    the universe as, 228

    of the Incarnation, 10, 12, 15, 57, 110, 123–24, 132, 239–40.

evolution

    biological, 11–13, 15, 71, 76–77, 80, 83, 104, 132, 168

    cosmological, *see* universe, evolution of

faith, 12, 30, 38–39, 41, 51, 56, 58, 99, 106, 171, 186, 198, 201, 240, 263

    and reason, 21, 30–31, 35–36, 63

Fall (as the postlapserian condition), 65, 73–78, 99, 116, 126–28, 130

Florovsky, Georges, 125, 127, 182, 186, 240

Frank, Simon, 32, 66, 74, 103, 140

Fromm, Erich, 67

God,

    as the creator, xii, 18, 20, 25, 32, 41–42, 51–54, 59, 105, 111, 113, 116, 119, 123, 126, 139, 143, 147, 166, 169, 179, 181, 186, 189, 194, 200–201, 207, 218, 224–25, 232, 235, 244–50, 253–54, 257, 259, 262, 264, 268

    communion with, xi–xii, 2–3, 7–8, 11, 17, 19, 23, 29, 37, 40, 44, 51, 56, 67–68, 77–80, 93, 95, 97, 105, 115–19, 125–26, 128–29, 132–33, 139, 161, 166, 169, 199, 224, 235–37, 239, 246, 248, 258–60, 263–64, 274

    experience of, 10, 36–37, 43–44, 48, 50–51, 151, 166, 169, 191

    faith in (*see* faith)

    Kingdom of, xii, 21, 90, 97–98, 100, 106, 117–18, 124, 132, 148, 188, 234, 239, 242

    praise of, 25, 62, 241–57

    Son (Logos, Word) of, *see* Christ, Logos of God

    Spirit of, *see* Holy Spirit

    wisdom and will of, 99, 186, 200–201, 208, 218–20

Grant, Edward, 240

Gregory of Nyssa, St., 52, 77, 101, 201–3

Gurwitsch, Aron, 35, 69, 175

Harrison, Peter, 240

Hawking, Stephen, 194

Heidegger, Martin, 43–45, 65, 168, 244, 275

Heller, Michael, 31, 207

Henry, Michel, 58, 64, 71–72, 87, 94, 111, 113, 139–41, 195, 203, 246, 268

history,

    of the universe (*see* the universe, history of)

    the order of (in contrast to the cosmic order), xi, 14, 16, 124, 185, 240, 251

    of salvation, xii, 152, 231–33

Holy Spirit, 11, 22, 101, 104–11, 113, 120, 126, 182, 200, 223, 242, 262–63
humanity (*anthropos*: human beings, man, men), xi–xii, xiv, 2, 4–6, 9–12, 14, 16, 17, 22, 24, 31, 33, 37, 41, 44–45, 47–49, 53, 55, 58, 60–80, 83, 90, 92, 95–97, 99, 100–103, 105–6, 110, 112, 116–18, 121, 125, 128, 132, 134, 137, 139–42, 145, 149, 150, 152, 163–64, 171–73, 176, 188, 192, 197–98, 212–13, 222, 228, 252, 258, 261
and the Incarnation, 231–43, 264
as a central theme of the dialogue between theology and science, 7, 9, 21, 27
as affected by the universe, 161
as archetype of the Logos (Word) of God, Christ, 216
as center of disclosure and manifestation (articulation, constitution), xi–xii, xiv, 13, 33, 37, 79, 136, 149, 166, 238, 248, 254
as consubstantial with the visible universe, 11, 144, 175, 260
as creature in communion 40, 58, 78, 115, 119, 125–26, 131–32, 180, 183, 188, 260, 267
as embodied (corporeal) creatures (bodies of), 53, 147, 150
as hypostasis of the universe, 21, 94, 129, 180, 230, 238
as Image of God (*Imago Dei*), xi–xii, 6–7, 14–15, 18, 20–21, 23, 33, 50–51, 54, 72, 77, 90, 108, 112–13, 115, 118–19, 125, 162, 169–70, 180, 186, 189, 220, 225, 230, 241, 256, 258, 266, 269
as microcosm, 9, 12, 128–29, 289
as personal (hypostatic) existence (personhood), 176,
as praising God, 247–50
as affectivity (self-affectivity) of life, xiv, 22–25, 32, 49, 58, 65, 71, 98, 107, 110, 113, 138, 140–48, 150, 154, 160–64, 166–67, 183, 198, 217, 222, 225, 228, 231, 244, 246, 248–49, 257, 260, 262, 265, 271, 277, 279–80
as transcendental subject, 161,
condition(s) of (human condition), 3, 73, 93, 107, 111, 119, 183
cosmological insignificance of, 169
deification of, 127–31, 218, 267
geocentric facticity of, 150–51, 154
goals of, 169
necessary conditions of existence of, 221, 247
origins (creation) of, 139, 162, 173, 181, 186, 204
sufficient conditions of existence of, 13, 84
paradox (dualistic nature) of (subjectivity), 23, 75, 103, 113, 116, 119, 133, 135, 138, 150, 152, 259
transfiguration of, 266–67, 269
unknowability of, xii, 21–22, 52, 61, 64, 79, 85, 91–92, 94–95, 133, 160, 178–79, 259
Husserl, Edmund, 68, 136–37, 140, 168, 170, 175

Incarnation, *see* Christ, Jesus of Nazareth, Incarnation, *and* Deep Incarnation, *and* phenomenality of the Incarnation
Irenaeus of Lyons, St., 111, 122, 231–32
Isham, Christopher, 194

Jaki, Stanley, 30
Janicaud, Dominique, 139
Jaspers, Karl, 65, 139, 168
Jeans, James, 203,

Kant, Immanuel, 46, 68, 91, 101–2, 115, 117, 134, 191, 209, 212, 214–15, 244, 264–65, 281, 286
Kierkegard, Sören, 90
Krauss, Lawrence, 168, 207
Kuiper, Franciskus, 89
Küng, Hans, 31

Ladrière, Jean, 167, 170–71, 190

INDEX 307

Life (as Divine), xii, xiv, 2, 20, 22–23, 31–33, 37, 58–59, 61, 65, 72, 94–98, 105–8, 110–13, 123, 125–26, 134, 139–40, 142, 144–45, 161–62, 164, 201, 217, 222, 228, 231, 233, 245–47, 256, 258, 261, 268–69
   self-affectivity of, 23, 147, 222, 235, 260
life (human) 1–2, 4, 6–7, 9, 13, 15–17, 19, 21–22, 24–25, 31–35, 37–38, 40, 42, 46, 49–50, 52–54, 57, 59–63, 65–67, 70–71, 73–78, 80–81, 83–94, 96–99, 101–7, 109–13, 115–16, 118, 122, 125, 131–32, 134–36, 138, 141–45, 148, 152–56, 161–64, 167–73, 177, 179–82, 188, 195, 201, 203, 212–13, 216, 221–23, 227–31, 233, 235, 239–40, 243–49, 256–58, 260–61, 263, 266, 268
   self-affectivity of, 142, 145–46, 150–52, 223
logos (*logoi*) (reason, rationality), 14, 59, 61, 109, 129, 184, 189, 218–21, 223, 252–55, 267, 274
Logos of God (Christ-Logos), 10–11, 14, 22, 25, 31, 40, 45, 58–59, 61, 72, 94, 97–98, 105–6, 108, 110–11, 113, 119, 122–23, 126, 128–29, 142–43, 147–48, 164, 179–80, 182, 187–89, 199–200, 223, 230–39, 250, 253, 254–56, 259, 262, 267–68
   (*see also* Christ; Holy Spirit)
Lossky, Vladimir, 14, 29, 30, 108, 129, 149, 151
Lyotard, Jean-Francois, 154

Marcel, Gabriel, 85, 88, 118, 145, 196
Marion, Jean-Luc, 45, 77, 87, 102, 155, 165, 227
Mathews, Freya, 172
Maximus the Confessor, St., 51, 72, 79, 126–31, 138, 148, 166, 169, 200–201, 206, 208, 217 221, 235–37, 239, 247, 254, 268, 274.
Merleau-Ponty, Maurice, 68, 71, 86, 178

Moltmann, Jürgen, 31, 65, 68, 174
multiverse (plurality of worlds), 82, 100, 121, 138, 150, 179, 198, 223, 230, 244
Munitz, Milton, 167, 172
Murphy, G. L., 11

natural attitude, 15, 23–24, 37, 50–51, 69, 81, 85, 92, 97, 109, 139–40, 144, 147, 155–56, 162, 164, 177, 181, 183, 189, 197, 199, 216, 222–24, 228, 230, 243, 250, 260–61, 264–65, 278
Newton, Isaac, 190, 206–7

Origen 187, 188

Pascal, Blaise, 59, 118, 256
Pannenberg, Wolfhart, 29, 31, 34, 106, 186
paradox of subjectivity, *see* humanity, paradox of dualistic nature) of (subjectivity)
Penrose, Roger, 82, 205, 219
Peters, Ted, xv, 130, 132, 152
phenomenality, xii, 31, 38, 43, 53, 107, 172, 243, 259, 271, 275, 277, 280, 282–83, 285
   of objects, xi, 1, 8, 22, 32, 45, 50, 55, 60, 63, 71, 98, 101–2, 104, 145, 153, 155, 165, 176, 181, 189, 195, 203, 205, 209–10, 214, 216, 224, 228, 246, 255
   of events, 45, 63, 81, 101–2, 123, 124, 139, 227, 229–30, 239
   of life, xi, xiv, 37, 47, 49–52, 96–97, 101, 104, 163, 176, 200, 210, 245–46
   of the Incarnation, 123, 239
   of the universe, *see* universe, phenomenality of
   of the world's and human origins, 179, 215, 222
phenomenology (phenomenological method), phenomenological 14, 37, 43, 48, 77, 97, 104, 109–10, 136, 139–40, 156, 170–71, 176, 195, 198, 222, 225–26, 246, 254, 260, 265, 271, 275, 277

phenomenology *(continued)*
  attitude (or philosophical) (as opposite to the natural attitude), 145, 177, 278–79
    (see also natural attitude)
  existential, 9, 37,
  reduction, 53, 136, 139–40, 155–56, 265, 277
  structure(s) (of subjectivity), xiv, 23, 111, 161–62, 203, 222, 260
    (see also, Gurwitsch, Heidegger, Husserl, Marcel, Marion, Merleau-Ponty, Ricoeur)
philosophy, 8, 22, 29–30, 34–36, 43, 47–48, 50–51, 53, 55–57, 62, 65, 67, 71, 104–5, 115, 133, 141, 146, 165, 200
  Greek, 184–85, 246
    (see also Plato, Thales, Heraclitus)
  negative certainty of, 3, 8
  perennial, 71
  phenomenological *(see* phenomenology)
  scientific (philosophy of science) 46–48, 53–54, 60, 62, 104, 170
  transcendental, 47–48
Plato (Platonic ideas, forms), 175, 184–85, 191, 195, 216–17, 290–91
Poincaré, Henry, 210
Prestige, G. L., 237,

Rees, Martin, 5, 91
Ricoeur, Paul, 86–87, 89, 135
Romano, Claude, 44–45, 54, 87,

Sagan, Carl, 256
Sakharov, Sophrony, St., 104, 182
Sherrard, Philip, 31
Soloviev, Vladimir, 72, 81, 123, 148

Teilhard de Chardin, Pierre, 10–12, 15, 17, 40–42, 68–69, 74–76, 81, 91–92, 119–20, 130–31, 146, 212
teleology, 38, 83, 91, 151, 221–22, 265
  of explanation (reason, research), 150, 155, 183, 212
  of human activity, 183,
Thales of Miletus, 185, 192, 229

theology, *in passim*
  as experience of God, *(see also* God, experience of), xii, xiv, 10, 36–37, 43–44, 48, 50–51, 151, 166, 175, 184
  patristic, 16, 24, 50, 217, 240
  philosophical, 43, 47
    (see also Christ, Christianity, Christian Church, faith, Incarnation, Logos of God, Holy Spirit)
time (and space), 75, 96, 102, 106, 108–10, 112–14, 118, 120, 122–23, 125, 130, 147–48, 150, 154, 157, 159, 169, 172, 174, 177, 182, 184, 187–89, 191–94, 196, 198–201, 204–8, 210–11, 213–14, 216, 218, 221, 224, 227–28, 238, 242, 251–53, 262
  beginning (origin, past) of, 214
  internal consciousness of, 113, 195
  pre-existent space and, 205, 207–9, 215, 217
Torrance, Thomas, 11, 31, 44, 55, 105–6, 109, 115, 120, 123, 126, 186

universe (the), *in passim*
  age of, 7, 31, 82, 132, 197–98, 201, 204–8, 211–18, 220–22
  as aesthetical idea (beauty of), 46, 184, 224, 252
  as event (in the phenomenality of events), 228
  as a construct (construct of), 175, 177, 229, 281,
  as contingent upon God,
    (see also, contingent facticity (contingency))
  as created, xi, 77, 110, 121, 128, 156, 179, 182, 187–88, 198, 205, 207, 222, 224, 233, 248, 250, 256, 263–66
  as hypostatically inherent in (enhypostasized by) the Logos of God, 108, 236–38, 262–63, 275,
  as intelligible, 139, 151, 163, 254, 279
  as rational idea ("object"), 46, 102, 225

as saturated phenomenon, 102, 153–57, 223, 227, 262–64,
facticity of, 16, 20, 91, 119, 189, 194, 198, 205, 207–8, 254
evolution of, 5, 14, 40, 75, 77, 80–81, 83, 119, 121, 130, 135, 165, 168, 186, 191–93, 196–98, 213, 253, 287
history of, 4, 5, 15, 41, 182, 212, 223
in the image (hypostasis) of humanity, xi, 104, 107, 169, 180, 229-30, 237
initial conditions of, 82, 91, 143, 205, 208, 219, 221, 287, (*see also* Big Bang)
instantaneous synthesis of, 10, 30, 138, 148, 161, 234, 258, 267
phenomenality of (as object, as event), 104–5, 155, 173, 181, 200, 205, 209–10, 243–44, 262–63
the order of (cosmic order as distinct from the human order) xi, 14–15, 74, 99, 120, 124, 173, 181–82, 188, 232
transfiguration of, 100, 131, 258
uniformity of, 269
(*see* cosmological principle)
visible, 253, 255

Weinberg, Stephen, 229
Wheeler, John Archibald, 197

Yannaras, Christos, 13–14, 31, 36, 55, 74, 76–79, 109, 118, 159, 196

Zizioulas, John, 36, 40, 66, 125, 128, 159, 236

www.ingramcontent.com/pod-product-compliance
Lightning Source LLC
Chambersburg PA
CBHW050620300426
44112CB00012B/1586